BEEN BROWN SO LONG IT LOOKED LIKE GREEN TO ME

THE POLITICS OF NATURE

Jeffrey St. Clair

Common Courage Press   Monroe, Maine

Library of Congress Cataloging-in-Publication Data is available
from the publisher on request.

ISBN 1-56751-258-5 paper
ISBN 1-56751-259-3 cloth

Common Courage Press
Box 702
Monroe, ME 04951

(207) 525-0900; fax: (207) 525-3068
orders-info@commoncouragepress.com

See our website for e-versions of this book.
www.commoncouragepress.com

First Printing

Printed in Canada

Contents

Dedication

For Dave and Anne Brower, Kimberly and the vanishing grizzlies of the Kootenai country, long may they ramble.

Opening Statements

The Map Is Not the Territory

Our house sits on the rim of a canyon sheathed in Douglas fir. The creek down below is roaring this time of year. Chinook salmon still climb its torrents, spawn and die. We find their carcasses, picked over by ravens. There are fewer dead salmon every year. This is not a good sign.

Osprey twist in the air on bent wings nearly every morning, cruising over the creek bed for live fish. Year after year they rear new broods in the craggy top of a broken hemlock, the nest an inverted igloo of found material—a model of organic architecture. The creek flows into the mighty Clackamas River a couple of miles away. At the confluence is an old mill site. The ground is saturated in creosote and PCBs, leaching remorselessly into the water, the flesh of salmon, the blood of osprey.

At least one cougar still prowls the canyon. Some nights we awaken to its eerie moaning. Dogs have gone missing. Big ones. But we hear the cat less often now. The city advances, glowing with light. The canyon is an island eroded by sprawl.

On clear days the stark pyramid of Mt. Hood flashes into view on the eastern horizon, its flanks draped with glaciers, pink as coho flesh. The glaciers are in retreat. The history of the forest is written on the face of those mountains, sixty miles distant. In winter, the clearcuts shimmer with snow, thousands of them, separated only by thin veins of ancient trees. This land is a battlefield. Perhaps, the largest in the nation. It sprawls over millions of acres. There have been so many losses. Stumps twelve feet across stand as headstones of the fallen. Still it rages. And the blood boils.

In 1990, Kimberly and I moved our family from the hill country of southern Indiana to Oregon. We were looking for someplace green, wet and foggy. We were told such weather was good for the skin, not a purely narcissistic consideration given the daily shredding of the ozone layer. There were other considerations, too: thousand-year-old trees, six-hundred-foot waterfalls, salmon, spotted owls, black bears, free-flowing rivers, progressive politics. The essentials of life.

Of course, the essentials aren't that easy to come by. The New Physicists have a saying: the map is not the territory. The conundrum is a metaphor for sub-atomic matter that rearranges itself so quickly that any depiction of its traces becomes obsolete before it is even drawn. When we arrived in Oregon, the Pacific Northwest was in the midst of the Great Change. Sure, Oregon still offered most of what we imagined, but there was less of it every day. In a word (Ed Abbey's), Oregon was being "Californicated": paved, smogged, subdivided, dammed, logged, mined, spiked with cell-phone towers, bankrupted schools, malicious rightwing politicos in the ascendancy. It even sported an ailing nuclear plant named after a condom: Trojan. But there was nothing remotely prophylactic about that demonic tower.

When you think of Oregon, you probably think of forests. The highway maps help pump the mystique, splashing wide swaths of green across the state. It's another illusion. Two-thirds of Oregon is desert, high desert: parched, austere, beautiful and vulnerable. The other third of the state, a thin 150-mile-wide band from the Cascade Mountains to the Pacific Coast, harbors the mightiest forest on the continent. Now it too is becoming a kind of desert, a biological desert, an ecological dead zone.

A century of unbridled clearcutting has taken its toll. By 1980, the Cascades, that lush volcanic range running from British Columbia to northern California, had been transformed into a patchwork of a hundred thousand clearcuts, a sight so surreal that it stunned even President Carter when he flew over Mt. St. Helens to survey the damage. Carter mistook the scars of logging for the blast of the volcano. There's a difference. The forests flattened by Mount St. Helens are starting to come back to life. The land leveled by the timber cartel isn't.

Many frail coastal mountainsides, punctured by logging roads and the forests shaved to the bedrock, simply collapse each winter in monstrous landslides, burying some of the world's most fertile salmon streams under mega-tonnage of rock and mud. This is the pillaged landscape of Ken Kesey's *Sometimes A Great Notion*. Never give an inch. Don't stop cutting until you reach the bone. Suck out the marrow and move on. There's never been a better guide to Oregon than that strange muddy novel.

But now the ravaged land of the Coast Range, in a kind of death spasm, is beginning to lash back. With a fearsome regularity, the winter landslides have begun crushing the new houses and trailers that regularly sprout up on logged-over forests. These days the clearcuts are killing more than salmon and owls.

Empires were built off the rape of these forests: Boise-Cascade, Georgia-Pacific, Louisiana-Pacific, Willamette Industries, International Paper and, mightiest of all, Weyerhaeuser. These corporations played a two-step game. Most of the companies owned millions of acres of their own land, acquired for pennies an acre through the Railroad Land Grants of the nineteenth century. Each one of those acres harbored tens of thousands of dollars worth of trees, mainly Douglas fir, the wood that built suburban America. Billions were made unfettered by law or morality or even common sense. A kind of capitalist anarchy swept through the woods; cut and run was its mantra. It is a theme that replicated itself across the mountains with the mercilessness of the parasitic beast in Ridley Scott's *Alien*, consuming its host forest and moving on to fresh ground.

In the early '60s, the timber behemoths had blitzed through their own vast holdings and turned their sights on the national forests. They got them. By 1970, logging on the public lands in the Northwest had more than doubled. The writing was on the wall for the spotted owl, marbled murrelet, coho salmon and 800 other species that depend on old-growth forests. By the time we arrived in Oregon, the timber industry was clearcutting more than 256,000 acres of national forest land in Oregon and Washington each year. Nationwide, the logged-over acres topped a million annually. These are national forests. Public lands. Your forests. Pissed off yet?

The timber barons are masters of the art of corruption and for decades they've had every politician in the Northwest firmly pocketed, liberal Democrats and rightwing Republicans alike. It's served them very well, indeed. When pesky laws like the Endangered Species Act blockaded their way, they had their politicians declare the logging exempt from such legal constraints. When federal judges ruled against them, they got Congress to overturn the injunctions. When Forest Service employees, such as my friend Jeff DeBonis, blew the whistle on illegalities, the timber industry got them transferred, demoted or fired. When Weyerhaeuser came under scrutiny by the Justice Department in a multi-million dollar timber theft case, the timber giant prevailed on the Clinton administration to quash the probe. Similar investigations into bid rigging, fraud and monopolistic practices got terminated from above.

With legal avenues of protest routinely annulled by Congress, forest defenders adopted more creative tactics. Along the Brietenbush River, Lew Herd buried himself up to his neck in a pile of boulders to block a logging road. Julia Butterfly and others took to the trees themselves, living in them as human shields against the chainsaws. At Warner Creek in the High Cascades, Earth First!ers built a makeshift fortress in the forest to fend off the loggers, squatting there through a winter that saw more than 500 inches of snow fall. George Atiyeh, a Vietnam vet and nephew of a former Oregon governor, held off Forest Service timber sale planners with a shotgun as they tried to mark for cutting the thousand year old trees at Opal Creek. A decade later, and despite all odds, those trees are still standing, now fully protected as a wilderness area.

Still the lost acres stagger the mind. Ninety-five percent of the primary forest, the ancient trees of the Northwest, had been liquidated by 1990, the year of the Earth Summit in Rio. At the global pow-wow, one American politician after another (except George Bush the First, who snubbed the entire show) rose to chastise Brazil for the destruction of the Amazon, where 75 percent of the primary forest remained intact. These same politicians, led by Democratic Party luminaries such as House Speaker Tom Foley, had underwritten the looting of the temperate rainforests of the Northwest and tried to crush any environmentalists who stood in their way. Of course, Foley is gone and greens helped to bring the titan down. So there's reason for hope.

We were somewhat prepped for the great struggle for the Northwest's forests, but nobody told us anything about Hanford. The last free-flowing stretch of the Columbia River cuts through a place of death and terror, the place where they assembled hydrogen bombs: the Hanford Nuclear Reservation. The bomb making there is largely over. But the horrific echoes of that age will never go away. It may be the most polluted place in the world, seething with tons of radioactive waste that will haunt the entire Northwest for millennia to come. There are easy no answers to the Hanford crisis. Indeed, there may well be no answers at all. The technology that built the bombs has no idea how to clean up the mess. In the meantime, the downwinders from Spokane to Portland pay the price. The price is cancer of the thyroid, of the lungs, of the blood. The Soviet Union is kaput, but the atomic clock is ticking in the middle of the American outback. Some Hanford investigators warn that the leaking tanks of radioactive debris may get so hot they'll explode—if the worst happens, it will be a dirty bomb we've dropped on ourselves.

The West is a vast place, but not nearly vast enough to handle all the demands laid upon it. Drive down any road in the Interior West and the ongoing ruination passes by your window in a grim montage: open pit mines a mile wide and a half a mile deep, leach piles of cyanide, bombing ranges, nuclear labs, and the internment camps known as Indian reservations. The interior West is America's own version of the Third World, a resource colony to be pillaged and abandoned. The timber and minerals are extracted as fast as possible and rendered into cash. Of course, the money doesn't stick around these parts. The boom and bust towns that sprouted up during the frenzies never boomed that big and when they busted they descended into a gloom as terminal as any Kurt Cobain song. Want a taste? Try the asbestos wasteland of Libby, Montana or the mining towns Elko, Nevada and Wallace, Idaho. Places that might even give David Lynch, director of *Twin Peaks*, the creeps.

You can graph the damage in tables and bar charts, but it doesn't do it justice. For that you need to get out there and witness the roughened edges of the West yourself: the orange flow of Iron Mike Creek, a Montana stream defiled by mining; the sound of F16s screeching across the Superstition Mountains; the omnipresent smell of cowshit in the Gila Wilderness; the feel of your fingers skimming over 800 growth rings on the stump of a Douglas fir along the Umpqua River.

There were fervent hopes that the election of Clinton and his slime green sidekick Al Gore would apply the brakes, pass new laws with sharp teeth, prosecute polluters, set aside wildlands from the dozers and the chainsaws, turn away from oil, uranium and coal and toward the sun. Instead, the Clinton/Gore era turned out to be a short-lived romance that ended in the environmental equivalent of date rape. For eight years, the forests, deserts and rivers took a beating, but the real loser was the environmental movement itself.

Oregon was a hotbed of environmental activism in the 1980s

and early 1990s. It's a big state with a small (though not small enough) population. But Oregon boasted more environmental groups than any other state, even more than that golden tragedy to the south of us, California. This was not merely a sign of an elevated consciousness. It was, to deploy the breathless language of Ashcroft, an indication of the dire threat level.

The threat hasn't diminished by any means, but the number of groups has shriveled. They couldn't survive the Clinton ice age. Many of the smaller groups simply flatlined. Meanwhile the mainstream groups got bigger and bigger and less and less effective. By the mid-1990s, mainstream environmentalism had become fattened and tongue-tied by foundation grants (many originating from the fortunes of big oil) and blindered by a reflexive loyalty to the Democratic Party. The new green executives sported six-figure salaries, drove around in limos and worked out of DC offices as plush as the headquarters of Chemical Manufacturer's Association. But the movement lacks heart and guts.

Along the way, I've come to disdain institutional environmentalism, as little more than soft-soled courtiers to entrenched power. Once the environmental movement was seen as a public interest movement of unimpeachable integrity—trusted by the left, despised and feared by the corporate right. After Clinton, many people rightly saw professional environmentalists as just another special interest lobby, obedient hand puppets of the DNC. The great Southwest writer and desert rat Charles Bowden says he'd never belong to any tax-deductible group, since the very tax status serves as a kind of seal of approval from the government. He's got a point. When the Sierra Club got too demanding in the 1960s, the IRS threatened to take away its coveted tax status. It promptly settled down.

As my old friend David Brower warned: "When we prevail, it's just a stay of execution. When the corporations win, they win forever. That's why we must be eternally vigilant." But eternal vigilance is wearying. The daily life of a grassroots green (as opposed to the DC subspecies) fighting big corporations is grueling and filled with vicissitudes. There are few rewards and many, many defeats, each one bitter and inconsolable. It's hard not to be worn down by it all. Now wonder so many enviros these days sound like glowering prudes, freighting a rhetoric of doomsterism. But we must fight against it, because it's unhealthy and no way to build a movement.

Brower himself never surrendered to the grave pessimism that is standard fare in the direct mail appeals of his former employer the Sierra Club and the other Beltway greens. Indeed, the last time I saw Dave was a few months before he died. We were in a parking lot overlooking that monument of evil: Glen Canyon Dam. Hundreds of young activists had joined us in the broiling Arizona sun, united in a single cause: the liberation of the Colorado River and the restoration of Glen Canyon. "Hell, I think we've really got a chance now," Brower said, his eyes sparkling with optimism.

Cling to that optimism that fired Brower's soul for 85 years. And remember Abbey's admonition to be a part-time warrior, sparing time to enjoy the offerings of the planet you're fighting to preserve. And it's okay to have a sense of humor. In fact, it's mandatory. At *CounterPunch* our motto is: be as radical as reality. Fight fiercely for what you feel passionate about, no matter how long the odds seem. But don't fret so much about the meta-crises, such as global warming or ozone depletion. It'll only weigh you down and drive you toward nihilistic despair.

This book is my attempt to come to terms with the way the West really works: the corporate mercenaries, corrosive politics and neutered environmentalism that have contributed to this dissolving landscape. These investigations seek to undermine the myths that propel the plunder, comforting but destructive illusions such as: the West as an edenic frontier, sustainable forestry, win-win solutions, acceptable risks. And the biggest lie of all: that the war on Indians is over. It's not. Far from it. As any Apache or Sioux will tell you. And they haven't given up on getting their lands back, either.

I remain an optimist, a callused utopian. There are vivid reasons for hope, most notably because down on the ground there are so many gifted fellow travelers out there shaking things up for the better: organizers, writers, litigators, fanatics, solo artists, malcontents, implacable assholes—nature lovers all. Here's a brief roll call of those whose work for the planet gives me cause for cheer. In Vermont, Michael Colby, editor of *Wild Matters*, fights the chemical agriculture industry and is never afraid to name names. In Colorado, my dear friend Pat Wolff works tirelessly on behalf of predators and Phil Doe battles the water vampires that would suck the rivers of the

West dry. In Montana, Mike Bader and Steve Kelly at the Alliance for the Wild Rockies stand up for the biggest wilderness we've got left and all the critters that depend on it, from grizzlies and wolves to bull trout and goshawks. In Tennessee, David Orr and his pals at Save Our Cumberland Mountains are fending off an unholy trinity: strip mine companies, chip mills and the KKK. Back in Hoosierland, my old comrades Andy Mahler, Libby Frey, Claude Ferguson, Mary Kay Moody, Tom Zeller, Leah Garlotte and Tim Maloney work tirelessly on behalf of the biologically rich hardwood forests of the Ohio River Valley, while John Blair, winner of the Pulitzer prize for photography, wages war on the coal mines and acid-belching power plants. In California, Patty Clary and her group CATS haunt the pesticide lobby's every move; Mark Palmer defends whales and dolphins and seeks to bring the grizzly back to the Sierras; and the good folks at Project Underground chase big oil around the globe. In Utah, John Weisheit and Owen Lammers at Living Rivers carry on Brower's quest to open the floodgates of Glen Canyon Dam and Denise Boggs at the Utah Environmental Center defends the precious forests of the Wasatch and Uintas. In Washington state, Dr. John Osborne and his associates at the Inland Empire Public Lands Council work to overturn one of the greatest swindles, the Railroad Land Grants, and Janine Blaeloch, at the Western Land Exchange Project, counters the moves to give even more public land away to corporations. In New Mexico, John Talberth at the Forest Conservation Council defends the rare forests of the high desert and Susan Schock is the bane of the ranchers and bankers. Over in Arizona, the folks at Dineh CARE fight for the forests and sacred sites of Navajoland; Ola Cassadore Davis speaks for the San Carlos Apache; and Dr. Robin Silver fights for goshawks, Mexican spotted owls and Gila trout. Up in Alaska, there's Pam Miller and the Community Action on Toxics; Buck Lindekugel and the folks at SEACC who defend the Tongass, the nation's largest rainforest; and in Fairbanks the Northern Alaska Environmental Center which battles to boot the oil companies out of the Arctic. Here in Oregon, Tim Hermach, the John Brown of the forest preservation movement, runs the Native Forest Council; Michael Donnelly defends the awesome Brietenbush Cascades and Larry Tuttle of Center for Environmental Equity revels in his role as the mining industry's biggest pain in the ass.

There are even some lawyers worth mentioning: Sharon Duggan in California, Mark Hughes in Phoenix, Scott Greacen in Montana, Tom Carpenter at GAP in Seattle, Jeff Ruch at PEER in DC, human rights lawyer Joanne Mariner and Michael Nixon, defender of Indian rights from Portland.

I've some great teachers in the classroom and in life. They need to be thanked: Laura Pilato, Jackie Snow, Jon Williams, Kermit Moyer, Thomas Cannon, Terence Murphy, Claude Ferguson, Elizabeth Frey and David Brower.

Let's not forget the writers. I'm not convinced we make that big of a difference, especially compared to the work of the people listed above. But there are a few that I enviously turn to again and again: Chris Clarke, editor of *Faultline*; environmental historians Donald Worster, Ted Steinberg, Michael Dorsey and Patricia Nelson Limerick; the desert trio: Ed Abbey, Charles Bowden and Terry Tempest Williams; Kurt Vonnegut, Thomas Pynchon and Lewis Shiner; Mailer and Vidal; Susan Davis, author of a wonderful book on the Disneyfication of nature; the poets Richard Hugo, James Wright, Simon Ortiz, Henry Taylor, David Vest and Daniel Wolff; Peter Mattheissen, the best nature writer we've yet seen; Leslie Marmon Silko; John Holt, the Hunter Thompson of trout fishing; economic theorists Doug Henwood (Marxist) and Randal O'Toole (libertarian); Ken Silverstein, Dave Marsh and Steve Perry; and, of course, my colleagues James Ridgeway from the *Voice* and Alexander Cockburn, with whom I co-edit *CounterPunch*.

This book was written under the influence of: Charley Patton, Howlin' Wolf, Thelonious Monk, Miles Davis, Hounddog Taylor, Sly Stone, The Clash, John Trudell and the blessed John Lee Hooker.

Most of all I must thank my parents for opening the book of nature for me, Zen and Nat for giving me a reason to fight for it, and Kimberly for riding point, no matter how heavy the incoming heat. I love you all.

There's a war going on just outside your window. It's a battle for life itself. So stow away this silly book and come join it. Remember: the map is not the territory. So burn the maps and get lost in the territory, while you've still got a chance.

PART I

The Politics of Expediency and Exploitation

One

Been Brown So Long It Looked Like Green to Me

Cast your memory back to the days of the Nixon administration, the glory time of American environmentalism. The country rallied to the cause of cleaning up the nation's waters and air, preserving its remaining wild lands and rivers, regulating the use and disposal of hazardous chemicals, rescuing wildlife from extinction.

Remember the first Earth Day: April 20, 1970. It was the brainchild of a United States senator, Gaylord Nelson of Wisconsin, who wanted a national teach-in on the environment. Nelson proclaimed that the environment "was the most crucial issue facing mankind." The teach-in became a media event, orchestrated by a young Harvard-educated lawyer, Dennis Hayes, who set forth the lofty protocols of the new movement: "Ecology is concerned with the total system—not just the way it disposes of its garbage."

That first Earth Day—when millions participated in demonstrations, clean-ups and rallies across the country—has been hailed as the largest organized event in American history and as a symbol of rebellion against pollution and the exploitation of natural America.

It didn't take Congress long to get the message. The House and Senate speedily decreed a new era of environmental law: 1970 saw the creation of the Occupational Safety and Health Administration and the passage of the Clean Air and National Environmental Policy acts, under which protecting earth, water and air legally became a priority for all federal agencies. Then in 1972 came the Clean Water Act, the first pesticide regulations, the Noise Control Act and a series of laws protecting marine mammals and coastal beaches. A year later Congress authorized the Endangered Species Act, regulated toxic chemicals and passed new green laws governing the use of public lands. Throughout the Seventies environmental standards stiffened, with legislation covering everything from Superfund (to finance clean-up of toxic dumps) to drinking water.

The environmental decade culminated in passage of the Alaska National Interest Lands Act of 1980, which protected about 110 million acres of wilderness, an area larger than California.

In those days Congress was well-stocked with conservationists: Ed Muskie, George McGovern, Jennings Randolph, Birch Bayh and Gene McCarthy. Even in the West, where states were still commonly thought of as resources to be exploited, environmentalism had its champions: Idaho's Frank Church, Montana's Lee Metcalf, Arizona's Morris Udall and Oregon's junior senator, Bob Packwood, an original sponsor of the Endangered Species Act. In his 1970 State of the Union address, Nixon himself embraced the green theme, proclaiming that "we must make our peace with nature" and reclaim "the purity of its air, its waters, and our living environment. It is literally now or never."

To be sure, that supple politician seized this chance to divert the attention of an increasingly restive middle class from the horrors of his war against Vietnam. Nixon understood that "the environment" could bring together every dreamer green enough to impale an avocado seed on a toothpick and raise it up in the thin light of the Me Decade. The environment might bring the beat legions of the counterculture together with the heavier left; it could ally those under 30 with those of more august years; it could make friends of radicals, senators, working people and the press. Forthwith Nixon created the Environmental Protection Agency, to which he named William Ruckleshaus as overseer. Ruckleshaus confronted industry polluters—he was one of the first federal bureaucrats to do so—before being drafted to his short-lived tenure as Attorney General, where he turned on his plucky boss.

In those heady days even the Supreme Court sheltered a radical conservationist, William O. Douglas. Douglas believed that nature should be afforded "rights." In 1972 he drafted a fierce dissent in the case of *Sierra Club v. Morton*, arguing in forceful and poetic language that wilderness itself deserved standing in federal lawsuits, so that before "priceless bits of Americana (such as a valley, an alpine meadow, river or a lake) are forever lost or are transformed as to be reduced to the eventual rubble of our urban environment, the voice of the existing beneficiaries of these environmental wonders should be heard." Douglas further suggested that conservationists who "have an intimate relationship with the inanimate object about to be injured are its legitimate spokesmen." Thus did Douglas give birth both to modern environmental law and, though he is rarely credited with it, the deep ecology movement.

The 1970s saw the green movement mature as a political force with a permanent DC presence, most notably with the creation of the League of Conservation Voters—an organization later headed by Bruce Babbitt—which, for the first time, tracked the environmental voting records of members of congress. Eco-lobbyists, operating largely from basements and scruffy offices on DuPont Circle, were considered the leanest and most effective on the Hill.

Meanwhile, a more confrontational and grassroots-based faction of the environmental community was beginning to organize, spearheaded by the Arch-Druid himself, David Brower. (Brower, dubbed the Arch Druid by John McPhee of The New Yorker, was fired by the Sierra Club because he was too radical, founded Friends of the Earth and was dislodged from that job for similar reasons.) Using the tactics of the civil rights and anti-war movements, this more radical wing of the environmental movement mustered in groups such as Friends of the Earth and Greenpeace, used aggressive media campaigns, civil disobedience and direct action against the corporations themselves.

The decade of the Seventies closed with another huge environmental demonstration, which was in its own way as prodigious as Earth Day. In the wake of Three Mile Island, 750,000 people gathered on the Mall in front of the Capitol to protest the evils of nuclear power, chanting "Hell no, we won't glow" along with the likes of Tom Hayden, Jane Fonda, Michael Harrington and Barry Commoner, who had decided to run for president on the green platform of the Citizens' Party ticket.

That bright afternoon on the Mall was the last light that shone on the DC-centered green movement. In two decades of Reagan, Bush and Clinton the environmental corps in DC has ripened to a complacent putty. The corporate counter-attack on greens began with the rise of the Sagebrush Rebels, an amalgam of ranchers, corporate executives, free-market economists and right-wing politicians who decried environmentalism as socialism-by-another-name and as a backdoor assault on property rights.

The Sagebrush Rebels were ignored until the election of Ronald Reagan, who bowed to the enthusiasms of Joseph Coors—the leading money dispenser of the far right and owner of substantial mineral claims on federal lands—and selected a suite of Sagebrush Rebels to fill important posts in his administration. These Reagan rebels, headed by James Watt (who ran Coors' Mountain States Legal Foundation) and Anne Gorsuch, called themselves "the Crazies on the Hill."

Watt, a millennialist Christian and rabid anti-Communist, was given the Department of Interior, which oversees the management of nearly 500 million acres of public land. He proclaimed he would make the "bureaucracy yield to my blows" and got off to a galloping start. Within a matter of months Watt proposed the sale of 30 million acres of public lands to private companies, gave away billions of dollars worth of publicly-owned coal resources, fought to permit corporations to manage national parks, refused to enforce the nation's strip mine law, offered up the Outer Continental Shelf oil reserves to exploration and drilling, ignored the Endangered Species Act and purged the Interior Department of any employees who objected to his agenda.

Rebel Watt defended his actions as being divinely inspired, arguing that conservation of resources for future generations amounted to a waste of "God's gift to mankind."

"I do not know how many future generations we can count on before the Lord returns," Watt warned. Use it or lose it.

In spite of his ravings Watt held on. He even survived his bizarre attempt to block the Beach Boys (in his fevered mind they represented the incarnation of the counter-culture, even though the group did fundraisers for George Bush) from playing a concert on the Mall, a stance that provoked an amusing rebuke from Reagan, who reminded Watt that the boys were all-American—and, more importantly, Californian. But like Earl Butz before him, Watt was undone by the racism that welled up invincibly within him. Attacking affirmative action, Watt complained that he couldn't set up a panel without finding "a black, a woman, a Jew and a person in a wheelchair." Although Watt was later indicted on charges that he bilked the Department of Housing, Education and Welfare out of millions, it was this remark that did him in.

Over at the Environmental Protection Agency, Watt's counterpart was Anne Gorsuch, a rough-hewn and ignorant Colorado legislator. Gorsuch, who later married Robert Burford, the rancher and mineral engineer Watt tapped to head the Bureau of Land Management, surrounded herself with a coven of advisors from the pollution lobby, including lawyers from General Motors, Exxon and DuPont. Her objective was to cripple environmental laws passed in the 1970s which, she argued, had created an "overburden" of regulations that "stifled economic growth."

To lead the toxic waste division of the EPA Gorsuch chose Rita Levelle, a public relations executive with the Aerojet General Corporation, a defense contractor with potentially vast hazardous waste liabilities. At news of her appointment many of the EPA's top scientists and administrators promptly quit.

Gorsuch and Burford left a miasma of suspended regulations, secret meetings with industry lobbyists, waived fines, and suppressed recommendations of agency scientists. In one piquant case Levelle refused—at the behest of Joseph Coors—to enforce new rules which prohibited dumping liquid hazardous waste into community landfills. Coors' breweries disposed of millions of gallons of such wastes near Denver.

The climate of cronyism that infected the EPA in those days had its source in the highest levels of the Reagan administration, which encouraged agency heads such as Gorsuch to pander to its political allies: Coors, Browning-Ferris Industries, Westinghouse and Monsanto.

Gorsuch's downfall came after congressional investigators requested records of her warm chats with companies under the EPA's jurisdiction. At the advice of a White House counsel she refused to give over the documents and was duly cited with contempt of Congress. When she was called to defend herself, the Reagan Justice Department refused to accompany her. Gorsuch resigned in disgust.

Meanwhile, the insipid and grossly naïve Levelle took the fall for the entire corrupt regime. She was eventually convicted on charges of lying to Congress and spent six months in federal prison.

Less heralded, though equally sinister, was Reagan's appointment of John Crowell as assistant secretary of agriculture, a critical position overseeing the operations of the Forest Service, which is one of the largest agencies in the federal government. As the former general counsel for Louisiana-Pacific, the nation's largest purchaser of federal timber, Crowell knew his duty. One of his first schemes was to suppress an internal investigation of his predatory former employer. Forest Service investigators had concluded that Louisiana-Pacific may have bilked the government out of more than $80 million by fraudulent bidding practices on the Tongass National Forest in Alaska.

Crowell then commanded the Forest Service to double its annual offering of subsidized timber, much of which was destined for mills owned by Louisiana-Pacific. He temporarily halted designation of new federal wilderness areas and squashed scientific reports suggesting that the relentless clearcutting in Washington and Oregon would wipe out the northern spotted owl.

Such useful objectives quickly accomplished, Crowell departed the Reagan administration for a more lucrative tenure at a Portland law firm, which specialized in clients such as the National Forest Products Association, which have a profound interest in exploiting the natural resources of the public domain.

The raw ideologues of the Sagebrush Rebellion over-reached, but their core message took hold: environmental regulations sapped economic growth. Environmental overkill became the excited talk of Washington's PR houses such as Burson-Marsteller and lobbying firms such as Akin, Gump and Patton, Boggs and Blow, which plotted a strategy of containment.

Often all that was needed was a kindlier visage. Take the case of James Watt's replacement at Interior, Donald Hodel. Shortly after Hodel took up his new duties he went hiking in Yosemite's meadows with David Brower. Brower, as militant as they come, returned to pronounce Hodel an "honorable man." Yet Hodel's policies at Interior were as pro-industry as Watt's, and far more effective. During his time there, Bureau of Land Management timber sales hit record levels, as did subsidies for the grazing and mining industries. Hodel was the man who objected to the Montreal protocol for restricting ozone-shredding chemicals, suggesting that to avoid skin cancer from increased ultraviolet radiation, people should simply wear sunglasses, hats and sunscreen.

Watt, Gorsuch, Levelle and Crowell were magnificent villains for fundraising: direct mail revenues for the top environmental groups exploded tenfold from 1979 to 1981. Green became the color of money, and the rag-tag band of hard-core activists who populated the Hill in the 1970s gave way to a cadre of Ivy League-educated lobbyists, lawyers, policy wonks, research scientists and telemarketers. Executives enjoyed perks and salaries that rivaled those of corporate CEOs.

By the end of the 1980s, Jay Hair was pulling down a quarter of a million dollars a year for overseeing the National Wildlife Federation's $80 million budget, and kept his limo engine running at all times, the air-conditioner grinding ozone at full-tilt against the moment he emerged from his office on an eco-mission or deal-making sortie.

Over at the Audubon Society a lawyer named Peter Berle commanded $200,000 a year. As he trimmed away at the muscle of the conservation staff, he gloated, "Unlike Greenpeace, Audubon doesn't have a reputation as a confrontational organization."

The Wilderness Society meanwhile passed into the grip of William Turnage, a Yale-educated manager, after the board of directors ousted Stewart Brandborg. Turnage vowed to transform the Wilderness Society into a "mainstream organization" devoted to policy analysis. Within three years, 37 staffers, denounced by Turnage as "young, radical, crusader types," had been kicked out the door, including Dave Foreman, who went on to found Earth First! The greens were replaced by Harvard-educated lawyers, such as Peter Coppleman (who went on to serve as deputy attorney general in the Clinton administration), conservative economists such as Alice Rivlin (tapped by Clinton to head the Office of Management and Budget), and industry foresters such as Jeff Olson, who formerly worked for timber colossus Boise-Cascade.

The big environmental organizations were by now well pickled in the political brine of Washington, with freshness and passion largely gone.

Early in his 1988 campaign George Bush attempted to distance himself from the environmental ethos of Reagan, who had said that if you saw one redwood tree you had seen them all. Bush's strategy was due mainly to the political instincts of Lee Atwater, who closely scrutinized polling data showing that support for green causes cut across class lines: more than 70 percent of voters wanted more government action to protect environmental quality. And they were willing to pay more taxes to see it would happen.

Thus, Bush proudly advertised that he intended to be "the environmental president." He went after Michael Dukakis, governor of Massachusetts and the Democratic nominee, over the dismal condition of Boston Harbor. Bush pledged to support the reauthorization of the Clean Air Act, including provisions aimed at controlling acid rain, and to take action to curb global warming. He actively promoted a plan for "no net loss of wetlands."

Soon after the election Bush followed up those promises by appointing William Reilly, the first professional environmentalist to head the EPA. Reilly had been the director of the Conservation Foundation, a staid environmental group funded by Laurance Rockefeller in 1948 to advance partnerships between industry and government.

Reilly's mantra at EPA became: "I don't care about the regulations, I want results." In practice, this meant that Reilly preferred consent decrees to punitive fines and criminal litigation, and voluntary compliance to mandatory regulations. He was also entranced by the notion that economic incentives could be used to achieve improvements in air and water quality.

Reilly's primary mission at EPA was to convince environmentalists to get on board the Bush administration's corporate-friendly overhaul of the Clean Air Act. For help, Reilly turned to Bush's favorite environmental group: the Environmental Defense Fund (EDF), a more svelte and modish version of Reilly's Conservation Foundation, packed with lawyers, lobbyists and scientists.

Nurtured on generous infusions of corporate grants and donations, the EDF grew into one of the most influential environmental groups in Washington. Operations are directed by Fred Krupp for the brawny sum of $125,000 a year. Krupp is known in some circles as the Michael Milken of the environmental movement, an allusion to the EDF supremo's tireless promotion of the "pollution credits trading" scheme, which allows industrial companies to sell their right to pollute to other companies through the Chicago board of trade.

Waggish environmentalists have dubbed Krupp's pollution credits "cancer bonds." For his part, Krupp doesn't have much use for grassroots activism, which he see as tarnishing the reputation of seri-ous environmental groups. Krupp liked to proclaim that "what the environmental movement needs is more scientists and engineers and economists." He prefers to work with such allies of the earth as McDonalds and General Motors, which are cordial to the idea that market mechanisms and technology can resolve nearly every envi-ronmental scruple.

All this lead to the development of a futures market in pollu-tion, where industrial polluters could sell or buy the right to spew toxins into the air and water of given communities. Unless they had enough money to buy off the polluters, the people living in those communities would be left no say in the quality of the air they were forced to breathe.

It was precisely these kinds of voluntary and market-oriented approaches that had attracted Reilly and Bush to Krupp in the first place. The whole scheme was laid out in a milestone white paper on so-called free-market environmentalism called, "Project 88," which EDF helped craft for Senators John Heinz and Tim Wirth. This doc-ument argued that environmental regulations were economically onerous and counter-productive. Hurt business, stifle economic growth and you deflate corporate interest in environmental quality. Such notions derive from the belief that environmentalism is a lux-ury concern toward which Americans turn their attention only in times of booming prosperity. The rhetoric of this fake construct is that the best way to protect wildlands, air quality and endangered species is to keep big business running in overdrive.

That such ideas percolated in an era that saw a steady accretion of environmental catastrophes—from Three Mile Island and Love Canal to Times Beach, Bhopal and Chernobyl; from the listing of the spotted owl as an endangered species and the decimation of commer-cial fish stocks on both coasts to the wreck of the Exxon Valdez—shows how thoroughly accustomed the mainstream greens had become to the enervating political climate of Washington, DC. Groups such as the National Wildlife Federation and Environmental Defense Fund had lent credence to the notion that environmental quality was a sec-ondary value, that the right to safe drinking water, clean air and func-tioning ecosystems could be compromised and mediated.

"Project 88" became a biblical text for Reilly, and many of its key provisions later resurfaced in the final version of the Clean Air Act. Heinz was killed in a plane crash in 1991 and a hefty chuck of his robust estate went to create the Heinz Foundation, which funnels millions of dollars to corporate-tolerant greens groups such as EDF. Tim Wirth later became ensconced in the Clinton administration as an advisor on environmental affairs at the State Department.

The anti-regulatory fervor of the Reagan era also thrived in the Bush administration. One particularly anti-environmental voice was Bush's budget director, Richard Darman, who zealously slashed planned spending for national park land acquisitions and hazardous waste cleanups. "Americans did not fight and win the wars of the 20th century to make the world safe for green vegetables," Darman thundered in a memorable lecture at Harvard. In lighter language his boss, Bush, lashed out at broccoli, on the grounds that he had been force-fed it as a child.

Meanwhile, over in the vice-president's office, Dan Quayle was running the White House Council on Competitiveness, a relay station for the complaints of corporate America. The Council was staffed by a young lawyer from Indiana called David McIntosh, subsequently elected to Congress in 1994, whose function was to review all new federal regulations with an eye toward how much each might impair the profitability of big business. "We're here to listen to the concerns of industry," McIntosh said. "The environmentalists have got the EPA as an audience for their complaints."

A typical example of the Council's chivalry is the case of the Louisiana black bear, an especially rare species that inhabits the backwoods swamps and bayous of the Mississippi delta. On learning that the Fish and Wildlife Service might list the bear as a threatened species, Louisiana-Pacific, Weyerhaeuser and Georgia-Pacific pleaded for the Competitiveness Council to intervene, arguing that the listing of the bear would prove a financial hardship to these multibillion dollar transnational companies. The Council sprang into action. The listing was delayed for more than two years, while the timber barons clearcut in the last remnants of the bear's habitat.

Meanwhile, the pro-development demeanor of the Interior Department, which was now under the control of Manuel Lujan, was only moderately less aggressive than during the frenzied days of Watt. Lujan was a former rightwing congressman from New Mexico with steely ties to the ranching and mining industries. He pushed hard to open the Arctic National Wildlife Refuge to oil drilling, continued Watt's push to accelerate exploratory activities on the Outer Continental Shelf, and resisted attempts to charge market prices for cattle grazing on federal grasslands, which under Lujan's tenure amounted to $200 million a year in subsidies to such needy public lands ranchers as Hewlett-Packard and the agribusiness magnate J.R. Simplot.

Under instructions from Bush, Lujan ordered the BLM to fast track the purchase of the Goldstrike Mine by American Barrick Resources, a Toronto-based company controlled by Canadian financier Peter Munk. The way thus lubricated, Barrick gained control of the 1,800-acre gold mine on BLM lands outside Elko, Nevada, for the princely sum of $9,500. By the time it is played out, the Goldstrike Mine will yield an estimated $10 million in gold. In 1995, in consideration for his favors, George Bush was invited to join Barrick's board of advisors.

Lujan also became the first Interior Secretary to challenge directly the Endangered Species Act. Lujan wanted to allow timber companies in Oregon and Washington to clearcut ancient forests inhabited by the northern spotted owl, which had been listed as a threatened species. The Interior Secretary fiercely opposed the court-ordered listing of the owl, saying, "If we've a species, I don't see why we have to save a sub-species, like the northern spotted owl. Maybe these subspecies just aren't meant to survive. Maybe they just can't adapt to their new surroundings." In an effort to override the Endangered Species Act's prohibition against logging in the owl's habitat, Lujan invoked the so-called God Squad, a panel of Bush administration appointees which could vote to "sanction" activities leading to the extinction of a listed species. The God Squad initially gave the owl a death sentence, but its extinction order was later overturned by a federal court.

At the close of the Bush administration, many high-profile environmental issues, including the fate of the Arctic National Wildlife Refuge and the ancient forests of the Pacific Northwest, remained gridlocked. But a quiet, vital change had taken place. The core idea of conservation and protection, that a strong federal regulatory system represented the best path to protect the American environment, was being quietly refuted by the leaders of the environmental movement.

Many of the old environmental heroes had moved on to strange new positions. William Ruckleshaus went from on from EPA to run Browning-Ferris Industries, the nation's largest solid waste company, and to sit on the board of the timber giant Weyerhaeuser and the agro-chemical empire Monsanto. Lee Thomas, one of Rucklehaus's successors at EPA, found an especially remunerative position as in the Atlanta headquarters of Georgia Pacific. The promiscuous Bob Packwood, now disgraced, traveled the roads of rural Oregon calling for the repeal of the Endangered Species Act, which, in another life, he had helped enact. Corporate criminal Louisiana-Pacific (which pleaded guilty to 16 felonies and misdemeanors in 1995) served as a proud sponsor of the 25th anniversary celebration of Earth Day.

In the Clinton era, the contours of the environmental politics in Washington settled into a triangulated landscape, bounded by the Executive Office Building and its agency outlet (where administrative fiats are handed down with devastating finality); the committee rooms of the Congress (where the chairs of the all-important appropriations committees dole out pork and pollution); and the gray mansions of the special interest lobbies, both environmental and industrial, which are stacked along K Street. Daily, the inhabitants of these centers of power determine the number of chinook salmon chewed up and spit out by the hydro-electric dams of the Columbia River, the gallons of dioxin flushed into the Mississippi, and the fate of animals such as the grizzly bear, whose habitat can remain protected or be transformed into cyanide-laced heap leach gold mines.

Clinton's years at the top of the Executive pyramid were defined by opportunism—his calling card as a politician. Environmental quality and economic progress can advance hand in hand, Clinton counseled. If they don't, well, there will always be time to fix the damage to the earth later. Remember, it's the economy, stupid.

When Clinton came to DC, he brought his old pal Mack McLarty with him as chief of staff. McLarty had been a chieftain of the natural gas behemoth ARKLA, Inc. and a golfing buddy of the tycoons of Arkansas. Along with the corporate lobbyist Vernon Jordan, McLarty played a decisive role in choosing Clinton's cabinet, including Leon Panetta and Alice Rivlin at OMB, Babbitt at Interior, Ron Brown at Commerce and former Gore staffers Carol Browner at EPA and Katie McGinty as supervisor of the White House Office of Environmental Affairs. All were cut from the same pro-business, anti-regulatory cloth spun by the Democratic Leadership Council. In a move that was later to yield useful dividends, the Clinton transition team also stocked the administration with a cluster of 24 top-level staffers from the ranks of DC-based environmental groups. At head was George Frampton, former president of the Wilderness Society, who was tapped as assistant secretary of Interior.

It didn't take McLarty long to exert his veto power over environmental policy. The administration's initial budget request to Congress included a provision to reform federal policies governing gold mining and subsidized grazing and timber sales on public lands. Widely backed by greens, the initiative would have protected millions of acres of forest and grassland from clearcutting and mining and would have saved the federal treasury nearly a billion dollars a year. Instead, it ignited a firestorm in the public lands states in the West. A posse of western Democrats, led by Senators Max Baucus of Montana and Ben Nighthorse Campbell of Colorado (who later skipped to the Republican side of the aisle), wrote an angry letter denouncing the plan and threatening to launch a filibuster against it on the Senate floor. McLarty invited the senators to the White House where he obediently agreed to pull the measure from the budget bill. (Bruce Babbitt, whose office had drafted the proposal, found out about McLarty's deal-making the next night at a cocktail party. His unlikely informant was Jay Hair, the head of the National Wildlife Federation. "The jerks didn't have the courtesy to ask me about it or even to tell me what they had done," Babbitt raged to Hair.)

McLarty's cave-in occurred on the eve of the first-ever presidential summit on environmental issues: the Presidential Conference on Northwest Forests, held in Portland, Oregon, on April 2, 1993. The timber summit, as it came to be known, had its roots in the controversy over the northern spotted owl and the clearcutting of ancient forests on federal lands in the Pacific Northwest.

The spotted owl, which nests only in old-growth trees, had been listed as a threatened species in 1990. The following year William Dwyer, a federal judge in Seattle, halted all logging on six million acres of old-growth forest in Oregon, Washington and northern California. The judge cited the government for a "systematic disregard" of the nation's environmental laws. The timber industry bellowed that the injunction was going to put them out of business and throw 100,000 millworkers and loggers out of work. Environmentalists responded that the decline of the owl would be just the beginning of a larger annulment of old-growth-dwelling species, including dwindling stocks of Pacific salmon—all threatened by logging. The most puissant predators in the forest, Weyerhaeuser, Georgia-Pacific and International Paper, which owned their own highly productive lands, were not affected by the injunctions and in fact had seen their earnings soar.

During his campaign swings through the Northwest, Clinton promised that within 90 days of taking office he would convene a summit to resolve the "timber crisis" once and for all. "I want to produce a legal plan for managing these forests," Clinton assured voters in Oregon. "And get the logs rolling back into the mills." So on April 2, Clinton summoned his top cabinet officials, corporate executives, millworkers, loggers, economists, bureaucrats, the Cardinal of Seattle, forest sociologists, academic and agency scientists and mainstream greens to Portland.

The timber summit itself was a piece of theater designed to allow Clinton to demonstrate his affection for nature and to show that he "felt the pain" of laid off millworkers. At the same time he humbly deferred to the true source of the millworkers' economic woes, Weyerhaeuser vice-president Charlie Bingham, who commands the exportation of billions of board feet of raw logs to mills overseas. Weyerhaeuser is also the largest landholder in Arkansas and Bingham and Clinton had known each other for years.

At the close of the session, Clinton bragged of taking the conflict out of the "courtroom and into the conference room" and promised to unveil a "scientifically credible and legally responsible plan" within another 90 days. The goal of the plan, Clinton murmured, was to provide a sure supply of timber to Northwest mills and to meet the requirements of the Endangered Species Act.

Insinuated into every line of Clinton's screed that afternoon was the promise that the whine of the chainsaw would be sacrosanct, immune from even modest attempts to mute the frenzied pace of the cut or the export of raw logs. And so it came to pass.

Clinton assembled a task force of federal scientists, headed by Forest Service research ecologist Jack Ward Thomas and forester Jerry Franklin, who also happened to be a board member of the Wilderness Society. The scientists devised eight options for the president to consider. None of them permitted enough logging to satisfy Clinton's political objectives. Clinton and Babbitt ordered the scientists to concoct another alternative, the infamous Option 9.

While Option 9 reduced the amount of logging allowed on national forests from the hey-day of the Reagan years, it failed to set aside any permanently protected old-growth forest preserves, and permitted clearcutting to continue in some of the most ancient groves in the region and in the most vital spotted owl and salmon habitat. In fact, the environmental analysis accompanying Option 9 admitted that this strategy places hundreds of species at increased risk of extinction, including the spotted, marbled murrelet and dozens of stocks of Pacific salmon and steelhead.

The scientists working on the project were prohibited from talking to the press, and Thomas and Co., under orders from the Clinton White House, promptly shredded documents that revealed the fake science behind Option 9.

Months later, Clinton picked Thomas to be the new chief of the Forest Service. Leaders of the DC environmental groups dutifully hailed Thomas's appointment as a major victory, despite his unsavory role in the development of Option 9. Their glee was short-lived.

Within months of assuming his post in the Clinton administration, Thomas approved the biggest timber sale in the modern history of the Forest Service. The so-called Prince of Wales timber sale on the Tongass National Forest in southeast Alaska called for the clearcutting of thousands of acres of ancient forest and the construction of more than 100 miles of road into a fragile and previously roadless landscape. The logging rights, bought by giant Louisiana-Pacific, had been strongly opposed by many biologists and geologists within the Forest Service.

In the spring of 1994, Thomas fired two Forest Service whistle-blowers. Ernie Nunn and Curtis Bates had stood up to the timber and mining companies in Montana, and first ran into trouble back in 1990, when they signed a letter which described the Forest Service as being dominated by the whims of the extractive industries and out of touch with the environmental concerns of the American public. That letter sparked such a revolt inside the Forest Service that the Bush administration attempted to sack the dissident forest supervisors. This Republican bid failed, rebuffed by congressional hearings and public outcry. Four years later, with a Democratic president and a Democratic congress, Thomas moved swiftly and with impunity to fire Bates and Nunn.

Despite these outrages, many of the big green groups remained locked in a necrotic embrace with the Clinton administration. The Sierra Club's Carl Pope, a long-time friend of Al Gore, hailed the Option 9 plan as "a fair and reasonable compromise." The National Audubon Society's Brock Evans, long touted as the best environmental lobbyist on the Hill, pronounced it "a shaky victory."

The Clinton administration floated a draft version of Option 9 before the public. Then Bruce Babbitt called on environmental leaders to annul the very injunction they had won in Judge Dwyer's courtroom against logging in spotted owl habitat. As "a gesture of goodwill" to the Clinton administration, Babbitt demanded that the environmentalists accept more than 100 timber sales in ancient forests. If they refused, Babbitt warned, the administration would ask Congress to overturn the injunction with what's known as a sufficiency rider, a tactic of the Reagan-Bush years. With such a rider, Congress stipulates that a law is "sufficient," overriding all relevant previous laws and regulations and is immune to future challenges in the courts.

Lawyers for the Sierra Club Legal Defense Fund (the self-proclaimed "dream team" of environmental law firms) forthwith coerced its clients into handing over several thousand acres of old-growth forest, and then, months later, the Dwyer injunction itself.

Grassroots greens vigorously resisted this surrender, which was quickly dubbed the Deal of Shame. But the Defense Fund, which holds a near monopoly on nonprofit environmental lawsuits, threatened to abandon any clients who refused to go along with its advice.

One of the strange pathologies afflicting contemporary environmentalism is that a conservation group without a law firm behind it
suffers extreme pangs of institutional impotence. "The problem was
that SCLDF's arguments stemmed from political, not legal, judge-
ments," says Oregon environmentalist Larry Tuttle. "And they were
shaped in large measure by their own economic self-interest (i.e.,
their right to sue and collect legal fees from the government), not
necessarily the future of the spotted owl."

Eventually, the enviros, pummeled by their own attorneys and
the Clinton administration, collapsed, and in the spring of 1994 the
cutting of ancient forest resumed for the first time in four years.
Things had indeed been better with George Bush and gridlock.

Bruce Babbitt's role in this deal shocked many greens. He had
been the president of the League of Conservation Voters, and many
had seen him as the green chevalier of the Clinton administration.
The stab in the back should have surprised no one.

Babbitt comes from a big-time ranching family fed and fattened
on the Western traditions of cheap water, free range and unregulated mining. And his record as governor of Arizona should have been
another warning sign. When mineworkers walked off the job citing
unsafe and unfair working conditions at the Phelps-Dodge silver
mine in the early 1980s, then-Governor Babbitt called in the
National Guard to crush the strike on behalf of the corporation,
which had long planned the confrontation in consort with the
University of Pennsylvania's Wharton School as a test case for
breaking strikes and unions with "permanent replacement workers."

Babbitt also strong-armed federal park officials in order to
secure approval of a resort complex on the rim of the Grand
Canyon. The resort is owned by a long-time friend and political contributor.

But Babbitt is perhaps most notorious for his single-minded
pursuit of Colorado River water to sate the thirst of real estate czars
in Tucson and Phoenix. While Babbitt supported mighty water allo-
cations to his state, he opposed them for his neighbors, vigorously
objecting to water claims made by California and Utah. These western water battles brought Babbitt into the embrace of Dick Carver,
a commissioner in Nye County, Nevada. Carver and Babbitt joined
forces in the quest for the waters of the Colorado. Carver later

became a key leader of the county supremacy movement, which asserts that the federal government does not have the constitutional right to own land. Carver has promoted his cause at gatherings of far right groups throughout the West, most notably at the Jubilee, organized by the racist Posse Comitatus and the Christian Identity movement.

In August of 1994, Carver ignited a war with the federal government when he mounted a bulldozer and plowed an illegal road onto the Toiyabe National Forest, nearly running over two Forest Service workers. Carver, who claims that he and Babbitt are close friends, threatened to shoot anyone who tried to stop him. Although harassment of a federal employee is a felony, punishable by a $250,000 fine and up to 10 years in prison, six months passed and the federal government took no action. Finally, only a civil suit was filed, and that was against the Nye County commission, not Carver. Local BLM and Forest Service rangers think Babbitt intervened with the Department of Justice to protect his old pal.

Other friends of Babbitt didn't fare nearly so well. Take Jim Baca, who comes from one of the oldest Hispanic families in the Southwest and who served for years as the lands commissioner for the state of New Mexico, where he acquired a reputation as a progressive and hard-nosed conservationist. But Baca's anti-cattle grazing stance earned him the seething enmity of ranchers across the West. Over the objections of the National Cattlemen's Association and the American Mining Congress, Babbitt selected Baca to oversee the BLM, the agency charged with administering about 250 million acres of public lands in the West—lands long viewed as the private dominion of cattle ranchers and gold mining companies.

Baca tried to make ranchers pay market rates for the use of public grasslands. (Currently, ranchers grazing cattle and sheep on federal lands pay less than a fifth of the rates charged on private and state lands—an annual subsidy of $200 million.) Then he went after the gold companies. Baca vigorously advocated the repeal of the 1872 Mining Law, which allows gold mining companies to claim title to public lands for as little as $2.50 per acre and then pay no royalties on the billions of dollars of minerals they remove. Baca fought for an 8 percent royalty rate on the mining of all public minerals and an end to the transfer of federal lands to mineral companies. Finally, Baca became the first BLM director to openly advocate for the need for more wilderness. He supported setting aside nearly 20 million acres of high desert and mountain country in Utah, Idaho and Oregon as wilderness, closed to logging, mining and road building.

This ran Baca athwart very powerful forces, many inside the Democratic Party. Baca's most prominent critic turned out to be the governor of Idaho, Cecil Andrus, former Secretary of the Interior under LBJ and a former employee of the Wilderness Society, where Baca had also once served as a director. In December of 1993, Andrus attacked Baca in a letter to Babbitt, pronouncing: "My friend, frankly, you don't have enough political allies in the West to treat us this shabbily." Later, Andrus, who after retiring as governor joined the boards of two mining companies, publicly fumed: "It's either Baca or Babbitt. One of them's gotta go!"

A few days later Babbitt announced in *The Washington Post* that Baca had been transferred from his BLM post to a new vague role as a policy adviser to Babbitt. There was a problem. No one had told Baca about the move. When he found out, he didn't like it and he resisted.

"I thought Babbitt at least owed it to me as a long-time friend to explain why I was being moved," Baca said. "I wanted him to ask me for my resignation personally." Chastened by criticism from the national press, Babbitt held off for a month. Then he called Baca into his office and told him either to accept the transfer or tender his resignation. Baca resigned. A month later, as he contemplated a run for governor of New Mexico, Baca said, "Babbitt doesn't stand up for his principles, because he has no backbone."

The Baca debacle was eerily reminiscent of a similar purge of federal land managers during the Bush administration, when chief of staff John Sununu engineered the removal of regional directors of the Park Service and Forest Service who had stood up to the timber, mining and oil and gas companies that wanted a free hand to plunder public forests adjacent to Yellowstone National Park. This crackdown on federal land managers sparked roars of protest from environmentalists, prompting congressional hearings and stories in the press and on TV. However, the national environmental community remained strangely mute following the ouster of Baca.

The man Babbitt picked to replace Baca, Mike Dombeck, was much friendlier to ranching and mining interests. Six months after his appointment, Dombeck drafted a secret memo to Babbitt outlining a plan that would have seemed radical during the tenure of James Watt. As a budget-cutting measure, Dombeck advised Babbitt that the BLM could either return 110 million acres of public lands to the states or sell them off to the highest bidder. A scheme earlier in the century to dispose of public lands and resources had sent former Secretary of the Interior Albert Fall to prison in the Teapot Dome scandal. Dombeck backed off the memo once its contents were leaked to *The Washington Post*.

Babbitt's right hand man at Interior was Tom Collier. Before joining the Clinton administration Collier and Babbitt worked together at the DC mega-law firm Steptoe and Johnson. The firm's roster of clients included many of the same companies Babbitt and Collier were in charge of regulating at Interior, including Burlington Northern, Canyon Forest Village Corporation, Alcoa, Canadian Forest Industries Council, Sealaska and the Forest Industries Committee on Timber Taxation and Valuation.

One of the companies previously represented by Collier and Babbitt is the Norwegian Cruise Lines, which held a permit from the Interior Department for cruise ship forays into southeast Alaska's Glacier Bay National Park. For years the company and Alaska Senator Frank Murkowski pressured the Park Service to increase the number of cruise visits permitted into the narrow fjords of Glacier Bay. The Park Service resisted, fearing adverse affects from the huge ships on orca, gray whales and other marine life—as well as the glaciers themselves. In fact, Park Service scientists were hoping to curtail the number of cruise ships permitted in the bay and enviros wanted to ban them outright. Then Babbitt and Collier intervened, overruled Park Service biologists, and upped the number of cruise visits, leading to millions in profits for their former clients.

Why was the reaction to Babbitt's various betrayals of the greens so subdued? Perhaps, like the Christian Right during the era of Bush, the Beltway greens felt there was nowhere else to turn. It is also clear that many still placed their hopes in Vice President Al Gore. Gore's reputation among the Washington press corps as an environmental titan was largely based on his grandstanding at the

Rio Earth Summit in 1992 and on his book *Earth in the Balance*, which stresses environmental discipline for the Third World, while gliding over the corporate looting of North America's forests, rivers and mountains. (This is nothing new. Heading the rush to the Amazon to denounce deforestation in the late 1980s were many US politicians who would be aghast at the thought of curbing timber companies operating in Montana or Oregon.) Gore is a DLC environmentalist, a tireless promoter of the free-market approach and the probable ghostwriter of Clinton's quip that "the invisible hand has a green thumb." Since the mid-1980s Gore has argued with increasing stridency that the bracing forces of market capitalism are potent curatives for the ecological entropy now bearing down on the global environment. He is a passionate disciple of the gospel of efficiency, suffused with an inchoate technopilia.

Several of Gore's protégés landed top posts in the administration, most notably Carol Browner as EPA administrator. Browner had served as Gore's legislative director from 1989 through 1991, before leaving to become the head of Florida's Department of Environmental Regulation. During her stint in Florida, Browner took two particularly high-profile stands. The first was a capitulation to sugar-growers and developers that allowed continued (though slightly filtered) dumping of pesticide-laced waters into the Everglades. Second, Browner allowed the Disney Company to destroy 800 acres of vital wetland habitat outside Orlando in exchange for a pledge from the eco-imagineers at DisneyWorld to recreate several thousand acres of "wetlands," a feat which remains well beyond the capacities of modern science.

At EPA, Browner wasted little time in promoting ideas, such as wetland trading, that during the Bush administration had met with howls of derision from the green lobby. One of Browner's first actions was to put the imprimatur of the EPA on the Everglades deal she had brokered a year earlier in Florida. This was a precedent of sorts—the first time the federal government had officially sanctioned the pollution of a national park.

Following Gore's lead, Browner initiated a campaign to "reinvent" the EPA by beginning to peel away "excessive environmental regulations"—the old refrain of the Gorsuch years. But Browner was playing from a slightly different book. Her theme echoes back to the late 1970s and the writings of Stephen Breyer, then an aide to Senator Ted Kennedy. Breyer drafted a book-length paper arguing that federal regulations should be evaluated through two tests: risk assessment and cost/benefit analysis. The costs of pollution control, under the Breyer scheme, would be weighed against the heavily discounted benefits of human health and environmental quality—a certain recipe for more hazardous waste landfills, dioxin-belching incinerators and higher cancer rates. In 1994, Breyer, of course, was elevated to a spot on the Supreme Court.

Browner's first target was the so-called Delaney Clause in the Food and Drug Act, which placed a strict prohibition against any detectable level of carcinogens in processed food. Though long the bane of the American Farm Bureau and the Chemical Manufacturer's Association, the Delaney Clause remained inviolate, even through the Reagan and Bush years. Yet within months of taking office, Browner announced that she felt this standard was too severe and moved to gut it. "We just don't have unlimited financial resources to enforce all these measures and that can create a blacklash," Browner complained. "So we need to be realistic. We need the strongest possible standards, but we need flexibility in how to achieve those standards."

Like the pliant Browner, Gore was in synch with the Clinton two-step. The prime example of this is the case of the hazardous waste incinerator in Liverpool, Ohio, operated by WTI. During the campaign, Gore vowed that the administration would never approve the toxic burner located just a few yards from an elementary school. Three months after the inauguration, Browner's EPA issued the lethal plant its operating permit. It turned out that the money behind WTI came largely out of the accounts of Arkansas financier Jackson Stephens, the Clinton/Gore campaign's biggest contributor. Gore said nothing.

On other crucial matters, Clinton used Gore to split environmentalists and thus advance pro-business policies, as in the fight over the North American Free Trade Agreement. The environmental defects of NAFTA were manifold and had helped to energize broad opposition to the trade pact, including a rare alliance between greens and big labor. When it looked as if NAFTA might crumble, Gore pledged to Clinton that he could wrest an endorsement of the deal from some top-rank environmental outfits.

Gore turned to his longtime friend Jay Hair of the National Wildlife Federation. Hair was the perfect figure to marshal support for NAFTA. He was the self-proclaimed leader of the Gang of Ten, executives of the 10 largest environmental groups, including the National Wildlife Federation, Natural Resources Defense Council, Sierra Club, Environmental Defense Fund, National Audubon Society, Izaak Walton League, World Wildlife Fund, League of Conservation Voters, Wilderness Society and Friends of the Earth. The Gang meets six times a year in such pleasing circumstances as Kodiak, Alaska; Telluride, Colorado; Jackson, Wyoming; and the beaches of Belize.

Hair knew he couldn't sell the other eco-executives on the meager environmental provisions of NAFTA, so he outlined the political calculus at work. Hair said that the green's endorsement of NAFTA would buy the administration's support for high priority environmental reforms at home, such as protection of ancient forests, reform of mining laws, stiffening of Superfund and reauthorization of the Endangered Species Act, which had been languishing for more than a decade. The more conservative and policy-oriented groups swiftly aligned themselves behind Hair, including EDF, NRDC, the World Wildlife Fund, the Nature Conservancy, Conservation Foundation and the National Audubon Society.

When the Sierra Club and Friends of the Earth refused to endorse NAFTA and instead joined the opposition, Hair threw a fit, dashing off threatening memos to the executives of both organizations, accusing them of treachery.

In the end, the resistance of the Sierra Club and Friends of the Earth didn't matter. The groups assembled by Hair were more than enough for the purposes of the Clinton administration. Days after the trade deal squeaked through Congress, John Adams, head of NRDC, claimed credit, boasting that he and Hair had "broken the back of the environmental opposition to NAFTA." A few months later the famous environmental "side agreement" to NAFTA was formally declared to be worthless.

Over the next four years, the Clinton administration continued to steamroll environmentalists: there was the Salvage Logging Rider, which suspended all environmental laws on national forests for two years; the weak-kneed Kyoto Accord on global warming; roll-backs in rules limiting ozone-depleting chemicals, such as methyl bromide; more deal-making with sugar barons down in the Everglades; exemptions from the Endangered Species Act for loggers and developers; and on and on.

A quarter-century after the first Earth Day, the corporate counter attack launched in the late 1970s is now nearly complete. As citizens virtuously warehouse their newspapers, seek redemption in glass and aluminum and recycle their direct mail pleas from mainstream environmental groups into properly labeled receptacles, they may be too busy acting locally to notice the grim climate that has settled over the national landscape.

Portland, 1996.

[An earlier version of this essay appeared in *Washington Babylon* by Alexander Cockburn and Ken Silverstein.]

Two

Bush, The Early Days

I'm both a compassionate conservative and a passionate conservationist," pronounced Interior Secretary Gale Norton in late February 2001, during a speech at Bob Packwood's Dorchester Conference, an annual confab on the Oregon Coast for western Republicans. "There are better approaches than top-down, Washington-based decision-making to protect our environment," she said. "I believe there are good ideas all over America. I respectfully disagree with those who say that to be good stewards of our national treasures, we must be willing to sacrifice jobs."

Norton didn't elaborate on what she meant by this. She didn't unveil her agenda at Interior, other than to say that she believed Snake River chinook salmon could be saved without tearing down the four dams that have brought them to the brink of extinction and that the oil that lies under the Arctic National Wildlife Refuge could be exhumed without so much as a stain on the tundra. But the people in the audience got her drift.

"When you compare Gale to Bruce Babbitt, you know that help is on the way," said Paulette Pyle, a lobbyist for pesticide and agribusiness concerns.

Take those national monuments created during the closing hours of Clintontime. Many right-wingers and latter-day Sagebrush Rebels want Norton to get rid of them. But that's not Norton's style. As she told *The Washington Post*, "I'm not Jim Watt. I've matured." Instead, Norton has decided to leave the designations in place, but she has signaled that it might be okay to explore for oil or coal inside them. That's how you can be "a good steward of our national treasures" without "sacrificing jobs." This cynical maneuver sets a template for the Bush approach to natural resource policy.

The early read on Norton is that she is a lot smarter and more politically savvy than her mentor Watt. Norton understands what many of the Republican ultras failed to notice: the national monument designations were mainly political fluff that imposed few real restrictions on commercial activities inside the boundaries.

Bush backed up Norton's nefarious scheme. "There are parts of the monument lands where we can explore without affecting the overall environment," mumbled Bush in an interview with the *Denver Post*. "It depends upon the cost-benefit ratio. There are some monuments where the land is so widespread, they just encompass as much as possible. And the integral part, the precious part, so to speak will not be despoiled. There's a mentality that says you can't explore and protect land. We're going to change that attitude. You can explore and protect land."

It's easy to see where this kind of boasting is headed. The Bush administration is advancing on multiple fronts, aimed at forcing the environmental community to blink and sign-off on a deal. Perhaps protection of the national monuments in exchange for limited exploration of the Arctic National Wildlife Refuge. Or vice versa. Some believe that the Bush inner circle (namely Cheney and Norton) is less anxious to drill in ANWR than it is to resurrect old Reagan era schemes involving the Rocky Mountain Front, the eastern flank of the mighty range running from north of Denver through Wyoming and Montana. Oil, coal, shale oil, and, if you believe the oil industry's press releases, the largest trove of natural gas on the continent.

Here's another example of the Norton two-step. Norton has offered as proof of her green bona fides a plan to boost the budget of the Land and Water Conservation Fund, a federal trust account that is used to purchase threatened lands with unique natural values. To the uninitiated this sounds like a laudable endeavor. After all, under past Republican administrations the billion-dollar LWCF has lain moribund: either unused because of rightwing opposition or juggled around in order to help conceal the size of the federal deficit.

But the kicker is that the LWCF is not financed through the general fund but by (surprise!) royalties from oil drilling on federal lands and the Outer Continental Shelf. So any hike in LWCF funding will necessarily involve an increase in public lands oil leases, an unyielding obsession of the Bush team.

Plus, there's another hitch. Norton adores the LWCF because it fits snugly into her free-market environmentalism mantra, which dictates that private property rights are sacred and not to be trampled upon by imperious federal regulations, such as the Endangered Species Act or Clean Water Act. According to her neo-Lockeian worldview, if the federal government wants to regulate use of private lands it should pay compensation or buy the property outright. Of course, this kind of cash-box conservationism spells a death knell for many environmental laws and, if taken to its logical extreme, is also a surefire way to bankrupt the federal treasury faster than the Bush tax cuts.

One of Norton's rare missteps so far was her pick for the number-two position at Interior: Steven Griles, an oil and mining industry lobbyist. Griles is one of those Washington political poltergeists who scurries back and forth between the government and private sector wreaking havoc for his cronies in the mining and oil industries. Under Reagan, Griles toiled in several different slots in the Interior Department, most deviously at the Office of Surface Mining, where he strove to obstruct any limits on the machinations of big coal. His tenure there, highlighted by an unyielding defense of even the most rapacious forms of strip mining, has earned him the lifelong enmity of anti-mining activists from Arizona to West Virginia.

For as much as the anti-federal government crowd excoriates Washington as a kind of post-modern Babylon, once they've settled inside the Beltway, few of them seem to return to their homesteads in the hinterlands even after their careers as so-called public servants have expired. Griles, for instance, cashed in on his expertise at manipulating the government in the service of industry by becoming a top corporate lobbyist at the coyly named National Environmental Strategies.

In tapping Griles, Norton snubbed Dick Cheney's flyfishing buddy John Turner, thought to be the frontrunner for the post. Turner, who lives near Cheney in Jackson Hole, Wyoming, served as director of the Fish and Wildlife Service during Bush I. Back then he was viewed as something of a moderate in a Department headed by the zany Manuel Lujan, who once opined that perhaps some species, like the spotted owl, simply weren't equipped to handle the

rigors of life in the modern world and should be allowed to graceful-
ly enter the oblivion of extinction. Ultimately, Turner's nomination
was sabotaged by Wise Use zealots and their congressional stooges,
most notably Senator Larry Craig, who chafed at his reluctance to
openly defy the edicts of the Endangered Species Act.

Here's why Norton's decision may backfire. Upon closer scrutiny, Turner's reputation as a conservationist, greatly abetted by mainstream green outfits, proves rather hollow. Grassroots activists recall
his efforts in the early '90s to suppress internal reports calling for the
protection of the spotted owl and Pacific salmon stocks, as well as
his willingness to entertain the notion of corporate sponsorship for
the national parks. Thus, it may have been easier for smooth-talking
Turner (still likely to land a lesser post in the Administration) to
move through the Norton/Bush agenda, than Griles, a self-proclaimed corporado, who will be ceaselessly attacked by the green
establishment as an industry puppet.

* * *

To get a better grip on where the Bush crowd is going, it's
important to look into some of the more remote corners of the
Administration, where much of the real dirty work will be hatched
and carried out. Take the decidedly unalluring Office of
Management and Budget. OMB seems likely to head a stealth attack
on environmental regulations, much as it did during the previous
Bush administration. "What regulations Bush won't kill outright,
they'll simply starve to death for lack of funds," predicts Larry Tuttle,
director of the Portland-based Citizens for Environmental Equity.

One of the more obscure outposts at OMB is the Office of
Information and Regulatory Affairs. It's the equivalent of a Star
Chamber for corporations seeking relief from pesky environmental
and safety standards. To head this outfit, which one Senate staffer
dubbed "the office of corporate ombudsman," Bush has nominated
John Graham, a long-time hired gun for polluting industries.
Graham now runs the Harvard Center for Risk Analysis, which has
received millions in financial aid from dozens of oil, timber, chemi-
cal and mining companies, including: ARCO, Boise-Cascade, BP,
Chemical Manufacturer's Association, Chlorine Chemistry
Council, DuPont, Electric Power Research Institute, General

Motors, Monsanto, National Association of Home Builders, and Waste Management.

Graham's routine is to solicit money from big corporations facing litigation or legislation to curb shoddy, toxic or dangerous business practices. He then writes a book, paper or article debunking the supposed dangers of the corporate misbehavior, citing "risk analysis" studies showing that the costs to the company of correcting the problem far outweigh the risk to the public.

For example, according to a report by Public Citizen, in 1991 Graham sought money for his center from Philip Morris. Five months later, Graham asked the tobacco company to review a chapter in his book on second-hand smoke. Since then Philip Morris has repeatedly cited Graham's work to undermine the EPA's efforts to regulate second-hand smoke.

Here's another example: Graham currently serves on the EPA's dioxin review board, where in 2000 he put forward the inane theory that small doses of dioxin might actually help prevent certain forms of cancer and urged the EPA to include in its profile of the deadly chemical a note stating that it was "an anti-carcinogen." Had Graham prevailed, this absurd footnote would have made it extremely difficult for EPA to hold the line on dioxin emissions.

"A person with such disdain for public priorities should not be given a last-ditch veto over the will of the public," warns Joan Claybrook, director of Public Citizen. "Installing an industry-funded flack in such a crucial position would harm the public for generations."

Despite toiling for biotech companies and the pesticide-happy agribusiness giants of California's Central Valley, Secretary of Agriculture Ann Veneman was thought by many liberal pundits to be something of a beacon of hope inside the Bush cabinet. She waltzed through her confirmation hearings and wasn't even confronted with a single nagging question on her plans for the largest and, frequently the most deviant, agency in the Agriculture Department, the US Forest Service. But two months into her tenure, things over at the Agriculture Department were beginning to look very bleak indeed.

Before Clinton left office, the US Forest Service completed its much-ballyhooed plan for roadless areas on national forest lands. An election-year scheme designed to boost Al Gore's standing with greens, the plan called for banning most new roads and some forms of logging in so-called roadless lands 5,000 acres and larger in the national forests. In the end, the proposal, which was riddled with loopholes, fell far short of the expectations of most environmentalists. Even so, the plan was wildly popular with the public and opinion-makers.

The roadless area rule was set to go into effect on March 13. But the timber industry, in the nadir of another of its frequent slumps, fumed at the idea and goaded Bush into slapping a hold on the plan soon after the inauguration. Then in separate suits the state of Idaho and timber giant Boise-Cascade asked a federal court in Idaho to overturn the rule, putting forth the fantastical theory that the plan hadn't been subjected to enough public review.

In fact, the case should have been dismissed outright, because the roadless area plan had gone through more public review than any environmental impact statement in the last 25 years. "There were more than 1.6 million comments and 600 public meetings," said Tim Hermach, director of the Native Forest Council, based in Eugene, Oregon. "This plan was studied to death."

But the Bush administration lawyers, put in the indelicate position of having to defend a plan they wanted to see abolished, simply threw up their hands, telling the judge they would be willing to suspend indefinitely implementation of the plan. "This was their first opportunity to defend the policy and they've come in with an offer to suspend it," said Tom Preso, an attorney for Earthjustice, which is representing numerous environmental groups that have intervened in the case. The Bush administration is giving every indication that they want to bring bulldozers back into the national forests. It's certainly a far cry from the vigorous defense of the rule promised by Attorney General John Ashcroft during his confirmation hearings."

In reality, this is an orchestrated winking game between the Bushies and their pals in industry—the suit and the pleadings were coordinated between the plaintiffs and the defendants. This incestuous scam points toward a key Bush strategy: let third-parties do the heavy lifting on the most controversial issues in order to deflect some of the political heat. A similar scenario played itself out in Alaska, where the Bush administration allowed the state's congressional delegation and governor, Democrat Tony Knowles, to take the lead on the heated issue of opening the Arctic National Wildlife Refuge to oil drilling, a scheme that enjoys little public sympathy. Indeed, the Administration quietly urged Knowles to push the state legislature into approving a $1.85 million appropriation to a front group, called Alaska Power, which would in turn lobby congress and unleash a nationwide public relations campaign backing oil drilling in the tundra.

* * *

Through the campaign, Bush reminded the "blue areas on the map" that he owned a ranch and sympathized with the plight of the small farmer. This was prefabbed pablum for the rural folks and Bush, aside from his antipathy for the estate tax, apparently didn't mean a word of it. In early March, family farm groups, already staggering from give-away trade pacts, chronically depressed prices and relentless consolidation, were dealt another blow when Veneman invalidated a referendum approved in 2000 to end a mandatory promotional program that farmers said was corrupt. The farmers charged that their own money was being used against them to pursue ecologically destructive and price depressing factory hog farms. "The vote proved that we don't want money going out of our pockets for factory farms and corporate control anymore," says Roger Allison, of the Missouri Farm Crisis Center. "But now they've sabotaged it, declaring war on the family farm and on democracy."

Most of the money from the check-off program funds the National Pork Producers Council, the trade association for the big pork processors that are putting small farmers out of business. The director of the council, Al Tank, served on George Bush's agriculture transition team.

Meanwhile, under the mantra of states' rights, the Agriculture Department and Christie Todd Whitman's EPA are moving to ease pollution rules on big industrial farms and feedlots. In Oregon, for example, dairy and beef cattle from factory ranches generate about 7.5 million tons of manure a year, much of it ending up in streams and rivers. In 1998, EPA found that 18 of the large ranches were violating the meager requirements of the Clean Water Act and began handing out fines and issuing corrective orders. Now the Republican members of the Oregon congressional delegation are asking Whitman and Veneman to withdraw the fines, halt inspections and turn enforcement over to the western states.

A similar move is afoot in Ohio, where the Farm Bureau and other lobbyists for the megafarms are telling Whitman to make EPA inspectors stay out of Ohio and other midwestern states and allow state agriculture departments (not even the environmental agencies) to decide how much pollution the meat factories can release into streams and rivers.

"Each state knows how to handle their situation better than the feds," said Ohio Farm Bureau president Terry McClure. McClure said he was encouraged by Bush and Whitman's receptiveness to the idea.

This is another key element of the Bush approach. Using code words such as state primacy, local control and bottom-up planning, the Bush environmental team is seeking to swiftly devolve regulatory power from federal to state and local authorities—bodies over which industry enjoys an even tighter stranglehold than they do the feds. Over at EPA, Christie Todd Whitman has lived a double life. On the outside, she has sounded like a perkier version of her predecessor, Carol Browner. Whitman bragged about getting the once taboo words "global warming" into Bush's first address to congress, publicly chafed about the decision to strip federal funding from groups that advocate abortion overseas, and, during a trip to Trieste, told European environmental ministers that the Bush administration, unlike Clinton/Gore, would pursue mandatory caps on carbon dioxide emissions. Whitman garnered glowing press coverage citing her courage and feisty independence.

Then the plank was sawed off behind her. Bush announced that there would be no carbon caps and told Whitman to stop referring to carbon dioxide as a "pollutant." Dick Cheney was rolled out of the hospital in time to do damage control, saying that Whitman had merely been a "good soldier" attempting to defend a "misguided" policy. Then Whitman herself was ushered forward to make a public retraction. She cited the looming energy crisis as the rationale for continued US intransigence on the build-up of greenhouse gasses.

The whole thing looked silly and amateurish. But it was actually a calculated maneuver. The Bush strategy is to hype up the

California power crunch into a national energy emergency, which they intend to use to advance their agenda on multiple fronts: increased drilling and exploration; suspensions of clean air rules; new tax credits for oil and gas companies; and more subsidies for nuclear power. The CO_2 retreat served as a kind of public sacrifice to illustrate their seriousness.

Less widely reported was Whitman's move to reduce existing air quality standards in the Great Lakes region. On March 18 2001, Whitman announced that the EPA would relax pollution rules for gasoline in Chicago and Milwaukee. Whitman said the move was needed in order to keep gas prices from "spiking" this summer. Of course, this merely creates another incentive for the oil companies to price gouge and offer up environmental regulations as a handy scapegoat.

Just how much of all this will the Bush team be able to get away with? Well, that depends on how well they execute what Gale Norton calls the "collaboration" approach, getting a few Democrats and one or two mainstream environmental groups to sign off an end-run around federal laws and regulations. It's already borne fruit. The carbon cap retreat was praised by three top Democrats: Sen. Robert Byrd, the coal companies' one-man praetorian guard, John Breaux, the dark knight of the oil lobby, and Rep. John Dingell, loyal servant of the Detroit automakers.

Of course, there's nothing innovative here. In Clintontime, it was known as triangulation. The new fusion politics looks a lot like the old variety.

Cheney's decision to steamroll through the Bush environmental agenda within the first 100 days may yet backfire. Handing out gifts to chemical companies, big oil, strip mining outfits, nuclear power and coal companies all in a month stinks of overkill. The decision to rollback newly imposed limits on arsenic levels in drinking water may prove to be a fatal miscalculation. Sure, there's a double standard. After all, Clinton waited eight years to impose the rule and Bush is taking the heat from the press and a newly energized environmental movement for junking it before it even went into effect. The fuss over the CO_2 caps represents a similar exercise in hypocrisy. But that defines the new reality. Bush will be held to a higher standard on these matters than Clinton. Each move to erode environmental regulations will be countered by acrid attacks from the likes of the Sierra Club and the Wilderness Society. And the big greens, so often tongue-tied during Clintontime, are top-notch at flaying Republicans.

But the more insidious problem for the Bush gang may reside within their own party. What the Republican leadership, in a blind fervor to repay its corporate underwriters, ignores at its peril is the growing sentiment toward environmental protection within the rank-and-file of their own party. Already, Republican senators Lincoln Chafee, Olympia Snowe, James Jeffords and Susan Collins have already chided some of the moves as misguided and dangerous for the future political health of the party—it took nearly four years to hear similar caveats about Clinton from Democrats.

Polls show that even Republicans oppose drilling in ANWR and loosening drinking water standards and that more than 50 percent support strengthening laws that have long been bugaboos of the industrial rightwing, such as the Clean Air Act and the Endangered Species Act. The evidence for this can be seen in the growth of a new environmental group that is already putting George Bush's feet to the fire: Republicans for Environmental Protection. These are really Republicans and hard core environmentalists. And they are gaining more clout inside the party with each Bush misstep.

"We're really disappointed in the president," says Martha Marks, president of Republicans for Environmental Protection. "Obviously, we were trusting he would live up to his campaign promise, but it seems like the wrong forces or the anti-environmental forces inside his administration are prevailing. But we've seen a strong spike upwards in membership after the Norton nomination and it really hasn't stopped. We've had several hundred more members sign up in the last two months. Maybe as many as 1,000."

Portland, June 2001

PART II
Wild Matters

Three

The Fall of Harry Merlo

A decadent, old-growth timber baron is chopped down.

Harry Merlo was brought down in the fall of 1995 by his hand-picked board because he was in the process of destroying both it and the company it was supposed to oversee. Toward the end, the 22-year chief executive officer and chairman of Louisiana-Pacific was a grotesque ruin, bellowing threats to relocate his company across the Columbia River from Portland, OR, to Vancouver, WA

Meanwhile, across four conspiracy-packed weeks, L-P board members plotted Merlo's ouster. Finally, they summoned him from his 40th floor eyrie in the tallest office building in Portland, hauled him halfway across the country to Chicago—where the timber industry was headquartered before it moved to the Northwest 80 years ago—and threw him out of the company and out of the 7,300-square-foot mansion furnished him by L-P.

What brought Merlo down?

The lawsuits in which L-P was mired break into five species. First are suits reluctantly brought by a federal government yearning to ignore the company's crimes. The feds charged willful violations of environmental laws such as the Clean Air and Clean Water acts. A grand jury indictment alleged tampering with emission monitoring equipment and alteration of plant records and fraud in presenting samples of siding for certification by an industry trade group.

Then there were civil suits brought by citizens living next to L-P's oriented strand-board mills, charging toxic emissions. There was the avalanche of suits from customers who had bought siding (Inner Seal brand, made from oriented strand board), only to find that after a year's exposure to humidity, L-P's patented siding warped, broke apart and exuded a poisonous gas. Finally, there were the L-P shareholder suits alleging manipulation and failure to disclose significant liabilities, estimated by some analysts to be as high as $5 billion. Pendant to these allegations came charges of sexual harassment against Merlo and his two top executives.

Most of these indictments, either actual or prospective, were inconveniences that Merlo and his board had lived with for years and which they regarded as a minor cost of doing business. The environmental counts concerning air and water regulations L-P faced in Virginia, Alaska and Colorado were no different from the suit brought by the Surfrider Foundation against L-P's pulp mill in Samoa, CA, six years ago. In that affair L-P took the fall, paid out $12 million and turned decades of flushing billions of gallons of dioxin-laced effluent into Humboldt Bay into a public relations coup, with a handsome grant from the feds to upgrade its facilities.

As far back as 1980, L-P had been convicted of monopolistic practices in southeast Alaska, in a suit brought by a small logging company, Reid Brothers, of the Tlingit Tribe. Today, L-P is the only company buying timber off the Tongass National Forest. In the meantime, another 80 small sawmills in that region have gone under, courtesy of these same monopolistic practices.

But under Merlo's manic autocracy, L-P had made serious enemies in recent years. As the largest logger of public forests in the country, L-P was often at odds with big timber landowners like Weyerhaeuser and L-P's own parent company, Georgia-Pacific. By pillaging the underpriced public resource, L-P drove down profits for companies taking logs from private lands. This trend began in earnest in the early 1980s when Ronald Reagan made former L-P general counsel John Crowell Assistant Secretary of Agriculture in charge of the Forest Service. Crowell promptly demanded that the national forests double their annual cut, much of it destined for L-P's mills.

Even on L-P's own lands Merlo brought predation to a new pitch by using what had been previously regarded as non-commercial junk trees: small-in-diameter piss fir, alder, live oak, aspen, and the like, giving rise to Merlo's famous quote: "We log to infinity."

In marketing the plywood and siding products from such timber, Merlo angered a second powerful force in the industry: the lumber wholesalers. Merlo was selling directly to national outlets like Home Depot, thus cutting out the wholesalers and stealing another edge on his competitors. Finally, Merlo infuriated trade groups such as the American Plywood Association, which L-P deliberately deceived, faking the durability of its Inner Seal siding.

One counterattack pondered by Merlo's corporate opponents

was a takeover. In the days before Merlo fell, there were rumors on Wall Street that either Weyerhaeuser or International Paper was maneuvering for such a bid. At all events, in his hours of extremity Merlo had no big-time corporate friends, despite receiving the 1990 Man of the Year award from Ron Arnold's Wise Use Movement.

What terrified Merlo's board above all else was the product with which Merlo had most closely identified himself and the company, namely oriented strand board, the second generation of L-P's wafer board, which had been used in plywood. Stories in *The Oregonian* in June 1995 enraged Merlo: they featured plant managers, cloaked in prudent anonymity, saying bluntly that they knew the product was worthless, Merlo knew the product was worthless, but was demanding that they run the mills at 120 percent of operating capacity.

Merlo may have thought that even $5 billion in potential liability payouts was something the company could live with. L-P has enormous cash reserves, something on the order of a half-billion dollars at any given moment. And he was planning to off-load the poisonous siding on Third World customers such as Vietnam and Bolivia.

Whatever his private calculation, Merlo lied to his board and L-P's stockholders. It is as though the chief executive of the Ford Motor Company, back in the 1950s, had refused to abandon the Edsel and was instead determined to make it the only available model for the next decade. Such was the degree of Merlo's obsession.

In that last week, a dark shadow fell across the path of the chief executive of L-P as he fought for survival. The shadow took the form of a corporate tyrant even more predatory and egotistical than Merlo himself: Pierre DuPont, a member of the L-P board, who had been conducting a private investigation.

In a traditional corporate interlock, L-P was giving most of its liability suit business to the DuPont law firm. After scrutinizing L-P's second quarter report, the DuPont law firm concluded that Merlo had inflated second-quarter earnings by nearly $30 million. Merlo was forced to issue a revised statement of second-quarter earnings, thereby in effect pleading guilty to the charges—which will undoubtedly materialize—of fraud on a majestic scale. This is what destroyed him. The board, had it permitted Merlo to continue his tenure, would have been complicit in his deceptions and therefore personally liable.

There have been some sentimental elegies in the corporate press about Merlo as the last of the timber barons, "rags-to-riches" giant in a Cloverdale, CA-to-Portland saga of rugged individualism, finally run aground by post-titan corporate America.

The truth is bleaker.

With the hearty sanction of his corporate accomplices and their political flunkies, Merlo presided over the looting of the public domain, the poisoning of people with the misfortune to live next to one of his plants, and the betrayal of his workers whom he abandoned as soon as he had savaged the resource or spotted cheaper labor farther south. He presided over criminal legal harassment of his opponents in the environmental movement and over the sale of rotten, dangerous products. He flourished amid all the crimes and was handsomely rewarded for them. He fell not because of his predations on the citizenry, but because he menaced the bank balance and the peace of mind of a financial interest more powerful than himself.

The man has gone. The corporate malpractices will survive him and Third World people will soon be breathing the fumes of Merlo's toxic legacy.

Portland, 1995

Four

The Chainsaw Hypocrite

(With Alexander Cockburn)

> "There is just one hope of repulsing the tyrannical ambition of civilization to conquer every niche on the whole earth. That hope is the organization of spirited people who will fight for the freedom of the wilderness."
> Robert Marshall, at the founding of the Wilderness Society in 1930

Through late February and early March of 1995 a hundred logging trucks carried $140,000 worth of old growth Douglas fir and ponderosa pine from the private ranch of G. Jon Roush, president of the Wilderness Society and a man paid $125,000 a year to preserve that "freedom of the wilderness" Robert Marshall pledged as the Society's credo 65 years ago.

Roush logged off the 80-acre patch of old-growth and mature forest on his $2.5 million dollar ranch outside the small town of Florence in western Montana at precisely the moment when environmentalists across the country had their backs to the wall, against a ferocious assault in Congress on federal laws protecting America's public forests.

Roush's chainsaw massacre strips the Wilderness Society of whatever shreds of moral authority might still adhere to a name once made glorious in the era of Marshall and Aldo Leopold. Not only has the Society's president flouted the preservation ethic he is paid to protect, but he has undertaken a timber cut nearly identical to one prevented from taking place on federal lands adjoining his ranch ten years ago. In his rush to get his own cut out, Roush appears to have breached state and federal regulations governing logging slash disposal and road use. And he sold his timber to Plum Creek, once described by a Wilderness Society adviser as a practitioner of "Nazi forestry."

The head of the Wilderness Society logging old growth in the

Bitterroot Valley is roughly akin to the head of Human Rights Watch being caught torturing a domestic servant. The 736-acre Roush ranch is bordered by the rugged Bitterroot National Forest. Roush executed his timber sale less than two miles from the boundary of the Selway/Bitterroot Wilderness and well within the boundaries of the Salmon/Selway Ecosystem—the largest wildlands complex in the lower-48 states and home to elk, black bear, mountain lion and gray wolves.

The low-elevation ponderosa pine forest Roush logged grew on rolling parklands above Sweeney Creek, a crisp stream that tumbles off the serrated snow-capped peaks of the Bitterroot Mountains. Sweeney Creek is one of the purest streams in western Montana, providing habitat for pure strains of rare westslope cutthroat trout and bull trout. The bull trout is currently being considered for listing as a federally threatened species. One of the major factors behind the decline in bull trout populations is increased sedimentation in the river caused by logging.

The timber cut from Roush's property was hauled off in about 100 log-truck loads across national forest land on Forest Service logging roads. These Forest Service roads are often built by logging companies using federal subsidies to reach clearcuts on nearby national forest lands. The Wilderness Society has been a particularly harsh critic of the Forest Service road building program, denouncing it as a form of corporate welfare that leads to destruction of wildlands and wildlife habitat. In a recent Wilderness Society fundraising letter attacking federal subsidies for timber sales and logging road construction, Roush railed against timber companies that "measure the value of land only in dollars, in board-feet of lumber."

In the mid-1980s, Roush successfully sued the US Forest Service when it sought to cut trees in the Bitterroot National Forest, citing the potentially disastrous effects that logging on the fragile soils there might pose to streams and rivers in the area. Indeed, Roush amassed testimony from geologists and foresters who said most of the Bitterroot Face area was unsuitable for logging. Back then Roush also complained about increased traffic from logging trucks on Forest Service timber roads that crossed both national forest land and his own property. It was those same roads that logging trucks used to haul off about 100 loads of timber from Roush's land following the latest cut.

The site was logged by Sun Mountain Logging, a small family-run company in Deerlodge, Montana. It did a careful job as these operations go. Still, there's no way to disguise the ecological damage done: compacted soils, sedimentation in rivers, increased likelihood of landslides in these landslide-prone mountains, lost habitat for elk, owls, and northern goshawk.

Incidentally, Troy Anderson, a manager at Sun Mountain, admitted that the logging operation may have violated Forest Service regulations, when they begin logging the site without applying for a permit to use FS Road 1315. "We didn't know we needed a permit," Anderson said. "We got one as soon as we learned it was required by law." Anderson's claims of ignorance sound genuine, but Roush, head of an organization dedicated to enforcing the laws protecting public lands, certainly should have known a permit was required.

Perhaps the darkest irony of this story involves the purchaser of Jon Roush's timber. Sun Mountain's Troy Anderson tells us that he delivered the Roush logs to a dimensional sawmill in Pablo, Montana. That mill, which is located on the Flathead Indian Reservation, is owned by Plum Creek Timber.

Among other notorieties, Plum Creek, a shadowy limited partnership spun off from Burlington Northern, is one of the leading log exporters in the Pacific Northwest, shipping 50 percent of the timber it cuts on its own lands to Japan and Korea without passing the logs through an American mill. Plum Creek is also a nonunion operation that has decimated its captive workforce during years of high profits.

But it is Plum Creek's reckless treatment of the land that has earned it the reputation as the nation's most ecologically deviant timber company. It was the late Arnold Bolle, former dean of the University of Montana's School of Forestry and a longtime advisor to the Wilderness Society, who once described Plum Creek's slash-and-burn rampage across Montana as "Nazi forestry."

"That the president of the Wilderness Society should log old-growth ponderosas on lands that should never be logged is bad enough, but to sell those logs to Plum Creek is truly nauseating," says Larry Tuttle, former director of the Wilderness Society's office in Portland.

One particularly interesting interlock here is with Jerry Franklin, a professor at the University of Washington and a member of the Wilderness Society's governing board. Franklin, it will be recalled, was the principal architect of Option 9, Clinton's corporate-friendly logging plan for the ancient forests of the Pacific Northwest. Several years ago Franklin was contracted by Plum Creek in an attempt to greenwash its image as a corporate Mengele with a chainsaw. Behind the distorting screen of Franklin's "new forestry," Plum Creek continued to log off two million acres of land across Montana, Idaho, and Washington.

By 1993 most of the mature forest on Plum Creek's land had been brutally clearcut and most of its smaller competitors driven into bankruptcy. However, in March, Roush's predecessor at the Wilderness Society, George Frampton (now at Bruce Babbitt's knee as Assistant Secretary of Interior for Wildlife and Parks) secretly fashioned a "conservation agreement" for the checkerboard landscape of northwestern Montana that will allow Plum Creek to traverse Forest Service lands and liquidate its few remaining sections of old growth in places like the Swan Range with impunity from the Endangered Species Act, even though the area is crucial habitat for the embattled grizzly. The Wilderness Society, of course, uttered nary a word of opposition to this latest capitulation by Babbitt's boys at Interior. Indeed, under Jon Roush's leadership the Society has never once raised its voice against the outlandish behavior of American timber corporations on private lands.

Plum Creek now holds a virtual monopoly on all timber from public and private lands in Montana. After logging nearly all the salable timber on its own lands, Plum Creek has been the loudest among those pressing for the opening of Montana's six million acres of de facto wilderness on federal land to intensive logging—a move that will probably doom the grizzly bear to extinction, but bring the limited partnership tens of millions a year in federal timber subsidies. (The story of Plum Creek's environmental rampage in Montana is brilliantly told by Richard Manning in his book *Last Stand*.)

Plum Creek has made a lot of money from the frenzied pace of its logging in the past three years, owing largely to the soaring values of private forest land, as appeals and lawsuits brought by grassroots groups such as Friends of the Bitterroot, the Ecology Center, and the Swan View Coalition temporarily smothered the flow of federal timber sales. Of course, other large landowners benefited from this trend as well, including Jon Roush, who certainly made a fine profit on his timber sale. This winter the going stumpage rate for ponderosa pine and Douglas-fir was between $350 and $550 per thousand board feet, meaning that Roush could have reaped at least $140,000 on his timber sale.

Bill Bradt, a privately retained forester who marked the sale for Roush, claims the logging was designed to "improve the ecological conditions" of the forest stand. Bradt, a former Forest Service timber sale planner, now runs Sapphire Realty and works as a private consultant. He suggests the stand was "overstocked" and needed to be "thinned" in order to keep it healthy. He admitted, though, that it contained no dead or dying trees and suffered from no insect infestations.

But "forest health" rationalization (the idea that forests need to be logged in order to protect them from fires, insects, and disease) is a notion that has been thoroughly discredited as a grim hoax by forest ecologists, including scientists on the staff of the Wilderness Society. Here's what Wilderness Society ecologist Gregory Aplet had to say about the forest health "crisis" in the Northern Rockies: "There is real concern that the forest health situation...is being exaggerated to create an atmosphere in which accelerated timber harvesting is encouraged in the name of ecological restoration."

This appears to be exactly what Roush did. At our request, Jake Kreilick, an ecologist with the Native Forest Network who toured the Roush site at the end of March shortly after the completion of the logging operation, described the landscape as being littered with big stumps and tall slash piles of lopped limbs and smaller trees. "The stand was heavily cut-over," Krielick said. "It looks like they took most of the biggest and best trees and left only the smaller stuff behind. There's no way this can be described as just a thinning operation. This isn't eco-forestry, it's just an attempt to cash in on valuable trees."

Ironically, the logging on the Roush ranch occurred as the US House of Representatives speedily passed the Taylor-Young Amendment to the Fiscal Year 1995 Recission Bill. Citing a "forest health crisis," the Taylor-Young Amendment mandates the logging of six billion board feet of timber on federal lands over the next two years, exempts those timber sales from compliance with federal environmental laws, and blocks citizen access to federal courts. A similar bill recently shot through the Senate. Much of this planned logging is targeted for roadless areas in western Montana and Idaho. The bill was strongly opposed by Wilderness Society staffers and lobbyists.

Unlike Oregon and California, the state of Montana lacks a state forest practices law to regulate how forests are logged on private lands. The only permit required for logging on private lands is a Slash Hazard Removal plan (which covers the disposal—usually by burning—of logging debris), which must be certified by the Department of State Lands. It appears that Roush's timber sale may be out of compliance even with this meager law.

"Legally, the plan is supposed to receive final certification *before* the logging starts," said Mark Lewing, Hamilton District Manager for the Montana Department of State Lands told us. "I understand they're finished cutting up there, but I haven't certified the plan yet." Lewing expressed amazement and dismay when told that Roush was president of the Wilderness Society.

In his single sale, Roush sold more timber than the surrounding northern half of the 1.6 million acre Bitterroot National Forest last year. Indeed, according to information provided to us by Karen Wandler, a timber staff officer with the Forest Service in Hamilton, Montana, since 1992 the Stevensville Ranger District, the portion of the federal forest adjoining the Roush ranch, has sold only 66.7 thousand board feet of timber.

"Jon Roush is doing what environmentalists haven't allowed the Forest Service to do for three years in the Bitterroot: conduct a roadless area timber sale," said Timothy Bechtold with the Ecology Center in Missoula.

Roush says that the cut was part of a separation agreement with his wife. He says he agreed in advance on the principles to be used in the logging. "If we had conducted the sale like a Forest Service sale, you'd be right to call me on it. But we did not." Astoundingly, Roush (the absentee forester) added: "The Wilderness Society wouldn't have much of a problem with the Forest Service if it logged in this manner." In fact, the Roushes cut the big, lucrative ponderosas and left the small ones behind—exactly what the Forest Service does in its so-called forest "health sales."

In an interview with *The Washington Post* prompted by our story, Roush called his timber sale a "model" for other landowners and denied that he logged any old growth, claiming "no trees older than 90 years were cut." Yet, the Wilderness Society's own ecologists endorsed the report of the Federal Ecosystem Management Assessment Team (largely authored by Wilderness Society board member Jerry Franklin) which describes any natural forest stands in the rain-drenched Pacific Northwest older than 70 years as late-successional/old-growth worthy of permanent protection. Most of the trees cut on the Roush ranch were between 80 and 90 years old and between 18 inches and 26 inches in diamter, easily qualifying for old growth status on the parched eastern slopes of the Rockies.

Back in 1993, Bill Arthur, head of the Sierra Club's Seattle, Washington office, logged off ten acres of his land in eastern Washington. Arthur sold the timber to Global Pacific, a log exporter, for $10,000 and used the money to help build a summer home. This disclosure outraged grassroots environmentalists as well as timber workers associated with the Wise Use Movement.

Both groups accused Arthur of hypercritical conduct. Arthur had testified for environmentalists at President Clinton's timber summit held in Portland, Oregon in April of 1992, where he broke ranks with the position of many environmental organizations and refused to endorse a ban on the export of raw logs from private and state lands in the West—a practice that forsakes 20,000 jobs in American timber mills every year.

The disclosures about Roush's logging off forest on his Montana ranch come in the wake the Wilderness Society's recent retreat from an injunction won in federal court halting all mining, logging, and grazing projects in salmon habitat on millions of acres of federal forest land in central Idaho. Under pressure from the Clinton administration and his politically-sensitive board members, Roush ordered the Society's lawyers to return to Judge David Ezra and have the injunction lifted. This action allowed clearcutting to proceed in the Cove/Mallard roadless area.

Roush, formerly Chairman of the Board of the Nature Conservancy (the wealthiest and most conservative national environmental organization) was named President of the Wilderness Society in 1993, replacing George Frampton. Since his appointment, Roush has maintained a close and uncritical relationship to the leadership of the Democratic Party. According to a disgusted Wilderness Society staffer, President Clinton personally thanked Roush for releasing the Idaho injunction.

The major foundations also continue to reward the Wilderness Society despite its repeated retreats. In March, the Pew Charitable Trusts issued a $350,000 check to the Wilderness Society to oversee a coalition of moderate environmental groups in a campaign to "protect" the Northern Rockies. Of course, the most aggressive grassroots groups in Montana and Idaho (organizations such as the Idaho Sporting Congress, Alliance for the Wild Rockies, and Friends of the Wild Swan) that have inflicted the most damage on the Forest Service timber machine are totally cut out of the deal—no doubt, a saving grace in the long run.

There's a particularly effective moment in Alfred Hitchcock's film of John Buchan's novel *The Thirty-Nine Steps*, where Richard Hannay, fleeing across the Scottish moors, at last stumbles into the house which he deems to be a sanctuary from his pursuers. His host suddenly holds up his hand. The top finger joint is missing—the sign that Hannay has given himself over to the enemy. Thus it is with Roush's Wilderness Society. Fundraising mailers by the millions pour from the Society's headquarters in Washington, which by 1998 will cost $6 million a year in lease payments. And thousands of Americans respond to Roush's impassioned appeals for money to save the wilderness. Meanwhile Roush is selling out to lumber giants in Idaho, playing footsie with the Clinton administration in its plan to clearcut ancient forest in the Pacific Northwest, and stripping his own lands of timber for private gain.

Portland/Petrolia, 1995

Five

The Floods of Forgetfulness

From February 4 through February 10 of 1996 an embedded low-pressure system sat over the Pacific Northwest, drawing warm waves of rain from the eastern Pacific. Coastal Oregon was drenched with over 23 inches of rain, Portland got 12, and the Cascade Mountains to the east about 18. The Cascades already had about a foot of snow at the thousand-foot level, with snow pack of up to 120 inches at the 6000-foot level.

The rains were some of the heaviest in thirty years. At the top of the seawall in downtown Portland the chocolate-colored Willamette River crested at 29 feet. Further upstream at Oregon City, where the riverbed is much narrower, the river crested at 44 feet, 22 feet over flood stage, inundating much of the town.

The Wilson River, plunging out of Oregon's Coast Range, met a high tide at Tillamook Bay and put the entire town of Tillamook under eight feet of water. Tillamook is in dairy country. More than 1,500 head of dairy cattle were drowned or got trapped in the mud and starved. The Santiam River which drains off of Mt. Jefferson in the Cascades reached record heights. Five thousand people had to be evacuated from the North Fork of the Santiam River canyon for fear the Detroit damn would fail.

The Columbia River, long believed to be tamed by mega-dams such as Bonneville and McNary, breached its banks and dozens of dikes, causing major damage in the river towns of Washougal, Vancouver, St. Helens, Kalama and Astoria.

In Washington state, the Lewis River, which slides off the south face of Mt. St. Helens, ran higher than it did following the eruption of the volcano in 1980 and flooded the town of Woodland, prompting a later visit from President Bill.

With the floods and the rains came an unprecedented number of landslides, closing 800 roads in Oregon and Washington, including all interstates. I-84 in the Columbia River gorge east of Portland vanished under ten feet of rock and mud.

The damage estimates thus ranged at anywhere from $2 to $3 billion.

The local press coverage was prodigious: 24-hour-a-day news bulletins; helicopter footage; intrepid reporters out in their Gore-tex storm gear. The newspapers ran special supplements over the next two weeks.

In all these thousands of stories, only one mentioned any possible connection between logging and floods. The closest *The [Portland] Oregonian* came was an enigmatic story—getting everything ass-backwards—in which the reporter discussed the damage the rains had done to the forest, with possible inhibitions on hiking next summer.

Down in Eugene in the very heart of Oregon's timber country, the *Register-Guard* did run an article discussing the relationship of the recent clearcuts to the floods. Most of the space was taken up with quotes from a Weyerhaeuser flack called Paul Barnum, who insisted, "It's preposterous to say that clearcutting causes flooding. And there's no definitive proof that clearcutting contributes to landslides. Flooding is caused by too much water for the earth to absorb." On that last point Barnum is right, thereby contradicting everything he said prior to that. Old-growth forests absorb about ten times as much water as the land does after the trees have been clearcut. This is a fact that has been known for a hundred years, since the very creation of the national forest system.

The silence in the press on the connection between clearcuts and floods stands in marked contrast to coverage back in the last big flood year of 1964, and indeed shows us how cowed or ignorant the reporters and their editors have become. In 1964 floods engulfed the whole of the North Coast from the Eel River in Northern California to the Quinault on the Olympic Peninsula. Then the connection was made very straightforwardly between such floods and the postwar logging boom that was still in its final phases on corporate-owned lands.

After the 1964 flood in the Willamette Valley, which drains the Cascades and Coast Ranges from Eugene to Portland, came the construction of 32 dams, mainly by the Army Corps of Engineers. This orgy of dam construction was a replay of a debate that attended the birth of the national forests.

Between 1892 and 1908 Gifford Pinchot—first chief of the Forest Service—fought a series of battles with opponents determined to destroy any rationale for publicly-owned forests and for any federal intervention in the management of private lands. Joe Cannon, the Speaker of the House, proclaimed that he would not vote "one damn cent for scenery." Cannon and his allies were eager to open up federally-owned lands in the West for settlement (i.e., corporate exploitation). In the East, Cannon and his allies wanted to keep the Feds out altogether.

Pinchot riposted that waterways lay within the federal government's constitutional purview and since waterways flooded from time to time, it was government's function to prevent such flooding, and hence in government's interest to create and conserve forests. At congressional hearings Pinchot would hold up a photograph of a clearcut hillside and pour a pitcher of water over the photo. The water would naturally run off at once. Then he would hold up a sponge, or what he called a "slopping blotter" and pour water over that, with a lecture on the absorptive capacity of trees. Forests, Pinchot concluded, prevent flooding.

After devastating floods in the heavily logged Ohio and Tennessee Valleys in the early 1900s, Pinchot's argument looked pretty good to Midwesterners and he made great headway. The big showdown came in the form of a stand-off between Pinchot and Hiram Chittenden, head of the Army Corps of Engineers. In those days, the Army Corps was in poor shape, partly from a series of financial scandals and partly from the fierce attacks the Corps had made on the idea of the Panama Canal. Chittenden was trying to restore stature and morale to the agency by arguing vigorously that in the end the only way to master hectic nature was to build dams: thousands of them.

In the short term, Pinchot got the better of Chittenden. He managed to win the passage of the Weeks Act of 1911, which allowed the government to buy forest land for the purpose of flood prevention. Though Pinchot—in contrast to John Muir—saw forests as zones for rational exploitation (i.e., the conservation ethic that Teddy Roosevelt appropriated), he did make protection of water quality and flood control centerpieces of his forest management practices. In consequence he didn't last long, was booted by President William Howard Taft when he attacked Richard Ballinger, the Secretary of Interior who wanted to give away the oil and coal rights to most of Alaska for corporate plunder.

After Pinchot's ouster, the Chittenden approach had the final victory. Pinchot's hope that privately-held corporate forests could be regulated was swiftly extinguished. These corporate lands were clearcut, amid environmental devastation, over the next half century. The Corps of Engineers and the Bureau of Reclamation began a dam-building race that caused further environmental devastation and doomed Glen Canyon and the salmon. By the early 1970s, even the Forest Service had joined in the rout of Pinchot's ideals. Pinchot favored selective cutting of forests, where trees are cut in groups of two or three leaving the forest itself relatively intact. But the Forest Service shifted from selective cutting to clearcutting in the 1960s, claiming that clearcuts increased water yield to the benefit of all, particularly in the arid West.

As those dams were going up, the forests were coming down. Between 1964 and 1996, 13 million acres of forest were clearcut in the Pacific Northwest. Along with the clearcuts, the Forest Service and the timber companies constructed 180,000 miles of logging roads (2.5 times as much as the interstate system begun in the 1950s). The end result is Oregon at the start of February 1996. In the Mapleton Ranger District of the Siuslaw National Forest west of Eugene, there were 183 landslides caused by the storm. All but three of them in clearcut terrain or on logging roads.

In unlogged watersheds, such as Opal Creek, the water ran swift and high, but stayed clear and held within its banks. The snowpack on clearcut terrain melted away quickly under the warm rains of the storm. But in the old-growth stands, the snow remains deep, sheltered by 200-foot-tall trees.

Billions of dollars were invested in flood control in the past thirty years so that hundreds of millions more could be spent logging off national forest land and building logging roads. The rainstorms that spawned the flood of '96 were nowhere near as protracted and fierce as the '64 storms, but the damage was much greater. The media circled the disaster without even the historical knowledge to ask the basic questions or look for the original causes.

Someone should sue the timber companies and get the questions asked in court. With all that talk about "property rights" and "compensations" and "takings" the timber lords should most certainly be made to pony up a hefty percentage of that $3 or $4 billion in damages from February's floods.

Oregon City, March 1996

Six

Ransoming Yellowstone

As President Clinton accepts the re-nomination of his party let us look at two of his most recent presidential deeds, an executive order on a proposed gold mine near Yellowstone Park and the signing of a bill advancing the deregulation of the oil and gas industry, both accomplished at his vacation headquarters in Wyoming. Clinton's press aide called the two initiatives "poetic symmetry." They tell us much of what we need to know about this man. For its part, the national press betrayed little interest in either the bill or the executive order, preferring to investigate who Clinton was playing golf with and whether the press pool was going to be allowed to accompany the first family on its rafting trip down the Snake River.

Turn first to Clinton's proclaimed salvation of Yellowstone National Park. The news headlines that evening and the next day confided merely that Clinton had arranged for Battle Mountain Gold, a subsidiary of the Canadian conglomerate Noranda, to abandon its plans to excavate for copper, gold and silver two and a half miles from the northeastern boundary of the nation's first national park in exchange for title to other federal lands. "We've all come to an agreement that Yellowstone is more precious than gold," Clinton declaimed under the rugged crest of the Absaroka Range.

What we actually had here was Bill Clinton paying off a gang of corporate hostage-takers and then passing them off as ecological heroes. The New World mining area, in the high country of Montana's Beartooth Mountains, came into the hands of the Noranda Corporation courtesy of the 1872 Mining Law, enacted the same year Yellowstone became a national park. The Mining Law gave away the public store to mining companies then and now, allowing them to patent (that is, take into private ownership) mineral rich public lands for as little as $2.50 per acre and pay no royalties on billions of dollars worth of public minerals. Under the Mining Law it is nearly impossible to force the companies to clean up their mess. There are more than 550,000 abandoned mine sites in the West containing 70 billion tons of highly toxic tailings piles and acidic mine wastes. An estimated 12,000 miles of streams have been killed off by mining operations.

Much of the concern about Noranda's New World project focused on the mine's monstrous tailings dam, meant to impound 5.5 million tons of mining wastes in a kind of cobalt-blue toxic reservoir. The design was experimental and, many engineers said, bound to fail. The Yellowstone country is a region stressed by bitterly cold winters and a geology prone to frequent and extreme seismic activities.

Noranda's environmental record is abysmal. Over the past 15 years the company, and its corporate offshoots, have racked up millions in fines for dozens of toxic spills, midnight dumpings of hazardous waste, falsified records, illegal discharges into rivers and lakes, air emission violations, dangerous working conditions, fish kills, and repeated failures to notify federal and state authorities of toxic releases. Any breach of the dam would have sent poisonous run-off gushing into the Clarks Fork of the Yellowstone River, one of the nation's most beautiful and famous trout streams.

But the mining company knew all along that blasting 800 million tons of rock out of the side of Henderson Mountain next to Yellowstone Park would never pass regulatory muster. Lawsuits against the company for violations of the Clean Water Act in its exploratory activities had already been filed and won. Moreover, the residents of Montana are poised to vote on (and, if the polls are accurate, pass decisively) a tough new water quality initiative that would doom the mine and many others like it throughout the state. Although Noranda never came close to receiving a permit for the mine, it huffed and puffed about moving forward with the project. Earlier this year, the mining company hired former Indiana Senator Birch Bayh (whose son Evan, the Clinton-lite governor of Indiana, will deliver the keynote address at the Democrats' convention in Chicago) and former Montana Governor Tim Babcock to extract the best deal possible for them in Washington. It didn't take long for the Clinton administration to fall down.

The easy, no-down terms of the Mining Law are quite lucrative, but Clinton and Co. soon offered the mining giant an even better deal: $65 million in other federal properties and a grant of immunity from prosecution for civil and criminal penalties amounting to

$135 million for their previous activities on the mining site, where many of the streams have been rendered as acidic as lemon juice. The environmental groups jumped in as well. Led by the politically malleable Sierra Club Legal Defense Fund and the foundation-dependent Greater Yellowstone Coalition, the greens agreed to drop a suit against the corporation that could have killed the mine out-right without any ransom payments.

As an added bonus, the mining company will be able to take a $30 million tax write off, another corporate subsidy that will ulti-mately be paid for out of the pockets of the American taxpayers. In total, the package amounts to a $230 million pay off to a renegade mining company that had threatened America's oldest national park with ecological ruin. This is a level of corporate welfare that even a Reagan-era defense contractor could appreciate.

Typically, the president praised the deal as a solution "where everybody wins," saying that it is symbolic of how the environment and the economy can work in harmony. "The way this was done should become a model for America's challenges," Clinton pro-nounced. "Not only in the environment, but in other areas as well." None of the reporters in the press pool queried the president on what this might do to the budget deficit.

In fact, the Yellowstone agreement sets a dangerous precedent. It encourages threats of destructive activities, such as mines, subdi-visions, and clearcuts, next to national parks and wilderness areas. The more vicious the threat, the more likely the government will pay you off. Look for new, high-profile mining claims to be filed next to Yosemite, Glacier, and the Grand Canyon in the hope of securing a handsome federal buy-out. "Yellowstone has been protected through a form of ransom," said Phil Hocker of the Mineral Policy Center. "But the kidnappers got away to seize another hostage."

Of course, this is not how Clinton saw the issue. Indeed, he praised Noranda as the very model of an environmentally responsi-ble corporation. "Mining jobs are good jobs and mining is important to our national economy and national security," Clinton said. "But we can't have mines everywhere, and mines that threaten Yellowstone, well, that's too much for the American people to bear."

Yet, Clinton's speech was notable mainly for its failure to men-tion the principal reason mines are popping up nearly everywhere in the West: the 1872 Mining Law. And, indeed, by paying off Noranda to abandon its claims to the New World site, the Clinton administration passed up a chance to use the impending threat to the world's most famous park as a way of forcing revision of the archaic law.

"Throughout the West there are people who are worried that toxic mines will destroy their watersheds, threaten their health, and disrupt their way of life," said Larry Tuttle of the Portland, Oregon-based Center for Environmental Equity. "But these people don't have Yellowstone next door. And by making this deal the Clinton administration lets itself off the hook for nationwide mining reform and hangs those communities out to dry."

Tuttle points out that the administration has already backed off two golden opportunities to reform the Mining Act, signed into law by Ulysses S. Grant to encourage settlement of the West. The first came only months into the Clinton administration's first year, when western Democratic senators convinced Clinton to remove from his first budget proposal a measure that would have prohibited mining companies from taking title to public lands and for the first time would have charged the companies royalties for minerals extracted off federal lands.

The second opportunity came at the close of the 1994 congressional session. Senator Dale Bumpers' mining reform bill was within only a couple votes of passing, when the Clinton administration suddenly backed off and the measure failed. Last year in Billings, Montana, Clinton explained his crucial decision not to push for overhaul of the Mining Act. "I support mining law reform," Clinton said. "But I want to see a kind of reform that doesn't drive companies out of business." It is interesting that Clinton's old friend from Arkansas, Dale Bumpers, wasn't invited to the celebration in Yellowstone. Also missing was Interior Secretary Bruce Babbitt, suggesting that perhaps even Bruce the Faintheart felt that the give-away was too unseemly.

Over the past five years, the Noranda mine has received an enormous amount of international attention. But the Noranda mine is only a relatively small-scale version of thousands of similar projects underway across the West. Currently, there are 200 applications pending for mining claims covering 140,000 acres of public land. If these parcels are patented to the mining companies, the federal treasury could expect to receive only about $700,000 for lands harboring an estimated $15.5 billion worth of gold, silver, and copper. Of course, this total doesn't account for the destruction of public wildlife habitat, streams, or wilderness areas.

Also missing from the presidential sermon was any mention of the Greater Yellowstone Ecosystem, the three million acres of federal, state, and private lands surrounding the park that are vital to the survival of the area's grizzly bears, wolves, elk, and trout. Interestingly, the New World mine deal requires the planned mining area to be turned over to the Forest Service, which even now is logging off thousands of acres of forests near Yellowstone's borders under the provisions of the salvage logging rider signed into law by Clinton a year ago.

None of these unpleasantries were allowed to intrude on the president's vacation or his press conferences. From his ranch outside Missoula, Conrad Burns, the right-wing senator from Montana, grumbled that the whole Yellowstone deal was about "feel-good politics." He pegged it about right. So did one of Burns' most aggressive adversaries, Jim Jensen, director of the Montana Environmental Information Center in Helena. "If a mine doesn't go forward, it should be because it doesn't pass the scrutiny of state and federal environmental laws," Jensen said. "And not because of some politician's desire to claim to have saved Yellowstone National Park."

In the end, it was about business and politics. Stock market analyst Jim Wah-Ngan of Smith Barney exulted that it was a great deal for the mining company since Wall Street "knew all along that the mine wasn't going to be permitted anyway." Predictably, the mining company's stock jumped 10 percent the day after the deal was announced. As Clinton himself made clear, Noranda's "shareholders win because their property rights were protected."

This ritual in Yellowstone signals that Bill Clinton has succeeded where Bob Dole failed—in ratifying the Wise Use Movement's position on regulatory "takings." Takings is an issue dear to the heart of corporate America, since it would require the federal government to compensate companies for not destroying the habitat of endangered species or damaging public lands or threatening public health. In other words, corporations have to be paid not to commit crimes against nature. Dole tried to maneuver a takings

bill through the senate in 1995 , but his efforts were crushed by a bipartisan coalition. Now Clinton has prevailed administratively and
has reaped praises for his "bold action" from the liberal press.
Perhaps that's why the ceremony was timed for the first day of the
Republican National Convention.

A good share of the blame for this debacle can be directed at
the *New York Times* editorial page, which concocted the ransom
strategy in a series of editorials written by Robert Semple over the
past two years. In the spring, Semple won a Pulitzer for his neoliber-
al pastorals. But it was the *Billings Gazette* and its excellent reporter
Michael Millstein that deserved the honors for exposing the grim
consequences of Clinton's Yellowstone deal. *The Gazette* decried the
administration's secret settlement for excluding the public from the
process. "Mr. President, these are public lands," the paper chided.
"And the public deserves a say in what happens to them." The
Gazette also reproached Clinton for creating "a precedent of government buyouts of controversial mine projects," while ignoring the
systemic cause of the problem, the archaic 1872 Mining Law.

A day later Clinton was back before the cameras in an elk-
trampled meadow near Grand Teton Park in Jackson Hole,
Wyoming, heaping honorifics on a smiling coven of oil company
executives as he signed into law the Federal Oil and Gas
Simplication and Fairness Act. The name of the bill (and the presence of the oil tycoons) should have signaled to the press that dirty
work was afoot. And indeed it was.

Approved by Congress on the last day of the recent session, the
bill does four things: it places a seven-year limitation on the auditing of oil company books recording income from drilling on public
lands; it turns over many of the auditing responsibilities concerning
drilling on federal lands to the states; it permits the oil companies to
sue the federal government to collect interest on "overpayments;"
and it allows those very same companies to set the "market price" of
the crude oil upon which the royalty payments to the federal government are based.

In reality, the bill legalizes a scam the big oil companies have
been running for decades, bilking the federal government out of billions of dollars by underpaying royalties on crude oil extracted from
federal lands. It turns out that in California alone the oil companies

have underpaid the treasury $1.5 billion. A quarter of that money should have gone to the state's cash-starved school system.

But Clinton cast the measure as simply a way of cutting government red tape and streamlining needless bureaucracy. "Many Americans don't know it, but a significant percentage of the oil and gas reserves in the United States are on federal lands," Clinton lectured. "Until today, regulatory red tape and conflicting court rulings had discouraged many companies from taking full advantage of these resources." He said he had been working since his first day in office to increase domestic energy production. This bill, Clinton remarked, was part of an overall strategy that "included lifting the 23-year old ban on Alaskan oil exports and efforts to increase production in the Gulf of Mexico." All done while protecting the environment, of course.

What the President chose not to mention is that many of the oil executives standing next to him in that meadow have applied for permits to drill for oil and gas all throughout the Rocky Mountains, including the oil rich area surrounding Grand Teton and Yellowstone Parks. Indeed, the Chevron Corporation has for years been pushing to open the Beartooth/Absaroka Range to full-scale oil and gas development, with dozens of drilling derricks clustered not more than a few miles from the site of the dreaded Noranda mine.

Clinton's signature on that fairness in oil leasing bill brings the prospect of oil wells and spills on the very threshold of Yellowstone that much closer. In this way, Yellowstone has been saved from a mining company which never intended to scrape out an ounce of gold and placed in the clutches of the big oil companies, which are primed to drill every last drop out of the Rockies.

Bozeman, Montana, August 1996

Seven

Oceans Without Fish

The Decline and Fall of America's Last Great Fishery

The Gijon cuts through the slate-colored swells, trailing a white V in the waters of the Bering Sea. The trawler lowers its giant pelagic net from the stern of the ship, and it unfurls into the dark waters below. The net, thousands of yards of lightweight nylon mesh, sweeps in a lethal curtain across the depths.

Hours later, the nets are cranked up to the piercing whine of straining engines. Inside: more than 400 tons of fish, crabs, and squid. A few Stellar's sea lions and fur seals, indiscriminately snared while foraging for salmon, are also part of the haul.

The sea lions and seals are not spared. Indeed, more than forty percent of the haul is considered worthless by-catch and will simply be ground up and spewed in bloody torrents of saturated chum from the bilges of the ship back out into the sea. Some 550 million pounds of marine life are wasted in this way in the North Pacific every year.

The Bering Sea is now the most productive fishery in North America. More than one-third of the United States' commercial catch comes from these cold waters near the top of the world. Among the species sought by the fishing fleets of the North Pacific are yellowfin, sole, herring, halibut, and perch. But the most cherished target is pollock, the tofu of fish. Pollock, craved by the Japanese for surimi, turns up in American markets as fish sandwiches at Burger King and McDonalds and as imitation crab in the fish freezers at Safeway.

The Gijon is registered to the Seattle-based American Seafoods Corporation, a subsidiary of Resource Group International, a Norwegian conglomerate. The ship is a floating factory, longer and wider than a football field. The $40 million trawler can process 80 tons of fish product a day, turning yellowfin sole into fish meal and pollack into surimi. The catch is stored in huge freezers, where it can stay preserved for months.

Resource Group International's primary competitor in the lucrative pollock fishing grounds of the North Pacific is the Arctic-Alaska Fisheries Company, another Seattle-based firm. Arctic-Alaska was acquired in 1992 by Don Tyson, the chicken mogul and Clinton patron from Springdale, Arkansas. Since then Tyson has bought up three other Alaska seafood operations and is fending off anti-trust investigations by the Federal Trade Commission.

The incursion of the big factory ships into the waters of the North Pacific began in the late 1970s and early 1980s. There are now 45 of the factory trawlers operating the Bering Sea fishery. The big boats are powered by supercharged diesel engines fed by massive fuel tanks that permit the ships to remain at sea for months without returning to home ports to refuel or off-load their catch. Often the processed surimi is simply off-loaded at sea to smaller ships owned by Japanese fish merchants. The long range of the factory ships allows them to operate in several distant fisheries in one season and evade the catch quotas that saddle smaller operators.

The arrival of the industrialized super-trawlers spell almost immediate cultural and economic disaster for the communities of coastal Alaska. For decades the flourishing Alaskan fishing industry had been characterized by independent ship owners and small processing plants, sprinkled down the coast in towns like Kodiac, Cordova and Ketchikan.

In the 1970s, nearly 80 percent of the Alaskan pollack catch was made by small operators. Now the situation is almost entirely reversed. More than 70 percent of the pollack in Alaskan waters is taken by the factory trawlers and dozens of independent boat owners have gone bankrupt. But it's the shore-based factories, making valued-added fish products, that have been hit the hardest by the new generation of trawlers. The canneries, surimi plants and frozen fish processing factories provided year-round high wage jobs, an important stabilizing force for rural Alaska's predominantly seasonal economy. Today many of those plants and jobs are gone, replaced by the factory trawlers, which increasingly tend to employ Mexican and Vietnamese laborers at sweatshop rates.

Many of Arctic-Alaska Company's ships now unload their catch not in Seattle, but in Shanghai, China, where Tyson purchased a fish factory in 1994 from the Chinese government. The deal was brokered with the help of Commerce Secretary Ron Brown and was backed by government insurance and loan guarantees from the Overseas Private Investment Corporation. In fact, the growth of the American factory trawler fleet was heavily underwritten by the US treasury, thanks to effective inside work by the congressional delegation from Washington state. Tyson's company alone received more than $65 million low-interest loans to fund the construction of 10 factory trawlers. In total, the Seattle-based factory trawler fleet has received $200 million in so-called Fisheries Obligation Guarantees and other federal subsidies.

The economic dislocation brought about by the invasion of the trawlers into southeast Alaska is grimly paralleled by an ecological catastrophe in the waters of the Bering Sea and North Pacific. Again most of the blame can be laid on the industrial behemoths. Using sophisticated sonar and electronic tracking devices, factory trawlers like the Gijon can quickly locate new spawning grounds and fish them to near extinction. This is called pulse trawling. An outrageous example of this practice occurred in the 1980s in the Shelikof Straight off the Aleutian Islands, when a newly discovered pollack stock was relentlessly fished to the point of collapse. According to a report on factory trawlers by Greenpeace, in less than a decade the Shelikof pollock fishery had declined from an estimated biomass of 3 million tons in 1981 to less than 300 thousand tons in 1988.

Each year since the factory trawlers have flocked to the Alaska waters the pollock season has closed earlier than planned. In the late 1970s, the pollock fishing season regularly ran for 10 months. In 1994, it closed after 70 days. It's not surprising. The annual harvest capacity of the trawler fleet may be greater than the entire pollack population of the Bering Sea. The ramifications of this rather dire situation were contemplated in an internal assessment by executives with American Seafood Company, "the catching capacity of vessels operating in the Bering Sea pollock fishery appears to be double or triple the annual quota." And these were quotas that most marine biologists believed to be dangerously inflated.

It's not just the commercial fish species, such as pollock and sole, that are being depleted. Crab, halibut, and arrowtooth flounder are also in trouble. The consequences extend even to fish-eating seabirds, such as puffins, thick-billed murres and black-legged kitti-wakes, and marine mammals, such as the Stellar's sea lion and fur seals. For example, pollock accounts for nearly 70 percent of the rare sea lion's diet. A recent report by the National Research Council warns, "It seems extremely unlikely that the productivity of the Bering Sea ecosystem can sustain current rates of human exploita-tion as well as the large populations of all marine mammal and bird species that existed before human exploitation—especially modern exploitation—began."

The trend toward over-exploitation of the Alaskan fishery will be difficult, if not impossible, to reverse. For one thing, even the strongest federal fishing laws have often only exacerbated the prob-lem. Take the Magnuson Act passed in 1976 as a way to protect American off-shore fishing grounds from growing incursions by for-eign fishing fleets. The measure, rammed through Congress by the acerbic Senator Warren Magnuson (D-WA), extended the federal government's jurisdiction over fish matters from 3 miles to 200 miles off the US coastline, a move that was bitterly denounced as an example of ecological imperialism by the Japanese and the Norwegians. In fact, it was simple economic protectionism.

The Magnuson Act established regional fish management councils to determine fishing seasons and allocate catch quotas. The councils, which soon came to be dominated by fishing industry lob-byists, were expressly exempted from federal conflict-of-interest laws, allowing industry members to direct as much of the haul back to their own companies and clients as they could get away with. And they did just that.

Exacerbating this situation is the archaic management philoso-phy of the federal agency charged with maintaining the health of ocean fish stocks: the National Marine Fisheries Service which, oddly enough, is under the purview of the Commerce Department. Instead of viewing marine ecosystems as being as vibrant, diverse and interconnected as an ancient forest in the Oregon Cascades, NMFS attempts to manage ocean fish stocks through a species-by-species approach. This benefits the bottom lines of the fishing fleets, but flies in the face of current ecological thinking. By focusing only on the commercial fish stocks, NMFS ignores the toll industrial fishing methods take on non-target species, such as sea lions and halibut, and on the marine habitat itself.

Medical researchers, backed by hefty grants from companies like Arctic-Alaska, continue to churn out reports touting the health-enhancing benefits of a diet laden with pollock, salmon and perch. Fish seems to lower bad cholesterol, reduce heart attack risks (especially for men), and suppress the advance of free radicals, those frenzied compounds that stimulate cancer cell growth.

All this is undoubtedly true. Yet, there are also health dangers associated with fish consumption. Fish can be contaminated with heavy metals, pesticides and other chemical toxins. One recent study estimates that consumption of PCB-laced fish from the Great Lakes may lead to 40,000 cancers over the next 25 years. Seafood products can also carry a host of foodborne pathogens, including listeria, vibrio vulnifcus and, yes, salmonella. Testing of fish for such dangers is even more lax and rudimentary than that in the beef industry. One local seafood merchant in Portland, Oregon says, "What it comes down to is smell. When it starts to stink we take it off the shelf. What else can you do?"

But even the most accomplished sole sniffers would be unable to detect that there is something terribly wrong with many of the fish being hauled out of the Bering Sea. Thousands of tons of perch, pollack and black sole taken by ships like the Gijon may—metaphorically, at least—glow; they may make Geiger counters erupt into a chilling stutter of clicks. In short, a considerable part of the haul from this last, great productive fishery may be radioactive.

What's going on here? The story dates back to 1971, during the glory days of the Nixon administration and the nuclear sabre-rattling leading up to Kissinger's detente with the Soviets. In order to send a message of "American resolve," Nixon ordered the Atomic Energy Commission and the Department of Defense to detonate the largest underground nuclear explosion in US history on Amchitka Island, a volcanic extrusion in the Bering Sea halfway down Alaska's Aleutian Chain.

The five megaton hydrogen "device" set-off on November 6, 1971 exploded with such force that the middle of Amchitka Island collapsed, forming what the mad scientist Edward Teller delicately termed "a nuclear-excavated lake." In the wake of the blast, hundreds of dead puffins were found with their legs driven through their chests, while sea lions, resting on sea rocks miles from the test site, were discovered with their eyes blown out of their sockets. Within months, there was ample evidence that the site, called Cannikian Lake, had begun to steadily leak radioactive waste, despite assurances from James Schlesinger, then head of the Atomic Energy Commission, that it would take "a thousand years or more" for transuranic radiation to dribble into the sea.

Thousands of recently declassified documents released by the Department of Energy to the Alaska Department of Environmental Conservation reveal that the Amchitka test began to leak iodine 131 and crypton 85 within two days of the blast, escaping into groundwater and then the sea through underground fissures in the island. Soon after these documents were disclosed, Senator Ted Stevens, the Alaska Republican, discreetly told Energy Secretary Hazel O'Leary, "Madame Secretary, we've got a problem up here. There's leaking from the Amchitka test site and it might endanger our North Pacific fisheries."

Now high levels of americum, plutonium and tritium are showing up in plant samples on the island. "If we're finding these levels of radioactive waste, then the potential for severe harm is there," says Pam Miller, a Greenpeace biologist who authored a recent report on the Amchitka situation. "This stuff appears to be leaking into the most important commercial fishery in the world."

Even so, executives at Don Tyson's fish company remain tranquil. "We've never once found any radioactive fish," said a spokeman for Arctic-Alaska Fisheries. Moments later, however, the PR man admitted that the company had never tested its fish for radioactive waste and had no plans to start. No wonder the surrealists adopted the fish as a symbol of their movement.

Seattle, May 1997

Eight

The Pulp Parachute

How Louisiana-Pacific Got Paid To Destroy the Tongass

One of the most lucrative and environmentally destructive deals in the history of the forest products industry was just closed out with an enormous golden parachute unfurled for a $2 billion-a-year timber company courtesy of the federal treasury. In February of 1997, the Clinton administration capitulated to the legal threats of the Louisiana-Pacific Corporation by agreeing to pay $250 million to settle a lawsuit over the federal government's cancellation last year of the company's long-term contract to log timber on the Tongass National Forest in southeast Alaska.

The buy-out may have been linked to the confirmation of Frederico Pena, Clinton's choice as Secretary of Energy. The nomination had been held up by Alaskan Senator Frank Murkowski, chairman of the Senate Committee on Energy and the Environment. Sources in the Senate say that Murkowski, who has been a virulent critic of the administration's environmental policies, threatened to block Pena's confirmation unless Clinton agreed to settle the Louisiana-Pacific lawsuit and guarantee higher levels of logging on the Tongass over the next five years. Pena's nomination was approved by Murkowski's committee the same week the Clinton administration announced the Louisiana-Pacific deal.

More than $140 million of the settlement will go directly into Louisiana-Pacific's corporate coffers. The remaining $110 million is scheduled to be distributed to local communities in southeast Alaska for the retraining of nearly 400 workers laid off from the company's closed Ketchikan pulp mill, although this portion of the deal must await Congressional approval. In addition, the Forest Service agreed to provide Louisiana-Pacific with a steady flow of old-growth timber from the Tongass for the next three years. A large portion of that timber will come from ecologically significant stands of old-growth forest on Central Prince of Wales Island near Ketchikan, which the Forest Service's own biologists have said should not be logged because of adverse impacts on salmon and the rare marbled murrelet, a forest-nesting seabird.

The pay-off caps a 40-year run in southeast Alaska, where the company was granted exclusive rights to log off more than one million acres of temperate rainforest on the fog-enwrapped islands of the Tongass, America's largest national forest. The Ketchikan mill, owned for the past 25-years by Louisiana-Pacific, was the beneficiary of an extraordinary deal hatched by the Forest Service back in the late 1950s. As an inducement to create year-round jobs in remote southeast Alaska, the Forest Service offered exclusive contracts to log old-growth timber off the Tongass rainforest for minimal costs to any companies that would build pulp mills in Southeast Alaska and operate them year-round.

By 1954, two pulp mills had been built in the region, one in Ketchikan by the Ketchikan Pulp Company, formerly owned by the gold mining giant FMC, and one in Sitka, controlled by a consortium of Japanese companies, including Mitsubishi and Sumitomo, operating as the Alaska Pulp Company.

The Ketchikan mill produced a bizarre assortment of pulp products, including rayon, fiber for disposable diapers, nitrocellophane explosives, food fillers and sponges. The Sitka mill mainly produced pulp for newsprint. After pulp prices took a nosedive in 1993, the Alaska Pulp Company closed its Sitka mill and the Forest Service terminated the company's contract. The Japanese-owned company then filed suit in federal claims court seeking nearly a billion dollars in damages. (After a decade-long court battle, a federal judge finally sided with the company. The feds have appealed the ruling.)

According to informants inside the Portland, Oregon-based company, Louisiana-Pacific had been attempting to unload the Ketchikan pulp mill for at least the last two years. When Louisiana-Pacific could find no buyers, the company shut the mill down, blaming the closure on the Forest Service for failing to provide enough timber at cheap enough rates to keep the mill running. The company also repeatedly lashed out at environmentalists, charging that efforts to protect old-growth forest stand and wildlife on the 16-million acre Tongass forest had created "a climate of uncertainty" over future timber cut levels.

Yet, most timber industry economists say that the real problem for Louisiana-Pacific had to do with the changing nature of the pulp market. Pulp prices, always erratic, have plunged to new lows over the past three years and, despite a few temporary spikes upward, have stayed depressed. Increased recycling, cheaper mills built in Mexico and China, and staggering environmental liabilities are only some of the factors undercutting the economic footing of aging pulps mills in the United States.

This situation was compounded for Louisiana-Pacific by the fact that the Ketchikan mill's equipment is outdated, inefficient to operate, and hazardous to workers and the environment. For nearly 40 years, the mill has flushed five million gallons of dioxin-laced wastewater into Ward Cove every day. Ward Cove, an inlet north of Ketchikan, was once a vibrant estuary filled with salmon, steelhead, humpback whales and orca, now it is a toxic dead zone. The company has not had valid air permit for the mill since 1990. From 1992 to 1997, the Ketchikan mill has been hit with more than $6 million in fines for violations of clean air and water laws. In 1994 FBI agents raided the company's offices and seized thousands of pages of documents. As a result of this investigation, Louisiana-Pacific was convicted on felony charges of falsifying pollution reporting data.

Louisiana-Pacific's decision to permanently close the pulp mill forced the Forest Service to terminate the long-term contract, since the timber purchasing agreement was predicated on the year-round operation of the mill. When the Forest Service voided the contract, Louisiana-Pacific rushed to the federal claims court in Anchorage, where it filed suit against the government. In court papers, the company alleged that the termination of the contract resulted in a governmental "taking" of the economic value of the pulp mill. The suit sought $400 million in damages. [They eventually settled for $140 million.]

"This settlement is a tremendous victory for the cause of property rights," says Ron Arnold, director of the Center for the Defense of Free Enterprise, a Bellevue, Washington-based Wise Use group. "The Clinton administration has validated our contention that the environmental regulations imposed on Louisiana-Pacific clearly damaged the company economically. The lesson is that the government can impose the regulations on companies, but they cannot escape paying just compensation for doing so, plus damages for bad faith dealing."

But most legal observers believe that Louisiana-Pacific's suit had little merit. Indeed, the suit sounds almost frivolous on its face. It almost seems as if there were some prior arrangement between Louisiana-Pacific and the Administration and the suit itself was just a pretext to a financial bail-out to a troubled company. The objective of Louisiana-Pacific for several years has been to shift toward the logging of lucrative old-growth trees without being burdened by the costly pulp mill operations.

Ironically, Alaska—where the logging scheme on the Tongass has been underwritten by Congress mainly as a rural jobs program—was exempted from the nationwide ban on the exportation of raw logs cut from federal lands. For the past ten years, Louisiana-Pacific's biggest money-making enterprise in Alaska has come from exporting yellow cedar to Japan. The company pays the Forest Service about $1.50 per thousand board feet for the right to log the cedar off the Tongass. Then it sells the cedar logs to Japanese timber merchants for as much as $1,500 per thousand board feet, all without running a single cedar log through an Alaskan mill. The Japanese are willing to pay such high prices because the Tongass cedar closely resembles Hinoyki cedar, which is considered sacred and is used to build Shinto temples.

"The Ketchikan Pulp Mill fifty-year contract thus ends up as the most expensive timber sale in Forest Service history," says forest economist Randal O'Toole. "The net loss from this one sale was close to a quarter billion dollars."

The infusion of federal cash couldn't have come at a better time for Louisiana-Pacific. It had been a turbulent three years for the timber giant. After experiencing record-setting profits in the early 1990s, Louisiana-Pacific was riding high, becoming a favorite of mutual fund managers and institutional investors. Then in 1993, the company was suddenly confronted with allegations that its executive offices resembled a kind of white collar brothel. A long-time executive assistant to LP CEO Harry Merlo filed suit against the company charging wide-spread sexual harassment of female employees. According to the complaint, the company only hired top female assistants if "they were young, blond, strikingly attractive and likely to acquiesce to sexual advances from the CEO."

The suit was largely ignored by Merlo and his hand-picked board, which that very same year rewarded him with a salary of $5 million and $48 million in company stock. But things were starting to fall apart in the company's Portland headquarters.

The problems centered on one of Louisiana-Pacific's signature products, Oriented Strand Board, known as OSB. The company marketed the siding as an environmentally-friendly replacement for plywood decking and siding for houses and apartments. According to LP's marketing PR, OSB is a "green product" because its manufacture does not require the logging of old growth. Instead, OSB can be constructed by chipping small diameter trees, including species that were previously considered to have little commercial value. The chips are then cooked up in a kind of toxic stew and pressed into siding panels.

The problem is that when exposed to moderate levels of moisture and humidity, OSB tends to disintegrate within two years. Moreover, as the OSB panels begin to break apart they release dangerous fumes from the glue used to hold the fiberboard together. This toxic phenomenon is known as out-gassing. It causes the insidious poisoning of people who occupy houses sheathed in OSB. The ailments suffered by victims of Louisiana-Pacific's deteriorating siding range from headaches and nausea to seizures and partial paralysis. In 1996, the company paid out nearly $500 million to settle class-action suits brought by homeowners who had purchased OSB products. Several states, including Oregon, Washington and Florida, are pursuing criminal investigations against the company for fraudulent testing and marketing of OSB. Two former employees have alleged that the company falsified testing results on the durability and safety of the OSB from 1990 through 1994.

As the OSB scandal reached its climax, the Louisiana-Pacific board called an emergency meeting in Chicago. There, Merlo was confronted with evidence that he had ordered the doctoring of proxy statements and SEC documents in an effort to conceal the extent of financial liabilities facing the company. After a hostile exchange, the board voted to remove Merlo from his position. The executive was escorted out of the meeting by armed security guards. Meanwhile, the locks on the doors of his penthouse office back in Portland, Oregon were changed and his files seized by company investigators and outside auditors.

Merlo was replaced as CEO of Louisiana-Pacific by former International Paper Company executive Mark Suwyn, an old friend of Louisiana-Pacific board member Pierre DuPont. But the problems for LP didn't end with Merlo's ouster. In the spring of 1997 , its stock price plunged after the company was forced to make a $300 million charge against its income. This announcement was followed by a new criminal investigation by the FBI into allegations of timber theft by the company on the Tongass National Forest. Forest Service whistleblowers had alleged that over the past 10 years Louisiana-Pacific has stolen over $24 million worth of federal timber.

Assigned the extraordinarily challenging task of running the public relations campaign over the past few years for the embattled company is a man called Thomas Hoog, general manager of the super-firm of Hill & Knowlton. Like many of the partners at Hill & Knowlton, Hoog's political ties are to the Democratic Party. He served as chief of staff for former Colorado Senator Gary Hart. Another Democratic powerbroker at Hill & Knowlton is the firm's CEO, Howard Paster, a golfing partner of President Clinton, who served for a year as director of legislative affairs in the Clinton White House. Hoog, who attended two of those White House coffee sessions, played a key role in persuading the administration to settle the Louisiana-Pacific case in Alaska.

Senator Frank Murkowski, the Republican from Alaska who now heads the powerful Energy and Environment Committee, has been a key player in defending Louisiana-Pacific's reign of terror on the Tongass for nearly two decades. During the 104th Congress, Murkowski authored legislative initiatives aimed at overturning environmental regulations on the Tongass in order to accelerate logging in areas under contract to Louisiana-Pacific. In the spring of 1995, it was revealed that Senator Murkowski owned more than $25,000 worth of stock in Louisiana-Pacific and that he was a major shareholder in the Ketchikan State Bank, one of the pulp mill's largest creditors.

It now seems that Murkowski used his clout as head of the committee responsible for reviewing Frederico Pena's nomination as Secretary of Energy to extract concessions on the Tongass. "Murkowski threw his weight around and the administration quickly caved in," said a Democratic staffer. "Everyone thought the fight on Pena's nomination was over the Yucca Mountain nuclear waste site. In reality, all the discussions had to do with logging levels on the Tongass and whether or not LP was going to be compensated for closing down the pulp mill."

The reaction of Alaskan environmentalists to the bailout of Louisiana-Pacific has been strangely supportive. "We are grateful that the contract is voided," said Tim Driscoll of the Southeast Alaska Conservation Council in Juneau. "Now the challenge for the Tongass is to shift toward a sustainable economy in the region. That means a smaller harvest which independent sawmills use to make value added products."

The problem with this rosy scenario is that there are few independent timber companies left in the region and almost no capital available to build new mills. Louisiana-Pacific is largely responsible for this situation. Native companies were hit the hardest by Louisiana-Pacific's near-hegemony over the regional timber market. In 1979, Reid Brothers, a small logging company owned by members of the Tlingit Tribe, filed a civil suit against both Louisiana Pacific and the Alaska Pulp Company. Among other things, the Reid Brothers alleged that the timber giants had rigged bids on Tongass timber sales, had conspired with local banks to manipulate the financing of small millowners, and had overestimated stumpage and logging costs to extract more subsidies from the feds. As a result of these predatory activities more than 100 small sawmills were driven out of business between 1970 and 1979. In 1981, the district court ruled in favor of Reid Brothers and the 9th Circuit Court of Appeals upheld the opinion that Louisiana-Pacific had violated anti-trust laws.

In the wake of the Reid Brothers case, the Forest Service began its own investigation of the pulp company. It determined that Louisiana-Pacific had defrauded the government out of more than $80 million. Yet, no action was taken against the corporation. Forest Service sources say that is because Assistant Secretary of Agriculture John Crowell had quashed the investigation before it reached the

Justice Department. Previously, Crowell had served as general counsel for Louisiana-Pacific.

Now, Louisiana-Pacific, a company with one of the longest eco-rap sheets in the nation, has finally achieved its goal of being the sole player in the lucrative Tongass timber market. And, as a surprise bonus, it has been handed by the Clinton administration $140 million in cash, which it will most likely use to expand its operations in Mexico, China and Bolivia.

Ketchikan, Alaska, November 1997

Nine

Why David Chain Died

David "Gypsy" Chain was killed on September 17, 1998 on Pacific Lumber land near Grizzly Creek off Route 36 in Humboldt County because he formed part of the last line of defense in a battle plan fatally betrayed by Democratic politicians and environmental executives cringing before a corporate predator from Chain's own state of Texas. A.E. Ammonds, the 52-year-old faller who put the tree down on Chain, crushing his skull, was the party immediately responsible for the young man's death. Ammonds was never charged and probably shouldn't have been. But the people who put him in the woods that day should bear the full brunt of penalties consequent upon a wrongful death.

The terrain where Chain died forms part of the Headwaters Forest, owned by Pacific Lumber, taken over some years ago by Maxxam, owned by Charles Hurwitz. As is well known, Headwaters is the largest private holding of old-growth redwoods in the world. When Hurwitz announced a few years ago that his crews would start logging, the most resolute plan against the tycoon was to have the US government penalize Hurwitz for his looting of a Texas savings and loan by taking Headwaters from him as compensation for his $2 billion heist. But this plan fell by the wayside, derided by the establishment enviros as far too extreme.

Next came a well conceived plan by former Rep. Dan Hamburg to have the US government buy out 40,000 acres of the entire 63,000 acre watershed for a substantial, albeit defensible sum. Although it was helped forward through Congress by two of the craftiest manipulators on the Hill—Vernon Jordan and Tommy Boggs, working for Hurwitz—the bill failed in the Senate.

Then came a well-conceived strategy by EPIC, the enviro group based in Garberville, to tame Hurwitz by rigorous application of federal and state regs. Thus, thousands of acres would be put off limits to the chainsaw in order to protect dwindling habitat for the marbled murrelet, the northern spotted owl and the coho salmon. Given the ravaged condition of Pacific Lumber's holdings after a decade of Hurwitz's onslaughts, the mandatory protections for these species would put most of the land out of Hurwitz's reach.

EPIC put its strategy into play with a series of lawsuits and petitions under the Endangered Species Act, and the strategy began to take effect. At this point, Hurwitz raised the stakes, announcing that in the face of these regulatory inhibitions, he was going to file a "takings" suit against the US government, suing it for hundreds of millions for preventing him from enjoying the rights and ravages of private property.

The Clinton administration and large environmental organizations such as the Sierra Club and the Wilderness Society took this threat as the tocsin for immediate retreat. Hurwitz, they quavered, might have a chance of victory in such a takings claim, which would encourage further "hostage taking" by corporations. So, they argued, the prudent course was to give Hurwitz more than he had ever dared dream when he had sent Jordan and Boggs up to Capitol Hill to work for the Hamburg Bill.

Enter Senator Dianne Feinstein. The California senator successfully lobbied Clinton to announce a deal whereby the feds and the state of California would pool money to acquire the minimal core area of Headwaters, less than 10,000 acres of the entire watershed. Of that, only 3,500 acres are composed of old-growth redwoods, for which the government offered to Hurwitz the astounding sum of $480 million.

One story going around Washington and Sacramento is that Hurwitz had argued that the acres were worth $900 million, roughly what he paid for the entire company, and the Department of Justice countered with a valuation of $20 million. At which point Tommy Boggs said, Why not split the difference?

By any measure this is surely one of Hurwitz's greatest financial coups. But there was a lagniappe. As part of the deal Hurwitz demanded that he be allowed to work his will on the rest of the entire 210,000 acres of his Pacific Lumber holdings. The US Department of Interior and the State of California duly agreed to sign off on a Habitat Conservation Plan or HCP proposed by Pacific Lumber. In the Clinton era, these HCPs have become the preferred corporate method of circumventing the Endangered Species Act.

Pacific Lumber's HCP will allow the company to largely liqui-

date the old growth and residual redwood and Douglas fir tracts outside of the 10,000 acres scheduled to be bought by the government.
The company is scheduled to receive a permit to kill as many as 340
marbled murrelets, the threatened seabird that nests in coastal old-
growth forest. This amounts to 17 percent of a total murrelet population in precipitous decline.

Right now on Pacific Lumber lands there are 116 pairs of nesting spotted owls. The HCP estimates that 16 pairs will be "taken,"
i.e., killed, and in the words of a California CDF consultant for the
plan, "the population [of owls] will be allowed to fluctuate with
changes in the landscape." Given that the spotted owl population
has been declining at as much as a 4 percent annual rate in Clintontime, none of this bodes well for the creature's long- or even middle-
term survival. On top of that, if the evidence shows that the owl and
the murrelet are disappearing at even higher rates, a "no surprises"
clause successfully demanded by Hurwitz means that nothing can be
done for 50 years, by which time the whole show will be over.

The coho salmon is probably the most complicated factor in
the whole deal and the species that could potentially keep most of
the remaining mature forest on Pacific Lumber lands out of the
sawmills. But instead of pushing an aggressive conservation strategy,
the government accepted the following brazen proposal in Pacific
Lumber's HCP: on what are called year-round salmon-bearing
streams, PL proposed a 30-foot no-cut buffer on each side. The federal guidelines for such streams in Washington, Oregon and
California require between 300 feet and 500 feet, depending on the
slope. On year-round streams without salmon that flow into salmon
streams, Pacific Lumber has successfully proposed a ten-foot "buffer,"
which is of course entirely meaningless.

At this level of protection the coho, once the mainstay of the
Indian economy, has no future at all.

There was a recent opportunity to lay this whole dreadful plan
low. The feds approved its $250 million slice of the $480 million last
year when Clinton signed the Interior appropriations bill. But the
deal still had to be approved by the California general assembly,
where EPIC was making a decent effort at monkey-wrenching the
process by fierce lobbying, stirring up fiscal conservatives at the huge
cost to the taxpayer and making environmentally minded legislators

writhe at the preposterousness of the HCPs.

But working the phones behind the scenes were conspirators in the drama which would end in David Chain's death. Dianne Feinstein and Tommy Boggs lobbied hard, and as the bill picked up legislative speed in Sacramento the one group which could have stepped forward and killed it in its tracks was the Sierra Club. Instead, in familiar fashion, the Club's executive director Carl Pope admitted later to his own board of directors that although it was "a close judgment call," the club "did not actively try to block (the bill's) passage, but rather put its energy into improving it." This would be all that was needed to inch the bill past the finishing post and the California General Assembly passed it on September 1, 1998.

Oh, and the improvements? The Sierra Club suggested that the coho buffer by expanded from 30 feet to 100 feet and from 10 to 30 feet, still far short of the minimum guidelines.

The stage was now set for its fatal denouement, and most likely a whole series of desperate and dangerous actions. Because of the deal finally ratified in Washington and Sacramento, there is no room left for regulatory inhibitions against corporate ravages. At the federal and state level, corporations can shove through Habitat Conservation Plans that are meaningless. The logging crews will be sent into the woods and the only restraint left will be direct action demonstrators like Chain. There is no alternative left.

After Chain was killed, the Sierra Club board piously passed a resolution of "outrage" against his end. The resolution was opposed by David Brower, who told the board that the Club should look at its own shared culpability, abandon ritual expressions of regret, cultivate "its rage and get its balls back."

Arcata, 1998

Ten

And Then There Were Three

The Second Extermination of the Lobo

The first Mexican gray wolf pup born in the wilds of the American Southwest in nearly fifty years is dead, presumed starved to death after its mother died in August of 1998. At the time its mother perished, the pup was only four months old and was incapable of surviving on its own.

Known as wolf 174, the pup's mother was one of 11 Mexican wolves, a subspecies of the larger North American timber wolf, released into the Gila Mountains near the border between Arizona and New Mexico by the US Fish and Wildlife Service in March of 1998. At first, the government suggested that the female wolf fell victim to an attack by a mountain lion, a rare way for a wolf to die. But later an autopsy revealed that the wolf had met a more traditional end: it had been shot.

The killing of a Mexican wolf violates federal and state laws and can carry a penalty of up to $100,000 and one year in prison. Typically, however, the Fish and Wildlife Service has been reluctant to pursue these types of cases against ranchers. An infamous example is the Montana case of a rancher who shot a federally protected wolf and the government declined to prosecute the case. The rancher later ended up jailed and fined for shooting a neighbor's dog.

Wolf 174 was the fourth of the Mexican wolves to have died after being released into the wild. Since her demise, at least two others have been killed and another is missing. The deaths have not been accidental. Instead, one by one the wolves have been deliberately killed, apparent victims of a vigilante campaign by angry ranchers in the remote mountains of Arizona and New Mexico. Of the 11 original wolves, only three now remain in the wild.

The Mexican wolf, known throughout the Southwest as El Lobo, is a diminutive subspecies of the timber wolf, which inhabits the northern Rockies and the North Woods area of Minnesota and Michigan. The lobos were hunted to extinction in the wild by the 1960s. After the passage of the Endangered Species Act in 1972, five lobos were captured in central Mexico and used to begin a captive breeding program. By the mid-1990s, zoos and other breeding facilities had generated 175 Mexican wolves. As a result of lawsuits by environmental groups, the federal Fish and Wildlife Service was forced to initiate a program to reintroduce the wolves into wilderness areas in eastern Arizona. Under the Mexican wolf recovery plan, the government has set a goal of having more than 100 wolves in the area by 2025.

When it was released in 1996, the government's reintroduction plan sparked fierce protests from ranchers, who lodged outlandish claims that the wolves would decimate their cattle and sheep herds. These assertions lacked any substance. Studies of wolf predation from Canada and Minnesota show that even in areas were wolves and livestock interact, wolves are reluctant to prey on domestic animals, preferring deer and elk, both of which are abundant in the Blue Mountains of Arizona. The Fish and Wildlife Service estimates that when more than 100 wolves have taken root in the area they will kill more than 10,000 deer and elk a year, while taking only from between one and thirty-four cows and sheep. Defenders of Wildlife has offered to compensate ranchers for any livestock losses to wolves.

The ranchers also claimed that the wolves posed a threat to humans. "We are afraid that some of these wolves are going to get hold of one of our children," Jesse Carey recently told the *Phoenix New Times*. Carey is a gun show owner and sheriff in Catron County, New Mexico, whose virulent anti-wolf rhetoric prompted federal law enforcement officials to seize guns from his shop to test against the bullets which killed the wolves.

"The notion that wolves will attack children is simply a scare tactic," says Dr. Robin Silver, a Phoenix physician and wolf advocate. "There's not one recorded instance of wild wolves preying on humans in North America. I don't think these wolves are going to change their evolutionary history."

The lobo has become the latest rallying cry for the anti-environmental movement. Despite national polls showing that more than 80 percent of the public supports wolf reintroduction, the antipathy for the wolf and its defenders is extreme across much of the rural west. The Southwest, in particular, has long been a breeding ground for some of the most virulent strains of the Wise Use Movement. Several counties have enacted ordinances challenging the federal government's authority to manage national forest lands and protection endangered species habitat. There have been armed confrontations with federal officials and environmentalists.

In 1993, Leroy Jackson, a traditional Navajo who had challenged the decimation of his reservation's forest by a white-owned timber company, received death threats and was later found dead in his van in a remote spot in northern New Mexico under mysterious circumstances. In 1997, Santa Fe environmentalist Sam Hitt received death threats and was hung in effigy outside the offices of the organization he heads, Forest Guardians. In December of 1998, the Santa Fe offices of the Animal Protection of New Mexico had its windows blown out by shotgun blasts. A group called the Minutemen claimed responsibility for the terrorist action. Police believe the attack was in retaliation of the group's support of wolf reintroduction.

One of the targets of this attack may have been Patricia Wolff, who works as a consultant for the group. Wolff has received several death threats, dating back to a 1992 incident investigated by the FBI. Wolff had recently released a tape-recording of a May 1998 conversation she had with a trapper named Jody Lee Cooper, who claimed that ranchers in Glenwood, New Mexico had wanted to hire him to kill the reintroduced wolves. Cooper, who refers to himself as "the predator's predator," said that he had been offered "$35,000 in cash to kill 'em all." Wolff took the tape to the Fish and Wildlife Service, which failed to follow up on the evidence. "I think he was truthful and credible," Wolff says. "He had no motive to lie to me."

The plan is to release 15 more wolves. The new wolves will be spray-painted orange, supposedly to differentiate them from coyotes, whom ranchers can legally kill. But in fact this glow-in-the-dark marking may just make the animals easier targets for the lobo killers.

Santa Fe, New Mexico, 1998

Eleven

The Ghost Bears of Idaho

The federal government maintains that the grizzly bear went extinct in Idaho more than fifty years ago. Two years ago the Fish and Wildlife Service announced an ambitious plan to bring the bears back in an expensive and controversial reintroduction scheme that would implant Canadian bears into the wildlands in the Selway/Bitterroot region of western Montana and central Idaho. But the plan came with a hitch. The reintroduced bears would be designated "an experimental, non-essential population." Under this status, the bears don't enjoy the full sanctions of the Endangered Species Act, meaning ranchers can kill them and their habitat is not reserved from development.

But old timers, wilderness enthusiasts and some bear biologists thought differently. They believed that the secretive bears had never been completely wiped out of Idaho, perhaps the wildest and most rugged state in the lower-48. There had been sightings of the great, hump-backed bear in the big Salmon-Selway wilderness of central Idaho and in the Great Burn roadless area to the north, on the crest of the Bitterroot Range.

"We believe there are grizzly bears back in that country, that there have been credible reports and that the very agencies responsible for recovering healthy populations of grizzlies have ignored those reports," said Mike Bader, executive director of the Alliance for the Wild Rockies. Bader's group and Wilderness Watch have asked environmentalists, hunters and outfitters to scour the 22,000-square-mile Salmon-Selway ecosystem looking for sign of grizzlies. Bader calls it the Great Grizzly Search and it has already produced results—scat and bristly clumps of hair. The scat and hair samples have been submitted for genetic testing to confirm they come from grizzlies and not the more common American black bear.

All of this has seemed to unhinge Chris Servheen, the head of the Interagency Grizzly Bear Task Force and the driving force behind the reintroduction scheme, which would strip the bears of the protections of the Endangered Species Act. In an interview with the *Missoulian*, Servheen angrily accused Bader and his allies of being conspiracy-mongers. "The idea that there is a conspiracy and we are not telling the truth is preposterous," Servheen said. "We have no reason on God's green earth to hide evidence of grizzly bears. What purpose would I have to hide evidence of grizzly bears? Grizzly bears are what I do."

But environmentalists point to two reasons why Servheen may have had a motive to cover up the existence of grizzlies in the Salmon-Selway country. First, there is the fact that naturally occurring bears enjoy the full protection of the Endangered Species Act. This means it is illegal to kill them or to destroy their habitat through clearcuts, mines, roads or cattle grazing.

Servheen's research has been partially funded by the National Fish and Wildlife Foundation, which receives grants from timber, mining and ranching concerns that have an economic interest in seeing all the grizzlies in the region designated as "non-essential and experimental."

Some environmentalists have taken to calling the grizzly reintroduction plan a "shoot-and-replace" program. "Servheen wants the public relations kudos of returning the bear, but without the burden of actually protecting them once they are back," says Steve Kelly, an organizer with the Friends of the Wild Swan. "These bears will be kidnapped from Canada, where the populations are already depressed, and dropped into Idaho, where they will meet near certain death. That's not conservation, that's just replenishing the targets in a shooting gallery."

When told that Bader had sent hikers and independent biologists into the woods to look for grizzlies, Servheen demeaned the effort and said he wouldn't accept as credible any of the evidence produced by the survey. "Somebody who says they saw a grizzly bear is not credible evidence," Servheen said. "We need a plaster cast of a paw print or a clear photograph. Or we need somebody who really knows grizzly bears who says they saw grizzly bears."

But there is mounting evidence that federal biologists and rangers with the Forest Service have seen evidence of grizzlies in the region and have passed the information on to Servheen. Bader has unearthed an October 27, 1998 memo from Forest Service biologist, Mike Hillis. "Last summer, two of our employees encountered grizzly bears in the Selway Bitterroot Recovery Area," Hillis wrote. The biologist reported that one employee spotted "a large brown-colored bear" with a "dish-faced profile" and a "a prominent hump." The other sighting was of a track of a hind foot "9.25 inches long by 8 inches wide" and the "claw marks that extended two inches past the toes," as is typical with grizzlies. Hillis concluded that both Forest Service employees "are experienced woodsmen and can be considered objective observers. Consequently, I feel that the sightings are in all likelihood those of a grizzly bear(s)." This memo was forwarded to Servheen.

On November 5, 1999, I talked to a Forest Service biologist who said he spotted a grizzly in the Bitterroot Mountains of Idaho in 1995. "And I'm not stupid," the Forest Service biologist said. "I know a grizzly when I see one." The biologist said he gave the coordinates of the sighting to Servheen and Servheen dismissed them out of hand. "He just didn't want to hear it," the biologist said.

The Forest Service certainly has no incentive to make up these claims. Finding grizzly bears in the woods only complicates their lives, making it much more difficult to do what the Forest Service does: plan timber sales.

Missoula, 1999

Twelve

The New Bison Killers

In the winter of 2000 Roy Koski and William Hill, a couple of retirees from Butte, Montana, were driving along Highway 287 near Hebgen Lake twenty miles from the northwestern border of Yellowstone Park. By the side of the road they saw five bison pawing through the snow trying to find some forage. The two men got out of their car to take some photographs. Soon a Montana Division of Fish, Wildlife and Parks truck pulled up beside them. Two rangers climbed out with high-powered rifles, knelt by their truck about 50 feet from the grazing bison, and shot them.

"We were looking at how pretty they were in the snow," says the 70-year-old Hill, who describes himself as an avid hunter. "Then, when the wildlife rangers suddenly shot the bison where they stood, I was so upset I started shaking and damned near cried. I thought, 'Isn't this a fine way to slaughter one of our national symbols?' Now, I think I'll stop hunting."

What Hill and Koski had witnessed has been a sadly familiar scene on the northern Montana edge of Yellowstone National Park in the frigid winter of 2000. Thus far, nearly 1000 bison have been shot or captured and then trucked to slaughterhouses by federal and state agents. This means that nearly a third of the total bison herd in Yellowstone has been exterminated since January. Hundreds more may perish before the June snowmelt.

The slaughter of the bison began as the result of a suit brought by the State of Montana and the Church Universal and Triumphant, a survivalist compound whose New Age leader is Elizabeth Claire Prophet. The Church, which maintains a huge arsenal of explosives and weapons, operates a large cattle ranch adjacent to the park's northern boundary near Gardiner, Montana.

The suit claimed that bison wandering out of Yellowstone might be carrying brucellosis, a disease of bacterial origin, which—when transmitted to cattle—can cause spontaneous abortions of the calves. Only a small percentage of the Yellowstone bison carry the bacterium and to date there has never been a documented case of brucellosis being transmitted from bison to cattle on the open range. Even if the Yellowstone bison herds were contaminated with the brucellosis bacterium in large numbers there would be little chance of them transmitting the disease to nearby cattle, says Dr. Jasper Carlton, director of the Biodiversity Legal Foundation, in Boulder, Colorado. That's because the disease is only transmitted through contact with infected, aborted fetuses or contaminated birthing fluids or tissue. Bison rarely experience abortion. In Yellowstone in the past 75 years, there have been only four bison abortions and it is not known if these were the result of brucellosis.

"The real absurdity is that when the bison, following their ancient migratory routes, return to Yellowstone in the spring to give birth, there are no cattle around to be infected," argues Steve Kelly, director of the Montana Ecosystem Defense Council.

It is one of the bitter ironies of this story that brucellosis is an exotic disease, passed on to bison in the 19th century by European cattle. Moreover, the brucellosis bacterium is now carried by most of the mammals in the Northern Rockies, from elk to field mice.

Despite all this, the suit was successfully brought. The motivation of the State of Montana is to assert increasing control over the management of Yellowstone, particularly its wildlife and its recreational activities. As part of its ideological battle with the federal park, the State of Montana, backed by timber, mining, and ranching interests, claims the right to kill not only bison, but also any grizzly bear or gray wolf that strays beyond Yellowstone's borders.

"Even if you buy the state of Montana's brucellosis threat argument, the rangers should at worst only be killing pregnant female bison," says Kelly. "But that's not what's happening. They are killing every bison that wanders out of the park."

The reason male bison and calves are being killed even though they pose no threat of transmitting the disease is that the Church Universal and Triumphant claimed in its suit that the wandering bison were knocking down its fences. Yellowstone Park sits on a high plateau and the natural migratory pattern is for the elk and bison to descend to lower elevations—such as that now occupied by the Church's ranch—in the hard winter months, when the park is buried under as much as twenty feet of snow.

Yellowstone is the first national park and the largest. Indeed, it is the only national park where the philosophy of natural regulation is supposed to hold sway. After the great bison extermination campaigns of the 1860s, Yellowstone was heralded as the last sanctuary of these shaggy creatures. This is the prime reason the bison became the symbol of the National Park Service and the US Department of the Interior. For decades, armed park rangers roamed Yellowstone's borders on horseback to protect the park's bison herd from poachers.

"Yellowstone was founded on the idea that there should be some places left where natural processes should not be interfered with," says Carlton. "The ongoing bison slaughter violates the prime directive of the park."

The bison observed by Hill and Koski had followed a new trail out of the park: a groomed path for the hordes of snowmobilers who have invaded Yellowstone in recent years from the western entrance. The reason the bison death count is so high—the original Park Service estimate had been that perhaps 200 animals might be killed—is because the packed snowmobile trails have allowed the bison to move quickly through what would otherwise be impenetrably deep snow.

Well aware that bison slaughter might attract unwelcome publicity, park officials have been trying to win credit by donating the low-fat bison meat to Indian tribes in the Northern Rockies and Great Plains. Rosalee Little Thunder is a Lakota Sioux woman who journeyed to Yellowstone to witness the capture and killing of the bison, animals which are sacred to her tribe.

"I saw them unloading truck after truck," Little Thunder said. "One bison was dead with its side ripped open to the ribs. Another bison was standing on top of the dead one. A third bison was dying. A fourth had a broken leg. The fifth had a large gore wound to its hindquarter and was bleeding profusely. State wildlife and slaughter-house workers poked electrical prods in sensitive areas of the bison, in their faces and testicles, to make them move out of the truck. This is the other side of the story. Certainly people are facing hard times and any food is appreciated. But our hunger does not justify the Yellowstone buffalo slaughter. The buffalo is far more important to the natural world than what the wildlife officials and the cattle ranchers are willing to see. The Lakota Nation has suffered great harm from humanitarian gestures in the past. Now we need not be fed the flesh of our own children."

After the retirees, Koski and Hill, watched the bison being shot near Hebgen Lake, they asked the regional wildlife ranger, Captain Jim Kropp, why those bison were killed. Kropp replied that his office had received a request from a nearby cattle ranch to remove the bison. The nearest cattle ranch is owned by movie star Steven Seagal, who recently proclaimed his commitment to the preservation of the Headwaters redwood forest. Not in his backyard!

Gardiner, Montana, 2000

Thirteen

To the Last Drop

When the Colorado Doesn't Meet the Sea

Fifty years ago Aldo Leopold hailed the Colorado River delta as North America's greatest oasis: two million acres of wetlands, cienegas, lagoons, tidal pools, jaguars and mesquite scrublands. Today it's a wasteland.

The mighty Colorado River no longer reaches the Sea of Cortez. Its entire annual flow has been diverted and spit out into hay fields, water fountains in front of Vegas hotels and thousands of golf courses. The Colorado has been sucked up to the last drop.

Its once lush delta is now a salt flat, as barren as Carthage after Scipio Africanus took his revenge on Hannibal's homeland. This estuary used to be one of the wonders of the world: a vast wetland, teeming with more than 400 species of plants and animals. In fact, like the Nile, another desert river, nearly 80 percent of the riparian habitat for the entire Colorado River was once clustered near the mouth of the river. The shallow lagoons in the delta region are home to the Vacquita dolphin, at four feet in length the world's smallest, which is now on the brink of extinction, with only 100 animals known to exist. Dozens of other endemic species are in the same shape.

And not just animals are in trouble. The delta was once the cultural mecca of the Copacha Indians, who made a good living fishing the estuary. But these days the fishing boats are beached and the Indians and Mexican residents are in grinding poverty, forced to work multiple jobs in distant tortilla factories, maquiladoras and wheat fields.

Perhaps the only legal framework as mind-numbing as the Law of Sea is the Law of the Colorado River. This thicket of deals, trade-offs, set-asides, subsidies and politically sanctioned thievery is nearly impenetrable to even the most seasoned and cynical observer. But from the Mexican side of the border, the law is devastatingly simple: the US retains 95 percent of the Colorado River's water and Mexico gets what's left over. Most years this is about 1.5 million acre feet, roughly the same amount that Sonoran desert farmers were using to irrigate their bean and onion fields in 1922.

Just before the Colorado crosses the US/Mexico border, 75 percent of its flow is diverted into the All-American canal. From there the water is flushed into wasteful irrigation systems and it eventually trickles down into the Salton Sea, once an important stop on the Pacific flyway for migratory birds now a toxic soup of fertilizer and pesticide runoff. Instead of a bird paradise, the Salton Sea has become a killing ground, the avian equivalent of cancer alley.

The water that eventually makes it to Mexico—much of it runoff from Arizona and California alfalfa and cotton fields—is nearly as salt-laden and toxic as that in the Salton Sea. The situation is so extreme that the Bureau of Reclamation was compelled to build a $211 million "reverse-osmosis" desalination plant at Yuma, Arizona. But that plant, built in 1992, has only operated for a year.

It comes down to consumption. People in the American southwest have yet to come to terms with the fact that they live in a desert. Per capita water use by the residents of California, Nevada and Arizona ranges up to as much as 200 gallons a day, more than 120 percent above the daily average for the rest of the nation. In Israel, for example, daily water consumption is less than 75 gallons.

But as stark as these numbers are the thirst of California agribusiness is downright vampirish by comparison. Nearly 80 percent of the Colorado's flow goes to corporate farming. Much of it to low-valued crops, such as alfalfa, cotton and even potatoes, that require lots of water. And because of their political clout they get the water cheap. Residents of Los Angeles, for example, pay as much as $600 per acre-foot for water from the Colorado. Big agribusiness is getting the same water for only $13 per acre foot.

For nearly 150 years, the attitude of the water users of the American West has been guided by one dictate: "use it or lose it." The notion of allowing any water to remain in the river, for fish, for birds, for rafters, or for Mexico, has long been anathema to the water lords.

"Scientists say we need at least one-percent to keep the

Colorado River delta on life-support," says David Orr, of the Moab, Utah-based Glen Canyon Action Network. "That's why we started the One-percent for the Delta Campaign. We're asking all of the water users in the Colorado basin to donate one-percent of their allocation to help restore the delta. One percent's not a lot to ask, is it?"

The question is rhetorical, because Orr knows better than anyone that the history of western water politics is based on this paradigm: use it or lose it. That's why the Colorado and its tributaries are dammed and diverted from Wyoming to the Mexican border. For the water lords' perspective, it's better to waste the water than to leave it in the river.

That's how we got Glen Canyon Dam, one of the world's greatest desecrations of nature. This concrete plug flooded nearly 300 miles of the Colorado, destroying one of the most glorious canyons on earth. But the impounded water—the equivalent of two years of the river's entire flow—just sits there. Lake Powell is what's known as a storage reservoir. It's there to merely keep the water from reaching the Sea of Cortez where it would be "lost."

But here's where we arrive at just how perverse the system has become. Because Lake Powell sits in the middle of a redrock desert, it loses a lot of water every year to evaporation. How much? More than a million acre feet. Moreover, another 350,000 acre feet are absorbed into the sandstone walls of the canyon. All told that represents ten percent of the Colorado's yearly flow. To put it in perspective: the evaporation loss in a single day is equal to the amount of water used by 17,000 homes in Phoenix over an entire year.

This grim fact has led to a radical but sensible idea: tear down Glen Canyon Dam, restore the canyon and let the water return to the delta, where it can replenish that once teeming oasis. To promote this outlandishly appropriate plan, Orr and his colleagues have taken to the road in a water-tanker truck, stopping at dams along the course of the Colorado, taking a bucket of water from each stop and into pouring the holds of the tanker, ultimately delivering it to the Colorado Delta. They've named their truck "Vacquita Rescue," after the rare porpoise.

This is the face of the new environmental movement: ethnically diverse, smart, theatrical, militant, and armed with a passion for social and ecological justice as well as a sense of humor.

Riding along with the truck on several of its stops in the Four Corners region was Thomas Morris, the head of the Navajo Medicine Men's Association. Morris sees the damming of the Colorado as an assault on the cultural and spiritual roots of native people throughout the Southwest. Many of the sites most sacred to Morris and the Navajo tribe are now buried under hundreds of feet of water, destined for Phoenix subdivisions and golf courses.

"Preserving our cultural traditions is more important but harder to do as time goes by," says Morris. "Indian people have worked hard to gain protection for our spiritual beliefs and practices, for the places where we make prayers, sing songs, and hold ceremonies. We have seen some progress, but there is still a long way to go. Imagine how it might feel if the great cathedrals were bulldozed for strip malls. The Bible tells how Jesus threw the moneychangers out of the temple. We can relate to that when we see our sacred places flooded and turned into tourist attractions."

Taking down Glen Canyon Dam would be a big first step toward righting old wrongs on both sides of the border.

Moab, Utah, 2001

Fourteen

Giving It All Away

Land Swapping in the New West

Back in early days of Reagantime, Interior Secretary James Watt, the nature-raping fundamentalist, hatched a dark fantasy to sell off millions of acres of public forest and parklands to private corporations. When this scheme leaked out to the press, it met with howls of derision and Watt was vilified even by members of his own party.

Now under the magic spell of the "win-win" solution, the land grab has been taken to heights undreamed of by Watt and his cronies. It began early on as a way to appease Republicans and tackle the federal debt, which had become an obsession of the bond market aficionados who were running the economic policy wing of the Clinton White House.

In the past five years, more than 1.5 million acres has been traded away in hundreds of swaps, sold to the public as a way to consolidate federal holdings. In reality, it's a wholesale privatization scheme. Another million acres in trades are awaiting completion. And some of the deals have been particularly lopsided. The West Utah land exchange is a particularly noxious affair. In this massive deal, the Interior Department acquired toxic lands near the Dugway Proving Grounds (a chemical weapons testing site) and surrendered land near the entrance to Zion National Park, where two golf courses will be carved into one of the most scenic spots on Earth.

In California, the Forest Service attempted to acquire a parcel of waterfront property on Lake Tahoe. After the deal was completed, they discovered that a title error had left an old mansion on the land in private hands. The owner of the mansion locked the gate blocking entrance to the new federal property. Ultimately, the Forest Service buckled to public pressure and simply purchased the mansion with cold cash.

The land swap frenzy can encourage a kind of hostage-taking by developers. In Colorado, for example, a developer acquired a privately-owned inholding inside of a popular wilderness area on national forest land. The developer threatened to put up a small ski resort on the site unless he was either bought out or given prime real estate near Aspen. The feds eventually paid him off.

"When we started looking into these land swaps in the mid-90s, nobody knew much about them and many enviros assumed they were benign transactions," says Janine Blaeloch, director the Western Land Exchange Project, a Seattle-based outfit that is one of the few environmental groups paying attention to this spasm of land trading. "So we started asking questions: how did they get chosen? Who makes the decisions? What are the ecological consequences? The answers we found were pretty ugly." Blaeloch's unflinching and feisty approach has made her a lot of enemies inside the agencies, big timber and, even big environmental groups, that have signed off on some the deals. "This is the future. I won't be surprised to see hundreds of thousands of acres of public lands traded away every year."

At the request of Rep. George Miller, the Democrat from California, the General Accounting Office launched an investigation of how the BLM and Forest Service had been administering their land exchange programs. After reviewing hundreds of transactions, the GAO concluded that both programs were so corrupt that an immediate moratorium on the swaps should be put in place and that a congressional investigation opened into improprieties committed by both agencies.

The GAO auditors found that most of the land exchanges favored private parties at the expense of the government and the environment. They also concluded that in many instances the BLM and the Forest Service failed to demonstrate that any public interest would be served by the exchanges and in many instances the government received abused land in exchange for top-notch habitat that would later be developed, clearcut or mined.

The BLM came in for particularly sharp criticism. The GAO investigators noted with amazement that the Bureau's accounting system didn't keep track of the value of the land exchanges, making it impossible to determine whether the deals were legal. But an analysis of some individual deals, especially in the state of Nevada, reveal the cozy relationship between agency land managers and private land developers.

In one exchange—which was noted in the files but not identified—the BLM traded to a real estate broker 70 acres of private land valued by agency appraisers at $763,000. Later that same day, the broker sold the same tract of land to a Nevada developer for $4.6 million. The same broker also made a killing on another BLM land swap. In this exchange, the broker acquired 40 acres of public land from the BLM at a value of $504,000 and sold it the same day for $1 million.

These sweetheart deals are the rule, not the exception. The GAO called on the BLM to "immediately discontinue buying and selling land under its land exchange program…and conduct an audit of financial records associated with the sales and purchases."

The Forest Service's record isn't any better. Over the past ten years, the agency has conducted more than 1,265 exchanges involving more than 950 square miles of land valued at more than $1 billion. But the GAO audit found that this was rarely a good deal for the government. "On average in an exchange, the Service acquired nonfederal land that was valued at about $780 per acre and conveyed federal land that was valued at about $1,415." In other words, even by the Forest Service's own often slanted accounting system the government was getting trading away lands that were nearly twice as valuable as what they were getting in return.

"Basically, the Forest Service was trading prime old-growth forest for lands that had already been clearcut," says Larry Tuttle, director of the Center for Environmental Equity, based in Portland, Oregon. "The agency is still controlled by timber beasts. They want to see these big trees cut and federal laws prohibit them from doing it. So they simply trade them off for lands that have already been logged over."

That was the case in one of the most contentious land exchanges of the past few years, the so-called Huckleberry exchange in Washington State. This deal found the Forest Service offering Weyerhaeuser 4,300 acres of natural forest land on Huckleberry Mountain for 40,000 acres of lands recently clearcut by Weyerhaeuser.

But the proposal was ridiculed by many environmentalists and fiercely opposed by the local community, which feared that landslides might follow in the wake of Weyerhaeuser clearcuts. The deal was also opposed by the Muckleshoot Tribe, which had long claimed that Huckleberry Mountain was a sacred site. This opposition may have been enough to scuttle the deal.

But Weyerhaeuser, one of the most politically devious companies around, hatched a dark scheme to greenwash the project. They devised a way to buy off the support of a high-profile environmental outfit: the Sierra Club. Although the land exchange was bitterly opposed by many Club activists, Weyerhaeuser executives targeted long-time Sierra Club official Charlie Raines as a potential ally. Raines spent much of his early career as an environmentalist working to create the Alpine Lakes Wilderness, a high-elevation landscape in the Cascade Mountains that is extremely popular with Seattle hikers. Indeed, in a well-known episode from the romantic folklore of Northwest environmentalism the boundary of the wilderness area was redrawn to include the spot where Raines first met his former wife.

Weyerhaeuser came up with the perfect trade bait. The company owned land inside the boundaries of the wilderness and offered to put it into the Huckleberry swap as an inducement to get Raines' support. It worked. Raines told the *Seattle Times* that the inclusion of the Alpine Lakes lands made all the difference.

So the Sierra Club's Raines became one of the land exchange's most fanatical proponents, often trotted out to dispute the concerns of other environmentalists and local residents. That was all the cover Weyerhaeuser needed. The deal went through.

"Charlie Raines worked for several years under the auspices of the Sierra Club's Cascade Chapter to facilitate the Huckleberry trade," says David Orr, a leader of the John Muir Sierrans, a grassroots cadre of activists seeking to reform the Sierra Club. "To many of us in the grassroots, the Huckleberry trade represents a horrifying abuse of power by the federal government, and it is made all the more troublesome by the interactions between Raines and Weyerhaeuser."

The deal had other problems that only became apparent after the transaction had taken place. The Forest Service told the public that the parcels being traded were both worth $45.5 million. But it turns out that the appraisers had grossly underestimated the economic value of the Forest Service's tract of old-growth and over-valued the cut-over and treeless lands put on the table by Weyerhaeuser. Two independent reviews concluded that the Forest Service had overvalued Weyerhaeuser's lands by more than 300 percent.

Moreover, Weyerhaeuser was given discounts on the Forest Service lands amounting to $30 million. This is a kind of risk insurance that the Overseas Private Investment Corporation ladles out to corporations doing business in so-called "unstable" regimes like Indonesia. But there was little justification for being so generous with Weyerhaeuser. In fact, even timber industry analysts shook their heads at the cushy deal.

Months later, however, the Ninth Circuit Court of Appeals ruled that the Huckleberry exchange violated federal law, since the Forest Service ignored the impact of the sale on threatened and endangered species, such as the northern spotted owl and marbled murrelet.

For many environmentalists trading off any public land is often seen as the equivalent of a museum deaccessioning a painting by Titian or a public library pitching its card catalogue system into the scrap heap. "They aren't making any more land," says Tim Hermach of the Eugene, Oregon-based Native Forest Council. "We need more land brought into the public domain, not less. There's no such thing as surplus public land. But the politicians have seen an easy way out with these landswaps. "

The initial solicitation almost always comes from the private landowner, a sign that the current system rarely has ecological considerations at the forefront. In fact, many of the federal bureaucrats that run the land exchange programs for the Forest Service and the BLM are more concerned about expanding the federal land base, or meeting land exchange quotas, than assessing the ecological or recreational value of the swaps. Thus, one Forest Service land exchange supervisor told the *Seattle Times*: "It's not the trees that matter, it's the land."

Many of these officials got their start as timber sale planners and were relocated to the real estate division after logging rates declined on the national forests in the wake of the spotted owl and salmon lawsuits of the early 1990s. These former timber beasts have retained a cozy relationship to their friends in the forest products industry and harbor deep grudges toward environmentalists and the endangered species, such as spotted owls or grizzly bears, that drove them from their chosen careers. One Forest Service fisheries biologist working in Oregon told *The Progressive*: "These guys might as well be real estate agents for the timber companies. They know where the remaining little pockets of old-growth are located and are only too happy to help them get their hands on it."

Why the dramatic movement toward land exchanges in the past decade? Inside the agencies, federal officials argue that the movement toward land exchanges was a consequence of the failure of the Congress and successive administrations to release money from the Land and Water Conservation Fund, the federal account funded largely by royalties from oil leases on the Outer Continental Shelf. But appropriations from LWCF have been meager for most of the last 15 years, in part because of a desire to use the multibillion trust fund to help conceal the true size of the budget deficit.

But there are two other factors at work. In the 1970s and 1980s, the timber companies in the Pacific Northwest and northern Rocky Mountains, spurred on by high prices and a lucrative log export market, went on a logging frenzy. By the end of the 1980s, most of the private lands had been liquidated of mature trees. The companies were desperate for supplies and turned increasingly to the national forests. But there was a problem. Logging across the region had placed hundreds of old-growth dependent species at risk of extinction, from the spotted owl and marbled murrelet to the Pacific fisher and coho salmon. The industry didn't want to deal with the environmental restrictions that went along with buying timber from the Forest Service. So they began proposing land exchanges instead.

"The big timber companies such as Weyerhaeuser and Plum Creek not only wanted the big trees from federal lands, they also wanted a free hand in how to log them," says Blaeloch. "And it's likely that after the timber companies log off the lands they get from the Forest Service they will turn around and try to trade them back for more old-growth," says Blaeloch.

In fact, that has already happened in Montana. In 1992, the Gallatin Land Exchange saw the Forest Service trade away forest lands outside Bozeman and near Yellowstone National Park. Within four years, most of the acreage was clearcut and in 1998 many of them came back to the Forest Service in another land swap with the same company.

At the same time, in the Southwest, another hotbed of land exchanges, a new spasm of land fever had broken out. The cities of the Southwest were booming: Las Vegas, Reno, Phoenix, Tucson, Santa Fe, and St. George, Utah. But the real estate barons confronted a problem. Many of these cities existed as islands surrounded by federal land, mostly under the control of the BLM. In Nevada, for example, more than 83 percent of the state is in federal ownership. In order to satiate the demand for new housing, the developers turned to the feds, offering land transactions that would make an arbitrageur blush with envy.

"The whole situation in Nevada is scandalous," says Blaeloch. "What you have are real estate brokers, BLM staffers and big developers making these deals behind closed doors with a smile and a handshake."

In many cases, the appraisers for both the public and private lands are picked and paid for by the corporations. Not surprisingly, the GAO found, this scenario almost always favors the corporations at the expense of the federal treasury and the environment.

Sometimes even the environmental impact statements that evaluate the swaps are farmed out to the corporations that will reap the benefits of the trade. For example, in Safford, Arizona, the BLM responded obligingly to the Phelps Dodge Corporation's request to expand its mammoth copper mine onto public lands adjacent to the Kneeling Nun National Monument. The BLM, saying that it was overworked, shunted the EIS off to a private contractor, whose fees were paid by Phelps Dodge. The mining company even kicked in money to pay the salaries of four BLM staffers who were overseeing the transaction. In this instance, the BLM approved a deal that giving the mining coming 20,600 acres of federal land for 4,000 of scrublands—a 5-to-1 ratio.

One of the land exchange program's biggest boosters is Interior Secretary Bruce Babbitt, the former Arizona governor. And, it turns out, several firms close to Babbitt have been on the receiving end of federal land swaps. Prior to becoming Interior Secretary, Babbitt worked for the mega-law firm, Steptoe and Johnson. One of

Babbitt's clients in those days was Canyon Forest Village, a scheme to build a Disneyland style resort outside Tuyasan, Arizona, near the entrance to Grand Canyon National Park. But since that part of northern Arizona is almost all federally-owned land, the project needed to land exchange to get off the ground. A complicated swap was put together years later, with Babbitt now ensconced at Interior, which included private lands formerly owned by the Babbitt family ranch.

This is not the only time Babbitt's former clients have benefited from a land trade. Babbitt also represented the Del Webb Company, the developers of Sun City and other planned communities and resorts in the Southwest. Del Webb was pursuing a project in the boomtown of Las Vegas. But nearly all of the available land in the Las Vegas Valley is owned by the BLM. With Babbitt serving as one of their lawyers, Del Webb approached the BLM with a land swap scheme. At the time, the BLM considered it a low priority. However, soon after Babbitt became Interior Secretary, the Del Webb exchange was pushed to near the top of the priority list.

All of this points to another critical problem with the way the program is currently run: the lack of public disclosure. Both the Forest Service and BLM have kept the public in the dark about some of the most crucial aspects of the land swaps, particularly the appraisal process. Citing the federal laws, such as the Privacy Act and the Trade Secrets Act, the agencies have refused to allow public interest groups to examine appraisal sheets until after the trade has been consecrated. "It's often impossible to determine whether the deal is actually in the public interest or even in keeping with federal law, until it's too late," says Blaeloch, whose group has recently won a landmark Freedom of Information Act case requiring the Forest Service to open its books in the Pacific Northwest.

Sometimes even government appraisers who object to land swaps favored by their agency or powerful real estate tycoons or corporations are made to pay a price. That was the case in the controversial Del Webb exchange outside Las Vegas, Nevada. In this case, the BLM's chief appraiser objected to a swap involving 4,776 acres, charging that the trade violated federal appraisal standards. The recalcitrant appraiser was promptly removed from the deal by officials at the BLM's headquarters and a new appraisal was initiated.

This time the Bureau hired a nonfederal appraiser who was recommended to the BLM by the developer. The appraisal was swiftly approved on terms favoring the company. But then the deal was leaked to the Inspector General of the Interior Department, who launched an investigation. The IG's office discovered that the deal would have given away federal lands at more than $9 million less than their market value.

Many of the deals are put together by third parties, land brokers and so-called land exchange facilitators. These middle men often make as much as 15 percent for the land swap commissions. Blaeloch believes that these brokered deals represent some of the worst trades. "These brokers put together incredibly complex trades, with 25-30 owners, and the agency," Blaeloch says. "The brokers end up making a big profit. Causes immense difficulty for us to understand what's going on. The more owners you have the more they protect themselves from exposure and legal accountability. There's no way the public is coming out clean in a trade where a broker takes 15 percent on the top."

Former politicians and Clinton administration officials are now getting into the act. A controversial land exchange in southern Oregon's Umpqua River Valley was promoted by former Oregon governor, Neil Goldschmidt and Tom Tuchman, the former point man for the Clinton administration on forest issues in the Pacific Northwest. Tuchman now runs a group called Forest Capital.

"The worst land exchange we've yet seen is the Steens Mountain deal in southern Oregon," says Blaeloch. Steens Mountain is wild landscape in remote southern Oregon that environmentalists have long wanted to protect as a national park. It is a rugged mountain landscape, but it is also riddled with private ranchlands. In 2000, Bruce Babbitt floated a proposal to declare the Steens a national monument and suggested a complex land swap to go along with it. In order to acquire 20,000 acres of new wilderness lands, the BLM traded away 100,000 acres of other lands to the ranchers. But that's not all. They also doled out nearly $10 million in cash and the BLM agreed that the feds would pay for new fencing and build all of their water developments—troughs, dams and holding ponds. It was a horrible deal that now has dozens of other ranchers begging for similar treatment, but nearly every environmental group in Oregon supported the deal, happy to have gotten 20,000 acres of wilderness land free from the depredations of sheep and cows.

"All of this may get much worse during the next four years under Bush," predicts Larry Tuttle. "But they will certainly have to thank Clinton and Babbitt for showing them the way to do it."

Las Vegas, Nevada, 2001

Fifteen

Chainsaw George

George W. Bush, fresh off a brush clearing operation at his Crawford ranch, snubbed the Earth Summit in Johannesburg for a trip to Oregon, where he vowed to fight future forest fires by taking a chainsaw to the nation's forests and the environmental laws that protect them.

In the name of fire prevention, Bush wants to allow the timber industry to log off more than 2.5 million acres of federal forest over the next ten years. He wants it done quickly and without any interference from pesky statutes such as the Endangered Species Act. Bush called his plan "the Healthy Forests Initiative." But it's nothing more than a giveaway to big timber that comes at a high price to the taxpayer and forest ecosystems.

Bush's stump speech was a craven bit of political opportunism, rivaled, perhaps, only by Bush's call to open the Arctic National Wildlife Refuge for oil drilling as a way to help heal the nation after the attacks of September 11. That plan sputtered around for awhile, but didn't go anywhere. But count on it: this one will.

Bush is exploiting a primal fear of fire that almost overwhelms the crippling anxiety about terrorists. In one of the great masterstrokes of PR, Americans have been conditioned for the past 60 years that forest fires are bad....bad for forests. It's no accident that Smokey the Bear is the most popular icon in the history of advertising, far outdistancing Tony the Tiger or Capt. Crunch.

But the forests of North America were born out of fires, not destroyed by them. After Native Americans settled across the continent following the Wisconsin glaciation, fires became an even more regular event, reshaping the ecology of the Ponderosa pine and spruce forests of the Interior West and the mighty Douglas-fir forests of the Pacific Coast.

Forest fires became stigmatized only when forests began to be viewed as a commercial resource rather than an obstacle to settlement. Fire suppression became an obsession only after the big timber giants laid claim to the vast forests of the Pacific Northwest.

Companies like Weyerhaeuser and Georgia-Pacific were loath to see their holdings go up in flames, so they arm-twisted Congress into pouring millions of dollars into Forest Service fire-fighting programs. The Forest Service was only too happy to oblige because fire suppression was a sure way to pad their budget: along with the lobbying might of the timber companies they could literally scare Congress into handing over a blank check. [For an excellent history of the political economy of forest fires I highly recommend Stephen Pyne's *Fire in America*.]

In effect, the Forest Service fire suppression programs (and similar operations by state and local governments) have acted as little more than federally-funded fire insurance policies for the big timber companies, an ongoing corporate bailout that has totaled tens of billions of dollars and shows no sign of slowing down. There's an old saying that the Forest Service fights fires by throwing money at them. And the more money it spends, the more money it gets from Congress.

"The Forest Service budgetary process rewards forest managers for losing money on environmentally destructive timber sales and penalizes them for making money or doing environmentally beneficial activities," says Randal O'Toole, a forest economist at the Thoreau Institute in Bandon, Oregon. "Until those incentives are changed, giving the Forest Service more power to sell or thin trees without environmental oversight will only create more problems than it solves."

Where did all the money go? It largely went to amass a fire-fighting infrastructure that rivals the National Guard: helicopters, tankers, satellites, airplanes and a legion of young men and women who are thrust, often carelessly, onto the firelines. Hundreds of firefighters have perished, often senselessly. For a chilling historical account of how inept Forest Service fire bureaucrats put young firefighters in harms way read Norman Maclean's (author of *A River Runs Through It*) last book, *Young Men and Fire*. In this book, Maclean describes how incompetence and hubris by bureaucrats led to the deaths of 13 firefighters outside Seeley Lake, Montana in the great fire of 1949. More recently, mismanagement has led to firefighters being needlessly killed in Washington and Colorado.

Since the 1920s, the Forest Service fire-fighting establishment has been under orders to attack forest fires within 12 hours of the time when the fires were first sighted. For decades, there's been a zero tolerance policy toward wildfires. Even now, after forest ecologists have proved that most forests not only tolerate but need fire, the agency tries to suppress 99.7 percent of all wildfires. This industry-driven approach has come at a terrible economic and ecological price.

With regular fires largely excluded from the forests and grasslands, thickets of dry timber, small sickly trees and brush began to build up. This is called fuel loading. These thickets began a breeding ground for insects and diseases that ravaged healthy forest stands. The regular, low-intensity fires that have swept through the forests for millennia have now been replaced by catastrophic blazes that roar with a fury that is without historical or ecological precedent.

Even so, the solution to the fuel problem is burning, not logging. The Bush plan is the environmental equivalent of looting a bombed out city and raping the survivors. The last thing a burned over forest needs is an assault by chainsaws, logging roads and skid trails, to haul out the only living trees in a scorched landscape. The evidence has been in for decades. The proof can be found at Mt. St. Helens and Yellowstone Park: unlogged burned forests recover quickly, feeding off the nutrients left behind by dead trees and shrubs. On the other hand, logged over burned forests rarely recover, but persist as kind of biological deserts, prone to mudslides, difficult to revegetate and abandoned by salmon and deep forest birds, such as the spotted owl, goshawk and marbled murrelet. They exist as desolate islands inside the greater ecosystem.

Even worse, such a plan only encourages future arsonists. The easiest way to clearcut an ancient forest is to set fire to it first. Take a look at the major fires of the West in the summer of 2002: the big blazes in Arizona and Colorado were set by Forest Service employees and seasonal firefighters, another big fire in California was started by a marijuana suppression operation, fires in Oregon, Washington and Montana have been started by humans.

In Oregon more than 45,000 acres of prime ancient forest in the Siskiyou Mountains was torched by the Forest Service's firefighting crews to start a backfire in order to "save" a town that wasn't threatened to begin with. The fires were ignited by shooting ping-pong balls filled with napalm into the forest of giant Douglas firs. By one estimate, more than a third of the acres burned the summer of 2002 were ignited by the Forest Service as backfires. That's good news for the timber industry since they get to log nearly all those scorched acres for next to nothing. Fire sales always come at a bargain price.

Far from acting as a curative, a century of unrestrained logging has vastly increased the intensity and frequency of wildfires, particularly in the West. The Bush plan promises only more of the same at an accelerated and uninhibited pace. When combined with global warming, persistent droughts, and invasions by alien insects species (such as the Asian long-horned beetle) and diseases, the future for American forests looks very bleak indeed.

Predictably, the Bush scheme was met with howls of protest from the big environmental groups. "This is part of Bush's irresponsible anti-environmental agenda," said Bill Meadows, president of the Wilderness Society. "The truth is that waiving environmental laws will not protect homes and lives from wildfire."

But they only have themselves to blame. They helped lay the political groundwork for the Bush plan long ago. And now the Administration, and its backers in Big Timber, have seized the day and put the environmentalists on the run.

The environmentalists have connived with the logging-to-prevent-fires scam for political reasons. First came a deal to jettison a federal court injunction against logging in the Montana's Bitterroot National Forest designed to appease Senator Max Baucus, friend of Robert Redford and a ranking Democrat. More than 14,000 acres of prime forest inside formerly protected roadless areas are now being clearcut. Then last month came a similar deal brokered by Senate Majority Leader Tom Daschle with the Sierra Club and the Wilderness Society that allows the timber industry to begin logging the Black Hills, sacred land of the Sioux, totally unfettered by any environmental constraints.

Grassroots greens warned that such willy-nilly dealmaking with Democrats would soon become a model for a national legislation backed by Bush and Republican legislators that would dramatically escalate logging on all national forests and exempt the clearcuts from compliance with environmental laws. We've now reached that point.

And there's no sign the big greens have learned their lesson.

The latest proposal comes courtesy of the Oregon Natural Resources Council and the Sierra Club. It's rather timidly called the "Environmentalist New Vision." There's nothing new about the plan, except that it is being endorsed by a claque of politically intimidated green groups instead of Boise-Cascade. It calls for thinning (i.e., logging) operations near homes in the forest/suburb interface. This is a pathetic and dangerous approach that sends two wrong messages in one package: that thinning reduces fire risk and that it's okay to build houses in forested environments.

In fact, there's no evidence that thinning will reduce fires in these situations and it may provide a false sense of security when there are other measures that are more effective and less damaging to the environment.

"Forest Service fire researcher Jack Cohen has found that homes and other structures will be safe from fire if their roof and landscaping within 150 feet of the structures are fireproofed," says O'Toole. "A Forest Service report says there are 1.9 million high-risk acres in the wildland-urban interface, of which 1.5 million are private. Treating these acres, not the 210 million federal acres, will protect homes. Firebreaks along federal land boundaries, not treatments of lands within those boundaries, will protect other private property. Once private lands are protected, the Forest Service can let most fires on federal lands burn."

As it stands, the Sierra Club's scheme will only result in more logging, more subdivisions in wildlands and, predictably, more fires. Any environmental outfit with a conscience would call for an immediate thinning of subdivisions on urban/wildland interface, not thinning of forests. Don't hold your breath. Too many big-time contributors to environmental groups own huge houses inside burn-prone forests in places Black Butte Ranch, Oregon, Flagstaff, Arizona and Vail, Colorado.

Of course, there's still resistance to these schemes. When Bush arrived in Portland to make official his handout to big timber, he was greeted by nearly a thousand protesters. On the streets of the Rose City, Earth First!ers and anti-war activists shouted down Bush and his plans for war on Iraq and the environment. The riot police soon arrived in their Darth Vader gear. The demonstrators, old and young alike, were beaten, gassed, and shot at with plastic bullets. They even pepper sprayed children. Dozens were arrested; others were bloodied by bullets and nightsticks.

This is a portent of things to come. When the laws have been suspended, the only option to protect forests will be direct action: bodies barricaded against bulldozers, young women suspended in trees, impromptu encampments in the deep snows of the Cascades and Rockies.

Not long ago, the occupation of cutting down the big trees ranked as one of the most dangerous around. Now, thanks to the connivance of Bush, Daschle and the big enviro groups, the job of protecting them will be fraught with even more peril.

Those brave young forest defenders, forced into the woods as a thin green line against the chainsaws, should send their bail requests to the Sierra Club and their medical bills to the Wilderness Society. They can afford it.

Portland, November 2002

Sixteen

Something Rotten in Klamath

More than 35,000 fish lay dead in the bed of the Klamath River and the death count continues to rise. These are not just any fish. They are wild salmon, both coho and chinook, the very totems of the Northwest. They suffocated from lack of cool water.

As the death toll mounted, Gale Norton, the grim boss of the Interior Department, acted befuddled and suggested that the die-off in these foul waters was a strange natural mystery.

But there's no need to call in a fish coroner. The slaughter in the Klamath River was a deliberate act, connived at by the White House, the Interior Department and the gang of Klamath River basin irrigators who have run riot down in southern Oregon for these many years.

"There are fish floating in every eddy," says Mike Belchick, a biologist with the Yurok Tribe. "Eyes popping out. Guts coming out. Scores of dead fish with moss on them. It makes me want to cry."

Now water is being released from the dams upstream near Klamath Lake. But it's far too late and will do little more than flush the stinking corpses downstream, along with the daily brew of pesticides, cowshit, and fertilizer that accounts for the normal effluent from the fields of the Klamath Basin.

Off course, it's the big fish kills that grab the headlines. And this was an unprecedented one: more than 30 percent of the entire salmon population of the Klamath wiped out in a single blow. Tribal leaders say there's no precedent for the death toll in history or myth.

But the salmon of the Klamath River, once one of the mightiest runs on earth, have been dying out for decades in a slow, steady slide toward extinction.

The gory frontpage photos of mass death send the wrong message, shocking, but oddly comforting to those responsible. They suggest a sudden catastrophic event, a singular tragic mistake. In fact, the salmon of the Klamath River, which flows some 200 miles from southern Oregon to the northern California coast, are the victim of a system that has conspired against them since the 1940s, at least.

It is a system of industrial agriculture, backed by the federal government, that has been given free reign to dewater the Klamath River to irrigate cheap croplands of alfalfa, potatoes and onions. More than half the annual income from these farms and ranches come from federal crop supports, but apparently that doesn't obligate them to save the fish.

The fact that the Yurok, Hoopa and Klamath tribes enjoy treaty rights to the river's salmon and depend on those fish for food, income and ceremonial rites has meant nothing to the masters of the river.

This is story of a death foretold. Biologists have warned since the 1970s that big changes in river flows were needed to avert extinction of coho and chinook salmon and the Klamath River suckerfish.

For eight years, Clinton and Babbitt did little for the salmon. Every proposal was a half-measure, which was denounced by the Klamath irrigators, and followed by a quick retreat. The salmon stocks declined, the delicate coho, which thrives in cold, clear water, tottered toward extinction.

By the time the Bush crowd took office, there was no margin for error. A nasty drought in the summer of 2001 exacerbated the problem. When federal biologists called for the Bureau of Reclamation to dribble out more water for the fish, the Klamath farmers threw a fit. They organized a so-called "bucket brigade," a raid on the dams and pumps that diverted water into their parched fields. Threats were leveled against federal biologists, environmentalists and Indians.

The sheriff of Klamath Falls joined in the fun, saying he wouldn't arrest any of the irrigators for monkeywrenching the water diversions. One of his deputies, Lt. Jack Redfield, even said at a rally of ranchers and farmers that he might tolerate some violence against Oregon environmentalists. Then he named two potential targets: Andy Kerr and Wendell Wood. "It won't take much from Andy Kerr or Wendell Wood or their like to spark an extremely violent response," said Redfield. "I am talking about rioting, homicides, destruction of property."

Environmentalists who engage in tree sits and roadblocks to stop timber sale are now treated like terrorists in several states, including Oregon and Idaho. Only last week, three Oregon forest activists were arrested on charges of torching logging equipment. They now face the possibility of 20 years in jail and $500,000 in fines.

But the Klamath water bullies are accustomed to having their way. They convinced the federal government to turn over almost half of the Klamath National Wildlife Refuge to them, which is now farmed at the expense of native wildlife. They've gotten away with destroying federal property, killing endangered species and threatening federal officials. Instead of rebukes and arrests, Oregon Senator Gordon Smith, the Republican frozen food magnate, called them heroes. They even got reimbursed by Congress for their trouble to the tune of $4 million.

The national press corps viewed this summer-long riot as a kind of quaint rural dust up, not much different than a fractious rodeo. At the time, the irrigators had conned the press into reporting that the water releases were all about saving the endangered suckerfish, a decidedly unsexy species also faced with extinction. The word salmon rarely made an appearance. In fact, the entire river system is a mess, on the brink of ecological collapse.

Last spring, the Bush crowd decided that the Klamath farmers could have all the water they wanted, regardless of the consequences for salmon. In a March ceremony, Gale Norton presided over the diversion of water to the irrigators. The tribes and environmentalists showed up to protest. But it was to no avail.

This summer was one of the driest and hottest on record. Biologists and tribes pleaded with Norton to release more water for the salmon. She refused. The Bush administration took the surrealistic position that fish don't need water. It's a position they still cling to. "If there is some evidence it's a problem, we'll take a hard look at it," said John Keys, director of the Bureau of Reclamation, only last week. "We've been saying since last year that we're not sure more water would do the fish any good."

By August, the temperature of the depleted waters of the Klamath River exceeded 70 degrees, a number considered lethal for migratory salmon. As the chinook and coho ascended the broiling river, they became disoriented, lethargic and began to perish from a host of diseases. Federal fisheries biologist Tom Shaw told his superiors that river conditions were "extremely lethal." His warnings were ignored.

"They played Russian roulette with our fish and our fish lost," says Troy Fletcher of the Yurok Tribe.

It wasn't so much a game, as a gameplan. All along the irrigators had plotted the final doom of the salmon, which were a looming impediment to their increasingly frail economic condition. With the troublesome fish out of the way, they believe that their precious system of dams, pumps and irrigation ditches will be safe from the lawsuits of the environmentalists and the tribes.

Now the dead fish are being scooped up with bulldozers and trucked to a plant in Eureka, California where they will be rendered into fertilizer and no doubt end up back on some of the very fields that lead to their demise.

Somebody should swipe a few of those carcasses from the banks of the Klamath, ship them to Washington and stuff them under Gale Norton's front porch, so that the unique odor of rotting salmon will haunt her the rest of her days.

Klamath Falls, September 2002

Seventeen

Going Critical

Bush's War on Endangered Species

The Bush administration has given up on the art of pretense. There are no more illusions about its predatory attitude toward the environment. No more airy talk about how incentives and markets can protect ecosystems. No more soft rhetoric about how the invisible hand of capitalism has a green thumb.

Now it's down to brass tacks. The Bush administration is steadily unshacking every restraint on the corporations that seek to plunder what is left of the public domain.

For decades, the last obstacle to the wholesale looting of American forests, deserts, mountains and rivers has been the Endangered Species Act. It has been battered before. Indeed, Al Gore, as a young congressman, led one of the first fights against the law in order to build the Tellico Dam. Reagan and the mad James Watt did violence to the law. Bush Sr. bruised it as well in the bitter battles over the northern spotted owl. Despite green credentials, Clinton and Bruce Babbitt tried to render the law meaningless, by simply deciding not to enforce its provisions and by routinely handing out exemptions to favored corporations.

But the Bush administration, under the guidance of Interior Secretary Gale Norton, has taken a different approach: a direct assault on the law seeking to make it as extinct as the ivory-billed woodpecker. Give them points for brutal honesty.

On May 28, 2003, Gale Norton announced that the Interior Department was suspending any new designations of critical habitat for endangered and threatened species. The reason? Poverty. The Interior Department, Norton claimed, is simply out of money for that kind of work and they've no plans to ask Congress for a supplemental appropriation.

It's no wonder they are running short given the amount of

money she's spending preparing oil leases in Alaska and Wyoming or mining claims in Idaho and Nevada.

Critical habitat represents exactly what it sounds like: the last refuge of species hurtling toward extinction, the bare bones of their living quarters. Under the Endangered Species Act, the Fish and Wildlife Service must designate critical habitat for each species under the law at the time that they are listed. It is one of three cornerstones to the law, the other two being the listing itself and the development of recovery plans.

The law hasn't worked that way for many years. Of the 1,250 species listed as threatened or endangered, the Fish and Wildlife Service has only designated critical habitat for about 400 of them. Despite what many mainstream enviromentalists are saying, the attempt to unravel critical habitat has a bipartisan history.

During the Clinton era, Bruce Babbitt capped the amount of money the agency could spend preparing critical habitat designations. Babbitt tried to wrap this noxious move in benign rhetoric, suggesting that designating the habitat wasn't as important as getting the species listed. Of course, it's the habitat designation which puts the brakes on timber sales and other intrusions into the listed species's homeground.

Babbitt's monkeywrenching was not viewed kindly by the federal courts, which issued order after order compelling the Department of the Interior to move forward with the designations. Those court orders piled up for eight years with little follow through.

Now the Bush administration has inherited the languishing court order and a raft of new suits, many filed by the Center for Biological Diversity in Tucson and the Alliance of the Wild Rockies in Missoula, two of the most creative environmental groups in the country. The Bush administration is not embarrassed about losing one lawsuit after another on this issue for the simple reason that it wants to engineer a train wreck scenario which will destroy the law once and for all.

The scheme to pull the plug on critical habitat began soon after Bush took office. Beginning in 2001, Norton ordered the Fish and Wildlife Service to begin inserting disclaimers about critical habitat into all federal notices and press releases regarding endangered species. The disclaimer proclaims boldy: "Designation of critical habitat provides little additional protection to species."

This is simply bogus as proved by the Fish and Wildlife Service's own data. In its last report to Congress, the agency admitted that species with habitat designations are 13 percent more likely to have stable populations and 11 percent more likely to be heading toward recovery than species without critical habitat designations.

Then in May of 2002, the Bush administration, at the behest of the home construction industry and big agriculture, moved to rescind critical habitat designations and protections for 19 species of salmon and steelhead in California, Washington, Oregon and Idaho. The move covered fish in more than 150 different watersheds, clearing the way for timber sales, construction and water diversions.

The next move the administration made against critical habitat was to begin redrawing the existing habitat maps to exclude areas highly prized by oil and timber companies. Since 2001, the Bush administration has reduced the land area contained within critical habitat by more than 50 percent with no credible scientific basis to support the shrinkage.

The Administration had practical motives. In coastal California, Norton ordered the BLM to speed up new oil and gas leases in roadless lands on the Los Padres National Forest near Santa Barbara, home to more than 20 endangered species, including the condor and steelhead trout. Where once the burden lay with the oil companies to prove that their operations would not harm these species, now it is reversed. Environmentalists must both prove that the listed species are present in the area and that they will be harmed by the drilling.

Next on the hit list was the coastal California gnatcatcher, whose protected habitat had already been shrunk to landfills and interstate cloverleafs under Babbitt. Carrying water for California homebuilders, Norton lifted protections for the bird on 500,000 acres of habitat in order to "reevaluate its economic analysis" from the habitat protection plan released in 2000. The administration also moved to rescind protections for the tiny San Diego fairy shrimp.

If you want a case study on how endangered species flounder without benefit of critical habitat designations look no further than the mighty grizzly bear of the northern Rockies. The grizzly was listed as a threatened species in 1975, but it has never had its critical habitat designated because a 1978 amendment to the Endangered Species Act granted the Fish and Wildlife Service the discretion to avoid making the designation for species listed prior to that year. The provision was inserted in the law by members of the Wyoming congressional delegation at the request of the mining and timber industry.

Grizzly populations are lower now than they were when the bear was listed. Tens of thousands of acres of grizzly habitat have been destroyed by clearcutting, roads and mines. Within the next 10 years, grizzly experts predict that key habitat linkages between isolated bear populations will be effective destroyed, dooming the species to extinction across much of its range. Even biologists in the Bush administration now admit that grizzly population in the Cabinet-Yaak Mountains on the Idaho/Montana border warrants being upgraded from threatened to endangered.

Now the terrible of fate of the grizzly is about to be visited upon hundreds of other species thanks to the Bush administration's latest manuever.

"When opponents of the Endangered Species Act seek to gut the critical habitat provision, they are gut-shooting endangered species, in direct offense to national public policy and our system of majority rule," says Mike Bader, a grizzly specialist with the Alliance for the Wild Rockies. "In their zeal to fatten corporate profits, they seek to bankrupt our national heritage."

Portland, July 2003

PART III

ToxicNation

Eighteen

The Risky Business of Life

The corporate push to dismantle federal protections against poisoners and polluters continues without check. The latest assault on the regulatory apparatus comes in the form of a report issued on June 16 by the Commission on Risk Assessment and Risk Management. This is a 10-member panel created by the 1990 Clean Air Act, which itself was harbinger of the "market-oriented" approach to regulation now carrying all before it.

Charged with analyzing risk assessment techniques in deciding policy on cancer-causing agents, the panel mostly consists of academic research scientists. Also aboard are representatives from Kaiser Permanente, the American Lung Association and Monsanto, the chemical giant. Their conclusion was hardly surprising: environmental laws are often too strict and not flexible enough. They also conclude that "good science" is often hampered by too much public participation. Risk assessments, the panel said, should replace some regulatory prohibitions because they allow companies and federal agencies to find cost-effective solutions to environmental problems.

Scarcely had the major environmental protection laws of the late 1960s and early 1970s gone onto the statute books before corporations and their squadrons of rent-a-thinkers began to devise ways to outflank the new regulatory structure. Bulking ever larger on their conference agendas were "risk assessment" and its love-mate, "cost-benefit analysis." The suggestion was that well-intentioned environmental laws were imposing absurd impediments on a vibrant economy. Was it really rational to ban carcinogens from food and water supplies if statistics showed that to spare one life the food industry might have to spend $100 million? Was it an accurate estimate of risk for humans to test carcinogens on lab animals, especially rats? Armies of corporate statisticians and kindred flimflam artists churned out numbers designed to discredit such laws as the famous Delaney Clause, which imposes an absolute prohibition on carcinogens in processed foods. The corporations recruited legal scholars such as Stephen Breyer (now on the Supreme Court) to denounce the inefficiencies of regulations. Also mustered were Chicago School economists like Milton Friedman to argue that regulations would be a disincentive to innovation.

Through most of the 1980s, environmentalists ridiculed this corporate campaign. With the arrival of George Bush in the White House the picture changed. Swaddled in corporate cash, the Environmental Defense Fund loudly proclaimed its conversion to the "market oriented" approach. EDF played a major role in drafting of the Clean Air Act of 1990 which engendered pollution credits, a market in cancer bonds, and "voluntary compliance." As the Act began the destruction of a quarter century's attempts to regulate air pollution, it also launched the Commission on Risk Assessment, charged with the task of drawing up guidelines on how the new "market" approach would operate in government agencies such as the Agriculture Department, Food and Drug Administration, Department of Energy, and Environmental Protection Agency.

As Theo Colborn writes in her recent book on pesticides and other toxic chemicals, *Our Stolen Future*, "the tool of risk assessment is now used to keep questionable compounds on the market until they are proven guilty. It should be redefined as a means of keeping untested chemicals off the market and eliminating the most worrisome in orderly, timely fashion."

This is not the direction recommended by the Commission on Risk Assessment.

Instead, the panel's recommendations are quite predictable. Topping the list is elimination of the Delaney Clause, a corporate dream since the early 1960s, and an obsession of EDF, EPA directorette Carol Browner, and President McMuffin himself. The panel recommends a similar down-grading of the Toxic Substances Control Act which strictly limits the use, storage, and transportation of dangerous chemicals. The panel urges down-grading of research on carcinogens conducted on lab animals. In an effort to undercut critics of incineration of military hazardous wastes, such as the corroding stockpiles of nerve gas, the panel urges that the risk assessment and cost benefit analysis studies be the prime navigational aids for the Pentagon and Department of Energy.

This sweeping assault on laws designed to save lives received an immediate clap on the back from the *New York Times*, which has been ardently in the corporate camp on these matters. The *NYT*'s Gina Kolata (Judi Bari's sister) began her June 14 story: "In a draft report that is winning praise from environmentalists and the chemical industry, a federal commission recommends that the system of assessing and regulating health hazards from environmental pollutants and other sources, like food additives, be overhauled."

Kolata duly quoted the approbation of the only environmentalists who had been shown the report, namely David Roe, an attorney with the EDF. Of course Roe praised the report as "a significant contribution and a major advance." In her second paragraph Kolata bannered the panel's conclusion that "the current highly fragmented adversarial system should be replaced with a system that enables health hazards to be considered in a broader context." Considered, that is, by corporate scientists and accountants unrestrained by strong environmental statutes.

Kolata, who was given an award by the chemical industry in 1994 for her stories discounting the dangers of breast implants, was apparently unable to locate a single critic of this brazen attempt to tear the heart out of what Peter Montague, editor of the newsletter *Rachel's Environment and Health Weekly,* calls "the only real anti-pollution laws we've got on the books."

Montague was savage to us on the subject of Roe and EDF's position on risk assessment: "Roe does an end run on questions of ethics, harm, profit, and democracy, and leaves these decisions in the hands of a half dozen data dweebs who will manipulate their numerical assumptions to reach any political conclusion they want." Montague ridicules Roe's claim, made in Kolata's article, that relief from regulatory requirements will create an incentive for corporations to make available proprietary information necessary to assess risk. As Montague points out, once corporations are allowed to follow voluntary guidelines, they are under no legal constraint to provide truthful data. Monsanto, for example, has a sordid history of fabricating scientific research on dioxin (which the company produced), enabling the company to duck thousands of lawsuits from Vietnam vets poisoned by Agent Orange. To trust a corporate scientist to provide truthful information is a foolish exercise.

Another spirited critic of the panel missing from Kolata's

rolodex is Michael Colby of Food & Water, the Vermont-based group. "Risk assessment," Colby says, "is the best club industry has to beat its way through the throng of victims awaiting redress."

The panel called for health hazards to be considered in a "broad context." The broad context of the panel's recommendations is not hard to discern: the climax of a 25-year long corporate campaign, a U.S. president and a high-profile environmental group in the pocket of the corporations, and a clamor for an end to "costly and frivolous litigation," meaning the use of the courts by citizens to obtain redress for grievous wrongs.

The next move will be the gradual implementation of the panel's program, mostly through administrative changes, undiscussed in Congress and unreported in the press. The world is changing and they don't want you to know.

Portland, 1995

Nineteen

Eve, Don't Touch that Apple!

Pesticides, Politics, and Acceptable Death

In 1900 cancer killed three people in America out of every hundred. Today, it's thirty-three out of every hundred and one out of every four Americans die from it. These figures come from Dr. Joseph Weissman, a professor of medicine at UCLA. Weissman reckons that a fair slice of this explosion in cancer mortality can be laid at the door of petro-chemicals, particularly those used by the food industry.

On August 1, the same day Bill Clinton announced his decision to sign the welfare bill, Congress passed—with the White House's glowing approval—the Food Quality Protection Act. In the House the vote was unanimous. In the Senate only one voice was raised against its passage. In consequence, a few years down the road Dr. Weissman or his co-researchers will have to recalibrate their numbers, for the worse. You wouldn't know it from the papers, from the radio or from TV, but this Food Quality Protection Act signals a retreat as momentous as the one on welfare, and once again, children will be paying much of the price.

The purpose of this bill, which was cosponsored by Rep. Thomas Bliley and Rep. Tom DeLay, respectively a mortician from Virginia and pest exterminator from Texas, is to overturn the Delaney Clause, in force since the 1950s and the only absolute prohibition against carcinogens in processed foods. This clause has been the target of the food industry since it became law. It was finally done in by the usual coalition: business lobbyists, the White House, pr firms, big green organizations, and the elite media.

Immediately after the Congress passed the bill, Clinton took the airwaves on his Saturday radio show to commend the Republican congress for rejecting "extremism on both sides" and finding the "common ground." "I call this the Peace of Mind Act,"

Clinton went on, "because parents will know that the fruits, grains and vegetables children eat are safe. Chemicals can go a long way in a small body."

But by throwing out the Delaney Clause, the federal government simply abandons any effort to prevent cancer provoked by pesticides and instead goes into the cancer management business by way of "risk assessment." Corporate and governmental statisticians will broker the "acceptable" number of people permitted to contract cancer from pesticides residues, comforted in the knowledge that most of these people will be poor and black or Hispanic. To put it another way, the government regulators are now set to determine how many people may be sacrificed in order for the food and chemical industries to make more money with fewer liabilities.

Amid all the talk about returning decision-making to the states, the new law explicitly prohibits states from adopting tougher safety standards than those required by the federal government. With the Delaney Clause dead on the floor of Congress, some 80 pesticides that were about to be outlawed as carcinogens will now remain in use. Call it the Dow-Monsanto bail-out bill, since these two companies make most of the chemical killers that were on the list to be banned.

The present calculation by the National Academy of Sciences is that between 30,000 and 60,000 people die each year from exposure to cancer-causing chemicals. Those at highest risk are children. The Academy's study found that for some children "exposures to just five pesticides found on eight foods could be sufficiently high enough to produce symptoms of acute organophosphate pesticide poisoning." Another recent report cautions that by an average child's first birthday, the infant has been exposed to more than eight carcinogenic pesticides in amounts that exceed the previous standards set for a lifetime of exposure.

The new standards for "acceptable risk" are to be set by the EPA, operating on recommendations of the food industry lobbyists, based on research from chemical industry scientists. "The new law brazenly codifies how many people the food industry can kill with pesticides," said Patty Clary, director of Californians for Alternatives to Toxics. "About as many a year as went down on Flight 800, per chemical." Clary adds that the Food Protection Act doesn't even address the topic of synergy, the toxic multiplier effect that occurs when more than one pesticide is involved.

Recent scientific research has shown that a cocktail mix of pesticides such as dieldrin, chlordane, and endosulfan is 1,600 times more toxic than the discrete chemicals administered separately. Dieldrin and chlordane are banned chemicals that persist in the environment at dramatic levels. Endosulfan remains in wide use. All are known to be endocrine disrupters and are linked to breast and uterine cancers, birth defects, and infertility.

This chemical soup is what children will now go on eating every day in products like raisins that are marketed directly at kids. "Chemicals go a long way in a small body," Clinton said. He could have been more specific. The new law now ensures that when children eat strawberries, they will also be ingesting the deadly chemical residue left by benamyl, captan, and methyl bromide. The average apple and peach has eight different pesticides embedded in it. Grapes have six and celery five. Children get as much as 35 percent of their likely lifetime dose of such toxins by the time they are five. Thus something intrinsically bad is happening when it does the most damage to growing bodies.

With the new pesticide law giving agribusiness the green light—within the flexible parameters of risk assessment—there's now scant incentive to transfer to other methods of ensuring high productivity in fields and orchards. But pesticides become less effective the more they are used. American farmers sprayed 33 percent more pesticides per acre in 1990 than they did in 1945. Over the same 45-year period crop losses from pests increased from 31 to 37 percent. The response has been every greater dosings with pesticides. Addiction to chemical-intensive agriculture has become so acute that bio-engineers at the Monsanto Corporation have concocted "Round-Up Ready" soybeans, that are resistant to massive doses of the pesticide, now required to kill pests. It is a deadly circle of poisons.

The risks from chemical-intensive agriculture come not only in the food but in the application of the pesticides, mostly in the form of aerial spraying. The federal Office of Technology Assessment reckons that more than 40 percent of the pesticides dumped by planes drifts off the target area, ending up in streams, schoolyards, and neighborhoods. Fluorescent tracers have shown that it takes only a moderate breeze to carry poisons such as 2,4-D and paraquat twenty to fifty miles. One study found poisons such as toxaphene, furan, and dioxin in the mud on the bottom of Lake Siskiwit, on Isle Royale—a wilderness island in the middle of Lake Superior. The pesticides had been wind-carried there for more than 200 miles.

Workers are the first to pay the price. In central Washington in 1995, 55 workers in an apple orchard became seriously ill after the wind shifted and they became exposed to the pesticide carbaryl. The EPA and the chemical industry claim that the regulations for the use of such pesticides will prevent any adverse health consequences. In their idyllic scheme, harvest spraying takes place in perfect windless weather, with workers decked out in the latest protective gear and with detailed warning labels emblazoned on the poison brews. Real life in the fields means planes dumping clouds of pesticide in the wrong place at the wrong time, no protective clothing, poisons mixed with bare hands, workers uninformed about the dangers of the chemicals they are told to handle. The instructions for the use of pesticides are usually printed only in English, while most field work-ers are Spanish-speaking.

This Food Quality Protection Act is the consummation of a campaign by the food and chemical industries that has stretched over decades, since Rachel Carson's *Silent Spring* alerted the public to chemical poisoning back in the 1950s. For years, the *Wall Street Journal*'s editorial pages have throbbed with denunciations of the Delaney Clause by industry flacks and think-tank whores. But the *Journal* was accompanied in its propaganda by the *New York Times*, not merely on the opinion pages but in the willfully purblind report-ing of such staff writers as Keith Schneider and Gina Kolata.

The Delaney Clause found its defenders in the National Coalition for Alternatives to Pesticides, Food & Water, Environmental Research Foundation, Mothers and Others for a Livable Planet, Cancer Prevention Coalition, and dozens of grass-roots groups across the country such as Californians for Alternatives to Toxics. In the end, they were no match for the forces arrayed against them. As Clinton was signing the bill into law, with a young-ster (one in four chances of croaking from cancer) at his elbow, Katie McGinty, head of the White House Council on

Environmental Quality, hailed the act as the dawning of a new age of environmentalism. "I truly believe that the president will go down in history for having put in place a new generation of environmentalism, based on cooperation, not confrontation; defining and securing the common ground, defining the common interest, not the special interest." McGinty should know all about special interests. At an earlier stage of her career, before she began ministering to Al Gore, McGinty was a lobbyist for the American Chemical Association.

But why wasn't there a fight from the big green groups inside the beltway over Delaney? Kurt Davies, of the DC-based Environmental Working Group, which backed the new bill, says it was about political realism. "An idealist would interpret the loss of Delaney as a retreat from environmental protection," Davies said. "But realistically, Delaney was going, and keeping it just wasn't a tenable battle. We just didn't have the voice. We weren't getting the thousands of letters needed to the Hill. Without that it was just bending to the enemy."

Of course the reason those letters weren't coming in to congressional offices was that the big green organizations had long since decided to give in on Delaney, trade it off in the interests of "realism." Organizations such as the unabashedly pro-corporate Environmental Defense Fund even attacked Delaney as an inefficient barrier to flexible environmental regulation. Groups like the Natural Resources Defense Council and National Wildlife Federation actually joined with lobbyists from Dow and Monsanto in testimony demanding the gutting of Delaney as a "sensible solution that goes a long way toward protecting the health of consumers."

Michael Colby at the Vermont-based Food & Water group calls this surrender "a classic case of activist malpractice. These organizations back legislation that gives corporations the right to pollute at the expense of the public health, while promoting the law as an improvement. Meanwhile, citizens are left to face the onslaught of more cancer risks, states are held hostage to weaker federal health standards, and the chemical companies and big environmental groups are laughing all the way to the bank."

Washington, DC, October 1996

Twenty

Dioxin for Dinner

For decades the Dow Chemical Company trotted out platoons of scientists and PR flacks to claim that the public had nothing to fear from background levels of dioxin that kept showing up in their blood, milk and food. These levels of the poison, Dow proclaimed, were merely naturally occurring phenomena that had been co-evolving with humans since the dawn of time. Dioxin, Dow said, was the harmless by-product of forest fires and volcanoes.

This hogwash was swallowed wholesale by state and federal politicians, bureaucrats, and important newspapers, such as the *New York Times*, whose environmental reporter Keith Schneider scribbled a series of articles in the late 1980s dismissing the environmental hazards and health perils posed by dioxin. These articles appeared in the wake of the environmental catastrophes at Love Canal in New York and Times Beach in Missouri, where entire communities had been contaminated by the reckless disposal of dioxins and PCBs. Schneider's cynical stories also came on the heels of revelations about serious health problems experienced by Vietnam veterans who had been exposed to Agent Orange, a dioxin-related pesticide. At the time, the chemical companies that had produced dioxin were facing billions in potential liabilities.

The whole preposterous thesis of dioxin as a discharge of Mother Nature was finally put to rest by scientists sifting through layers of sediment dredged up from the bottom of Lake Superior. The layers of the lake bed record the history of the environment. When the muck was analyzed in the early 1990s, it transpired that there were no traces of dioxin found before 1940.

Dioxin is a true child of the twentieth century. Its chemical family was created in 1900 in the laboratory of Herbert Dow, founder of Dow Chemical. Dow used jolts of electricity to extract chlorides from huge brine deposits outside Midland, Michigan. The first commodity attained by this process was chlorine bleach, which brought in tens of millions for the young company.

By the 1930s Dow, Dupont, and Monsanto had discovered

another lucrative use for these chlorines. By combining chlorine atoms with petroleum hydrocarbons (waste products from oil and gas operations), the companies created a toxic smorgasbord of chemicals known as chlorinated hydrocarbons. These formed the basis of pesticides, solvents and plastics. When heated in a pesticide processing plant or burned in an incinerator these chlorinated compounds release dioxin, the deadliest known family of chemicals that includes 210 toxins ranging from PCBs to furans and TCDDs.

The noxious nature of these chlorine compounds began showing up in the labs of Dow and Monsanto in the early part of the century. The most common toxic reaction to the chemical was chloracne, which resembles a severe case of teenage acne, except it covers the entire body and persists for years. Indeed, some reactions can be so severe that they totally disfigure people who have been exposed to the chemical.

Back in 1947, Dr. Raymond Susskind described a white male patient who had contracted chloracne after exposure to dioxin at a Monsanto plant in West Virginia: "He has given up all social and athletic functions and remains in his house for months on end. Several times he has been mistaken for a negro and has been forced to conform with the racial segregation customs of the area. This has happened on busses and in theaters." Susskind served as Monsanto's company physician and his notes on the toxic reactions of workers to the chemical were buried in the company's corporate archives.

Those background levels of dioxin written off by Dow's rent-a-scientists in the 1970s and 1980s had in fact developed as part of a toxic fallout from a nationwide network of incinerators, iron smelters, chemical and cement plants, paper mills that use chlorine bleaching, and factories making polyvinyl chloride (PCV) plastics.

The EPA has known of the serious health consequences of dioxin in the environment since 1971, but has taken scant action, aside from some ineffectual initiatives on dioxin exposure at the workplace. Even these meager moves have been under constant attack from the chemical lobby and its political allies. In 1991 the paper industry (the main source of dioxin releases into the nation's water supply) and the Chlorine Council, a dioxin-users trade association, prevailed on Dan Quayle and his Competitiveness Council to intervene with the EPA and relax even those frail regulations. The EPA duly complied, announcing that loosening of standards was part of a long-term assessment of the toxicity of dioxin.

The results of that study, commenced in 1992, are now in. They are not what the chemical industry had been bargaining for. In fact—short of major nuclear accidents—dioxin now ranks as the most toxic threat to the general population of the United States.

Nearly everyone in the country is already carrying what is called a "body burden of dioxin" that is 500 times greater than the "acceptable risk" level for carcinogens.

Dioxin can be considered a sort of environment hormone that ravages the endocrine system, distorting cell growth. In men, dioxin elevates testosterone levels, reduces sperm counts, and leads to increased rates of diabetes. In the last 50 years, sperm counts have declined by more than 50 percent, while incidences of testicular cancer have tripled.

In women, dioxin seems to prompt endometriosis, a painful uterine disorder that now afflicts 5 million women a year. Dioxin exposure has also been linked to breast cancer, a disease that has more than doubled since 1960. Pregnant women are especially vulnerable, since the daily level of dioxin intake is enough to cause long-term damage to fetuses, giving rise to birth defects, disrupted sexual development, and damage to the immune system. If you live in the Great Lakes region, your body burden of dioxin may be two to three times greater than that of someone living on the West Coast. Both weather patterns and clustering of chemical plants produce this additional exposure.

In surveying the dangers of dioxin, the EPA's current risk assessment process focuses only on the immediate area surrounding individual sources of dioxin emission, such as incinerators or pulp mills. The agency assumes that exposure can be associated only with drinking water, air and dioxin-contaminated soils. The impression left by most of these assessments is that the greatest risk of dioxin exposure comes from workers at chemical plants and people who live near dioxin-emitting facilities. But a new two-year study of dioxin in the Great Lakes region by a team of scientists at Queens College, New York City, led by Dr. Barry Commoner shows a different story.

- The greatest source of exposure to dioxin does not stem from proximity to a chemical plant or incinerator, but from consumption of contaminated food.
- Less than 10 percent of dioxin particles settle to Earth within 30 miles of its source, i.e., an incinerator.
- At least half of the dioxin falling on the fields, lakes and dairies of the Great Lakes states comes from incinerators located up to 1,500 miles away.

Such environmental regulations as are in place fail to deal with any of the realities disclosed by Commoner's team. For one thing nearly all of our exposure to dioxin comes from food, not from breathing contaminated air or drinking dioxin-laced water. Dioxin is a fat-soluable chemical, meaning it bioaccumulates up the food chain. For example, fish from Lake Michigan show levels of dioxin more than 100,000 times higher than the surrounding water, plants, and sediment. Two-thirds of the average American's exposure to dioxin comes from milk, cheese and beef, a result of cows eating contaminated food crops.

"The risk to the people of Chicago is not so much from inhaling dioxins emitted by the city's trash-burning incinerators," Commoner said. "But rather from ingesting milk and cheese produced from farms in Wisconsin and Minnesota. Moreover, these foods are likely to be contaminated not just by the emissions from the Chicago incinerators, but by incinerators in Indiana, Texas, and Florida."

Tracing sources of contamination from their area of research around the Great Lakes, Commoner and his colleagues were able to identify 1,360 culprits, as far afield as Utah, Florida and Texas. The biggest culprits are the least regulated: medical waste incinerators. There are 623 of them in the Great Lakes region, in the form of hospitals, nursing homes, funeral homes, medical labs, blood banks, veterinary clinics, and crematoria. One reason they are such a high source of dioxin is modern medicine's increased use of chlorinated plastics.

In most hospitals, waste is divided into black bag and red bag categories. Black bag waste consists of discarded paper, plastic, glass, metal, and food waste—not so different from what you might find in household trash. This accounts for about 85 percent of the medical waste stream. Then there is red bag waste, which includes anatomical waste, gauze pads, catheters and infectious or pathological materials. The per-patient yield of red and black bag waste is about thirteen pounds a day. Pleading poverty, the medical and funeral lobby have persuaded the EPA to hold off from any burdensome supervision of the way they incinerate this avalanche of dioxin-suffused matter.

The second leading source of dioxin in the Great Lakes region comes from 57 municipal waste incinerators, burning 12 million tons of trash a year. Every load of trash dumped into those solid waste incinerators contains plastics, solvents, and chlorine-based products that when burned create dioxin. In fact, recent research shows that incinerators actually synthesize dioxin, producing from the smokestacks nearly 500 times the amount of dioxin chemicals as were present in the source material. Most of the dioxin now coursing through the bodies of Americans was actually created by the incinerators.

Of the eight Great Lakes states, Minnesota ranks behind only Michigan in the number of hospitals with an on-site incinerator. There are 113 such incinerators in Minnesota burning more than four thousand tons of infectious waste a year. In addition, Minnesota has 20 cremortaria and a commercial medical waste incinerator.

Minnesota also ranks second in the number of municipal solid waste incinerators with 13, including the massive Hennepin incinerator in Minneapolis. Altogether, the Minnesota incinerators burn three million tons of waste a year. Only New York incinerates more trash.

According to Commoner, nearly all of the dioxin emitted from these incinerators could be eliminated, either by intensive recycling or with landfills. Commoner estimates that switching to these methods could save cities $350 million a year. By the same token, black bag medical waste can also be safely recycled, while the red bag medical waste can be sterilized through autoclave technology and then landfilled.

Not surprisingly, the EPA has shown little interest in moving toward the elimination of dioxin-spewing incinerators. Instead, the agency has adopted the strategy of pollution control, relying on scrubbers and other expensive technological fixes that cannot reduce dioxin emissions to zero. "The Clinton administration and some of its acolytes in the Washington environmental community, like the Sierra Club and the Natural Resources Defense Council, are spending their scarce resources jousting in court over the meaning of things like 'maximum control technology' and not even discussing real pollution prevention, which requires not emitting dioxin to begin with," charged Dr. Peter Montague, director of the Environmental Research Foundation in Annapolis, Maryland.

Montague points out that many of these national environmental groups endorsed the repeal of the Delaney Clause, which prohibited the addition of carcinogens to processed food. The zero tolerance standard of Delaney will be replaced by a risk assessment strategy that allows supposedly safe levels of carcinogens in the food supply. But risk assessments, particularly in the case of chemicals such as dioxins, vastly underestimate the actual cancer risks by looking at the health consequences of individual sources of pollution, instead of examining what Commoner calls the "entire ecosystem of carcinogens."

"This is the painful lesson that ecology teaches," Commoner said. "The danger of dioxins is vastly greater than the risk assessments have led us to believe; it threatens entire populations with unacceptable risk of cancer and poses grave hazards to fetal development."

Of course, there are powerful forces arrayed against any move to zero-out dioxin emissions, led by multi-billion dollar chemical giants such as Dow, Monsanto, and DuPont. These companies maintain huge political action committees. Combined, they dole out more than $2 million a year to federal candidates of both parties.

The big trash disposal companies, such as Waste Management and Browning Ferris Industries, also have an enormous economic stake in keeping the incinerators running, despite the dire dangers to public health. These companies hold lucrative contracts from large cities to burn municipal trash and both have spent tens of millions of dollars greenwashing their mephitic business, including dumping loads of cash into the coffers of large environmental groups. Waste Management's CEO Dean Buntrock has served for years on the board of the National Wildlife Federation, which supports incineration as an ecologically sound method of waste disposal.

As a result, both political parties are beholden to the dioxin lobby. Bob Dole has been the prime legislator for the chemical-agriculture industry and has opposed any attempts to rein in the production of dioxin-allied chemicals. His running mate, Jack Kemp, whose congressional district adjoined the dioxin-saturated Love Canal, downplayed the toxicity of the chemical and dismissed local activists such as Lois Gibbs as hysterical housewives. Kemp voted repeatedly to ditch the Superfund law and has railed boisterously against Community Right-to-Know statutes.

Similarly, Bill Clinton has maintained a long-standing relationship to the hazardous waste incineration business. One week prior to his election as president, Clinton gave the go-ahead for the Vertac incinerator which has poisoned the town of Jacksonville, Arkansas with lethal levels of dioxins and other toxins. A month into his administration, Clinton over-ruled EPA scientists and betrayed his own campaign promises by giving the green light to WTI's deadly PCB incinerator in Liverpool, Ohio. For nearly a decade, Hillary Rodham Clinton collected $30,000 a year as a director of the Lafarge Corporation, one of the nation's biggest cement manufacturers, which heats its massive, dioxin-seething kilns with millions of gallons of toxic sludge. The cement industry continues to enjoy an exemption from key environmental laws governing the incineration of hazardous waste, an exemption that owes much to the influence of Hillary Clinton in the late 1980s and early 1990s.

Lois Gibbs, now director of the Citizens' Clearinghouse on Hazardous Waste, sees the problem as a failure of the political process to deal with the growing power of multinational corporations. "We can't shut down the sources of dioxin without finding the courage to change the way government works," Gibbs said. "We have to explore how people became powerless as the corporations became powerful. We have to figure out a way to speak honestly and act collectively to rebuild our democracy."

Portland, 1996

Twenty-One

The Monsanto Machine

For years, Monsanto, the agrichemical giant, has regularly popped up on the *Forbes* and *Fortune* lists of the most respected American companies. Their image is carefully cultivated with a sophisticated public relations campaign, portraying the St. Louis-based firm as the small farmer's friend and a dedicated leader in the fight to end global hunger. "Doing well by doing good" is the company motto, spread across glossy magazine ads and discreetly placed television spots.

But Monsanto's reputation in the international community is distinctly less favorable. Last year, the European Union (EU) moved to block imports of the company's genetically engineered products, such as soybeans and bovine growth hormone (rBGH). And in the developing world, Monsanto has been fiercely attacked for decimating native ecologies by introducing so-called test-tube crops and dousing them with heavy doses of pesticides and fertilizers, all with the backing of the US government.

In the mid-1990s, Monsanto came under fire for pushing so-called "Terminator" seeds in India and Africa. The Terminator is a genetic technology that sterilizes natural seeds in plants, forcing farmers to depend on Monsanto's patented, genetically engineered crops. The company also promotes its Round-Up Ready seeds as "insect resistant." But, in fact, the patented seeds are genetically designed to survive heavy doses of toxic pesticides.

The financial stakes are high. The haul from Monsanto's Round-Up Ready soybeans, potatoes and corn, and its Terminator seeds could mean tens of billions of dollars. "Monsanto is the most perfect example of what is so evil about the corporate mentality," says Patty Clary, head of Californians for Alternatives to Toxins, an Arcata-based group that monitors the use of pesticides. "They developed these genetically engineered crops with the sole objective of forcing farmers to use Round-Up."

Monsanto always has been able to count on the aid of the US government to sedulously promote its products. With the ceaseless encouragement of the Department of Agriculture, American farmers have planted more than 50 million acres of Monsanto's genetically engineered crops over the past four years. The Food and Drug Administration (FDA) has also played along, acceding to the company's demand that genetically engineered crops not be labeled as such.

When faced with the almost certain prospect that the EU would ban the import of Monsanto's genetically engineered corn in 1998, the company unleashed an unprecedented lobbying effort, flying a group of critics to the United States, where they visited corporate headquarters. Then the writers were taken to Washington, where they were given a tour of the White House, including a rare visit to the Oval Office.

Top Clinton aides—including US Trade Rep. Charlene Barshevsky, Secretary of State Madeleine Albright, Secretary of Agriculture Dan Glickman and Secretary of Commerce William Daley—also have lobbied their European counterparts on Monsanto's behalf. Even Bill Clinton and Al Gore got in on the act, engaging in some last minute arm-twisting of Irish Prime Minister Bertie Ahren and French President Lionel Jospin. Both the French and the Irish caved in to the pressure.

This spring, Monsanto's genetically engineered corn will be planted in Europe for the first time. Toby Moffett, the former liberal congressman from Connecticut and now a Monsanto political strategist, smugly bragged about the victory to the *St. Louis Post-Dispatch*: "I'm 54 years old and I've been in a lot of coalitions in my life, but this is one of the most breathtaking I've seen."

How can Monsanto's extraordinary leverage be explained? Political influence often comes down to the judicious application of campaign cash. Monsanto—a $7.5 billion company—has poured nearly $200,000 a year into the coffers of candidates for federal office and the two major parties. This is a relatively paltry amount compared to the millions pumped into the system by big oil or even by its chemical rivals, DuPont, ICI and Dow. Instead, Monsanto has realized the efficacy of a well-financed lobbying strategy.

In 1997, the chemical giant invested $4 million for lobbying Congress and the White House on issues ranging from the federal tax code and agricultural subsidies to hazardous waste laws and food safety regulations. To protect its tax loopholes, Monsanto retains the services of David Bockorny, a former legislative affairs specialist in the Reagan White House, and Catherine Porter, former chief trade and tax counsel to Sen. John Chaffee, the powerful Rhode Island Republican.

On the troublesome matter of patents—a huge issue in the genetic engineering field—Monsanto has recruited the help of Dennis DeConcini, the former Arizona Democratic senator. DeConcini's firm, Parry & Romani, has carved out a specialty in the field of agricultural and pharmaceutical trademarks, and the libelous practice of staking property rights to native seed stocks. Similar work is done for Monsanto by Timmons and Company, a Democratic lobby shop that includes Ellen Boyle, former press secretary to Tip O'Neill; William Cable former deputy assistant for legislative affairs to Jimmy Carter; and John S. Orlando, who served as chief of staff to John Dingell, the senior Democrat in the House.

Perhaps no American company has so zealously exploited Washington's revolving door as Monsanto, which has seized on ex-Clinton aides and federal bureaucrats to advance its interests. Consider the case of Michael Taylor: after graduating from law school in 1976, Taylor went to work for the FDA, rising through the ranks. He left the federal government for a post in the high-powered Washington law firm of King and Spaulding to become their FDA specialist. During his tenure there, Taylor represented Monsanto's efforts to gain FDA approval for rBGH. Taylor left the firm in 1991 to rejoin the FDA, this time as deputy commissioner for policy. In that position, he wrote the guidelines on the use and marketing of rBGH, which turned out to be very favorable for Monsanto. The FDA guidelines exempted milk producers from labeling dairy products from cows that had been treated with rBGH. Now Taylor has resumed to Monsanto, working on what the company calls "long range planning."

During his days at King and Spaulding, Taylor also authored more than a dozen articles critical of the Delaney Clause, a 1958 federal law prohibiting the introduction of known carcinogens into processed foods, which had long been opposed by Monsanto and other chemical and pesticide companies. When Taylor rejoined the federal government, he continued advocating that Delaney should be overturned.

In the fight to bring down Delaney, Monsanto also secured the services of the Duberstein Group, the lobbying firm of Ken Duberstein, former chief of staff under George H. Bush and a close friend of Gen. Colin Powell. Duberstein's outfit is a sterling example of the bipartisan nature of lobbying, since its roster of lobbyists includes former Reagan and Bush administration officials, an adviser to former Vice President Walter Mondale, a former aide to Senate Majority Leader Trent Lott and House Democratic Whip David Bonior's former chief legislative aide.

Monsanto's lobbying apparatus even has penetrated the ranks of a nonprofit consumer group, the Safe Food Campaign, which advocates tougher food inspection standards. The group was founded by Carol Tucker Foreman, who served as an assistant secretary of agriculture in the Carter administration.

Ironically, Foreman also represents the Beef Council, Procter and Gamble and Monsanto. Foreman used her close ties with the Clinton administration to get Virginia Weldon, Monsanto's former public relations chief, appointed to Clinton's Committee of Scientific Advisors and Gore's Sustainable Development Roundtable—entities that recommended the Delaney Clause be replaced with more flexible legislation.

But the company may have secured its biggest coup in 1997, when it brought onto its board Mickey Kantor, the former secretary of commerce and one of Bill Clinton's closest advisers. Kantor joined two other Washington insiders on the Monsanto board— William Ruckleshaus, former director of the EPA, and Gwendolyn King, former head of the Social Security Administration.

Monsanto compensates its directors handsomely: Kantor receives nearly $100,000 a year. But that relatively small investment brings Monsanto lucrative returns. It was Kantor who opened the doors to the White House and pushed the administration to pressure the EU over Monsanto's genetically engineered grain.

Kantor's new law firm, Mayer, Brown & Platt, watches out for the company's interests in matters of international trade, food safety and product labeling. Prior to Kantor's arrival at the firm in 1997, one of Mayer, Brown & Platt's top lobbyists was William Daley, whom Clinton tapped to fill Kantor's spot in the cabinet. In that capacity, he has led the charge for Monsanto on several continents.

When you've got friends like this, you don't have to concern yourself with your enemies.

Postscript: In October of 1999, Monsanto caved to global public pressure and vowed that it would not commercialize its Terminator. The announcement came in a letter from Monsanto's CEO, Robert Shapiro, to the Rockefeller Foundation. "Though we do not yet own any sterile seed technology, we think it is important to respond to those concerns at this time by making clear our commitment not to commercialize gene protection systems that render seed sterile." Environmentalists were cautious, noting that Monsanto was desperate to counter the negative press that had dogged the company and that there was nothing to prevent the biotech firm from marketing the technology at a later date.

Portland, 1999

Twenty-Two

Inside Big Meat

All is not right at the IBP Inc. plant in Pasco, Washington, one of the nation's biggest slaughterhouses. According to workers, meat at the plant is routinely contaminated with cattle feces because workers on the processing line are not give enough time to wash their hands. Under pressure from aggressive plant managers, meat that falls on the floor, which is often littered with meat byproducts and entrails, is often immediately placed back on the line without being cleansed. Cutting tools and conveyor belts, workers tell *CounterPunch*, are also regularly coated with pus from abscesses and tumors that haven't been properly cut out of the meat. Meat cutters at the plant also told me that often cows are not rendered unconscious before being sent down the line. Instead, workers say they often hear cows frantically mooing as they are skinned and dismembered alive.

All of these problems are a function of the excessive speed of the meat processing line, a complex and dangerous network of conveyor belts and overhead chains and hooks. "They keep that line moving as fast as possible and they don't want it stopped for any reason," an IBP worker told us. "They don't care about the cows or the cow shit on the meat. They've got quotas to meet." IBP plants, workers say, aren't slaughterhouses so much as meat factories.

Workers say that IBP doesn't give them adequate breaks and cheats them out of pay for the 30 minutes a day it takes to put on and remove the protective clothing, glasses and gloves they must wear to work the cutting line. According to union shop steward Maria Martinez, many workers are often denied bathroom breaks, forcing them to urinate in their pants so they won't fall behind.

The workers know that when they fall behind they risk being fired. Early in the morning on June 4 2000, IBP managers yanked a meat cutter of the cutting line, saying that he wasn't keeping up with the flow of the meat. When his fellow workers saw him being taken away, twenty of them followed him to the plant manager's office. Many of them carried their knives with them. The production line came to a halt.

The workers told the manager that all of them were having problems doing their jobs safely because the pace of the line was too fast. "The velocity of the machines was so fast, we couldn't work properly," said Malquiadez Perez, another shop steward. But the managers didn't want to hear any of this. They told the meat cutters that they had 60 seconds to return to their places on the line or they would be fired on the spot.

Maria Martinez, an organizer with the TDU, told the IBP managers that the group would go back to work if all of them could return, including the meat cutter who had been fired for not keeping up with the pace of the line. The manager told Martinez no, demanded that they workers turn over their knives and told them they were fired.

This action led 800 other workers at the plant to walk off the job as well, carrying their knives with them. The action effectively shut down the slaughterhouse. On June 8, the union voted to go on strike.

The strike was settled on July 7, when after heavy-handed tactics from James Hoffa's national office of the Teamsters, workers narrowly approved a new contract on a 276–258 vote. Under the terms of the deal, union members will be given a say in the composition of the plant's safety committee and wages for most workers will be increased by $1.32 an hour. But many union leaders opposed the contract, saying it failed to address the key issues that prompted the walk out.

"This strike was never about money," says Maria Martinez. "It was about worker safety and consumer protection. And we didn't get what we were fighting for."

However, the issue is not over yet. In response to letter from Martinez and others, the USDA's Food Safety and Inspection Service has opened a probe of IBP for possible violations of worker safety, meat quality and animal cruelty laws. The Humane Slaughter Act of 1958, for example, prohibits companies from butchering animals while they are conscious.

For its part, IBP denies all the charges against it. The Dakota Dunes, a South Dakota-based company says that it recently installed a "steam vacuum system" that will "sanitize" the meat even if it becomes contaminated by feces and pus on the line. IBP claims that the June 4 walkout was a set up and had nothing to do with the dismissal of the meat cutter. Company spokesman Gary Mickelson says that the IBP security people had "picked up rumors the night before that the workers were planning an action the next day." Mickelson says the entire affair "was staged by the union."

But this is far from the first time the $13 billion company has been accused of shoddy practices and worker safety violations. Indeed, since its founding in 1960 (then called Iowa Beef Packers), the company has gained a reputation as being fiercely anti-worker and for being quick to call in scabs and violent strikebreakers. In the early 1969, the company's confrontations with its workers reached a bloody crescendo when it closed down three Iowa plants, increased automation and tried to bust the United Food and Commercial Workers when it demanded a 20 cent an hour pay raise for workers. The following year, the Federal Trade Commission hit the company with an antitrust suit, which prohibited IBP from acquiring any new plants in South Dakota, Minnesota, Iowa or Nebraska. As a result, IBP invested in the Pasco plant in Washington and several others in the Pacific Northwest and Texas.

In 1972, IBP's founder and former CEO, Currier Holman, was convicted of paying a New York mob boss $1 million to insure that unions would not disrupt the distribution of IBP meat on the east coast. More investigations for monopolistic practices followed, even after the company was acquired by Armand Hammer's Occidental Petroleum in 1981. In 1985, OSHA hit IBP with a then-record $2.6 million fine for manipulating data on the high rate of worker injuries at its plants. Of particular concern for OSHA was the design of IBP's cutting machines, which caused repetitive motion disorders in hundreds of IBP workers.

After Hammer died in 1990, IBP was spun off in a public stock offering. Today, Archer-Daniels-Midland is the IBP's biggest shareholder, owning more than 14 percent of the company. This didn't change the company's practices much. Although IBP executives appeared at a press conference with Clinton administration officials in 1996 denouncing the practice of hiring illegal foreign workers, a few months later the company was busted for employing 64 undocumented meat cutters at its huge pork plant in Storm Lake, Iowa. But the firm's cozy relationship with high level figures in Congress and the Clinton administration probably save it from prosecution.

The IBP board hosts the dreadful Wendy Gramm and JoAnn Smith, Assistant Secretary of Agriculture for Meat Inspection during the Bush presidency. Gramm and Smith are handsomely compensated at the tune of $30,000 for a week's worth of work for the company.

Although IBP claims that it pays its meat cutters for a full day's work, factory workers say that they must come in a 5:30 each morning to begin sharpening their knives and putting on the cumbersome gear, about half an hour before the meat line cranks up. At the end of the day, another half-hour is spent cleaning up the workstations, gear and knives. Workers say they are not compensated for this time nor are they given two 10-minute breaks required by federal law for laborers who work more than an eight-hour day. IBP calculates the "official" workday at 7 hours and 56 minutes and claims it is only required to give the workers one 15-minute break and a half-hour lunch break in the grueling day. In 1997, the Tenth Circuit Court in suit brought by workers at a different plant ruled that IBP was required to pay workers at that plant for the time spent putting on and taking off the cutting gear and preparing the knives and workstations. A similar suit was recently filed against IBP's Pasco factory.

Allegations about contaminated meat coming from IBP plants has put the company on the defensive and has prompted it to invest heavily a new PR campaign disguised as a "food safety initiative." On May 17, IBP spent $150,000 to start up the "Safeguarding Our Last Links Campaign," which will be run the Food Marketing Institute, the meat industry's trade association. The Last Links campaign will not focus on the growing crisis of e.coli contamination in meat plants, but on teaching consumers how to keep meat "safely" stored in refrigerators and how to clean countertops and silverware. The campaign, IBP's CEO Robert Peterson said, is designed to "help consumers learn safe food handling practices."

Of course, this might be a tough sell, coming from a company whose workers say they are forced to urinate in their pants on the factory floor as they butcher live cows and put meat coated with pus and feces on the packaging line.

Spokane, 2000

Twenty-Three

Killing the Tisza

In the spring of 2000, a dam break in Central Europe set off a spill of 100 tons of cyanide-tainted slurry from a gold smelter in northern Romania. The poison eventually worked its way down the 1000 km length of the pristine Tisza to where the river runs into the much larger Danube in Serbia, creating what scientists called a "wave of death."

As a result, one of Europe's most important river systems has turned into a death trap with fish, wildlife, micro-organisms and plants killed all along its length. Hungary and Yugoslavia have pulled at least 100 tons of dead fish from the water. Drinking water was poisoned. People worked feverishly to keep livestock and game from drinking the river water. Biologists predict it will take from 10-20 years for river life to return to normal with some of the damage irreversible. Some 62 types of fish and 20 protected species have been affected. Concentrations of cyanide measured 2.7 milligrams per litre of water several hundred miles from the spill source. That's 130 times the safe limit. Because cyanide decomposes quickly its effect upstream promises to be short-lived, and since it dilutes quickly, the Danube should be spared. But the real problem is that leaking out along with the cyanide are quantities of toxic heavy metals which can stay in the Tisza's muddy bottom for as long as five years. These toxic metals don't kill immediately, but are concentrated in fish and waterfowl, leading to disease and cancer further up the food chain. Tom Popper of the Regional Environmental Center, based in Hungary, said, "In terms of complete destruction to one ecosystem this is probably worse than Chernobyl."

The Danube, Europe's Mississippi, is a mess. The river is 2,850 km long and has a drainage basin that touches 17 countries. Running West to East, from the German Alps to the Black Sea, the river's natural course has been thrown off by dams, and its natural wetlands inundated. Spills such as the recent one on the Tisza are frequent in Central and Eastern Europe, and the World Wide Fund for Nature estimates that a quarter of all rivers in southern and eastern Europe are heavily polluted, often by toxic wastes. The pollution has been aggravated by NATO's bombing of the bridges crossing the Danube at Novi Sad in Serbia during the recent war. The damage has closed the river, shutting down traffic. Additionally, bombing a big chemical and oil complex outside Belgrade is thought to have set loose dioxins and other toxic chemicals into the surrounding air and water whose effects are likely to be damaging over the long term.

The ecological travesty in Romania is nothing new to the gold mining industry and it is not a problem that is peculiar to the developing world. Indeed, the United States has seen its share of toxic mining accidents. In 1990, the Brewer Gold Mine in South Carolina spilled thousands of gallons of toxic wastewater into the Lynches River, killing thousands of fish. Nearly 1,000 birds perished in Nevada when they drank cyanide-tainted water at a gold mine owned by Echo Bay, a Canadian company. A cyanide spill at the Richland mine in South Dakota's Black Hills destroyed a blue ribbon trout stream, killing more than 10,000 fish.

All of these situations have occurred at relatively new mining sites that were using the "new generation" of mining technology. Ironically, the new mining techniques are much more dangerous to the environment and human health than more traditional methods. Long gone are the days of the pick-ax miner or the deep shafts that tapped rich veins of gold miles below the surface of the earth. The new gold rush is carried out with chemicals and it was largely developed in the United States by the Department of the Interior and American mining companies.

One of the big problems with gold mining had always been its inefficiency. Older mining practices were able to extract less than 60 percent of the gold from the ore. On top of this, the old gold mines were very labor intensive operations, which wasn't a problem in countries such as South Africa with maintained a largely captive and cheap labor pool. This began to change in the early 1970s, when the Denver, Colorado-based Newmont Mining Company, with help from the US Bureau of Mines, developed a new mining technique "heap-leaching," using a sodium cyanide solution. Under this controversial practices, giant holes are gouged into the earth (sometimes more than two square miles in size), the rock is excavated, pulverized and soaked in a solution of sodium cyanide which leaches flecks of gold from tons of rock. The cyanide-laced water is then left behind to evaporate in tailings ponds.

Although the new method is economically efficient, it is fraught with environmental perils: acid drainage, ground water contamination, toxic spills, and a scared landscape. These are mammoth operations that often leave an open pit in the earth, a mile wide and more than 1,500 feet deep. The operations are big because it requires enormous quanities of rock to produce a pound of gold. For each ton of gold an average mine produces, it will also generate three million tons of waste rock or tailings. Homestake Mining Company's Ruby Mountain mine in Nevada, will yield less than one-tenth of an ounce of gold from each ton of rock. Nevada is the epicenter of the new gold rush in the US. There are over 36 large-scale heap-leach mines in Nevada alone. Nationwide there are more than 150 cyanide heap-leach mines. Under current law, US mining companies are not required to reclaim these pits or do much with the tailings.

There is another built-in problem with new mining techniques. These kinds of chemical mining operations consume massive amounts of water. Thus the poisonous chemicals and the toxic tailings ponds are often stored perilously close to rivers and lakes or above aquifers that often provide drinking water to communities downstream. Accidents are common and leaking is inevitable. American rivers have paid a heavy price for past mining practices. According to the US Department of Interior, more than 12,000 miles of streams have been fouled by mining wastes. One of the most notorious mining disasters happened in Colorado in 1986 when a dam broke at a gold mining site in Summitville spilling a stream of cyanide and other toxic chemicals into the Alamosa River. The poisonous wastewater poured at a rate of 3,000 gallons a minute, effectively killing off life in an 18-mile stretch of that mountain stream. The company that ran the mine, Galactic Resources, closed down, filed for bankruptcy and left the United States. The site is now on the Superfund toxic waste site list and may end up costing taxpayers more than $150 million to clean up.

"With cyanide they can extract gold from nearly every site on Earth," says Larry Tuttle, director of the Center for Environmental Equity, a Portland, Oregon-based group that monitors mining operations. "Because they are so toxic and so fraught with the potential for disaster, the new breed of mining companies is looking for the places where they are welcome politically and relatively free of environmental standards." For the past few years the price of gold has hovered at record lows, causing more and more mining companies to migrate to the places where it is cheapest to do business: Africa, South America, Indonesia, the former Soviet Union and eastern Europe. Cyanide is one of the most lethal chemicals know to man. It is deadly in minute amounts, particularly to fish and birds. But humans are also vulnerable. Cyanide is the poison that killed hundreds in the Jonestown, Guyuna mass-suicide and the tylenol-tampering case. Operating in third-world nations incurs a degree of political and financial risk. As a result, global mining firms have sought help from famous politicians and investment bankers. Soon after George H. Bush left office he joined the advisory board of Barrick Resources, a Canadian mining conglomerate. Henry Kissinger has a spot on the board of Freeport-McMoran, which operates a controversial gold mine in Indonesia.

Esmeralda Exploration brought onto its board of directors, Michael Beck. Beck is currently the managing director of Rothschild Natural Resources, a branch of the Rothschild financial empire. He was also a former investment officer at the International Finance Center for the World Bank. The IFC is a financial backer of gold mining ventures around the world. This is far from the first ecological disaster caused by a breached dam from a mine site. In 1985, a dam at a cyanide tailings pond in Guyani busted open, killing more than 80 miles of the Essiquibo River. The mine was a joint venture of Cambior (Canada) and Golden Star Resources (Colorado). In March of 1996, a dam breached at a mine in Marcopper, Philippines, forcing the evacuation of 1,200 residents and contaminating thousands of acres of agricultural land. The mine was owned by Canadian mining giant Placer Dome. A year earlier, 12 people were killed in the Philippines when a toxic flood released from a gold mine run by the Manila Mining Company. In 1998, a cyanide spill at the Kumtor mine in Kyrgyzstan contaminated miles of river. The Kumtor mine, like the Aurul, was promoted by the IFC. In addition, it received more than $192 million in "political risk" insurance from the US government's Overseas Private Investment Company.

The main producer of cyanide is the DuPont Corporation, which refuses to release annual production figures. But we can get a rough picture from Nevada alone, where gold mines use more than 80 million pounds of the toxic chemical each year.

There are signs that public attitudes toward chemical mining are beginning to change in the United States. In 1998, outrage over plans to put a giant mine near Yellowstone National Park sparked Montana citizens to approve a ballot initiative banning new cyanide mines in that state. Similar measures are planned for Oregon and Colorado. In the meantime, there's nothing to prevent a Romanian-type spill from happening in the United States.

Portland, 2000

Twenty-Four

The Drug War According to Dr. Mengele

BioWarfare in the Andes

Hostile intentions toward the people of another country. Deployment of chemical weapons and biological agents. Pursuit of a scorched earth policy. Sound like Saddam's Iraq? Think again. This neatly sums up the Bush administration's ongoing depredations in Colombia, all under the shady banner of the war on drugs.

The big difference is that Saddam's hideous use of poison gas against the Kurds and, possibly, against Iran occurred more than 15 years ago. Since the Gulf War, Saddam's mad pursuits have been more on the order of chemistry experiments in bombed out basements. But the Bush administration's toxic war on Colombian peasants is happening now, day after day, in flippant violation of international law.

Indeed, as Bush offers pious homilies on Iraq's possible hoarding of so-called Weapons of Mass Destruction, his administration and its backers from both parties in Congress are poised to unleash a new wave of toxins in the mountains of Colombia, including a dangerous brew of biological weapons its proponents rather quaintly call mycoherbicides, Agent Green.

The leading germ war hawk in the congress these days is Rep. Bob Mica, a Republican from Florida. In mid-December 2002, Mica called on his pals in the Bush administration to uncork a currently banned batch of killer fungi and begin a campaign of saturation spraying. "We have to restore our mycoherbicide," Mica fumed. "Things that have been studied for too long need to be put into action. We found that we can not only spray this stuff, but we found that we can also deactivate it for some period of time—it will do a lot of damage—it will eradicate some of these crops for a substantial period of time."

Of course, Agent Green also kills everything else it touches. There's not even a pretense to call these germ bomblets "smart fungi." This is the drug war as it might be waged by Dr. Mengele. Mica's bracing call for an unfettered germ war on Colombia should be jotted down by junior legal eagles with dreams of becoming future prosecutors of war crimes.

But Mica is far from a lone crazed voice. Even the perpetually conflicted Colin Powell is on record supporting the use of biological agents as a key part of Plan Colombia. Indeed, Anne Peterson, the US ambassador to Bogota, testified recently that she believed bio-weapons had already been deployed in Colombia. Bizarrely, she later retracted this chilling observation, saying that it had been made under duress. Ms. Peterson didn't say who had applied the thumb-screws.

Then there's Rand Beers, one of the few holdovers at the State Department from Clintontime. It's easy to see why this biowar zealot appealed to the Bush crowd. Back in the late '90s, Beers was all for using germ weapons on crops in drug-producing countries. Now, as Assistant Secretary of State for narcotics, Beers trots across the globe to various international conferences where he invariably is forced to defend this toxic footnote to Plan Colombia against critics who charge that it violates, among other treaties, the Biological Weapons Convention. Beers often says that the toxic weapons are needed to fight international crime syndicates. This heady bit of sophistry is hardly an exemption from the prohibitions, which, it must be point-ed out, the Bush administration doesn't believe in anyway, even though they are trigger-happy to invoke its provisions against enemy states, such as Iraq.

So, as in Macbeth, sin plucks on sin.

Agent Green is a genetically engineered pathogenic fungi, con-jured up by the US Department of Agriculture's experiment station in Beltsville, Maryland. It is now being produced with US funds by Ag-Bio Company, a private lab in Bozeman, Montana and at a for-mer Soviet bioweapons factory in Tashkent, Uzbekistan. The labs are brewing up two types of killer fungi, Fusarium oxysporum (slated for use against marijuana and coca plants) and Pleospora papveracea (engineered to destroy opium poppies).

The problem is that both fungi are indiscriminate killers, posing threats to human health and to non-target species. Add to this the fact that when sprayed from airplanes and helicopters, Agent Green will be carried by winds and inevitably drift over coffee plantations, fields, farms, villages, and water supplies.

Agent Green also threatens the ecology of the Colombian rainforest, one of the most biologically diverse on the planet. These forests harbor a greater variety of species per acre than any country's. But the Colombian forests are already under frightful siege from gold mining, oil companies, logging outfits and cattle ranching. By one count, Colombia has already lost more than a third of its primary forest and continues to lose forest at a rate of 3,000 square miles (or nearly 2 million acres) a year. It's possible that the Agent Green operation may saturate more than a million acres of Colombian rainforest, with potentially devastating ecological consequences for endemic wildlife and plants.

So it's likely that Amazonia could become collateral damage in the Bushites' bio-war adventurism.

This grim prospect may place the US squarely in violation of yet another international treaty with which Bush, the former cocaine tooter, is charmingly unacquainted: the Convention on the Prohibition of Military or Any Other Hostile Use of Environmental Modification Techniques (ENMOD). ENMOD grew out of the worldwide outrage sparked by the use of Agent Orange and other environmentally malign potions plastered across Southeast Asia during the Vietnam War. Adopted by the UN in 1976 and signed by the US, ENMOD prohibits any signatory nation from using the environment as a weapon of war, which the spraying of Colombia constitutes by definition.

The US bio-bomblets can't even be made to stay in Colombia, but, like the pesticides and fumigants already dropped, will inevitably stray across the Colombian border into Ecuador and Peru. Both nations vehemently oppose the US biowar plan and charge that it violates international law. Specifically, they cite a non-proliferation section of the Biological Warfare Convention that prohibits the transfer of germ weapons and technology from one nation to another. Presumably, the Bush administration now considers Colombia a wholly owned colony, where even remote Andean valleys are in the toxic grip of the US empire.

"If Agent Green is used anywhere, it will legitimize agricultural biowarfare in other contexts," says Edward Hammond, director of The Sunshine Project, the anti-biowar group that has done excellent work in exposing the environmental consequences of toxic spraying in Colombia. "Reasoning in a similar manner as the US, others might prepare a biological attack on the US tobacco crop, which poisons millions worldwide, or those opposed to alcohol might target grapes or hops."

Eradication programs are a foolhardy way of addressing problems associated with drug consumption. It doesn't work, it oppresses the weak, and merely plays into the pockets of the drug profiteers, from the cocaine generals to the drug cartels and the banks who launder the money.

"In much of rural Colombia, there is simply no way to make a legal living," says Adam Isacson, of the Center for International Policy. "Security, roads, credit, and access to markets are all missing. The most that many rural Colombians see from their government is the occasional military patrol or spray plane. When the spray planes come, they take away farmers' illegal way of making a living, but they do not replace it with anything. That leaves the farmers with some bad choices. They can move to the cities and try to find a job, though official unemployment is already 20 percent. They can switch to legal crops on their own and risk paying more for inputs than they can get from the sale price. They can move deeper into the countryside and plant drug crops again. Or they can join the guerrillas or the paramilitaries, who will at least keep them fed."

Of course, the drug war has little do with the real motives of this ghastly program. The truth of this can be divined in the numbers. Billions in US aid and thousands of gallons of chemical pesticides have been poured on Colombia with little dent in coca production. In fact, the flow of drugs from Colombia is increasing at a rapid clip.

Back when the Clinton administration was pushing a somewhat reluctant congress to approve its multi-billion project dubbed Plan Colombia, none other than Rand Beers swore that the spray and burn tactics would "eliminate the majority of Colombia's opium poppy crop within three years." Congress bought Beers' song and dance, approving $1.3 billion dollars. (As a pre-condition for receiving the money, Congress required Colombia to begin operational testing of bioweapons. Bowing to world pressure, President Clinton waived the requirement.)

In the past five years, nearly a million acres of land in Colombia has been blitzed by pesticides and fumigants, rendered them as sterile as the fields of Carthage after Scipio Africanus' last cruel visit. But over the same period, production of cocaine in Colombia has more than tripled. Opium production is also soaring, increasing by more than 60 percent since 2000. Colombia now accounts for more than 30 percent of the heroin consumed in the US.

The reason for this will be obvious to anyone who has read the book I co-authored with Alexander Cockburn, *Whiteout: The CIA, Drugs and the Press.* War, especially covert ones, and drugs go hand in hand. Colombia is mired in a three-way civil war, with each side, guerillas, paramilitaries and the government troops, funding their operations from proceeds from the sale of drugs. The bloodier the conflict, the greater the flow of drugs.

But from the beginning Plan Colombia was only ostensibly about drugs. It was really a way to use the drug war to underwrite the Colombian military's savage war against the FARC and other rebel groups and secure US control over Colombian oil, gas and mineral reserves. The so-called eradication programs have targeted areas controlled by the FARC, rather than even larger swaths of land held by paramilitaries, serving as vicious proxy-warriors for the Colombian government.

According to Rep. Bob Barr, since the implementation of Plan Colombia at least 22 US helicopters have been shot down by Colombian rebel groups—a figure the Pentagon coyly refuses to confirm or deny. However, the State Department confirmed that last month three US planes were struck by groundfire on the same day.

The US presence in the war is being waged under the jurisdictional banner of the State Department, so often in the past a sign of the darker presence of the CIA and other covert warriors. In December, Colin Powell revealed his intention to up the permanent fleet of US attack helicopters in Colombia to 24. The State Department informed congress that new pilots were being trained at "a classified location" in New Mexico.

Now, it appears that the Bush administration has given Congressman Mica the green light to work his dark magic on the reauthorization of Plan Colombia, where he would insert language once again requiring the use of Agent Green as a condition of the Colombian government getting its hands on US billions. These days they don't even go to the bother of trying to hide the strings.

There's plenty of evidence that the Colombian government is now totally under the sway of Washington and will be only too happy to oblige, even if that means allowing the US to launch biological warfare attacks on its own peasants.

In a bracing irony, Colombia now presides over the UN Security Council, which is poised to clobber Iraq for hiding its history of bioweapon development. Indeed, it was the Colombian delegation that made the controversial call to hand over an early copy of Iraq's weapons declaration, which the US generously returned a week later—minus 8,000 pages.

This scandalous project drones on under the radar of the mainstream press, ever loath to tackle seriously any topic wrapped in the holy robes of the drug war. Yet, what it really adds up to is a form of environmental terrorism. The toxic wasteland and human suffering left in the wake of these operations is not accidental, not, to use the fetching term of the economists, a uncomfortable externality of an otherwise benign project. Instead, it is a calculated tactic, designed to evoke fear and terror—the carpetbombing of the drug war.

Don't say the toxic warriors in the Bush administration aren't bibliophiles. Obviously they've read *Silent Spring*. Only not as the stark warning Rachel Carson intended, but as a war plan which they are now bent on putting into global action.

Portland, January 2003

PART IV

Power Plays

Twenty-Five

Oily Wedlock

You'd think that a merger of two oil giants giving the new partners a 15 percent armlock on the domestic fuel market would arouse some public comment, if not outrage and obloquy. In the old days, members of congress—particularly from the Northeast and Midwest—would be turning out furious press releases and invoking the Sherman Anti-Trust Act, but thus far...nothing. Back in 1973, the year the US Senate almost voted to break up the oil industry, Rep. John Dingell from Michigan held a hearing on the topic of "White Collar Crime in the Oil Industry." Those were more turbulent days. No politician uses that kind of language now.

Shell Oil and Texaco, among the largest oil companies on the planet, are now well along in an engagement to be finalized in 1999. Scheduled for merger are the US refining and marketing operations of the two companies. When it come to selling gasoline, the new entity will be the largest company in the US.

Thus far no one in any position of regulatory oversight has seen fit to raise a bleat, which is all the more surprising given the fact that earlier this year gas prices suddenly shot up amid much headscratching on the TV new shows and in newsrooms across the country. The real reason, of course, was never even hinted at: the big oil companies were simply doing what came naturally to them—fixing prices. The merger of Shell and Texaco will only increase the frequency of similar "inexplicable" increases in the future.

The only cautionary note sounded by the Clinton administration came from Deputy Energy Secretary Charles Curtis. Last week he addressed oil company executives at the annual confab of the American Petroleum Institute. Curtis wagged the most deferential of fingers. "Domestic energy prices have grown brittle, with troubling results," Curtis said politely. "Investors and consumers don't like surprises, but that's what they're getting. Public confidence in the free market erodes when prices suddenly increase. Too much volatility will create demand for political solutions that are shortsighted and ill-conceived."

Far more agitated than Curtis are employees of Shell. They have told company executives that they fear the merger may well bring unwelcome Texaco policies, in the form of discriminatory hiring and promotion practices, such as those that recently cost the company $176 million in a settlement of a class action suit. During the suit, lawyers for the plaintiffs released a secret tape recording made by a vice-president of Texaco where executives of the company referred to black employees as "porch monkeys," "orangutans," and "Aunt Jemimas."

Shell's vice president, Jim Morgan, responded to these fears with a letter to Shell employees sent on November 21. "I want to assure you that we have no intention of entering into any relationship that is not based on high ethical standards and the utmost respect for individuals," Morgan wrote. "Compatibility in values and standards of integrity between two parties considering entering into a relationship are critically important."

Noble sentiments indeed, albeit somewhat undercut by some unwholesome chapters in Shell's treatment of its own black employees. Shell is now facing two class action suits alleging that the company discriminates against them. No black employee in the company's retail marketing division has ever made it into Shell's senior or executive ranks. In the entire history of Shell Oil USA only two African-Americans have ever been promoted to senior management in any part of the company.

As at Texaco, when black employees have confronted management about the apparent impossibility of rising up Shell's corporate ladder, they have been met with contemptuous rebuffs. One of the most honored Shell employees is a black engineer named Jimmy Hunter, a Shell man since 1979. He's twice been given Shell's top company honor, the Laurel Society Award. But the expected promotions never followed. When Hunter questioned his supervisor, he says he was told, "I don't know why you still have shackles around your ankles."

Another plaintiff in the class action suit against Shell is Sharon Ambeaux. She developed a sales and marketing program called "Crazy Days." The program was a huge success. But Ms. Ambeaux remained mired at a near entry level pay grade after 17 years of service.

Vociferous in denunciations of Texaco has been Jesse Jackson. When the infamous Texaco Company tapes first surfaced, with racist remarks by Texaco executives played on Ted Koppel's *Nightline*, Jackson called for a boycott of the company, for drivers to cut up their Texaco credit cards. Then he warned of a nationwide stock divestiture campaign if Texaco did not change its ways.

However, no such fulminations have come from Jackson in the case of Shell. The reason may have to do with one of the foulest chapters in Shell's history: its role in the destruction of Ogoni tribal lands in Nigeria, and in the execution of the premier Ogoni political activist, Ken Saro-Wiwa and eight of his colleagues. Exactly a year ago, Saro-Wiwa and his friends went to the gallows, not long after Royal Dutch Shell (parent to the American subsidiary) warned the Nigerian government that Ogoni protests over its environmentally destructive drilling practices and tribal demands for a share of the billions in past oil revenues must be quelled, otherwise Shell would pull out of Nigeria altogether.

In the weeks after Saro-Wiwa and his compatriots were sentenced to death, the international campaign fighting for their lives implored Shell to take a public stand. Shell did nothing, thus signaling the Nigerian dictatorship run by General Sani Abacha that it was safe to proceed.

Right after the execution, Randall Robinson of TransAfrica sent a letter to Bill Clinton calling for fierce US sanctions against Nigeria. The US buys nearly half of Nigeria's oil exports (oil revenues provide 80 percent of the nation's budget) and could thus cripple the regime if it led an oil embargo. But the administration responded with only token sanctions, involving delays in some arms sales and a scolding of the country's diplomats.

Senator Nancy Kassenbaum of Kansas and Rep. Donald Payne of New Jersey denounced this as inadequate and introduced a bill in Congress calling for a full embargo. The administration was horrified. "There's plenty of oil [available on world markets]," said one US government official in an off-the-record talk. "But there's only so much Bonney Light." He was referring to Nigeria's coveted sweet crude oil, which is extremely pure and economical to refine.

At this moment pressure from Jackson would have counted for something. But he remained silent. His fellow Chicagoans, Senator

Carole Moseley-Braun and Louis Farrakhan, went off to Nigeria under the supervision of US lobbyists retained by General Abacha for more than $10 million. One of the key firms hired by the Nigerian regime was Symms, Lehn and Associates, headed by former Idaho senator Steve Symms. Another key player was Shell's lobbyist Tommy Hale Boggs, brother of news diva Cokie Roberts and Clinton golfing pal. Using a PR strategy developed by these firms, Nigeria began a nationwide advertizing blitz that included full-page ads in the *New York Times* implying that Saro-Wiwa was a terrorist and that the environmental problems of oil drilling in Nigeria had been cured.

Meanwhile, Moseley-Braun and Farrakhan returned from their Nigerian "fact-finding" mission saying that an embargo would be premature and counterproductive. Moseley-Braun testified in the Senate against the embargo bill, and told colleagues (falsely, it turns out) that the Congressional Black Caucus was evenly split on the issue. Randall Robinson then revealed that he personally had rejected an attempted bribe of $1 million by Abacha's operatives to change his position. "Oil money makes a huge difference," he said, "because it puts spunk in the spine of your enemy."

An unpublicized part of the anti-embargo campaign was the intense lobbying effort by American oil companies, including Mobil, Amoco, Chevron and Texaco, which are planning a $4 billion natural gas project in Nigeria. As a result of all these pressures, the Kassenbaum/Payne bill never even got out of committee. This came as a disappointment but not a surprise to Ken Saro-Wiwa's brother, Dr. Owens Wiwa, who has recently filed a multi-million dollar suit against Shell, charging it with crimes against the environment and human rights. "The evil alliance between Shell and the military dictatorship could only have been broken by an international embargo," Wiwa said. "Oil is the only thing that keeps the regime in power." Today, 18 other Ogoni activists await execution for their efforts to drive Shell Oil Company from their homeland. The Clinton administration remains silent.

The trend towards concentration in the energy industry is accelerating rapidly. Even if there was any disposition in the White House or in Congress to try to represent the public interest here, in terms of controlling prices, limiting environmental destruction and human rights abuses, such intervention is getting a great deal harder. Oil power has grown again to levels of invulnerability reminiscent of the 1880s and the 1920s, cutting down any who dare stand in its path.

Oregon City, 1996

Twenty-Six

Crude Aspirations

The New Alaskan Oil Rush

(with Alexander Cockburn)

Forget the favors to Lippo. Forget those nightly rentals of the Lincoln bedroom. By far the biggest scandal in town, entirely unreported, is the new Alaskan oil rush. It is a multibillion dollar giveaway reminiscent of the Teapot Dome fiasco in 1922 when Albert Fall, President Warren Harding's Interior Secretary, secretly leased off a Naval Oil Reserve north of Caspar, Wyoming to oil man Harry Sinclair. After it was disclosed that Sinclair had given him as much as $400,000 during his tenure in office, Fall became the first member of a presidential cabinet to do time in federal prison.

How is this contemporary version of the Teapot Dome being brokered? In Alaska everything was going fine for the oil cartel until the Exxon Valdez struck Blighe Reef in 1989. After eleven million gallons of crude coated Prince William Sound, public esteem for the oil companies, never robust, shriveled abruptly, even in Alaska where each resident receives a $1,200 check every year from the oil earnings of the North Slope companies. Even the companies' urgent cries that the Prudhoe Bay wells were running dry and the country would soon face another oil shortage could not convince Congress to open the Arctic National Wildlife Refuge to oil leasing, a decade-long goal of ARCO, British Petroleum and Exxon, which are the three major players in the state.

Stalemated, the Alaskan oil cartel did a 180 degree spin. In 1994, they announced the discovery of more oil in the Prudhoe Bay fields than had been previously imagined. Enough oil, in fact, to keep the pipeline running for another 30 to 50 years. The problem wasn't a shortage, the oil companies argued, but a glut of crude, which, because of laws prohibiting the sale of Alaskan oil to lucrative foreign buyers, meant the companies might have to scale back production and lay off hundreds of workers.

In the spring of 1996, the Clinton administration handed the oil industry a gigantic favor worth billions, amid a sphinx-like silence from the press. It overturned the 30-year old ban on the export of Alaskan crude oil. The oil companies would now be able to market the crude to Japan, South Korea, Taiwan and China. The opening of the North Slope to oil drilling, and the construction of the leaky 820-mile-long Trans-Alaska Pipeline to transport the crude from Prudhoe Bay to Valdez, was sanctioned by the US Congress *only* because the oil was intended to buttress America's energy independence. Exports of raw crude were explicitly banned. At the time Senator Walter Mondale warned that the oil companies would eventually have the ban overturned, saying they had always intended it to be the "Trans-Alaska-Japan pipeline." Mondale correctly foresaw that the oil companies would export large shipments of the Alaskan crude to Asia in order to keep winter heating fuel prices high in the Midwestern states. Now, nearly three decades after this prediction, the oil companies have the jackpot in their grasp.

The winning strategy to lift the export ban was hatched by Tommy Boggs, the Rasputin of American lobbyists, whose firm, Patton, Boggs, represents a thick portfolio of oil companies, including Exxon, Mobil, Shell, and Ashland. In this instance, Boggs was the advance man for Alyeska, owned by the Alaskan oil consortium. Alyeska operates the Trans-Alaska Pipeline and supervises oil extraction on the North Slope. Alyeska is owned by the consortium of companies doing business in northern Alaska. In an August 1995 memo to a prospective client, Boggs, a golfing pal of Bill Clinton, boasts of his bipartisan expertise in moving the measure through Congress: "We have a very good working relationship with the Alaska delegation, having led the private-sector effort to get exports of Alaskan North Slope oil approved by the 104th Congress and signed by President Clinton." Boggs' normal price tag is a robust $550 per hour, which translates into $22,000 for a 40-hour week.

Barely was the ink dry on Clinton's executive order allowing sale of Alaskan oil to Asian customers before he handed the Alaskan oil cartel another amazing gift, once again without a whisper of interest in the corporate press. This was the demurely named Federal Oil and Gas Simplication and Fairness Act. The title of the bill was signal enough that dirty work was afoot. And indeed it was.

Approved by Congress on the last day of the 1996 summer session, the law does four things: it places a seven-year limit on the federal auditing of oil companies records of their income from drilling on public lands. It turns over many of the auditing responsibilities concerning drilling on federal lands to the states. It permits the oil companies to sue the federal government to collect interest on "overpayments" and it allows those very same companies to set the "market price" of the crude oil upon which the royalty payments to the federal government are based.

The next public intimation that among the federal properties leased by ARCO and Exxon is the Clinton administration came in the vulgar surroundings of Jackson Hole, Wyoming on lands formerly owned by the Rockefeller clan. Here, amidst his pre-convention jaunt to the Rockies, Clinton found time to play host to a platoon of oil company moguls. At that day-long session under the shadow of the Grand Tetons, executives from the Alaskan oil cartel took the opportunity to brief the president on an even grander scheme to boost domestic oil production: open the National Petroleum Reserve in Alaska to oil leasing. And here's where we find Teapot Dome *redivivus*.

West of Prudhoe Bay lies the 23-million-acre National Petroleum Reserve, set aside in 1923 by executive order. Back then it was known as the Naval Petroleum Reserve and the oil was held in store against a national calamity. William Hard, writing in *The Nation* in 1923, described the purpose of the naval oil reserves: "[to conserve] oil in the ground for the use of the government at some future time when the customary commercial supplies of oil might be insufficient and when some great impending national emergency might demand a governmentally reserved and controlled abundant source of fuel for our fighting ships."

For decades, the oil companies and their allies in the Interior Department lobbied to open the Alaskan reserve to private leasing and exploitation. Decade after decade, the admirals fought them off. Even during the fraught hours of World War II, the Navy resisted calls by Standard Oil and Texaco to open the Arctic fields for reasons of national security.

In the early 1970s, shortly after the Prudhoe Bay discoveries,

ARCO, Exxon and British Petroleum redoubled their efforts to gain entry in the Petroleum Reserve, Senator Adlai Stevenson warned that "history is repeating itself, except that the stakes could make the raid on Teapot Dome a petty misdemeanor by comparison." All through the frenzied days of the energy crisis, the Navy stood firm and the gates to the Arctic reserve remained closed.

In 1980, Jimmy Carter changed the name of the area to the National Petroleum Reserve-Alaska and, in a possibly fatal move, transferred authority for the reserve from the Navy to the Interior Department. Still, the function of the reserve remained very much the same. The oil was to be held back for use in a national crisis. Even during the ebullient years of the Reagan/Bush era, when the oil companies made vigorous efforts to attain their goal, the Alaskan oil reserve remained sacrosanct. In 1981, James Watt and his forces at Interior geared up to open the Alaskan reserve to oil leasing and development, but were held off by a lawsuit brought by two Eskimo elders, who argued that oil drilling in the reserve would damage their subsistence rights to hunt caribou and fish the area's lakes and rivers for Arctic char and whitefish. Bill Clinton and Bruce Babbitt are now set to accomplish what Reagan and Watt could not.

Students of the political economy of the Clinton White House are correct in assuming, as this narrative unfolds, that the billions handed over by Clinton to the Alaskan oil cartel were predicated on a substantial river of slush coming the other way. The fundraisers at 1600 Pennsylvania Avenue were not disappointed.

After all, ARCO—expected to be the prime beneficiary of the new Alaskan oil bonanza—is one of the preeminent sponsors of the American political system. The oil giant maintains a hefty federal political action committee. In the 1996 election cycle, the ARCO PAC handed out more than $357,000. But this is only the beginning. Over the same period, ARCO pumped $1.25 million of soft money into the tanks of the Republican and Democratic national committees. The company contributed at least another $500,000 in state elections, where corporations can often give directly to candidates.

Robert Healy is ARCO's vice-president for governmental affairs. On October 25, 1995, Healy attended a White House coffee "klatch" with Vice-President Al Gore and Marvin Rosen, finance chairman of the Democratic National Committee. A few days before the session, Healy himself contributed $1,000 to the Clinton/Gore re-election campaign. But from July through December of 1995, largely under Healy's direction, ARCO poured $125,000 into the coffers of the DNC.

The man who does much of ARCO's political dirty work in Washington, DC is Charles T. Manatt, former chairman of the Democratic Party. Manatt runs a high-octane lobbying shop called Manatt, Phelps, Rothenberg and Evans, formerly the lair of Mickey Kantor. The lobbyist attended a White House coffee with Clinton on May 26, 1995. In 1995 and 1996, Manatt alone doled out $117,150 in hard and soft money. Members of Manatt's family threw in $7,000. His law firm kicked in $22,500 and the firm's PAC another $81,109.

Inside the Clinton cabinet, Manatt's former partner, Kantor became the most strident agitator for lifting the export ban on Alaskan oil, promoting it as a vital prong in the administration's Asian trade policy. Kantor, who recently resigned his position as Secretary of Commerce, intends to resume his law practice with the Manatt, Phelps firm.

ARCO's former CEO, Lodwrick Cook, is a personal friend of Bill Clinton. In 1994, Cook celebrated his birthday at the White House. The President himself presented the oil executive with a towering cake. Cook traveled with Commerce Secretary Ron Brown on a trade junket to China in August 1994. During that trip, Cook and Brown negotiated ARCO's investment in the huge Zhenhai refinery outside Shanghai. The refinery is now ready to process Alaskan crude, which suggests that at least two years before Clinton's executive order on oil exports in the spring of 1996, ARCO had inside knowledge of what was to come.

A key role in this affair also has been played by Alaska's governor, Tony Knowles—a bizarre hybrid of Clinton and oilman Lloyd Bentsen, known by some Alaskans as the Governor of ARCO. Knowles, who proudly asserts that in his youth he was a "roughneck" in the oil fields of west Texas, is the first Democrat to run the state in many years and his campaign received more than $30,000 from ARCO, the largest producer on the North Slope. In recognition of this munificence, Knowles has pushed the oil industry's agenda in his frequent meetings with the Clinton crowd.

"The Knowles administration told Clinton and Al Gore that if they wouldn't allow the Arctic National Wildlife Refuge to be leased to the oil companies, then they must open the National Petroleum Reserve." So says Sylvia Ward, of the Northern Alaska Environmental Center in Fairbanks. The Clinton administration had vowed to veto any measures to open the 17-million acre Alaska National Wildlife Refuge to oil drilling, but to the disappointment of Alaskan environmentalists it has refused to back efforts to protect the coastal plain as wilderness.

Knowles accurately saw this as an opening and he made haste to exploit it. For the governor and the oil companies, accelerated drilling in the National Petroleum Reserve will be a kind of testing ground for the more lucrative fields that lie under Alaska National Wildlife Refuge. "We'll show them that we can do it right," Knowles says.

This was almost certainly the message Knowles and his Lt. Governor Fran Ulmer delivered to Clinton during their sessions at the White House. Ulmer was the guest of the Clintons for a morning coffee in the mansion's Map Room on February 28, 1996. Knowles, and his wife, also spent an evening in the Lincoln bedroom.

In his January state of the state address, Knowles boasted that he had successfully convinced the Clinton administration to cleave the way open for more oil drilling in Alaska. The governor's claims were soon confirmed by no lesser a notable than the Secretary of the Interior, Bruce Babbitt.

On February 7, Babbitt announced that he was ordering the preparation of an environmental impact statement on the leasing of the Reserve. Babbitt went further, saying that "oil leasing is absolutely the goal of the environmental studies." This statement is indicative of the utter lawlessness of the crowd now running the country. As the National Environmental Policy Act stipulates, environmental review comes first, and a decision second. Babbitt is brazenly indicating that the preparers of the EIS have been told in no uncertain terms where their duties lie.

"Babbitt's promise to conduct an oil leasing environmental review undercuts the purpose of NEPA," Jim Sykes, director of Oil

Watch, an Anchorage environmental group.

Typically, Babbitt rationalizes this effrontery by gesturing toward a new kind of consensual politics that does not require the pesky corsets of legal obligation: "We'd like to break away from the adversarial style and see if we can put together some new way of doing business with the oil industry. I think we've got lots of possibilities."

What kind of place is the National Petroleum Reserve? Nothing less than the largest expanse of undeveloped public land in North America, a wilderness bigger and just as ecologically fragile as the more high profile Arctic National Wildlife Refuge located two-hundred miles to the east. This 36-thousand square mile expanse of Arctic land is crossed by the Colville River, which sweeps in a giant arc from its headwaters in the Noatak National Park across the Anuktuvuk plateau to its delta at the icy Beaufort Sea. Grizzlies gather at the river in astounding numbers to feast on grayling, Arctic char, and whitefish.

As the river makes its final bend toward the Arctic Ocean, it slides along a mighty escarpment, a 60-mile long palisade of cliffs, eroding away at the base to reveal mastodon tusks and the fossilized bones of dinosaurs. Two hundred feet up in these limestone bluffs nest peregrines, gyrfalcon, and rough-legged hawks, making the Colville drainage the most prolific raptor habitat in the Arctic. It is this escarpment that the oil companies cherish most.

By far the region's most dominant ecological force is the Western Arctic caribou herd, which roams across the reserve to grazing grounds in the Brooks Range on migratory routes unimpeded for millennia. The 500,000-head herd is the largest in Alaska, three times the size of the famous Porcupine herd in the Arctic National Wildlife Refuge. In the wake of the caribou come the wolves, ravens, wolverines and native hunters, feeding on the detritus of this massive rush of life.

David van der Berg is a carpenter from Fairbanks and one of the few people to have floated the entire 450-mile-long course of the Colville, the river the Eskimo call Kuukpik, the big waters. "The Colville country has a severe and austere beauty," says van der Berg. "It is unquestionably the wildest place in North America. The oil companies have occupied nearly every other tract in northern

Alaska. Yet true wilderness is now so much scarcer than oil. This land should be left to the grizzlies, the caribou, and the Eskimo."

The Arctic Reserve encompasses an area the size of Indiana; yet the entire region is home to fewer than 5,000 people, most of whom live on the Reserve's peripheries in the Eskimo villages of Barrow, Wainwright, Atquasak, and Umiat.

On the eastern border of the Reserve is the hamlet of Nuiqsut, a relatively new village of 450 people built on the site of an ancient Eskimo settlement. By the early 1960s, many of the Eskimo had been moved off their traditional lands, relocated to Barrow, the northernmost town in the United States. But in 1974, 27 families left Barrow, saying they were going to reclaim their traditional lands at the mouth of the Colville River, near the ruins of old dwellings made of sod and whalebone. Their neighbors shook their heads in amazement, thinking they would surely perish. The Eskimo families spent their first winter living in tents. Then, two years later, the Arctic Slope Regional Corporation, a consortium of the native groups of northern Alaska, donated the money to build the small town at Nuisquit. This year the town is celebrating its twentieth anniversary.

But now ARCO has come to Nuiqsut, looking for help in gaining entry into the reserve. The oil flacks have promised money and jobs. And indeed the people of Nuiqsut would certainly like the money, but fear the cultural and environmental repercussions of an enormous oil field development over which they would have no control.

To transport the crude from the well-heads, the Trans-Alaska Pipeline would be extended from Prudhoe Bay west to the village of Nuiqsut and across the twenty mile-wide delta of the Colville River. From there, smaller feeder lines would branch inland linking up with the drilling sites. With the pipeline and the oil wells will come roads, camps, alcohol and dumps.

For anyone who thinks that a bit of oil drilling would leave scant scars on a virtually uninhabited place the size of Indiana, consider what's already happened on the North Slope. The 500-plus wells in Arctic Alaska produce 840,000 gallons of waste each year. In 1985 and 1986 the Alaska Department of Conservation recorded 953 spills involving oil and other liquids. The contents of more than 250 reserve pits, each filled with 13 million gallons of toxic pollutants, are pumped onto gravel roads or the open tundra. A January 1997 report by the Alaska Forum for Environmental Responsibility disclosed that British Petroleum had been illegally injecting hazardous waste, including oil, solvents, paints, paint thinners, hydraulic fluid, and glycol, into its wells near Endicott Island, one of the most productive oil fields in Alaska. When an oil worker refused to dispose of the waste in this manner, he was chided by his superiors and told that illegal dumping didn't matter because "no one lives on the North Slope anyway."

The pipeline itself has leaked almost from the day the crude began to flow. In 1976, it was learned that one of the Alyeska's contractors had falsified x-rays of faulty welding on much of the pipeline. In 1979, one of those welds broke and more than 235,000 gallons of oil spilled into the Atigun River high in the Brooks Range. Since then, the situation has deteriorated and now the pipeline averages a major incident every ten days. Many of these problems have been brought to the attention of the company and federal officials by Alyeska employees. The oil company's response wasn't to fix the problems, but to go after the whistleblowers.

"In 1990, Alyeska hired a special arm of the Wackenhut Corporation security firm to conduct an industrial espionage campaign, ostensibly to identify and harass the whistleblowers," says Richard Fineberg of the Alaska Forum. "When the pipeline company's espionage escapades came to light, Alyeska issued a public apology and eventually settled lawsuits against six Alaskans who were objects of the spying effort."

From Nuiqsut on a clear day it is possible to see the foul haze of the operations at Prudhoe Bay 60 miles away. The industrial sprawl surrounding Prudhoe Bay is the best reason to keep the oil companies out of the Arctic Reserve. These days Prudhoe Bay is something of a toxic armed encampment, entry to the area is totally controlled by the security forces of the oil companies.

The man assisting in the possible doom of the Reserve intends to visit it this summer. Bruce Babbitt plans to go to Alaska and hike over the 23 million acre reserve. "I want to get out on the ground and I want to look at every square inch of National Petroleum Reserve. My plans now are to fly to Anchorage, change planes for Barrow and then I want to disappear into the NPR for as much time as I need, to understand every geological structure, every lake, every wildlife issue so that I will be prepared to be a meaningful participant in this process." Perhaps, in his extended peregrinations Babbitt will come across the bones of Hale Boggs, the former oil Congressman from Louisiana, whose plane disappeared in the Alaskan outback in 1972. It would be an appropriate discovery. Boggs, after all, navigated the original Alaskan oil bill through Congress as a favor to his friend Edward Patton, the Exxon executive who became the CEO of Alyeska, now represented in Washington by Hale Boggs's son Tommy.

How much oil is buried beneath the tundra? According to explorations in the early 1970s by Navy geologists, the Alaskan reserve may harbor as much as 35 billion barrels worth nearly a trillion dollars if drilled to the last drop. The estimate is almost certainly conservative. ARCO knows more precisely the subterranean wealth at stake, because it has done extensive testing in the area and has just struck a 300-million-barrel oil field on the Reserve's eastern border, near the village of Nuiqsut. In fact, the oil companies have been poaching crude off the Alaskan Reserve for years, siphoning its hidden reserves by slant drilling within the two-mile wide buffers established in 1923 by the Navy. But ARCO—which swallowed up old Harry Sinclair's oil company in 1969, the same year it struck oil in Alaska—says that to divulge what it knows about the oil in this public property would be to reveal proprietary information.

"Some conservationists might be tempted to trade off the largely unknown ecological treasures of National Petroleum Reserve for a delay in the leasing of the Arctic National Wildlife Refuge," Sylvia Ward warns. "But that would be a tragic miscalculation. In Alaska we've come to learn that the oil companies won't stop until they have it all. "

Petrolia/Oregon City, 1997

[Postscript: In the end, the oil companies fared damned well under Clinton. They didn't get into ANWR, but they probably didn't expect to get that prize just yet. In exchange, they won access to the vast Naval Petroleum Reserve, and off-shore leases in the Beaufort Sea and the Gulf of Alaska. These reserves dwarf the amount oil that may (or may not) exist under ANWR.]

Twenty-Seven

Blowing Smoke

Clinton and Kyoto

To all those who expressed a sense of shock and dismay upon learning of the Clinton administration's rollover on global warming, I say: cherish those feelings, because such unvarnished displays of political naivete are so rare in these days of cultured cynicism. Demonstrations of pure outrage, however untutored by Beltway brahmins, indicate that at least some people believe things could be different in this battered Republic.

In case you missed it, in late October of 1998 Bill Clinton, after much consultation with the omnipresent White House pollsters, announced his position on global warming for the International Convention on Climate Change to be held this December in Kyoto, Japan. In a nutshell, the US will argue that global warming shall not stand in the way of economic growth. The icecaps (and Rhode Island) be damned. The US, Clinton confessed, would solemnly renege on its previous pledge to reduce greenhouse gases to 1990 levels by the year 2000. The President decided that the fossil fuel lobby deserved another eight years to get its act together, calling for greenhouse gas emissions to "be stabilized" sometime between 2008 and 2012. The date 2008 is scarcely plucked from thin air, since by then Al Gore will have safely finished his second term (assuming, that is, he's not on parole).

Clinton also expressed his fatigue with the cumbersome pleas made by environmentalists for binding emissions targets, for rules with regulatory teeth and sanctions for violators. Such notions are archaic, the President concluded. In their place, Clinton offers up a Friedmanesque economic contraption, replete with vows of voluntary compliance, tax incentives (what few are left for the loophole-laden energy industry) and a global system of tradable pollution credits. Under this system, companies that close polluting factories in say Illinois or Louisiana could gain credits to construct equally toxic plants in places like Honduras or Indonesia.

As for the recalcitrant posture of China on global warming, the Clinton position displayed an eerie simplicity: we can help the Butchers of Beijing cut their emissions by selling them nuclear power plants. This elegant solution helps our pal Jiang Zemin out of a jam and comes to the rescue of Westinghouse's ailing nuclear division.

In contrast, the European Union proposal calls for a 7.5 percent reduction in carbon dioxide emissions by 2005 and a 15 percent reduction by 2010.

For their part, the fossil fuel industry pumped millions into a tired TV campaign that mimicked the medical lobby's Harry and Louise ads, which broke Hillary's heart four years ago. The themes were achingly familiar: the "theory" of global warming is based on unproven scientific speculations; cutting greenhouse emissions will cost billions of dollars and thousands of jobs; and an international treaty on climate change will represent an unprecedented intrusion of governmental powers into the lives of average Americans.

The real damage was done by one of the craftiest lobbyists on the Hill, Donald Pearlman, a senior partner at the powerhouse firm of Patton, Boggs. Pearlman a former high official in the Reagan Energy and Interior Departments oversees an industry group known as the Climate Council. Pearlman has deftly recruited Third World nations to act as stalking horses for the fossil fuels lobby. In 1996, the Kuwaiti delegation to the Geneva summit delivered a blistering denunciation of a proposed global warming treaty. According to *Der Spiegel*, the delegation's submission to the council was written in Pearlman's handwriting.

There's no debate that the Earth's climate is warming dangerously and inexorably. No scientist whose pockets are bulging with corporate cash disputes the cause: burning of fossil fuels. There's only a kind of ritual quibbling over how fast the change is occurring.

Organized labor, despite pledges of a revived green consciousness, sat on the sidelines for this one. It's not hard to see why, given the enviro-lobby's lethargic efforts to block fast track and other issues dear to working folk. It's too bad, because both issues are inextricably linked. They share the same bottom line of the globalized economy that profits off the export of jobs and pollution.

Nobody even mentions the oil companies any more, although their grip on the economics of our everyday lives is more insidious and concentrated than ever.

The Energy Department is now under the control of Frederico Pena, the man who certified ValuJet as safe to fly.

"Five years ago Bill Clinton and Al Gore accused the Bush White House of being the 'lone holdout' and an 'obstacle to progress' after it refused to support mandatory curbs on greenhouse gases," says Kalee Kreider of Greenpeace. "Now, it is Al Gore and Bill Clinton who are the obstacles."

The retreat on global warming must be put next to Clinton's unconscionable stance on land mines as yet more evidence of the US government's steady degeneration from leader to renegade.

Oregon City, 1998

Twenty-Eight

For Enron Size Does Matter

[Note: I started covering Enron in 1994, when the company was mutating from a natural gas pipeline company to the great new thing, a kind of dot.com of the energy industry. It didn't take much investigation to come to the conclusion that the core of the company was rotting faster than it seemed to be growing. Like Nike, Enron was great at public relations. Its CEO Ken Lay also knew how to play the political game. It showered money everywhere, which not only opened doors but bought wholesale changes in the law. The rise and fall of Enron is really a metaphor for the frenzy of deregulation that occurred during the Clinton administration, all under the mesmerizing mantra of giving consumers more choices. Even though Enron crashed and burned, its executives have walked away unscathed and the deregulatory mindset that helped spur one of the largest financial implosions in corporate history continues unabated.]

When Enron pounced on Portland General Electric in 1997, few ordinary people in Oregon were familiar with the $20 billion Texas company. It was variously described as a natural gas company or an energy wholesaler. This is a potentially dangerous misperception. At the time of the Enron takeover of PGE, a Wall Street analyst observed: "A lot of people don't understand what Enron is. They are a finance company. They're trying to set themselves up as the Salomon Brothers of the energy business."

In fact, Enron is multi-tentacled conglomerate, a Y2K version of the old bandit John D. Rockefeller's Standard Oil Trust. Enron isn't primarily an energy company, its a combine for the cyber generation, with interests in oil and gas fields, nuclear power, coal plants, wind power, solar technology, telecommunications, exotic financial instruments such as temperature futures, billing and metering systems, pipelines, water companies and electric utilities. Enron hedges its bets so that it always ends up on top, more often than not at the expense of its customers and neighbors.

But what is this Texas company and what does it want in Oregon? Enron is run by Ken Lay, a former Nixon aide, with a in-bred loathing for any kind of government regulation that interferes with his company's profit-making instinct. When Lay took over Enron in 1984, he focused the company's operations on what he calls "unregulated markets" and vowed to undermine federal regulation of the gas and electric power industries. Using his intimate ties to politicians such as George Bush, Tom DeLay and Phil Gramm, backed by millions in political contributions, Lay largely accomplished his goals by 1996, with a series of orders deregulating the natural gas and utilities market. Enron quickly capitalized on the new energy environment by doubling its annual sales. It used its new-found wealth to gobble up a variety competitors and prized assets, such as Zond wind systems, Solarex and PGE.

The day-to-day operations of Enron are run by the company's president, Jeffrey Skilling, a man even *Fortune* magazine describes as arrogant. Skilling is a corporate tycoon in the mold of Chainsaw Al Dunlap, who believes that profits should come at the expense of workers. "You must cut jobs ruthlessly by 50 or 60 percent," Skilling thundered last year. "Depopulate. Get rid of people. They gum up the works." And, in fact, Enron has followed this vicious course of action. From 1991 to 1995, Enron's profits and stock price more than doubled. Yet over that same time frame the company slashed more than 10 percent of its jobs.

While Enron's workers were getting laid off, Ken Lay was becoming a multimillionaire. From 1996 through 1997, the CEO made more than $4 million in salary, benefits and bonuses. Even more astounding, he enjoys more than $156 million in Enron stock options. Other Enron benefits have accrued close to home. In 1997, Enron paid $1.9 million in commissions to a travel company owned by Lay's sister, Sharon. In that same year, Enron also bought out a paper products company owned by Lay's son, Mark. Enron paid off more than $1 million in the company's debts, hired Lay's son for a salary of $150,000 a year, plus a $100,000 signing bonus and a guaranteed $100,000 annual bonus, plus 20,000 shares of Enron stock options.

Concern for the environment, human rights and social justice don't rank high on Enron's corporate agenda. Instead, these issues are largely viewed as tiresome impediments to the accumulation of profits. Under Enron's tight-fisted control, don't expect PGE to exhibit much sensitivity to the concerns of low-income consumers, the subject of energy conservation and renewables or the plight of salmon and steelhead.

Instead, it seems increasingly likely that the profits from Enron's ownership of PGE—profits largely guaranteed by its status as a utility—will undoubtedly be re-channeled into the company's burgeoning international operations. Over the past five years, Enron has struck a series of lucrative deals with some of the world's most repressive regimes, including China, Pakistan, Turkey, Guatemala and Indonesia. In India, Enron's security forces have violently suppressed popular protests against the firm's Dabhol power plant, earning the company a stern rebuke from Amnesty International.

While Enron exhibits a profound distaste for government oversight, it always seems to be panhandling for government handouts and tax breaks. Many of its international projects have enjoyed billions of dollars worth of financing from the federally-funded Export-Import Bank and the Overseas Private Investment Corporation. When fiscal conservatives and environmentalists joined together earlier this year in an effort put these two purveyors of global misdeeds out of business, Enron rallied to their defense, arguing that it unless it received federal backing for these projects it would be forced to use German or French labor and technology. So far OPIC and the Ex-Im Bank have survived.

For Enron, as with Godzilla, size does matter. Lay has brashly said he wants to make his company the world's biggest energy conglomerate. The path toward this grandiose vision will be paved on the back of residential customers, government regulations and the environment.

Oregon City, 1998

Twenty-Nine

Old King Coal Still Reigns

It may have been the most revolutionary environmental decision by a federal judge since William Dwyer handed down his first injunction stopping the logging of ancient forests in the Pacific Northwest. On October 20, 2000, federal judge Charles Haden ruled that the industry could not bury its mining waste in valleys containing streams that flow year-round or seasonally. The ruling, which was based on provisions in the Clean Water Act, effectively puts a halt to the latest form of coal mining: mountain-top removal. Mountain top removal mining makes strip mining look like laser-eye surgery by comparison. In this technique, mountains are simply decapitated, the coal extracted and the waste dumped in the nearest valley. Since 1986, more than 470 miles of West Virginia streams have been buried in these "valley fills."

In a plainspoken and tough 48-page ruling, Haden wrote: "When valley fills are permitted in intermittent and perennial streams, they destroy those stream segments. The normal flow and gradient of the stream is now buried under millions of cubic yards of excess spoil waste material, an extremely adverse effect. If there are fish, they cannot migrate. If there is any life form that cannot acclimate to life deep in a rubble pile, it is eliminated. No effect on related environmental values is more adverse than obliteration. Under a valley fill, the water quality of the stream becomes zero. Because there is no stream, there is no water quality." The suit was brought by one of the most tenacious groups in the nation, the West Virginia Highlands Conservancy.

Senator Robert Byrd, the coal mining companies' best friend on the Hill, found the judge's ruling irksome. The senator threw a tantrum on the floor of the Senate and vowed to pin a rider to the Interior bill overturning the judge Haden's injunction. Byrd was backed in this hardball tactic by Sen. Jay Rockefeller, Rep. Nick Rahall and Gov. Cecil Underwood—all Democrats. Underwood's rhetoric was especially heated as he urged Byrd on. "I don't see how you can mine any coal if Haden's decision is upheld," Underwood fumed. "Carried to the extreme, it would virtually shut us down. It will take statutory correction to change it permanently. If the law is changed, the court decision is moot."

Rahall, a vocal critic of gold and silver mining practices in the western states, also attacked Haden's ruling, saying it put West Virginia at competitive disadvantage. "There's some urgency in addressing this issue," said Rahall. "What this decision does, then, is undermine one of the basic tenets of the Surface Mining Control Act, which was to provide a level regulatory playing field among all the states."

"What can be more ironic?" says Jim Sconyners, a mining organizer with the WV chapter of the Sierra Club. "From mining reformer to defender of the worst mining abuses in America. The transformation is breathtaking."

Byrd made calls to George Frampton and the White House and on October 29, Clinton sent word to Byrd that he supported the senator's measure to bail out the coal mining companies and keep tearing apart the mountains in the coal mining states of West Virginia, Kentucky, and, yes, Al Gore's home state of Tennessee.

Kathy Karpan, the head of the Office of Surface Mining (a part of Bruce Babbitt's Interior Department), was quick to leap to the mining industry's defense. Within hours of Haden's ruling, Karpan told the Martinsville *Daily Mail* that she was willing to change the regulations so that they could get around the judge's order and resume blasting the tops off mountains and burying the mining waste in streams. But she noted that other agencies would have to join hers in the effort. "That is on the table, whether the stream buffer zones can stand," Karpan said. "What complicates this is, it's not just an issue for our agency. We have to talk to the EPA and the Corps of Engineers."

Karpan need not worry. On the issue of coal mining, the Clinton administration has put up a united front, in part owing to Al Gore's longstanding ties to the strip miners. And, in fact, the big coal companies have prospered in West Virginia during the Clinton administration. According to a recent report by Jim Truman, a coal market analyst for Hill and Associates, a management consulting firm in Annapolis, Maryland, the state's coal production has increased by 30 million tons since 1992. Moreover, the coal industry has rapidly consolidated. In 1995, the eleven largest companies in the Appalachian coal region (West Virginia, Kentucky, Virginia and Tennessee) produced less than half the coal, with the largest company excavating 25 million tons a year. Just three years later, the top 11 companies produced more than 70 percent of the region's coal, with the three biggest firms hauling out more than 40 million tons each. The frenzy of strip mining has depleted the region's coal reserves, according to Truman. He estimates that at current rates West Virginia's coal supply will be exhausted in about 25 years.

Members of the Citizens Coal Council, an anti-strip mining coalition, went to Washington to air their concerns to Frampton. They asked the head of the Council on Environmental Quality (and Gore's top environmental adviser) why the administration would consider signing the Byrd rider when it had pledged to veto all anti-environmental measures attached to year-end funding bills. Frampton was blunt. He said simply, "We don't consider this an environmental issue." As one of the enviros at the meeting said, "If Clinton and Gore don't consider strip mining an environmental issue, what the hell is?"

Joe Lovett, the Charleston lawyer who argued the case for the Highlands Conservancy, thinks Clinton and Gore will never cross Byrd. "The White House is hedging," Lovett said. "Byrd's rider is a blatant attempt to remove the most important stream protection provisions from the Clean Water Act and the Surface Mining Control Act. But my guess is that Clinton's not going to veto it."

He didn't.

So much for the greatest environmental president since Teddy Roosevelt.

Martinsburg, 2000

Thirty

Enron Has Fallen

In 1997, I wrote a story about the new wave of electric utility deregulation sweeping the United States with the aid of the Clinton
administration and a cadre of neo-liberal environmental outfits. At
the center of the narrative was a Texas natural gas pipeline company that had recently been "liberated" by state and federal regulators
to enter whole hog into the new go-go energy market. I warned that
this particular company symbolized nearly everything that was
wrong about the frenzied rush to deregulate the nation's electric utilities: it was unreliable, profit-obsessed, arrogant, politically-wired,
relentlessly expansionist, brutal to its workers and hostile to the
environment.

A few days after the story hit the streets, I got a call from this
company's vice-president for public relations. He said I'd gotten
them all wrong. They were the good guys, he averred, who would cut
red tape, lower energy prices, move away from nukes, coal and other
environmentally-malign power sources and look out for the poor
during the cold winter months as part of its charitable duty. He
spoke of his company the way Steve Jobs used to talk about Apple
Computer: it was the future, an energy company for the people that
was primed to do battle against corrupt and bloated utilities. He
spoke of new market opportunities in energy futures and even the
weather. "Five years from now we will have revolutionized the energy market," he predicted.

That company, as you've probably guessed, was Enron, now fled
to the financial bomb shelter known as federal bankruptcy court, a
flight that the company's executives had the temerity to blame on its
workers whose pension funds those same executives had destroyed.

Rarely has a company rocketed to such heights and fallen to
rubble so quickly. Enron was once the darling of Wall Street. Now it
represents the largest (at $50 billion in assets) bankruptcy in histo-
ry to date and its executives may face criminal charges for an elaborate cover—up of the company's ruinous financial condition. As a
parting shot, on December 4, Enron summarily fired 4,000 employ-

ees, more than half its workforce. The employees, some of whom were dismissed by pre-recorded telephone calls, were told to expect no more than $4,500 in severance pay, regardless of how long they had worked for the company. This comes on top of the news that those very same Enron workers had seen their life savings turn to dust as the company's 401(k) plan, heavily invested in Enron stock, has proven to be worthless.

Even those workers who saw something coming, when word leaked out about the frailty of the company's finances back in February, couldn't take action to protect their assets. During the boom on Wall Street, 401(k) plans were hailed as a way for working people to get rich. Advocates of Social Security privatization pointed to the soaring value of the 401(k) plans as a justification for turning Social Security over to Wall Street. For a while this seemed to hold some truth, as mutual funds mushroomed during the 90s, many workers envisioned themselves retiring as millionaires. But of course it didn't last. The market has crashed and across the country workers' retirement plans withered. As Paul Krugman noted in his *New York Times* column, if the Clinton/Bush plans to convert Social Security into a defined contribution system are placed into effect: "the fate of Enron's poor employees, victimized by a management team they thought was on their side, may truly be the shape of things to come."

At Enron the situation is even worse than it is for other workers who have seen their retiree funds shrivel in the Wall Street meltdown. Half of the stock in Enron employees' 401(k) retirement plans was Enron stock, contributed as a "company match." This was a business move for Enron. It didn't cost the company anything and they enjoyed generous tax deductions for each contribution to employee retirement accounts. Then when Enron went into its fatal tailspin executives froze the stock in the 401(k) plans during a crucial period, so that Enron workers couldn't take any action to salvage their retirement funds. During that time, the value of Enron's stock plunged from $32 to $9 a share. When a full damage assessment had been made, Enron's employees were distraught and outraged. The company responded by sending in teams of "anger management" counselors.

Enron executives, however, were under no such constraints.

Over the past year, Enron's top executives made over $100 million in profits from insider sales of the company's stock. As the *Oregonian* noted, "at this point employees are better off working with lawyers than grief counselors."

When the feds hit town, the scene inside the company's Houston headquarters was surreal, as workers were ushered out of the 50-story office tower by armed guards and the management of the company was in hiding. "Almost everyone is gone," says Pedro Manrige, a risk manager for the company. "Upper management is not talking. No managing directors are around. Police are on every floor."

Many of the people now snickering at Enron's fate are the same professional soothsayers who only a few years ago were hawking it as the maverick of the new breed of energy traders. The *Oregonian*, for example, which fervently backed the company's takeover of Portland General Electric is now suggesting that Enron executives be held criminally liable for looting the company. "They should turn over every rock," the *Oregonian* editorialized on December 4. "The bottom line is that Enron lied to its employees as surely as it lied to all of its shareholders and government agencies. Enron may be able to throw itself on the mercy of distant New York bankruptcy courts, but it shouldn't be able to slither away from damage it's caused to workers who put their trust in their company."

Of course, the *Oregonian* could have cast a more critical eye on the company when it really counted: three years ago when Enron swaggered into Oregon to gobble up Portland General Electric for a cool $3.2 billion. Instead, the *Oregonian* and the *Wall Street Journal* delicately referred to the deal as a merger, which would be great for PGE's customers and shareholders alike. But this quickly proved to be a wild misnomer. There was no question who the dominant partner is in this relationship, Enron. It's a company that never accepts a subservient role and doesn't tolerate anyone telling it how to behave.

Initially, Wall Street mavens scratched their heads at the merger. What interest would Enron, a global energy giant, have in PGE, a moribund electric utility saddled with a defunct nuclear reactor? The answer came soon enough. Enron's sights weren't on Oregon, but its neighbor to the south, the 31 million residential electric consumers in California, and the high-tech, aerospace and defense factories that make the state one of the world's most power-hungry regions. This is the motherlode for the new energy robber barons. But to enter this lucrative market Enron needed credibility as a power provider. But like an apex corporate predator Enron also had its eyes on PGE's assets, cheap hydro-power that it could sell across the West at huge mark ups, power plants and dams that it could auction off, and a network of transmission lines that led right into the high-priced California market.

As for PGE's problem child, the Trojan nuclear reactor, Enron's acquisitions analysts believed it would prove only a minor irritant. There was a sure-fire solution: stick the ratepayers with a large share of the costs of this misbegotten venture and dump the nuclear waste, and the attendant risk, on the federal government. This was the age-old strategy of privatizing the profits and socializing the costs.

Enron begrudgingly admitted to all this at the time in one of their filings with the Securities Exchange Commission, where Enron's CEO Kenneth Lay confirmed that the acquisition of PGE "has allowed Enron to expand its West Coast power marketing operations and has assisted in establishing entry into retail markets in other parts of the country." In other words, PGE customers are funding Enron's global expansion plans.

But the target was not just California. Enron truly has a global reach. In fact, more than 35 percent of the company's income derived from its international operations, pipelines across the Amazon, oil wells off the coast of Venezuela and Trinidad, power plants in Indonesia, China and India, and natural gas fields in Russia. The guaranteed profits from PGE can be channeled into any of these overseas operations, where Enron expects to make as much as 50 percent of its profits by the year 2002.

Enron has a reputation for getting what it wants and doing whatever it takes to get the job done. In September of 1999, Enron was splashed across the front pages of the British press in a money scandal involving Tony Blair and his Labor Party. It seems Enron has been caught funneling large sums of money to the Labor Party in an attempt to win government support for its planned $2.2 billion takeover of Wessex Water, one of Britain's largest public utilities. The disclosures have blackened the eyes of Blair's party and prompted a government review of the merger and Enron's future business intentions in Britain.

But it is the purchase of PGE that presents a microcosm for how Enron operated on a global scale. The first strategy was to lubricate the political system with generous infusions of campaign cash. Enron is one of the nation's top sponsors of both the Democratic and Republican parties, pouring over $3 million into their coffers since 1989. This investment has yielded the company tremendous rewards, including government-brokered and financed deals worth billions in China, Indonesia, the Philippines and India. In Oregon, Enron lavished contributions on the state's congressional delegation, supporting both Gordon Smith and Ron Wyden. Neither senator uttered a critical peep about the Texas takeover of Portland's electric utility.

The second tactic was to buy off the potential opposition, preferably as cheaply as possible. In Enron's power deals in India this took the form of political bribery. The PGE deal was a fairly straightforward operation. Enron pledged $20 million to local charities and promised to contribute an additional $10 million to Oregon environmental groups and conservation projects, effectively muting any uncomfortable questions about how the Texas company planned to deal with such homegrown issues as salmon conservation and low-cost electricity. It also formed a cozy relationship with Ralph Cavanagh, the energy expert at NRDC, who testified in favor of the company before the Public Utilities Commission hearings on the merger.

When philanthropic disbursements don't quell all the critics, Enron didn't hesitate to reveal its dark side. The company has a well-earned reputation as one of the most aggressive in the energy business. "They play with steel elbows," one bruised competitor said. In Oregon, Enron wasted no time in going after the Public Utilities Commission when the PUC had the temerity to question the public benefits of the merger. The energy conglomerate rushed to the Oregon legislature, promoting a bill that would eviscerate the PUC's regulatory power. Ultimately, the PUC buckled under the pressure and approved the deal.

Soon the true price tag of Enron's takeover of PGE began to be seen: as deals were cut to ensure that the lowest electric rates went to largest and most wasteful consumers of power, the pulp mills and aluminum plants. Meanwhile, some of PGE's most prized assets were auctioned off to the highest bidder, with the ratepayers being expected to make up any losses. For the residential consumer and the salmon, the honeymoon for the ignominious marriage between PGE and Enron was over years ago.

There was some relief amid the gloom in Portland on December 4 after it was learned that Enron had not included PGE in its bankruptcy filings. That didn't last long. The next day it was learned that Enron had used the utility as collateral for a $1.5 billion loan it had submitted for approval to the bankruptcy judge Arthur Goldberg.

"Now we have the prospect of them selling PGE off piecemeal," says Larry Tuttle, director of Citizens for Environmental Equity, one of the few groups to fight the PGE/Enron merger. "Who will bear the brunt of the clean up of the Trojan nuclear reactor? Will it even be covered? In what manner? Obviously, criminal and civil proceedings against Enron executives. But they can't stop there. They need to investigate of PGE executives, too. Sometime in the last couple of years they had to know the true financial condition of Enron. The fact they didn't use their due diligence to inform PUC or their consumers of the fragile nature of company and the fact that it was being looted by its top executives is a criminal act."

Portland, 2000

Thirty-One

Whistling in the Dark

The first planned blackouts since World War II. Classrooms in the dark. Computers crashing. Medical equipment in private houses and nursing homes put at risk. Traffic signals on the blink. Outrageous fuel bills, triple the normal rate and rising. Price gouging by independent suppliers. Political fingerpointing. And a mounting feeling of impotence and outrage among residential consumers. Welcome to California and the wild west of the deregulated power grid.

The California power crisis is not an aberration and shouldn't be surprising. It is, in fact, the logical outcome of the kind of deregulation that the state enacted four years ago, at the behest of utilities, big power consumers, financial houses, and even some environmental groups.

Many predicted just this scenario and were ridiculed as doomsters. Nettie Hoge, from the utility watchdog group TURN, warned that the deregulation bill would lead to "unregulated oligopoly power," soaring prices, increased pollution and unreliable supplies. Backers of the bill dismissed such claims out of hand, proclaiming that the forces of the free market would be entirely virtuous, leading to cheaper electricity, greater consumer choice and better service.

When a coalition of consumer and environmental groups, led by consumer lawyer Harvey Rosenfeld, TURN, California PIRG, the Sierra Club and Friends of the Earth, launched a ballot initiate in 1998 (Proposition 9) to undo some of the damage, the utilities spent more than $30 million to defeat the measure.

Now even Governor Gray Davis is saying the deregulation was a mistake. But he's going soft on the real culprits: California's big private utilities. Instead, Davis is pointing his the finger at "out of state suppliers" who are gouging California ratepayers. True enough. But only in part. To capitalize on California's travails, independent power producers have jacked up the price, sometimes holding the juice hostage. The average spot price over the past year has been about 15 cents per kilowatt hour. But in December and January that price has catapulted, with Southern California Edison making one power buy at $1.50 per kilowatt hour.

Even so, California has been fortunate. The Clinton administration ordered the Bonneville Power Administration, which operates hydroelectric dams on the Columbia and Snake River systems in the Pacific Northwest, to sell cheap power to the state, averting an initial round of blackouts. But this power diversion can't last long. For one thing, it's been a dry winter in Oregon and Washington, with only 40 percent of normal precipitation. For another, the releases of water needed to generate power for Californians have a higher purpose: providing flows needed for runs of endangered salmon.

When the BPA reached its limit on January 18, the lights went off in northern California. Now, with California sucking power from every available sector, the entire western power grid may be at risk. Already, the price of electricity in neighboring states is on the rise, primarily due to California's straits. In Oregon, electric prices are expected to increase as much as 30 percent over the next year.

Predictably, the utilities are clamoring for another bailout and the California general assembly and Governor Davis have been more than willing to come to their rescue. The credit ratings of the state's two dominant power companies, Southern California Edison and PG & E, have been downgraded by Moody's to the level of junk bonds. Southern California Edison was poised to default on a $215 million debt to the California Power Exchange Corporation, until the Federal Energy Regulatory Commission intervened. The utilities both claim they are on the very of bankruptcy, victims, they claim, of the very deregulation legislation they spent millions to force into law. The FERC also came to the rescue of PG & E, shielding the company's profitable subsidiaries from any bankruptcy action. Now, the State of California wants to buy power on long-term contracts and sell it to the utilities at a subsidized rate.

But again all is not as it appears. As Harvey Rosenfeld, president of the Foundation for Taxpayer and Consumer Rights, said: "Whenever they've got a gun to your head, it's a bad time to cut deals." Rosenfeld has threatened to sue to halt any bailout for the utilities.

These utilities already huckstered their way into a $28 billion ratepayer financed bailout for their misguided investments in nuclear power plants as part of the 1996 deregulation bill. And they used that money to create a maze of subsidiaries allowing them to build and operate power plants across the country, from which they have made a handsome profit. A new report by the Critical Mass Energy Program, part of Ralph Nader's Public Citizen, shows that both Southern California Edison and PG & E have gone on a spending spree in the past few months, doling out more than $20 billion for out-of-state power plants, at the very time they are poor-mouthing Californians.

Nader's group believes that instead of bailing out the utilities, the state should seize these assets. "California got into this mess by writing deregulation's rules on terms dictated by the power companies," says Wenonah Hauter, director of the Critical Mass Energy Program. "Consumers helped pay for those billion dollar investments under deregulation, so these assets—not taxpayer funded credit guarantees—must be the first line of defense against deregulation's failure."

Of course, all of this plays right into the hands of the gang of oil barons now in control of the White House and the Congress. Listen to Senator Frank Murkowski, chair of the Senate energy committee, a fanatical proponent of deregulation. "Before there is going to be meaningful corrections, the California consumer has to feel the hit," said Murkowski. "That hasn't occurred yet." Murkowski dismissed the blackouts as merely an "inconvenience."

His associate, Sen. Pete Dominici, of New Mexico, took a similar line, saying that California needs to be taught a lesson. What lesson? That it's reluctance to build new coal and nuclear power plants because of environmental concerns was foolhardy. "They've got to change their 'we don't want any power plants attitude.'"

Notice once again how the victim is being blamed: the residential consumer. Not the power companies. Not the big industries.

You can see where Murkowski's going. He wants to use the issue of an energy shortage to press his fondest dream: opening up the Arctic National Wildlife Refuge to oil drilling. And he won't stop there. Murkowski would also like to see the Pacific Coast opened to oil and gas rigs as well.

The nuclear power industry is also licking its chops. Since the early 1980s, the nuclear industry has been on its death bed, struggling to maintain expensive and unreliable reactors and accumulating mounds of radioactive waste. But the power crunch and the spike in prices has given the nukes a second chance.

The dirty secret of this whole affair is that several environmental outfits must shoulder much of the blame for the mess that now confronts Californians. The Energy Foundation, Environmental Defense Fund, Planning and Conservation League and, most notably, the Natural Resources Defense Council have all to varying degrees backed energy deregulation and opposed attempts to regulate utilities, such as Proposition 9.

These groups represent a new breed of environmentalists, which have embraced market-oriented solutions to environmental problems. In essence, they want to use pricing as a weapon to bludgeon consumers into adopting conservation measures. The scarcer the resource, the higher the price. The higher the price, the less people will be inclined to use it. (Except, of course, for the wealthy.)

In the energy sector, this is called Demand Side Management, or DSM. NRDC's Ralph Cavanagh is the main guru of this scheme. He has become a darling of the think-tank world and the utilities' favorite enviro. (One of NRDC's founders is John Bryson, currently CEO of Southern California Edison.)

Cavanagh denounced Proposition 9's attempts to rein the utilities and cap their rates as "an invitation to vote yourself a 10 cent hotdog." This is typical of the free-market environmentalists' cavalier attitude toward consumers.

But if NRDC is nonplussed about the plight of residential consumers, they've been more than willing to help the big utilities in their hours of need. Cavanagh has been canoodling with the utilities for more than a decade. In 1989, he was the impresario behind the California Collaborative, a secret pow-wow between utility executives and like-minded environmentalists to find a compromise on energy-efficiency issues. Cavanagh later admitted that "collaborative" was a poor choice of words, because, he said, "collaboration still has overtones of Vichy, France."

But collaborator is a precise descriptor of Cavanagh's unrepentant dealmaking with big business: where he has endorsed mergers between corporations such as Enron and Portland General Electric and ratepayer bailouts of failed nuclear plants. "I've never seen anyone give away so much and get so little in return," said Lennie Goldberg, a lobbyist with TURN.

Californians are starting to wake up. A recent *Los Angeles Times* poll showed that more than two-thirds of Californians believe that energy deregulation was a mistake and they favor re-regulation by a 2-1 margin.

In the long run, there are only two solutions to the power crisis: public ownership of the electric power sector (such as is the case in Sacramento) and unplugging from the grid entirely by going solar. In the meantime, here's an idea: the next time you receive a utility bill mail it off to NRDC and ask them to pick up the tab: 71 Stevenson St., #1825, San Francisco, CA 94105.

San Francisco, 2001

Thirty-Two

The Big Prize

(with Alexander Cockburn)

W hen it comes to oil politics and Alaska the Bush administration and the environmental movement are already treading the measures of a familiar dance. President Bush is insisting on the urgency of drilling for oil in the Arctic National Wildlife Refuge. He points to a supposed oil shortage that has somehow darkened homes and businesses up and down the West Coast. The environmental movement is already ramping up its national mail campaign rallying supporters for the battle to save the Refuge.

The actual game is bigger and more sinister.

Let's start by disposing of some myths. Start with the ludicrous claim of the Bush crowd that California's energy crisis can be solved by oil drilling in Alaska. Nationwide, oil provides only three percent of the source fuel used to generate electricity. In California, the figure is less than one percent.

Bush grandly offered California exemptions from its supposedly onerous clean air rules, claiming that once freed from such red tape the state's power producers could build a new generation of plants powered by fossil fuels. The Refuge's oil won't be much help here, since the US Geological Survey Office estimates that, even on an expedited schedule, oil won't flow from the Refuge until the year 2015.

Nor is the oil companies' problem in Alaska a shortage. Recall that back in 1995, British Petroleum, ARCO and Chevron entreated President Clinton to cancel the 20-year ban on export of crude oil from Alaska to other countries. Congress had made such a ban a precondition of permitting the construction of the Alaska pipeline. The intent of the ban was to ensure Alaska's oil would help stave off any shortage of oil on the West Coast of the US. The oil companies wanted the ban lifted because they had a glut on their hands and required new markets.

Clinton readily assented and the oil companies began exporting Alaska crude oil forthwith to Japan, South Korea and China. The extremes to which they went in using Clinton's waiver to bilk American consumers came to light a few weeks ago when The *Oregonian* newspaper won a Freedom of Information Act lawsuit, gaining access to 4,000 pages of documents in the Federal Trade Commission's files concerning the merger of BP-Amoco with ARCO.

An FTC economist had concluded that BP-Amoco was selling oil to Asian refineries at prices lower than it could sell to US refineries on the West Coast, in order to manufacture a US shortage. As evidence the FTC had e-mail traffic passing between BP managers who talked about "shorting the WC [West Coast] market" in order to "leverage up" the prices there. Another BP manager called this scheme a "no brainer." The FTC reckoned that this ploy allowed BP to hike prices at West Coast pumps by as much as three cents a gallon.

So the oil companies' strategy is to exploit the electricity crisis to seize at last a number of long-sought objectives: not just access to the Arctic National Wildlife Reserve, which would be a great symbolic victory, but also tax breaks worth billions for oil and gas extraction from wells across the country.

Just to take Alaska, such tax breaks would mean that the oil companies could start pumping oil out of the West Sak field, near Prudhoe Bay, estimated to contain as much oil (though more viscous and sandy) as Prudhoe Bay itself. The oil companies are also pushing for a reduction in their royalty payments for oil and gas extracted from public lands.

The big prize for the oil companies in North America isn't the Refuge, but sites off the Alaskan coast and the Gulf of Mexico: "Deepwater," says Jeff Kieburtz of Solomon, Smith Barney, "is where the real, pure exploration is going in this country." Here we come to one of the lesser known legacies of the Clinton era. Under the encouragement of Bruce Babbitt's Interior Department, deepwater drilling operations more than doubled in the Gulf of Mexico in the year 2000 alone.

Among those roaring their protests at this activity is Gov. Jeb Bush of Florida who, three days after his brother's inauguration, implored the new team to place a moratorium on deepwater wells in the eastern Gulf of Mexico, saying that "Florida's economy is based on tourism and other activities that depend on a clean and healthy environment."

Right now the Interior Department is looking at 668 lease applications that piled up in the Clinton years for new offshore oil development, from the Gulf of Alaska, to the Copper River Delta (perhaps the greatest remaining salmon fishery in the world), to Cook inlet (flanked by the Katmai National Park and the Kenai peninsula) to Bristol Bay, to the Chukchi Sea up by Point Hope, to the Beaufort Sea.

In other words, the entire coast of Alaska is in play. Small wonder that Gov. Tony Knowles of Alaska boasted to the press at the start of January that it is his hope to make Alaska "a one-stop shopping" site for America's energy needs.

At the national level the big environmental groups are focussed entirely on the Arctic National Wildlife Refuge, which is indeed in peril. But they would be advised to learn the history of that very refuge. It was originally set aside in 1957 by President Dwight D. Eisenhower. In the same package, Ike's Interior Secretary, Fred Seaton, opened up 20 million acres of Arctic coastline to oil development.

In Alaska there are local groups, from the Gwich'in trying to save the Refuge and the National Petroleum Reserve west of Prudhoe Bay, to the Inupiat Eskimos seeking to defend their whale hunting grounds against oil derricks in the Beaufort Sea to the Northern Alaska Environmental Center in Fairbanks taking on the oil companies' grand plan. They understand the stakes more clearly than the national green groups, with the laudable exception of Greenpeace.

As for the Wilderness Society, National Audubon Society and the others, rapt in their fixation on the Refuge, they seem to be ceding without a fight the rest of the Alaska coast, the Gulf of Mexico and maybe even the Rocky Mountain front. Just listen to Deborah L. Williams, executive director of the lavishly funded Alaska Conservation Foundation. She recently journeyed to the Refuge with Lesley Stahl of CBS's 60 Minutes and vowed that not one oil rig would ever rise on the plains of the Refuge.

But at the same time Williams told the *New York Times* that she supports oil drilling in the National Petroleum Reserve which is eight times as large and just as pristine as the Refuge, because "I drive a car and use petroleum products and we all have to responsible and balanced." Williams, it should be added, was working for Bruce Babbitt at the Interior Department as his Alaska specialist when he okayed test drilling in that very part of the Alaskan tundra.

Petrolia/Portland, 2001

Thirty-Three

Atomic Trains
in a Post-9/11 World

For years environmentalists have warned that shipping high-level nuclear waste across the country on rails or highways was a program fraught with peril. They pointed to the near certainty that eventually a train would derail or a truck would crash, spilling radioactive material into streams, fields or cities. They warned that the US was embarking on a path that would inevitably led to "a kind of mobile Chernobyl." They even pointed to the possibility that the nuke trains made an inviting target for terrorists, who could turn the locomotives into a high-speed radioactive weapon that could be derailed in the heart of several of the nation's largest cities, putting the lives of millions at risk.

These concerns were dismissed as the ravings of anti-nuke Cassandras by the Department of Energy and, to a large extent, the national press corps. Indeed, the atomic boosters had become so confident of their scheme that they were poised to greenlight the largest rail shipment of nuclear waste in US history for a 2,000 mile journey from New York to Idaho. Then came 9/11 and suddenly the anti-nuke organizers didn't seem so hysterical after all.

The Department of Energy's nuke train plan came to a grinding halt, marking yet another salutary reappraisal of US environmental policy following the terrorist attacks of September 11. The atomic waste train was scheduled to carry 125 highly radioactive nuclear fuel assemblies from West Valley, New York through ten states to Idaho. The move has now been postponed until at least April 1, 2002.

"Actions speak louder than words, so although DOE will not admit it publicly, it's clear the West Valley shipment was suspended due to terrorism and security concerns," said Kevin Kamps of Nuclear Information & Resource Service (NIRS). "We're relieved DOE has recognized the extreme danger this proposed shipment would have created and chose instead to suspend the shipment. But the threat such shipments pose is not going to go away in a few months. Proposals for shipping tens of thousands of high-level radioactive waste containers by train and truck through 43 States past the homes of 50 million Americans to national dumpsites in Utah and Nevada must be re-examined in light of the potential for terrorist attacks."

The twin 20 foot-long, dumbbell-shaped metallic atomic waste containers were scheduled to leave DOE's West Valley Demonstration Project near Buffalo as early as mid-September. But due to concerns about additional potential terrorist attacks, Energy Secretary Spencer Abraham suspended DOE nuclear waste and materials shipments the day after 9/11, capitulating to concerns that environmentalists and anti-nuke groups had been raising for years.

Even so the DOE's suspensions were only temporary. By the end of September, the Department began raising the possibility that the West Valley shipment might still roll by Halloween. Because metal gaskets on the two containers have not been certified for cold weather conditions, DOE had agreed to deliver the shipment to its Idaho National Engineering and Environmental Laboratory no later than October 31 in order to avoid encountering freezing temperatures.

Then on October 7, the DOE reinstituted its suspension of nuclear waste shipments, citing concerns of potential reprisal attacks in response to the initiation of US military action in Afghanistan that day. Despite this, DOE's West Valley site director Alice Williams told the *Buffalo News* on October 16 that the nuclear train might still roll by the end of the month despite on-going national terrorist threats. However, the very next day, orders were sent to Williams from DOE headquarters in Washington explicitly suspending the shipment until next spring, according to an October 19 *Buffalo News* article. The two containers will now be off-loaded from the on-site railcars, where they sat outdoors since May, and will spend the winter inside the West Valley facility.

"Energy Secretary Abraham's decision to halt this high-level nuclear waste shipment, not once, not twice, but three times clearly shows that the Energy Department itself acknowledges atomic waste trains like this one are potential terrorist targets," said Tim Rinne, State Coordinator of Nebraskans for Peace.

"Attorney General John Ashcroft and the FBI have warned

about additional terrorist attacks. Trucking firms and railroads have been put on highest alert against attacks upon hazardous and radiological shipments. Recently, airports around the Three Mile Island nuclear plant were shut down due to a terrorist threat. The DOE shipment ban should be extended indefinitely, and expanded to cover commercial high-level nuclear waste shipments as well," said Kay Drey of the Missouri Coalition for the Environment.

Despite the current shipment ban, Energy Secretary Abraham appears ready to approve the national high-level atomic waste dumpsite targeted at Yucca Mountain, Nevada. DOE closed its public comment period on the Yucca proposal October 19, and has announced Abraham will make his recommendation to President Bush by the end of the year or early next year.

In recent days, the US Nuclear Regulatory Commission publicly announced its "concurrence" with DOE's Yucca Mountain siting guidelines, and in recent weeks finalized its own Yucca licensing regulations. At the same time, the NRC is reviewing a nuclear power industry license application to "temporarily store" all currently-existing irradiated fuel at the Skull Valley Goshute Indian reservation in Utah, which would launch 200 high-level atomic waste trains per year throughout the country as early as 2004.

"It is hypocritical for DOE to put the brakes on the West Valley shipment while rushing ahead to give its thumbs up to Yucca Mountain," said Dave Ritter, policy analyst at Public Citizen's Critical Mass Energy and Environment Program. "Approval of the Yucca Mountain repository proposal would launch tens of thousands of high-level atomic waste trucks and trains onto our roads and rails. Inadequately addressing potential terrorist threats to such shipments is rash, irresponsible, and reckless."

DOE studies show that 50 million Americans in 45 states live within a half mile of projected highway and train routes to Yucca Mountain.

Critics also point to an August 27, 1998 letter written by Abraham, then a US Senator from Michigan, to then-Energy Secretary Bill Richardson regarding plutonium shipments. In the letter, Abraham wrote "I am sure you will agree that the ramifications of an accident are too serious to consider anything less than the very best emergency response preparedness."

"Just as police and firefighters were on the front line of the 9/11 attacks, so would emergency responders be called upon to protect our communities in the event of an atomic waste transport accident or terrorist attack upon a shipment," said Chris Williams, executive director of Citizens Action Coalition of Indiana. "They need to be thoroughly trained and well equipped to deal with radiation emergencies, and not caught off-guard as our government agencies have been by the bio-terrorism attacks."

Greens want the NRC to address terrorist threats to atomic waste transport containers. Commercial high-level atomic waste shipments, such as those to Carolina Power and Light's Shearon Harris reactor storage pools in North Carolina, have continued to roll despite the DOE ban.

In a September 21 response to the September 11 terrorist attacks, the Nuclear Regulatory Commission admitted that "the capacity of shipping casks to withstand such a [large aircraft] crash has not been analyzed."

In June 1999 the State of Nevada filed a "Petition for Rulemaking" to the NRC, charging that safeguards against terrorist attacks on high-level radioactive waste shipments were woefully inadequate or non-existent. Nine state governments and the Western Governors Association endorsed the petition. Despite officially agreeing to act on the petition in September 1999, the NRC has yet to do so.

"Large scale movement of radioactive waste on the roads and rails would create tens of thousands of potential targets, in virtually any scenario a terrorist might choose, whether major metropolitan areas, suburbs, or the agricultural heartland, near schools, hospitals, or water supplies," said Corey Conn of Illinois-based Nuclear Energy Information Service.

Portland, 2002

Thirty-Four

From "Senator Lunkhead" to Energy Czar

A Year in the Life of Spencer Abraham

When Spencer Abraham toiled as the junior senator from Michigan, he wanted desperately to do away with the Department of Energy, a federal outpost that the Republicans have railed against since its creation under Jimmy Carter. In his six years in the senate, he never missed a chance to vote to abolish the department and to accuse its administrators and employees of an hysterical range of misdeeds, from treason (Wen Ho Lee) to using the banner of environmentalism as a cover for bringing about a new age of solar socialism. Abraham was trounced in his 2000 senate reelection bid and, rightfully thinking that his prospects for employment in the private sector might be bleak, he faxed his frail resume (highlighting his stint as part of Dan Quayle's brain trust) to the Bush transition team—meaning, as in all other matters of import, Dick Cheney. When word came that Bush and Cheney were set to offer Abraham the post as the nation's energy czar, Abraham reportedly threw something of a tantrum. Apparently, he had his heart set on the slot at the Department of Transportation, where, no doubt, he believed he could do some major league damage for the captains of industry in Detroit and Dallas.

But time heals all wounds. Now that he finds himself in charge of the DOE, Abraham seems to have become entranced by its political utility. The Energy Department, Abraham soon discovered, was not some green bunker plotting the solar conquest of the energy market. No. It was a clearinghouse for the oil and nuke industry, a kind of federally-endowed lobby, which occasionally dispensed token handouts to the energy conservation crowd. In recent years those tokens have gotten smaller and smaller.

Let's review Abraham's first year directing the energy policy of Big Oil's newest favorite administration (recall that the last one wasn't all that bad for the likes of ARCO and Chevron). At the top of the list is the ceaseless maneuvering to break open the Arctic National Wildlife Refuge to exploration and drilling. The Refuge (only the pro-drilling claque insists on calling it ANWR, which sounds frightfully like an oil company moniker) sits on the arctic tundra in the northeastern corner of Alaska. Long a prize of the oil lobby, the Refuge is the last unsullied swath of coastline in the American arctic, home to polar bear, wolves, caribou, salmon, raptor nesting colonies and the Gwich'in tribe.

Even though by bureaucratic right the Arctic Refuge is part of Interior Secretary Gale Norton's empire, Spence Abraham made the transfer of the wildlife refuge to the oil industry the top priority on his energy agenda. Upon reflection, it wasn't a particularly smart move, even if higher-ups like Cheney were telling Abraham to go for it.

But Spence isn't the brightest bulb in the Bush cabinet. Indeed, during his tenure in the senate Abraham was known by senate staffers—the biggest gossips on the Hill—as being jovial but clueless. One Republican senate staffer told *CounterPunch* they referred to Abraham as "Senator Lunkhead"—that's a certain kind of distinction in a chamber populated with the likes of Rick Santorum and Sam Brownback.

Drilling in the Arctic Refuge is a battle that Abraham simply can't win. And mightier men than he have tried, from James Schlesinger (the first energy secretary under Carter, now a pimp for Big Oil) to the arch-villain himself, James Watt. It's the third rail of environmental politics, the Death Star for Big Oil's deepest desires. The Big Green groups are likely to capitulate on everything from the Everglades (witness the recent sell-out by National Audubon Society on Jeb Bush's developer-friendly plan) and Superfund to ancient forests and the Endangered Species Act. But they will not relent on the Arctic Refuge. Why? Easy: it's the biggest fundraiser they've ever come across and they'll fight to the death to keep it. (That also means, of course, that many of these green groups want the Refuge to remain perpetually at risk of development.)

Last week in a desperate attempt to secure enough votes to

override a senate filibuster of the bill to open the refuge, Abraham played the Iraq card, alleging that Saddam Hussein's threat to cut off oil sales to Israel's allies necessitated opening the refuge to Exxon and Chevron. Of course, Abraham didn't explain Saddam's threats would have the slightest impact on US oil supplies, which have maintained an embargo against Iraqi crude since the Gulf War. Even former CIA head and Iraq hawk James Woolsey didn't buy that one. "The bottom line is that we'll be dependent on the Middle East as long as we are dependent on oil," said Woolsey, who served as Director of the Central Intelligence Agency from 1993 to 1995. "Drilling in ANWR is not a recipe for America's national security. The only answer is to use substantially less petroleum."

But Abraham wasn't through. He had a bad hand, but he was determined to play all his cards anyway. The secretary hatched a scheme with Senator Frank Murkowski to lure the votes of Democratic senators by proposing to add a bailout for steelworkers to the energy bill. While the measure may have attracted the attention of some Dems from the steelbelt, it foundered when conservative Republicans condemned it as a boondoggle for big labor. After six years in the senate, you'd have thought that Abraham would have at least learned to check these kinds of vote swaps over with Trent Lott first and not simply take the word of Murkowski, who is deranged on the subject of oil drilling in the Arctic.

Earlier this week Abraham's department came up with another stupid idea: blame it on the Indians. The DOE launched a despicable attack on the Gwich'in, the Arctic tribe that has opposed drilling in ANWR out of concern for the impacts on fish and wildlife, particularly caribou, that they depend on for sustenance. Abraham dredged up a 20-year old exploration arrangement on the Venetie Reservation outside the small town of Arctic Village, signed off on by some tribal members. The exploration site was not in caribou habitat and proved to be lacking in oil reserves, but Abraham went out of his way to portray the impoverished tribe as a band of duplicitous hypocrites in the press, as if hypocrisy were a moral defect unknown to Big Oil.

For their part, the Gwich'in remain undeterred. The Refuge is a centerpiece of their spiritual cosmology, revered as "the sacred place where life begins."

"We depend on the caribou, as Gwich'in people, for food, clothing, medicine, tools and spirituality," says Sandra Newman, a council member for the Vuntut Gwich'in First Nation. "And in return, the caribou depend on us to take care of the land for them so they can continue to be free."

It was all for nothing. On Thursday April 18, the pro-drilling forces fell 14 votes short of invoking cloture. But true to his nature, Abraham vows to fight on.

At the same time Abraham was bashing the Gwich'in, he was going to bat for the big boys in Detroit, helping to defeat once again new fuel efficiency standards for American automobiles. Under the rosiest scenario, the oil reserves under the Arctic Refuge will yield roughly 3.2 billion barrels. And it would take 10 years for that oil to reach the pump, and even when production peaks—in 2027—the refuge would produce less than two percent of the oil Americans are projected to use. By contrast, Detroit automakers have the technology right now to boost fuel economy standards to at least 40 miles per gallon. By phasing in that standard by 2012 the nation could save 15 times more oil than the Arctic Refuge is likely to produce over 50 years.

When tougher fuel efficiency standards came up for a vote before the senate in mid-March, Abraham was there to denounce the measure and lobby senators to defeat the package. He was so persuasive that fourteen Democrats jumped over to his side, including Baucus-MT, Bayh-IN, Breaux-LA, Byrd-WV, Carper-DE, Cleland-GA, Conrad-ND, Dorgan-ND, Feingold-WI, Kohl-WI, Levin-MI, Lincoln-AR, Mikulski-MD, Miller-GA, Nelson-NE, and Stabenow-MI. (Nearly all of these Democrats were certified as good greens by the League of Conservation Voters and the Sierra Club's political action committee.)

Then there's Abraham's cozy relationship with Enron, a bond forged during his senate term that continues to this very day despite the company's leprous reputation. Even after the Enron scandal blew up, the DOE and the State Department have continued to go to bat for the energy conglomerate, particularly on the issue of the Dabhol natural gas plant in Maharashtra State, India. This monstrosity was neither needed nor wanted by the Indian people, but came about through a combination of bribes and arm-twisting, led by Frank

Wisner, Jr. (son of the famous CIA official and suicide) who served as Ambassador to India under Clinton and then made a bee-line for Enron's board. When the plant predictably went under, Enron begin desperately badgering the Indian government to cover its estimated $200 million in loses. Cheney and Abraham were recruited to do the shattered company's bidding. And they did, even as India was being recruited as a fellow traveler in Bush's war on terror. To its credit, the Indian government told the Bushies to take a hike.

But the defense of Big Oil is never done, a loss for one is a loss for all. Thus, a couple of weeks ago, the Bush team was still going to bat for Enron, as the State Department and the DOE warned the Indian government once again that its failure to "live up to its contractual agreements" on the Dabhol plant might limit future investments in the nation by US energy firms. A prospect that the Indian people (if not the government) must be greeting with a sigh of relief.

[By the way, just how phoney was Enron? This nugget gives a pretty good idea. It seems that the company ran a mock trading floor in its Houston headquarters, complete with desks, flat-panel computer displays and teleconference rooms. The idea was to fool visitors and prospective investors into believing that Enron traded commodities full-time, in a kind of 24/7 frenzy. In fact, the equipment was only hooked up internally, and the employee-"traders," who appeared to be frantically placing orders, were merely talking to each other—no doubt about how they could unload the soon-to-be-worthless Enron shares clogging up their 401(k) plans.]

On the nuclear front there's Yucca Mountain, the austere stretch of Mojave desert 100 miles north of Las Vegas where the DOE and its masters in the nuclear industry want to dump the radioactive waste that is piling up relentlessly at the nation's commercial nuclear reactors. During the 2000 campaign, Bush pledged to Nevada voters that he would hold firm against any attempt to make Yucca Mountain the nation's nuke waste dump.

That promise certainly helped Bush win a tight race in Nevada and (along with the Supreme Court) the White House. But it turns out that Bush was just kidding. Within weeks of taking office, the leaders of the nuclear industry were given free access to the White House and the DOE and quickly went about writing a game plan for seizing Yucca Mountain. Anyone who'd taken the time to look at where the nuke industry's political money was flowing couldn't have been surprised at Bush's political pirouette.

A new report by Public Citizen spells it out pretty clearly. The nuclear industry contributed $82,728 to Abraham during the 2000 election cycle, when he was a US senator, and spent even more money lobbying on issues dear to the industry's bottom line, including the ill-conceived nuclear waste dump proposal. In 2000 alone, leading nuclear energy interests that helped bankroll Abraham's unsuccessful Senate campaign spent more than $25 million to hire some of the highest-powered lobbyists in Washington, DC, including top officials from the Reagan and Clinton administrations, records show. Eight of the lobbying firms hired made *Fortune* magazine's recent list of the 20 most influential firms in Washington.

But the nuke industry didn't stop there. They also spent more than $25 million lobbying congress and federal agencies on the matter—that's about a half-million a week, every week of the year. The nuclear industry flooded Washington with a strike force of lobbyists, totaling more than 53 different lobbying firms, for a combined total of 199 individual lobbyists. This doesn't include the in-house lobbyists working for utilities and other nuclear industries.

And these were no run-of-the-mill K-Street lobbyists. Nearly half of the lobbyists hired by Abraham's top nuclear contributors previously worked for the federal government. The roster includes seven former members of Congress; former acting Energy Secretary Elizabeth Moler, who also was former chair of the Federal Energy Regulatory Commission; Gregory Simon, the chief domestic advisor to former Vice President Al Gore; Haley Barbour, political affairs director in the Reagan White House and former chair of the Republican National Committee; and James Curtis, who served on the Nuclear Regulatory Commission.

These people can work political magic. For example, Abraham and Homeland Security head Tom Ridge came to the remarkable conclusion that shipping high-level nuclear waste across the nation by rail and truck presents no special terrorism risk. No wonder Ridge doesn't want to answer any questions during his appearances before congressional committees.

Of course, Ridge does have a point. Terrorism probably isn't the biggest concern when it comes to hauling all that radioactive waste across country. It's much more likely that an American city will be nuked by accident when one of the atomic trains derails and spills its lethal cargo into rivers and neighborhoods and onto streets. In fact, it's a statistical certainty.

Remember, as my friend David Vest points out, this scheme to ship nuclear waste by rail from every corner of the country to the Nevada outback is being pushed by many of the same people who threw a fit over busing kids a few blocks to improve educational opportunities for urban students. And, by and large, they are the same cadre of politicians who want to pull the plug on Amtrak as a burdensome federal subsidy.

Then there's the Bush/Abraham/Cheney energy plan, the creation of which has been the subject of brutal litigation between the White House, the General Accounting Office and environmental groups. Two recently released documents give an idea of how closely the Bush energy plan followed the industry's script:

A March 20, 2001 email from the American Petroleum Institute to an Energy Department official provided a draft Executive Order on energy. Two months later, President Bush issued Executive Order 13211, which is nearly identical in structure and impact to the API draft, and nearly verbatim in a key section.

In March 2001, a Southern Company lobbyist emailed a DOE official suggesting "another issue" for inclusion in the energy plan: so-called reform of the Clean Air Act and related enforcement actions. The suggestion was incorporated into the energy plan, launching the Administration's controversial effort to weaken the Clean Air Act and retreat from high-profile enforcement actions against the nation's largest polluters, including the Southern Company.

While Abraham, Cheney and the other Bush bigwigs huddled repeatedly over a period of months with the energy elite, environmentalists were largely locked out. Abraham himself met with more than 100 representatives from the energy industry and trade associations from late January to May 17, 2001, when the task force released its report. But when enviros, lead by the corporate-friendly Environmental Defense Fund, asked for a meeting with Abraham, his scheduler, Kathy Holloway, stiff-armed them, saying that Abraham was too busy for a face-to-face.

One of the DOE documents released by order of a federal court on April 10, 2002, shows that the Energy task force gave one of its staff members 48 hours to contact 11 environmental groups to obtain their policy recommendations. The environmental groups were given 24 hours to provide written comments. Another DOE memo notes that staffers should endeavor to closely scrutinize the greens' comments and "recommend some we might like to support that are consistent with the Administration energy statements to date." There was a final blow. In order to print up the oil/nuke energy plan, Abraham chose not to waste a cent from his multi-billion dollar drilling budget. Instead, he plundered $135,615 from the DOE's mothballed solar, renewables and energy conservation budget to produce 10,000 copies of the White House energy plan released in May 2002. The solar funds were even raided to pay for the Administration's energy lobbyist Andrew Lundquist's air ticket to Alaska to strategize on drilling in the Arctic Refuge.

But Abraham's going to have to find a new printing account next year, because those funds probably won't be around much longer. The energy plan that the solar funds financed the printing of calls for slashing the renewable energy program by more than 50 percent. Maybe old Spence has a sense of irony after all.

Portland, October 2002

Thirty-Five

Shafts of Death

Remember the Quecreek coal mine disaster in Pennsylvania in the summer of 2002? It left nine miners trapped 300 feet underground in rushing, frigid waters for more than three days. Bush rushed from his Crawford Ranch for a photo op with the rescued miners in Somerset County, Pennsylvania looking for a repeat of his performance at Ground Zero, the crowning moment of his presidency. "What took place here in Pennsylvania really represents the best of our country, what I call the spirit of America," Bush proclaimed. Then he sped off to a $1.5 million dollar Republican fundraiser in Philadelphia.

What took place in Quecreek was no "accident," merely lethal normalcy, business-as-usual for the industry in the coal fields of Appalachia, where mine-and-run corporations send their workers down to extract every last yard of from dwindling coal seams.

The Black Wolf Mining Company, a non-union operation, tried to pin the blame for the disaster on bad maps provided by the state of Pennsylvania, which led the mining crew to drill into the adjacent Saxman mine, abandoned in the 1950s and filled with 60 million gallons of water, which sluiced at 60 miles per hour into the Quecreek mine.

But that excuse won't wash. For one thing, officials at the company and federal regulators at the Mine Safety and Health Administration had been aware since at least 1999 that those maps were dangerously inaccurate. And in the days leading up to the disaster, the miners themselves had warned the company.

"The mine was wet from the very beginning," says Ronald Hileman, one of the rescued miners. Hileman testified to senate investigators that the crew boss had told executives at the mining company about the bad condition at least twice before the collapse.

Black Wolf has been described in the press as a struggling local company. This is nonsense. It's part of the coal industry's echo to Enron's structure, a series of shell-corporations and subsidiaries designed to maximize profits for the partners and shield them from liability.

Black Wolf, which has only been around for a year and has already racked up 21 serious safety violations, operates the mine. It's run by David Rebuck, an executive at Mincorp, an international mining conglomerate. Mincorp owns PBS Coal, which has operated in Pennsylvania for decades. PBS Coal controls Quecreek Mining, which owns the mine. Quecreek subcontracts the operations of the mine to Black Wolf. The parent company, Mincorp, is a spinoff from the British coal giant, Burnett and Hallamshire, once the darling of international financiers. It went belly-up in an Enron-style accounting scandal in the late 1980s.

The mining company's executives didn't even call the miners after they were pulled from the pit. Instead, they whined to the press that liabilities from the catastrophe might force them into bankruptcy unless they could find a way to cut costs.

Cost-cutting in mining means injury or death for the men down the shaft. The miners well knew Bush's plans to slash safety funding by more than six percent, most of it coming from the coal mine enforcement division. The man Bush picked to head the Mine Safety and Health Administration, David Lauriski, is a long-time coal industry executive and lobbyist.

Shortly after taking office, Lauriski bragged to a group of coal industry executives that his regulatory agenda "is quite a bit shorter than some past agendas." Indeed, death warrants usually tend towards brevity. Part of Lauriski's abbreviated agenda is to reduce the number times a mining company has to sample coal dust levels inside the tunnels, a move that is certain to increase incidence of black lung disease. And yes, Lauriski wants to get rid of the chest X-ray program that tests miners for black lung disease.

Lauriski also wants to slash the number of mine inspectors by 25 percent, even though the lack of inspections may have been partially responsible for the Quecreek disaster. Under current guidelines, the MSHA is required to inspect mines at least four times a year. But an investigation by a Pittsburgh television station revealed that it had been more than a year since federal inspectors had visited the Quecreek mine.

In addition to Lauriski, Bush also tapped Stan Suboleski for a seat on the Mine Safety and Health Review Commission. Suboleski is an executive with the A.C. Massey Coal Company which, according to the United Mineworkers, has one of the worst safety records in the industry. Massey is also the company responsible for the annihilation of more than 70 miles of streams in eastern Kentucky, when 300 million gallons of coal sludge spilled from one of its mines. It was the worst ecological disaster in the US since the Exxon Valdez oil spill.

The planned dismantling of the MSHA comes at a time when coal-mining deaths are on the rise, 132 since 1999. In the early part of the century, more than 1,000 miners a year perished in the shafts. A US soldier during World War I had a better statistical chance of surviving the year than did a miner in the coal mines of West Virginia. Unions and mine safety laws turned things around.

But now the tide seems to be sliding back, abetted by an administration that is hostile to workers, unions and mining regulations. In September 2001, 13 miners lost their lives in a coal mine explosion in Brookwood, Alabama. In the preceding months, federal mine inspectors had cited the mining company 31 times for safety violations, including citations for accumulations of free-floating coal dust that may have led to the fatal explosion. The feds issued warnings, but never took action against the company, following the Bush administration's script of voluntary compliance.

The United Mine Workers say the latest trend in the industry is to import low-wage workers from Latin America to work the tunnels of Kentucky and West Virginia, workers who don't join unions and who can't read maps, assuming these have any relation to reality.

Portland, 2002

Thirty-Six

A Shock to the System

Blackouts Happen

"The Dark Ages: They haven't ended yet."
Kurt Vonnegut, Jr.

The most shocking thing about the reaction to the power outage that darkened the Northeast on August 14, 2003 (aside from the spasm of self-congratulatory mewling of New Yorkers for surviving a whole 16 hours without electricity, as Baghdad enters its powerless fifth month) is that people were shocked that the lights went out.

Let's face it, blackouts happen. There's nothing new about that. Even New York City, whose citizens seem to think they are immune from such unsettling intrusions of reality, goes dark with the regularity of the arrival of locusts. That's the nature of the gridded power system.

Of course, some things *have* changed. The intervals between system crashes are getting more frequent and the outages themselves more prolonged. And the explanations are becoming more convoluted. When they bother to explain at all.

We are days after the latest big event and no one really knows what happened. That's because no one's actually in charge of the chaotic system that shuttles power to half of the nation. Welcome to the world of laissez-faire electricity. Follow the blinking hand.

Here's all we really need to know: something tripped. The current in the Erie Loop jolted backwards, feeding on itself in an act of electric cannibalism. It's an apt metaphor for the nation's electric system. So get used to it. Oh, yeah, and open your checkbook.

Some of us have been down this road before.

Much of the West went dark in August of 1996—though New Yorkers may have missed the great event. There seems to have been a news blackout on that power outage, which presaged the great California outages of 2002. It's too bad the press didn't look more closely at the causes of the 1996 blackout, which hit more than two million homes, because that meltdown in the power grid revealed the profound defects lurking in the system and how those inherent problems were exacerbated by the deregulatory frenzy of the 1990s.

You can see why the press bypassed the issue. Stories on utilities are about as exciting as a root canal. They are difficult to write and even more demanding on the readers, who are more inclined to wade through a story on genocide in Eritrea than to try to make sense of the political economy of the US electric power system. All in all, it's easier to keep people in the dark about such matters.

Plus, in the go-go 1990s electricity deregulation seemed to be the great bipartisan project, promising consumer choice, lower rates and the opportunity to plug in to greener energy. Even environmental groups, such as EDF and NRDC, went along for the ride hawking the virtues of freewheeling companies such as Enron over the public utilities, which were portrayed as palsied dinosaurs in an era of brawny dot.coms.

On the national political scene, Ralph Nader stood nearly alone in warning about the impending tragedy of jettisoning the system of regulatory mechanisms that had held the power companies in check for the past half-century in favor of a scheme that resembled a Vegas casino game. But with Clinton and NRDC backing the deregulatory mania, Nader was easily dismissed as a grumpy doomsayer.

Of course, in hindsight handing over the electrical power system to companies that have the moral sensibility of telemarketers and derivatives traders and then freeing them from most government oversight doesn't seem like the brightest idea.

When George Bush finally interrupted his swing of California fundraisers to enlighten us on the crisis, he described the Northeast blackouts as a "wake up call." For once he's right. But he was somewhat less forthcoming on precisely what are we waking up to. Namely, an ever dimmer future of blackouts, brownouts and rising electric rates. It's a scenario that Bush and his cronies helped broker. Pay more, get less. That's the cruel equation of deregulation.

Ironically, Bush has been helped somewhat by the skidding economy. With many factories idled, the demand for power has been relatively low since 2002. If the economy ever rouses itself from the doldrums, the nation's frail power system will be taxed even more and rolling blackouts may become a regular feature of American life, like those taunting tapes from Saddam Hussein and Osama bin Laden.

But at root this isn't a problem of demand. In fact, there's an overcapacity of electricity. When the lights went back on in the Northeast, they did so without one kilowatt coming from a nuclear power plant. All 21 had been shut down. Let's keep them that way.

No, it's not an energy crisis we face, but a crisis of accountability. Regulated monopolies were overthrown in the 1990s and replaced by unregulated monopolies who would much rather stuff their profits into dividends and gaudy executive bonuses than sink them into long-term investments in an aging transmission grid.

In his brief speech, Bush, who mistakenly referred to the Northeast event as a "rolling blackout," also pointed to the anachronistic grid as a problem. "We'll have time to look at it and determine whether or not our grid needs to be modernized," mumbled Bush. "I happen to think it does, and have said so all along."

Hold on, Mr. President.

Far from always saying the electric grid needs to be modernized, in June of 2001 our amnesiac leader threatened to veto a bill in congress that would have appropriated $350 million to upgrade the transmission grid. However, Bush didn't have to resort to the veto. The Republican-controlled House of Representatives voted the measure down twice, largely along party lines.

Bush delicately avoided any mention of the probable culprit in the grid crash: FirstEnergy, the Ohio-based utility. Bush's discretion is understandable. After all, on June 30 FirstEnergy's CEO, H. Peter Burg, hosted a fundraiser for Bush that netted his campaign more than $600,000. The featured speaker at the event was none other than Dick Cheney. The company's chief operating officer, Anthony J. Alexander, is also an old pal. Indeed, he was one of Bush's famous "Pioneers." He contributed $100,000 of his own to the 2000 Bush campaign and raised at least another $100,000. Other executives at FirstEnergy have contributed more than $50,000 to the Bush reelection bid. That kind of money may not talk, but it sure buys silence.

So now we know. The system has shorted out and there's no simple fix. Indeed, there may be no fix at all. And, more intriguingly, there's no political mechanism to demand or oversee an upgrade of system that nearly everyone agrees is broken. That's because the electric power safety net, erected after the power company scandals of the 1920s, was giddily cut loose during Clintontime. Like welfare, once the regulatory framework is dismantled it's gone for good. Score another one for Bill.

Today, there are scarcely any rules to follow and compliance with the few guidelines that remain is merely voluntary. There are no penalties levied when things go terribly awry. There's not even anyone to levy the fines. In many cities, public utility commissions, which once acted to restrain the baser instincts of electric utilities, have been abolished or simply stripped of all authority. Many of the power companies are now located far out of state. In Montana, electric power is delivered by a company headquartered in Philadelphia. In Portland, Oregon, power was provided by a bankrupt company from Houston, Texas, lately looted by its own executives: Enron. And on and on it goes.

The electrical system of post-regulatory America is a Hobbesian morass of open markets, emasculated regulators and predatory corporations who are supposed to be providing a basic human service but act as if they only owe allegiance to the bottom line.

Across much of America (though, perhaps, not midtown Manhattan), blackouts are a regular pre-planned event, courtesy of the electric companies. In the deregulated environment, low-income families have little recourse when the bills pile up and you have to choose between paying the water bill, the doctor bill or the power bill. A 2002 report by Dr. Meg Powers estimates that more than 27 million low-income families in America face electricity shut-offs every year. Imagine being laid off in Bush's wrecked economy and having to place your family at the beneficence of Enron, ConEd or Duke Power.

Instead of punishing the private power generators and utilities, Spencer Abraham, Bush's goofy Secretary of Energy, wants to penalize the customers who were hurt most by the blackout and the failed promises of cheaper rates made by the zealots of deregulation. "The grid's got to be upgraded and the consumers are going to have to be willing to pay for it," warned Abraham.

When it comes to energy policy, compassionate conservatism means keeping the public in the dark until they pony up the money to put the power companies in the black.

Portland, August 2003

PART V

On Native Ground

Thirty-Seven

Showdown at Big Mountain

In 1979, Katherine Smith, a Navajo grandmother, confronted tribal police and Bureau of Indian Affairs fencing crews near her hogan with a shotgun. She fired a blast over their heads. This was the first shot in a resistance to the forced relocation of some 12,000 Navajo from their traditional lands on Big Mountain in northern Arizona. "The federal government took me to prison because I wouldn't relocate," Smith said. "But I will go to prison again if they try to take me from my land."

And, in fact, that fate is precisely what more than 200 other Navajo families now face, after two decades of resistance to forced eviction. The whole affair has been played in the press as a century-old land dispute between the Navajo and the Hopi, dating back to 1882 when President Grover Cleveland created a 1.5 million joint-use area on borders of the Hopi and Navajo reservations. The truth is somewhat different.

Back in 1863, when they were being exterminated by Kit Carson and his US Army units, the Hopi invited the Navajo refugees up to the sanctuary of Big Mountain and the two tribes lived amicably together from that time to the late 1960s. "It's not a Navajo-Hopi land dispute," says Rose Helliger, a Navajo. "We were more interdependent than enemies. This is about multinationals pushing native peoples off their lands to make a profit. Why do they have to relocate us? The coal."

The coal in question lies on Black Mesa, a hundred square mile seam of low sulfur coal that is the richest deposit in North America. In fact, coal and oil had been discovered on these Indian lands in the late-nineteenth century by US government surveyors, but the ardent desires of mining and oil companies to extract the treasure was thwarted by the Navajo's initial refusal to lease the land and by the fact that the Hopi culture did not recognize a central government authority.

Enter John Boyden, a Mormon attorney from Salt Lake City operating on behalf of the companies chasing the coal. Boyden ingratiated himself with Hopis, offering to be their attorney for little compensation. He soon concocted a "Hopi Tribal Council" consisting of pro-mining leaders from only three of the twelve Hopi villages. Even so, no similar Navajo group could be whistled up to join with Boyden's Hopi front in selling out to the energy companies.

So in 1962, Boyden got his Hopis to file a suit demanding that the federal government concede that the Hopis had equal rights to the coal deposits under Navajo-controlled lands on Black Mesa. The suit prevailed. In 1966, Boyden led the Hopis to sign leases to the coal on Black Mesa to Peabody Coal Company. The Navajo Tribal Council, not wanting to be left out, quickly endorsed similar deals. It soon emerged that Boyden was operating not only on behalf of the Indians, but also as a hired agent of Peabody Coal.

The leader of the traditional Hopis, Thomas Banyacka, vigorously opposed the leases and tried to stop them through the courts, but he soon found out how ingenious Boyden had been in constructing his pseudo-tribal government. Banyacka, the acknowledged Hopi leader, found he had no legal standing to sue.

Boyden then pressed forward with a strategy practiced by British colonialists and by the Romans before them: divide and rule. In order to consolidate the mineral wealth for the coal companies, Boyden wanted to partition the joint-use lands on Big Mountain occupied by both Hopi and Navajo. To further this aim, he needed a reluctant Congress to pass a law realigning the reservation boundaries. Boyden hired a PR firm, Evans & Associates, to concoct a scenario of perennial Hopi-Navajo enmity. The firm produced films and feature stories successfully planted in *Life* magazine, buttressing the theme that the only way to prevent an internecine range war was to divide the land between the tribes.

Boyden's strategy was successful. In 1974, Congress passed the Navajo-Hopi Land Settlement Act, spitting the 1.8 million acres between the two tribes. Any member of either tribe caught on the wrong side of the new line was forced to pick up stakes and move across. There were about a hundred Hopi on what was now Navajo land, and no less than 12,000 Navajo on lands now officially Hopi. Coincidentally, the Hopi side contained most of the known coal reserves. The language of the bill was largely written by Boyden.

What followed was the most savage compulsory relocation

since the removal to internment camps of Japanese-Americans during the Second World War.

As an inducement for the Navajo to relocate speedily, the law passed by Congress required an immediate 90 percent reduction in livestock grazing on lands now assigned to the Hopi, a devastating financial blow to these pastoralist families. Hopi tribal police were given the right to impound Navajo sheep caught grazing out of designated areas. Navajo families were offered $5,000 to abandon their hogans and move to government-built tract housing on the periphery of the reservation. Several thousand Navajo took this offer. Many ended up on the so-called "new Navajo lands" along the Rio Puerco, near Sanders, Arizona. The property, near an abandoned Kerr-McGee mine, had been recently given to the Navajo by the feds, but the soil was contaminated by the largest uranium spill ever to have occurred in the United States.

Many of the relocated Navajo were ill-equipped to make a go of things in an urban economy. The $5,000 was soon spent and many lost their homes. These relocated Navajo now suffer from shockingly higher rates of unemployment, alcoholism, and suicide than other Navajo. "The situation is worse than apartheid," says Bruce Ellison, an attorney for the Navajo resisters. "It's government sanctioned ethnic cleansing."

In 1991, traditional Navajos brought a lawsuit against the US government, challenging the relocation on religious grounds. The suit, known as *Manybeads v. the United States*, prevailed, forcing the Feds, Navajo and Hopi into a court-ordered mediation on the future of the joint-use lands. In early 1993, the outlines of a preliminary settlement emerged, whereby Navajo families not already evicted would be allowed to stay on Big Mountain. In exchange, the Hopi would be given 450,000 acres of nearby federal lands, including the San Francisco Peaks, a range of extinct volcanoes sacred to the Hopi and now part of the Coconino National Forest north of Flagstaff.

This proposal was swiftly shot down by three powerful interests: the Sierra Club, which refused to tolerate the notion of national forest land being returned to its original stewards; the family of Bruce Babbitt, owners of the CO Bar Ranch, one of the largest livestock operations in northern Arizona, which did not want to lose its grazing rights; and of course Peabody Coal, whose every move is being plotted by Boyden's successor, no a less a power than Washington super-lobbyist Tommy Boggs, Jr.

The suit brought by Manybeads was thrown back to the federal mediator, a judge from the Ninth Circuit Court of Appeals who advised the plaintiffs that they had better accept reality, that resistance was futile and might only lead to "another Waco."

The mid-1970s saw coal mining on Navajo and Hopi lands accelerate to full-tilt, with the 200 Navajo families still clinging on to their ancestral homes harassed by the Hopi Rangers, the uniformed bully-boys of the Hopi Tribal Police, also by the Bureau of Indian Affairs, and by goons from Wackenhut, the security firm hired to patrol Black Mesa by Peabody Coal Company. By the early 1980s, the war on the Navajo prompted no less a military strategist than President Ronald Reagan to declare that under his authority National Guardsmen and US Marshals could smash the Navajo resistance and complete the relocation of the hold-out families in no less than thirty minutes.

Despite such fire-breathing declamations and the belief of Reagan's Interior Secretary James Watt that all Indian reservations represented socialism by stealth, Reagan did little. Neither did the Bush regime. The Navajo families stayed put while their relocated brothers and sisters pined away amid misery and social dislocation in pre-fab towns of Tuba City and Sanders.

As Clinton campaigned his way through 1992, he raised Navajo hopes. The Arkansas governor held much-publicized meetings with leaders from Indian Country, including Navajo tribal president Peterson Zah. In 1993, the Clinton White House issued a flurry of executive orders on protection of Native American sacred sites, environmental justice and civil rights matters. There seemed to be an encouraging move to take some of the responsibilities on environmental issues from the hated Bureau of Indian Affairs and give them to the EPA. Perhaps most promising was the appointment of an Indian leader, Ada Deer, as Assistant Secretary of Interior for Indian Affairs.

Such hopes were soon dashed. On August 5, 1993, the federal mediator in the Hopi/Navajo dispute, Judge Harold McCue, ordered the resisting Navajo families to agree to a settlement, either relocating to the Navajo reservation or signing a restrictive 75-year lease that would give nothing more than squatters rights on the land that had been theirs for generations. The families speedily rejected the proposal, thus prompting McCue to exclaim that another Waco might be in the offing, in which the Navajo would encounter the same fate as David Koresh and the Branch Davidians.

The Hopi Tribal Council, ever in the pocket of Peabody Coal, demanded that the Bureau of Indian Affairs put the squeeze on the Navajo families. The Clinton administration responded with cruelly coercive tactics. With winter approaching, Hopi Rangers and BIA agents began confiscating the Navajos' stacks of firewood, along with their axes and saws. The agents claimed that the firewood had been illegally cut without permits from the Hopi Tribe and the BIA. They demolished all new Navajo construction projects, including barns, corrals, and additions to existing homes. In November of 1993, the BIA began daily raids, rounding up all the free-range Navajo livestock they could find, mostly sheep. The agency increased the release fee imposed on the Navajo to recover their animals tenfold, from $100 to $1,000 for each haul.

This federal policy signed off on by Secretary of the Interior (and Arizona rancher) Bruce Babbitt, soon bankrupted more than a dozen Navajo families. In a letter to Zah, Ada Deer claimed that the livestock raids were merely part of a nationwide crackdown to protect grazing resources. Deer asserted that the feds had no intention of specifically targeting the Navajo pastoralists. As for the outrageous increase in impoundment penalties, Deer said "It is part of a similar policy for assessing livestock impoundment fees that is followed throughout Indian country by the Bureau."

But a few weeks later, attorneys at the Justice Department's solicitor's office admitted in open court that the crack-down was designed to pressure the Navajo families to abandon their fight. This disclosure prompted the often demure and cautious Navajo Tribal Council to unwonted anger. Peterson Zah wrote a furious letter to Ada Deer: "I often feel that your advisors are unable to understand the human and Navajo side of this dispute, and a recommendation to 'turn up the heat' on the families in order to get them to make more concessions is a fundamental misreading of what will be necessary to win the trust and the assent of these families. Unfortunately, the stepped up enforcement is having exactly the opposite effect and has deepened the families' suspicions that the purpose of the United States' participation in the mediation is to have Navajo families forcibly evicted from their homes." Zah's letter had little effect on the federal harassment campaign.

All the while, the mining on Black Mesa continues apace, in one of the ugliest forms of extraction in an industry not known for ecological delicacy. Peabody Coal is owned by the English conglomerate Hanson PLC, which bought the mining company in 1990 from Boeing and Bechtel. Peabody operates two large mining sites on the reservation, the Kayenta mine and the Black Mesa mine. Seven million tons of coal are gouged out of the Kayenta deposit each year. The coal is hauled by an electric railroad to a coal-fired generating plant at Page, Arizona, overlooking Glen Canyon. The Black Mesa mine yields five million tons of coal a year which is sluiced through a 300-mile pipeline in a slurry mix of coal and water. The water is drawn from the now rapidly shrinking Navajo aquifer. More than 50 springs in this desert area have vanished. Peabody dismisses any concerns remarking in a company publicity statement that the 1.3 billion gallons of water pumped out a year is a "teaspoon from a bucket."

The degradation of the area is not merely a matter of aquifer depletion. Over the past fifteen years there have been numerous poisonings and die-offs among Navajo livestock drinking water from springs and wells near the mines. Tests show that the water had been contaminated with high levels of lead, arsenic and copper. The company has also been cited for illegal dumping and for leaky underground storage tanks. The constant shroud of coal dust on the mesa has proven a health hazard for livestock and people. One of the big problems has been the effects of blasting, with the shock waves leveling Navajo hogans.

When Peabody won its coal leases, the company was given an exemption from the Antiquities Act, allowing it to mine on burial grounds. The only proviso is that a medicine man should be brought in to perform a perfunctory ceremony in the general area of the land to be excavated. 1993 was a particularly horrifying year for the Navajo, in which no less than four burial grounds were mined. "The remains of our ancestors are being dug up and shipped to the place where they burn the coal," says Louise Benally of the Navajo Dineh Nation.

All the problems at the coal mines prompted the resisters in the Navajo Dineh Nation to file an administrative suit alleging Peabody had violated federal mining laws. The Indians got no help from local environmentalists. Leaders of the northern Arizona Sierra Club Chapter said the events on Black Mesa "were not an environmental concern." Even so, the Dineh Nation prevailed, when the judge ruled that Peabody's mine and its slurry pipeline (which is co-owned by natural gas giant Enron) violated the National Environmental Policy Act and the Surface Mining Control Act. Frustrated by this unusual setback, the US Attorney in the case, Jon Johnson, turned to the Navajo elders mustered in the courtroom for the final hearing and said, "I guess its time for the C-4 and the automatic weapons." Peabody Coal and the Clinton administration rushed to federal court were the ruling was duly overturned on a technicality.

With the Navajo hold-outs still displaying unbending resistance, the Clinton administration propelled a law through Congress last November requiring that the Navajo families agree to the mediated settlement by April 1 of this year. The legislation also took care to exempt the settlement from compliance with the Native American Religious Freedom Act.

So now the Navajo families face a brutal choice: they can either move to wretched circumstances in Tuba City and Sanders. Or they can sign the lease, whose terms translate as enforced relocation by another route. The ongoing aim of the quisling Hopi Tribal Council is to open Big Mountain to Peabody Coal. The tribal council has already developed maps showing where the strip-mining will occur. The terms of the 75-year leases are designed to be untenable. The Navajo families must agree to limit their activities to within 13 acres of their existing homes sites and to confine their livestock to designated grazing areas, the classic enclosure technique to evict herders. They cannot live away from their home sites for more than two years, on penalty of losing them. They cannot sublease their home or operate any kind of business from it. The most tell-tale proviso is that the Navajo must renounce any claim on sacred sites in the area and they are prohibited from burying their dead on the land where they lived for so long, a stipulation which strikes at the very core of Navajo custom.

The Navajo families fight on notwithstanding, and deserve all

the support that can be mustered. "Our way has no word for relocation," says Roberta Blackgoat, a Navajo leader of the resistance. "It
means the same as death. To go away from your home and to never
come back."

Financial support for the Navajo families on Big Mountain can
be sent to the Sovereign Dineh Nation, PO Box 1042, Hotevilla,
AZ 86030.

Kayenta, Arizona, 1997

[Update August 2003: The situation on Big Mountain continues to
deteriorate. Families have been forcibly evicted. Hogans have been
bulldozed. Livestock has been impounded. Meanwhile, the operations of Peabody Coal continue to gouge mammoth holes in the
heart of Black Mesa, the coal dust darkens the skies for miles. The
UN Commission for Human Rights was called in to investigate
abuses in the forced relocation. All to little avail. In April of 2002,
Roberta Blackgoat, who lived her entire life on Big Mountain, died.
In one of her last messages to the supporters of the Navajo families
on Black Mountain she wrote: "My ancestors sat here and there and
there and there. We don't know how thick the soil is with their (our
ancestors) bones are, so the land is out of the ancestors turned to
soil. We don't know how many centuries they have been sent by the
great spirit here. So that's why I can't leave this ancestral land. Their
graveyard is our roots."]

Thirty-Eight

Star Whores

Astronomers & the Vatican vs. Apaches on Big Seated Mountain

We waited for a night when the moon was obscured by clouds. It sounded like a silly plan here in the heart of the Arizona desert, where Oregonians stream each year to worship the unrelenting sun.

But the wait was only two days. Then the sky clouded up, just as the Apaches predicted. These weren't rain clouds, just a smoke-blue skein, thin as morning fog, but dense enough to dull the moonlight and shield our passage across forbidden ground.

We were going to see the scopes. The mountain was under lockdown. Armed guards, rented by the University of Arizona, blocked passage up the new road and patrolled the alpine forest on the crest of Mount Graham. Only certified astronomers and construction workers were permitted entry. And university donors. And Vatican priests.

But not environmentalists. And not Apaches. Not at night, anyway. Not any more.

Yet, here we were, skulking through strange moss-draped stands of fir and spruce, displaced relics from a boreal world, our eyes peeled for white domes and trigger-happy cops.

It says something about the new nature of this mountain, this sky island, that we heard the telescopes before we saw them, a steady buzz like the whine of a table saw down the block.

The tail-lights of SUVs streamed through the trees, packing astronomers and their cohorts towards the giant machine eyes, on a road plastered over the secret middens of the mountain's most famous native: the Mount Graham red squirrel.

The tiny squirrel was once thought to be extinct. In 1966, federal biologists said that they had found no evidence of the squirrel in the Pinaleno Range (the strange mountains of which Mount

Graham forms the largest peak) since 1958. Then five years later a biologist working in the shaggy forests at the tip of the mountain found evidence of at least four squirrels. A wider survey showed an isolated population on the mountain's peak. In 1987, the squirrel finally made the list as an endangered species.

Still, the squirrel population fluctuates wildly from year to year, in cycles largely tied to the annual pine cone crop. But these days the population spikes rarely top 500 animals on the entire planet— which for them constitutes the upper flanks of Mount Graham, the same swath of forest claimed by the astronomers. But the trendlines for the squirrels all point down: down and out. And the astronomers just keep coming. And so do the clearcuts. The new campsites. The unnatural fires. Extinction looms.

We edged along the road, under the cover of a beauty-strip of fir trees, until we came to a fence, tipped with razored wire, and beyond it a clearing slashed into the forest. And there before us crouched one of the mechanical space-eyes, set within a white cube, sterile as a hospital. The structure is so cold and lifeless that it could have sprung from the pen of Richard Meier, the corporate architect responsible for the dreadful Getty Museum blasted onto the crest of the Santa Monica mountains outside LA.

My guide calls himself Vittorio. "That's Vittorio with a 't'," he says. "Like the Italian director." But he calls himself Vittorio in honor of the great Apache leader Victorio. He was 19 when I met him in the mid-90s, hip deep in snow, at a place called Enola Hill in the Cascade Mountains fifty miles or so from Portland. Enola Hill is a sacred site for many of the tribes of the Pacific Northwest—a bulge of basalt covered with Douglas fir, where from a narrow thrust of rock you can look up a fog-draped canyon to Spirit Horse Falls and beyond to the white pyramid of Mount Hood.

Enola Hill has been a vision quest site for centuries. But the Forest Service, despite brittle platitudes from Bill Clinton about his sensitivities to native peoples, schemed to blast a road through the heart of the hill and clearcut it to the bone.

Vittorio haunted the forests of Enola Hill for weeks, along with a few dozen other Indian activists and environmentalists, bracing themselves in front of dozers, cops and chainsaws. Some were hauled off to jail; others, like Vittorio, faded into the forest, to fight another day. But eventually, the Forest Service had its way. The logging roads went in and the trees came down. But the experience brought us together. It is a friendship sealed in sorrow and anger. And humor, too. Vittorio, who studied art at UCLA on what he calls "a guilt and pity scholarship," is not a grim person. He has a wicked sense of humor and an unerring eye for beauty.

Vittorio mainly grew up in east LA. His mother died young in a car crash with a drunk driver outside Safford, Arizona when he was five. Vittorio was in the car and he still bares a scar, a purple semi-colon hanging above his left eye. He was taken in by his grand-mother, a Mexican-American. For a time she cleaned the house of Jeff Chandler, the cross-dressing actor who once played Cochise.

Vittorio's father is a San Carlos Apache from Tucson. He went off to Vietnam, came back shattered in his head, and addicted to smack. It wasn't long before he ran into trouble. He is now parked in the bowels of Pelican Bay, the bleak panopticon-like prison in northern California, another victim of the state's merciless three-strikes law.

"My old man was born with two strikes," Vittorio said. "Just like the rest of us. But after Vietnam, he couldn't run and hide anymore."

That's been the fate of too many Apaches since whites invaded their lands: chased, hunted, tortured, killed, starved and confined. And then blamed for the misery that had been done to them. The Apaches have been relentlessly demonized, perhaps more viciously than any other tribe. Here's how General John Pope described them in 1880: "a miserable, brutal race, cruel, deceitful and wholly irreclaimable." This description, of course, bears little relation to the Apache, but is a fairly apt portrait of their tormentors.

But that's how they were treated, as irreclaimable subhumans, even after they agreed to submit to life on the reservations. Young Apache men were forced to wear numbered badges, just like the Jews of Nazi Germany. Minor violations of arbitrary rules, such as the ban on drinking Tizwin, an Apache homebrew, meant exile to Leavenworth, often a death sentence. Apaches weren't recognized as citizens until 1924. They were prohibited from practicing their religion until 1934 and couldn't vote until 1948.

But still they resist and their resistance earns them even more rebukes from authorities and locals yahoos. Until the 1960s, it wasn't uncommon to see signs outside stores, diners and bars throughout southern Arizona saying: "No Dogs or Apaches Allowed." Now, ain't that American?

In the hip-deep snow on Enola Hill, Vittorio told me this story about his namesake, the great Chihenne Chief, Victorio. "Victorio was revered by his band and by most other Apaches," Vittorio said. "When he was gravely wounded by federal troops during a raid on his camp in the Black Range, the soldiers called on the Chihenne women to surrender, probably so they could be raped and then sent to their deaths. The women shouted back their refusal and vowed to eat Victorio's corpse should he die, so that no white man would see his body or abuse it."

At the time, the Mexican government had put out a $50 bounty for each Apache scalp and offered the then grand sum of $2,500 for the head of Victorio. The Apache leader survived the battle of the Black Range, but was eventually tracked down, ambushed and killed in the mountains of Chihuahua.

* * *

In the spring of 2002, Vittorio invited me to Arizona to tour the San Carlos Reservation and make a covert visit to the Mount Graham telescopes. At the time, the University of Arizona was in the midst of constructing the $87 million Large Binocular Telescope, billed as the largest optical telescope on Earth.

That's right, $87 million. Put this outlandish figure in perspective. That's double the entire annual income of all Apaches in Arizona. The astronomers and priests have never experienced anything approaching life on the San Carlos Reservation, where grinding poverty is the daily fare. And it's been that way since the beginning in 1872, when this bleak patch of land along the Gila River was established as a reservation/prison by the grim Indian killer Gen. George Crook.

The non-treaty Apaches, those who refused to sign away any of their traditional lands to the whites, have always hated the place for its brackish waters, infertile soils and robust population of rattlesnakes. The site was a malarial barrens where many Apaches died of what the Army called "quotidian intermittent fever." Here's how Daklugie, the son of the great Chiricahua leader Juh, recalled the early days of life on the reservation:

"San Carlos! That was the worst place in all the great territory stolen from the Apaches. If anybody ever lived there permanently, no Apache knew of it. Where there is no grass there is no game. Nearly all of the vegetation was cacti; and though in season a little cactus fruit was produced, the rest of the year food was lacking. The heat was terrible. The insects were terrible. The water was terrible. What there was in the sluggish river was brackish and warm. At San Carlos, for the first time within memory of any of my people, the Apaches experienced the shaking sickness."

Of course, that was the point. The Army and the Interior Department weren't on a humanitarian mission. The reservations, especially for the Apaches, were always more like concentration camps carved out of the most desolate terrain in a barren landscape. American death camps. Black holes on Earth.

And so 140 years later, San Carlos remains one of the poorest places in the nation. The per capita income is less than $3,000. More than 50 percent of the people who live there are homeless. More than 60 percent are unemployed. Less than half the Apaches have a high school diploma and only one in a hundred Apache kids go on to college. The University of Arizona, so anxious to defile a sacred Apache mountain in the pursuit of science, has done almost nothing to help the dire situation at San Carlos, except to raid the reservation for cultural artifacts and to submit the people there to remorseless interrogations by university anthropologists.

* * *

Our way up Mount Graham seemed simple enough when tracing the route on the map. We traveled logging roads, traversed deer and bear trails and made a steady bearing up a crumpled ridgeline toward the forests of Emerald Peak. Naturally, I was lost within an hour.

Perhaps, it had to do with the otherworldliness of the ascent, moving out of searing desert through chaparral, scrublands and finally into ever deeper forest. As the astronomers trained their lenses deep into the past toward the light of dead stars, we walked through a living relic; the journey up the slopes of the mountain was a trip back into ecological time.

Mount Graham is a sky island, a 10,700-foot-tall extrusion from the floor of the Sonoran desert, which has traveled its own evolutionary course since the last ice age, more than 10,000 years ago. The mountain is a kind of continental Galapagos, featuring seven different biomes, stacked on top each other like an ecological flow chart.

At the very top of the pyramid (and the mountain) is a cloud forest of fir and spruce, the southernmost manifestation of this biome. This is an ancient forest, as stout and mossy as the fabled forests of Oregon. That's where the squirrels hang out. Of course, the forests has been gnawed at over the years by loggers and the like, but there was still more than 600-acres of it left when the astronomers laid claimed to the area, with the ironclad brutality of a mining company.

From an ecological point of view, the astronomers couldn't have picked a worse site in Arizona—partly because the only rival to Mount Graham, the densely forested San Francisco Peaks north of Flagstaff, holy ground for the Hopi, has already been defiled by ski slopes and powerlines. There are more than 18 plants and animals that are endemic to Mount Graham. There are nine trout streams tumbling off its slopes. Numerous cienegas, those strange desert marshes. Rare northern goshawks and Mexican spotted owls. And more apex predators, cougars and black bears, than in any other place in the desert Southwest. When you've got the big predators, it's usually a sign the ecosystem is humming along in a functioning state—an all-too-rare condition in the American West these days.

But there's a problem. And it's a big one. It is the curse of ecological islands to suffer from high extinction rates, even in a relatively natural state. But when outside forces, such as clearcuts, powerlines, roads, and telescopes, rudely penetrate the environment these rates soar uncontrollably.

The reason is fairly straightforward: the species that live in these isolated habitats have evolved in a kind of vacuum and aren't equipped to handle the shock of such drastic changes to their living quarters. And there's another complicating factor. When endemic animals and plants are wiped out by chainsaws and bulldozer, there's no nearby population to fill the void: a sea of hostile desert separates Mount Graham from the archipelago of sky islands arcing through northern Mexico and southern Arizona.

In a way then, the plants and animals of Mount Graham share this striking vulnerability with the Apache people, who, although masters of desert life and highly skilled warriors, had no ultimate defense against the waves of disease and alien technology marshaled into their realm by whites.

* * *

Mount Graham attracted astronomers for some of the same reasons it harbors unique wildlife and is revered by the Apache: it is wild, remote, tall and steep. Indeed, although it's not the tallest mountain in Arizona, Mount Graham is the steepest, rising more than 8,000 feet off the desert floor.

The University of Arizona fixed its attentions on Mount Graham in the early 1980s. It had gotten into the astronomy game in the 1920s and had put observatories on several of the peaks in the Santa Catalina Mountains outside Tucson, including Mount Lemmon, Mount Hopkins and Kitt Peak.

The University's Seward Observatory touts itself as one of the top astronomy centers in the world. It not only mans observatories, but also has its hands in the lucrative business of building and polishing the giant mirrors used by modern telescopes.

But the star-gazing business is akin to the expanding universe: staying on top means constantly building new scopes, claiming new, higher peaks, extending your empire.

The University's Seward Observatory had run into another problem. The observatories closest to Tucson had become increasingly less efficient over the years, the image quality marred by smog and light pollution. So they went looking for a new peak and quickly settled on Mount Graham, 100 miles northeast of Tucson. Of course, they told the Apaches nothing about their intentions.

It turns out that Mount Graham isn't a very good place to probe the secrets of the heavens. There are updrafts of warm air pushing off the desert that distort the images, making them as jittery as the first snaps that came back from the Hubbell space telescope. Plus, Mount Graham is a sky island and though it rises out of one of the driest stretches of land on the continent it is often cloudy on the peak.

"Any Apache could have told the astronomers that," says

Vittorio. "It is a stormbringer mountain, summoning up all the moisture from the desert below, pooling it at the peak in a nimbus of clouds."

In fact, the University of Arizona knew that Mount Graham was a poor choice for the deep space telescopes from the beginning. In 1986, a team from the National Optical Astronomy Observatory conducted a two-year investigation comparing Mount Graham and Mauna Kea, Hawai'i as possible telescope sites. The Arizona peak fell far short. "There was no comparison," concluded Mike Merrill, an astronomer at the NOAO. Indeed, the study advised that there were 37 other sites ranking better than Mount Graham for observing stars—even the smog-shrouded Mount Hopkins topped Mount Graham.

This troublesome bit of news didn't deter the University of Arizona. In 1988, it announced plans to turn Mount Graham into a kind of astronomical strip mall, featuring seven telescopes at a cost of more than $250 million. They rounded up a bevy of partners, including the Vatican, several universities in the US and Europe and the odious Max Planck Institute, which in an earlier incarnation as the Max Planck Society gave assistance to the murderous experiments of Dr. Mengele.

This peculiar consortium ran into immediate legal hurdles, the biggest being the small Mount Graham red squirrel. It was a now federally protected endangered species and its last refuge was the very cloud forest the astronomer's claimed for their avenue of telescopes. Biologists from the Fish and Wildlife Service announced that the project would jeopardize the squirrel's very existence. It's not hard to figure out why they reached this conclusion. The observatory scheme would destroy nearly 30 percent of the squirrel's best remaining habitat.

But the University wasn't going to let extinction stand in the way of science. It took an aggressive and belligerent approach. Officials badgered and intimidated federal biologists and when they wouldn't back down the University and its lawyers went over their heads. For example, in May of 1988, the University summoned Michael Spear, then regional head of the Fish and Wildlife Service, to a closed-door meeting at the Tucson airport, for a session of backroom arm-twisting. Spear emerged a few hours later having agreed to order agency biologists to conclude that the telescopes could go forward regardless of the effect on the squirrels. Which is, in fact, what they did.

"Procedurally, it was incorrect," Lesley Fitzpatrick, a US Fish and Wildlife biologist, later testified. "And it was in violation of the law, and therefore it is incorrect regardless of whether its procedural or substantive."

In other words, the Fish and Wildlife Service had committed a fraud and everyone there knew it while they were doing it. And they got caught and even then it didn't matter. Why? Well, a diminutive squirrel doesn't pull at the heartstrings of most Arizonans, who seemed unruffled at the fact that the state's rarest species was slated to become political roadkill.

More tellingly, the University got its way because it has powerful politicians in its pocket, ranging from Bruce Babbitt to John McCain, and they used them relentlessly, especially the vile McCain.

The university tapped McCain to push through congress the so-called Idaho and Arizona Conservation Act of 1988. This deceptively-titled law was actually a double-barrel blast at the environment: it gave the green light to illegal logging in the wildlands of Idaho and for the construction of the Mount Graham telescopes, shielding them from any kind of litigation by environmentalists or Apaches. To help sneak this malign measure through congress, the University shelled out more than a half-million dollars for the services of the powerhouse DC lobbying firm Patton, Boggs and Blow.

The bill passed in the dead of night and, in the words of one University of Arizona lawyer, it gave the astronomers the right to move forward "even if it killed every squirrel."

It also exempted the project from the National Historic Preservation Act and other laws that might have made it possible for the Apaches to assert their claims to the mountain, giving the University of Arizona the dubious honor of becoming the first academic institution to seek the right to trample on the religious freedoms of Native Americans.

In the spring of 1989 with the squirrel population in freefall, the Forest Service, which oversees Mount Graham as part of the Coronado National Forest, began to raise questions about the project. Worried that the astronomers' road might spell the squirrel's demise, Jim Abbott, the supervisor of the Coronado forest, ordered a halt to construction at the site. The delay infuriated McCain.

On May 17, 1989, Abbott got a call from Mike Jimenez, McCain's chief of staff. Jimenez informed Abbot that McCain was angry and wanted to meet with him the next day. He told Abbott to expect "some ass-chewing." At the meeting, McCain raged, threatening Abbott that "if you do not cooperate on this project [bypassing the Endangered Species Act], you'll be the shortest tenured forest supervisor in the history of the Forest Service."

Unfortunately for McCain, there was a witness to this encounter, a ranking Forest Service employee named Richard Flannelly, who recorded the encounter in his notebook. This notebook was later turned over to investigators at the General Accounting Office.

A few days later, McCain called Abbott to apologize. But the call sounded more like an attempt to bribe the Forest Service supervisor to go along with the project. According to a 1990 GAO report on the affair, McCain "held out a carrot that with better cooperation, he would see about getting funding for Mr. Abbott's desired recreation projects."

Environmentalists lodged an ethics complaint against McCain, citing a federal law that prohibits anyone (including members of Congress) from browbeating federal personnel. The Senate ethics committee never pursued the matter. When the GAO report condemning McCain surfaced publicly, McCain lied about the encounter, calling the allegations "groundless" and "silly."

In 1992, environmentalists Robin Silver and Bob Witzeman went to meet with McCain at his office in Phoenix to discuss Mount Graham. Silver and Witzeman are both physicians. The doctors say that at the mention of the words Mount Graham, McCain erupted into a violent fit. "He slammed his fists on his desk, scattering papers across the room," said Silver. "He jumped up and down, screaming obscenities at us for about 10 minutes. He shook his fists as if he was going to slug us. It was as violent as almost any domestic abuse altercation."

Witzeman left the meeting stunned: "I'm a lifelong environmentalist, but what really scares me about McCain is not his envi-

ronmental policies, which are horrid, but his violent, irrational temper. I wouldn't want to see this guy with his finger on the button."

* * *

Despite lawsuits and fierce protests, including a daring attempt
to block the access road by a young Apache mother named Diane
Valenzuela, who suspended herself from a tripod, the Vatican and
Max Planck scopes went up.

Then the opponents began another tact: a global campaign
against universities seeking to invest in the Mount Graham
Observatory. It was brilliantly executed and wildly successful. More
than 80 universities announced they would have nothing to do with
the observatory and 50 prominent European astronomers signed a
letter requesting that the project be halted "so that the unique environment and sacred mountain of Mount Graham can be saved."
Even the Max Planck Institute scaled back its investment.

All of this began to wear on the head of the Mount Graham
project, Peter Strittmatter, the chief astronomer at the University's
Seward Observatory. He lashed out repeatedly at the Apaches and
greens, referring to them as "essentially terrorists." That's an old slur
for the Apaches, going back to the conquistadors, and an increasingly common one for environmentalists. (By the way, Strittmatter's
special focus is the all-important subject of..."Speckle
Interferometry.")

But the University pressed on, deploying tactics that seemed
cribbed right out of the Dow Chemical Company's playbook: they
brought in former FBI agents, including veterans of the bureau's
noxious COINTELPRO operation, to train campus police; they
tried to infiltrate and disrupt opposition groups; and they hired a PR
firm to write phony letters, supposedly drafted by Arizona students,
to local papers attacking the Apaches and the enviros.

Then in 1993, the astronomers finally confronted the technical
problem that had loomed for so long. The original site for the Large
Binocular Telescope was simply untenable. It was too windy and too
cloudy. So the astronomers announced they were going to move it
to a new site on the mountain, even deeper into the forest.

The enviros and Apaches argued that this sudden change in
plans would reactivate environmental laws that had been neutered

by the 1988 legislation. But in the pre-dawn hours of December 3, the University unleashed a pre-emptive strike: they clearcut 250 old-growth trees on the new site before the environmentalist could get before a judge. They didn't even tell their own biologist, charged with monitoring the project's impacts on the red squirrel. He found out about it on the evening news.

When the environmentalists finally got into a federal court, the judge agreed with them and halted the construction of the big scope, ruling that the project needed to undergo a formal environmental review. The university appealed and lost.

Then in 1996 the Apaches turned to President Clinton. Despite Clinton's pledges to protect the environment and honor the religious practices and sacred sites of Native Americans, he bowed to the demands of the University and signed another piece of legislation overturning the court injunctions and shielding the new site from environmental review and litigation. So even when you play by the rules and win, you can still lose through political connivance and trickery. It's a lesson the Apaches learned long ago.

So work on the big scope resumed, followed by the construction of a 23-mile long powerline corridor up the flank of the mountain. By 2003, the sacred mountain of the Apache had been fully electrified.

* * *

As we crept through the lush montane forest to the crest of the mountain, Vittorio pulled a small pouch from his pocket. He said it was a medicine bundle that he wanted to bury at the telescope site.

"What's in there?" I asked. "Sage and sweetgrass?"

"Hell, no," he chuckled. "Squirrel shit."

"Uh," I asked nervously. "Do squirrels carry Hanta virus?" [I was referring to the disease rodents in these parts carry that is fatal to humans.]

"One can always hope."

He dug a small trench beneath the fence, slid the pouch under, buried in it fir needles and said something in Apache that I couldn't begin to translate, though it sounded more like a curse than a prayer.

"The priest said if they spotted aliens in those scopes, it would be their mission to convert them," Vittorio said, speaking of Father George V. Coyne, the head Vatican astronomer. "But they are the aliens here and they're too fucking self-righteous to realize it."

Here's a taste of Father Coyne's cosmic eschatology: "The Church would be obliged to address the question of whether extra-terrestrials might be brought into the fold and baptized. One would want to put some questions to him, such as: have you ever experienced something similar to Adam and Eve, in other words, original sin? Do you people also know a Jesus who has redeemed you?" And this spaced-out priest has the nerve to denounce the Apache religion as primitive?

The Apache know Mount Graham as Dzil nchaa sian, Big Seated Mountain. The mountain is an anchor point of the Apache cosmology, as vital to their tradition as Chartres, the Wailing Wall or the temples of Angkor Wat. It orients the world, presages the weather, nurtures healing plants and serves as a sanctuary from bands of killers, so often riding under the auspices of the Church. What more do we require of holy places? That they be handmade? Commissioned?

Ironically, that's the position of the Catholic Church. Coyne himself has sneered that unless there are physical relics on the site it can't really be considered sacred, except as a kind of paganistic nature worship which the church finds anathema.

"Nature and Earth are just there, blah!" the cosmic priest wrote. "And there will be a time when they are not there... [The Apaches and militant greens] subscribe to an environmentalism and religiosity to which I cannot subscribe and which must be suppressed with all the force we can muster."

Of course, over the past four hundred years the Church has done its damnedest to eradicate any remnant of Apache culture: villages, clothing, language, ceremonies and the Apache themselves.

"On this mountain is a great life-giving force," declared Franklin Stanley, a San Carlos medicine man, in 1992 as the bulldozers prepared to dig the footings for the scopes. "You have no knowledge of the place you are about to destroy."

But the priests manning the $3 million Vatican Advanced Technology telescope dismissed Franklin and the other Apaches. They prevented Apache leaders from meeting with the Pope and even went so far as to suggest that were being used as part of a Jewish conspiracy. "The opposition to the telescopes and the use of Native American people to oppose the project are part of a Jewish conspiracy that comes out of the Jewish lawyers of the ACLU to undermine and destroy and undermine the Catholic church," the Rev. Charles Polzer told Indian activist Guy Lopez in 1992. Polzer, a Jesuit priest, was the curator of ethnohistory at the Arizona State Museum. "Two Phoenix doctors, Robert Witzeman and Robin Silver, are examples of this conspiracy," Polzer told Lopez.

Polzer was as wrong about Witzeman and Silver as he was about the sacred nature of Mount Graham. Witzeman is a Lutheran; Silver is a Mormon. Silver has been a friend of mine for many years. He's also the busiest man I know. He's a gifted tennis player, an emergency room physician, a father and the most prolific environmentalist in the Southwest. "Apaches, Jews and greens we're all the same to the Church and the University of Arizona," says Silver.

The astronomers even made it illegal for the Apaches to conduct prayer ceremonies on the summit without a permit and arrested Wendsler Nosie, a member of Apaches for Cultural Preservation, when he exercised his constitutional right to pray there without one.

"These space priests have the same old prejudices that the inquisitors did back when they went after Galileo," says Vittorio. "What's bizarre is that the tables have turned. Now the Church is being used by the scientists to legitimize their rampages. They even have the gall to name their sacrilege the Columbus Project."

Several universities, including the University of Minnesota and Virginia, offered to buy off opposition from the Apaches. It didn't work. "They're asking us to sell our spirit," said Wendsler Nosie. "The answer is 'no, we don't want anything they're offering to us financially.'"

* * *

In October of 1992, I attended a Columbus Day rally against Mount Graham at the University of Arizona's Seward Observatory outside Tucson. As an Apache leader was giving a speech, a goon squad of University police charged into the crowd, tackled and tried to drag away one of the Native American student leaders. Robin Silver, who among his other pursuits is a first-rate photographer, began clicking shots of the assault. Then the cops turned their attention on him. He was arrested and his camera seized.

Silver wasn't there to protest, but to document. Still, the University cops recognized him immediately as a chief nemesis. Since 1988, there's been more than a dozen lawsuits filed against the telescope project. Silver has had his hand in crafting most of them. Unlike many environmentalists, Silver also deals honestly and respectfully with Native Americans.

For the university, this is a dangerous mix. And they've repeatedly tried to discredit Silver in the press and with politicians. When that didn't work they sent their cops out to intimidate him. But emergency room physicians don't scare easily and the arrest blew up in the face of the University—Silver also knows how to work the press.

But the university (surely one of the sleaziest institutions in the US) didn't relent. In 1993, it hired the Snell & Winter law firm to dig in to the possibility of filing racketeering charges against environmentalist and Apache opponents of the telescopes. And on and on it goes.

Why would the university go to these extreme lengths? Well, the Mount Graham telescope complex isn't just about the pursuit of "pure science"—as if any science could ever be pure—or, as one astronomer put it, "peering through the dark avenues of time to witness the creative spark of the Big Bang."

Astronomy isn't a benign science. Indeed, it's often difficult to separate the discipline from its unseemly ties to military applications. Galileo's first telescopes were designed for the war lords of Venice, who used them to spot enemy ships and troops. The giant mirrors that power the Mount Graham scopes have also been touted for their dual use nature: both as stargazers and as a potential component in the Star Wars scheme, wherein the mirrors would reflect laser-beam weapons on satellites and incoming missiles.

Of course, it's also about money. Lots of money. And we're not just talking about the enormous cost of the project. Telescopes are big business. The investment partners for the Mount Graham Observatory are selling viewing time for $30,000 a night. The actual fee per night might drop when there is an online experience competing with it. But that online product will indeed make the total revenue climb when the Large Binocular telescope goes online—if it does. Then there's the stream of federal research grants, guided to them by political patrons such as McCain, which the University hopes will tally in the tens of millions a year.

"These guys don't just have stars in their eyes," quips Vittorio. "They've also got dollar signs."

Robin Silver calls them simply "the Star Whores."

All in all, the maligned art of astrology does rather less harm and provides a good deal more human solace.

* * *

"Hey, you, assholes!" We'd been discovered. "Freeze, damn it!"

A green tunnel of light swept towards us, like a dragnet scene in a bad James Cagney movie. A corpulent cop rumbled toward the fence, dragging a bum leg and carrying what looked to be an assault rifle.

"This way," Vittorio whispered and took off running. I jogged after him as he bounded through the forest like a bear harassed by hornets. He descended a rough deer trail, then cut cross country, topping a razor-thin ridge and down into a cove of moss-bearded spruce. I stayed within sight of him for a few minutes, but soon lost him in the darkness, as my lungs began to seize. I'm a lowlander and the 10,000-foot altitude took its toll with a vengeance.

Exhausted and disoriented, I tripped over a downed tree and plunged headfirst into a snow bank. Suddenly, I felt overcome with doom. I laid there in the snow, gasping for air that wasn't there, waiting for the fat cop with the club foot and the rubber bullets to come haul me away to some shithole in Tucson…or worse.

"Psst. Down here." Vittorio to the rescue once again.

He was crouching in a narrow gorge, about 20 feet below me. I pulled myself out of the snowbank and worked my way down into the ravine. We walked a few hundred yards in silence, absorbing the intoxicating vanilla-like scent of the forest, until the gorge came to an abrupt end at a cliff, towering a few hundred feet above a broad flank of the mountain below us.

We sat down on the ledge, our feet dangling in a kind of space. A rush of air from below warmed our faces. The sky had cleared of clouds. To the west, the desert rolled on in the darkness beneath us toward the Galiuro and Santa Catalina Mountains and the distant flickering tumor of Tucson.

"Look!" Vittorio whispered, pointing to the midnight sky, suddenly streaming with stars. "How much closer do we really need to be?"

San Carlos, Arizona, 2002

Thirty-Nine

The Battle for Zuni Salt Lake

For the Zuni, this place is the center of the world. For the Department of the Interior under Gale Norton, it's just another coal seam, 18,000 acres of wasteland just waiting to be strip-mined.

The pueblo tribes of the Southwest call this place the Zuni Salt Lake sanctuary. The Interior Department and the mining company insist on calling it by the less alluring Fence Lake.

Located about 60 miles south of Zuni pueblo, Zuni Salt Lake is a rare, high desert lake. It's extremely shallow, with the depth varying from four feet to only a foot and a half. During the summer months, much of the water evaporates under the scorching New Mexico sun, leaving behind beds of salt.

For centuries, the pueblo tribes of the Southwest, including the Zuni, Acoma, Laguna, Hopi and Taos pueblos, have made annual pilgrimages to Zuni Lake to harvest salt, for both culinary and ceremonial purposes. Ancient roadways radiate out from the lake to the various pueblos. The lake itself is considered sacred, home the Salt Mother deity, who the Zuni call Ma'l Oyattsik'i.

The land surrounding Zuni Salt Lake has always been considered a sanctuary zone, a kind of inter-tribal commons were hostilities are lain aside, purification ceremonies are performed and the sacred salts are gathered. Anthropologists say these areas, termed Neutrality Zones, are rare in North America and the Zuni Lake site is one of the most prominent and well preserved.

Most of the traditional lands of the Zuni Pueblo, including the salt lake, were seized by the federal government in the 1880s. The lake itself was designated a federal salt mine. The Zuni began fighting for the return of their most sacred site around the turn of the century. Finally, in 1977 the Carter administration relented to mounting pressure and decided to return Zuni Salt Lake to the pueblo. But, except for 5,000 acres of land immediately surrounding the lake, the remainder of the Zuni Salt Lake sanctuary stayed in federal hands, under the control of the Bureau of Land Management.

The Zuni Sanctuary has the geological misfortune to straddle the San Augustine coal formation, which stretches from Zuni Salt Lake north toward the Jemez Mountains. In 1986, the Zuni Tribe learned that the Salt River Project, an Arizona utility with close ties to Bruce Babbitt, had applied for a permit with BLM to gauge an 18,000-acre strip mine at Fence Lake, 11 miles north of Zuni Salt Lake, in the heart of the sanctuary zone.

One of the big concerns raised by the Zuni at the time focused on the effect of the strip mine on the Dakota Aquifer that underlies Zuni Salt Lake. Coal mines are massive consumers of water. One estimate suggests that the initial proposal for the Fence Lake Mine requires the extraction of 600 gallons of water from the aquifer every minute over the 50-year life span of the mine. The Zuni rightly feared that this would do lasting damage to the aquifer and the lake itself. They asked the US Geological Survey to investigate.

Typically, the USGS took its time, partly because of the innate sluggishness of the agency and partly do to political interference from political appointees in the Reagan and Bush I administrations. When the report finally appeared in 1992, the Survey's hydrologists estimated that the strip mine could lower the aquifer by at least four feet up to ten miles away. The report concluded that the survival of Zuni Salt Lake itself could be put into question.

But by then, the Salt River Project utility had been granted two strip mine leases by the ever-compliant Bureau of Land Management. Things came to a pause, however, when archaeologists with the Park Service stepped in, determining that more than 55 percent of the land the BLM had given away to be strip mined by the Salt River Project qualified for protection under the Federal Register of Historic Places.

Archaeologists working for the Park Service and the tribes estimated that the sanctuary zone, which includes about 187,000 acres surrounding the lake, contains more than 5,000 archaeological sites, including burial shrines, ceremonial areas and other structures. It turned out that despite a decade of protests from the pueblo tribes the BLM hadn't screened any part of the area for cultural or archaeological sites, areas it was ready to consign to dynamite and giant shovels.

The BLM knew better. In 1988, Dr. Clara Kelly, an independent anthropologist working for the Acoma Pueblo, interviewed elders with the tribe who told her that the Acoma considered most of the land slated for strip mining as being sacred. They also told her that the Zuni, famed for their reticence on these matters, believed the sanctuary zone extended over an even larger area. When Kelly tried to follow up, the BLM apparently interfered and she wasn't granted permission to talk with the Zuni elders. Her initial report was found in the BLM's files.

Kelly wasn't the only scientist to find her warnings buried. Earlier this year, a hydrologist for the Bureau of Indian Affairs filed a complaint with the Equal Employment Opportunity Office, claiming that a supervisor had harassed him after he cited hydrological studies saying that the strip mine would harm Zuni Salt Lake.

The Clinton administration could have halted the project, but it didn't. In fact, the 1990s were largely a time of the Zuni tribe, and environmental groups, fighting off the BLM and the Salt River Project with one administrative appeal after another. Despite the high-minded rhetoric from Clinton and Babbitt about environmental justice and Indian sovereignty, the administration steam-rolled the concerns of the tribe and were ready to give final approval for the mine as the clock ran out on the Clinton White House.

For awhile, it looked like the Bush II administration, under fire and facing contempt of court citations for its ravaging of the Indian Trust Funds, might reverse course and can the project. But on May 17, Gale Norton quietly gave final approval for the strip mining to begin.

Under the Norton plan, the Salt River Project will be permitted to strip mine more than 18,000 acres over the next 40 years, extracting as much as 40 million tons of coal. To suppress dust and process the coal, Norton will allow the company to pump water from the nearby Atarque Aquifer.

The coal is destined for the aptly named Coronado Generating Station near St. Johns, Arizona, a main power source for metropolitan Phoenix that spews out a gray swirl of smoke visible for 50 fifty miles. In order to get the coal to the power plant, the SRP will build a 44-mile long railroad from the strip mine, which will cross federal land and destroy many ancient roadways to Zuni Salt Lake. The utility says its on schedule to begin construction of the railroad in the spring of 2003 and will begin mining coal in January of 2005. Zuni tribal leaders say that the mine will destroy more than 500 burial shrines.

The Zuni and other pueblo tribes have few options left, but they are resigned to fight in the courts and, if necessary, through civil disobedience. On July 17, runners from Hopi, Acoma, Taos and Laguna pueblos led a protest at the headquarters of the Salt River Project then ran to Zuni pueblo, a ceremonial reenactment of the ancient pilgrimages to Zuni Lake.

"Everyone must learn to respect this place," said Bucky Preston, from the Hopi Nation, who had just completed the 250-mile run from Phoenix. "We must start disciplining ourselves. If we don't, greed will destroy us all."

The governor of Taos Pueblo, Vincent Lujan, was somewhat more direct. He reminded the officials of the Salt River Project utility about the Pueblo revolts of 1680, when the pueblo tribes pushed back the Spanish and warned that they were in for a similar battle.

"It took us 60 years of fighting to get back our sacred Blue Lake at Taos," Lujan said. "Now we are embarking on a similar battle. There's meaning in what these runners do here. We were here before you. We're going to be here forever. This is where our ancestors shed their blood."

Zuni Pueblo, 2002

Forty

Black Deeds in the Black Hills

Tom Daschle Dooms
the Sacred Land of the Sioux

If there was even the smallest doubt before, it's been eradicated now. The Black Hill National Forest in South Dakota, where Crazy Horse and Black Elk went on vision quests, must be returned to the Lakota Sioux for its own survival.

In 1868, the federal government signed a treaty with the Lakota Sioux granting the tribe ownership of most of western South Dakota, including the majestic Black Hills. Six years later, the US tried to coerce the tribe, under threat of starvation, to cede the Black Hills back to the government so that they could be ravaged for gold. The tribe wouldn't yield, thus prompting Custer's rampages against the Sioux and his eventual demise at Little Big Horn. Eventually, the government seized the land anyway, assassinated Crazy Horse and Sitting Bull, and confined the Sioux to the enforced poverty of the Pine Ridge and Rosebud reservations, which functioned for years as little more than concentration camps to house some of the most destitute communities in the United States.

Much of the Sioux land ended up in the hands of the federal government as part of the 1.5 million acre Black Hills National Forest. The Black Hills, the tallest mountains east of the Rockies, are an isolated range that rise up like shadows off the sun-baked flatlands of South Dakota. The flanks of the mountains are a kind of botanical crazy quilt, blending Rocky Mountain species with those found in Great Plains, Midwestern prairies and eastern deciduous forests. The Black Hills are the eastern limit of the Ponderosa pine forests and about the only place you can find unadulterated patches of montane grasslands.

For decades, the Sioux have pressed for the return of these lands. Environmentalists, largely, have refused to support the transfer, saying that the mountains would be better off in the hands of the Forest Service. It's the old paternalism that has stained mainstream environmentalism since John Muir helped to evict the last remnants of the Southern Miwok tribes out of Yosemite so that the Park Service could run the show (Yosemite is Miwok for "some among them (i.e., the whites) are killers"). These days it's okay to quote Native American spirituality in your fundraising letters, another thing entirely to trust the tribes to take care of their own lands.

But this condescending line should no longer wash with even the most gullible green. Now the sacred mountains, which the Sioux call Paha Sapa, are being laid to waste in a final frenzy to log off the little wild forests that remain and environmentalists and top rank Democrats must share the blame. In early July, two big time environmental groups, the Sierra Club and the Wilderness Society, connived with the top Democrat in the Senate, Tom Daschle, to doom some of the last wild forests in these sacred lands to logging. Worse than that, the deal exempted the clearcutting from compliance any environmental laws.

Under the Daschle/Sierra Club/Wilderness Society deal, which was again attached as a rider to the Defense Appropriations Bill, the Forest Service will allow timber companies to begin logging in the Beaver Park Roadless Area and in the Norbeck Wildlife Preserve. These two areas harbor some of the last remaining stands of old-growth forest in the Black Hills. All of these timber sales will be shielded from environmental lawsuits, even from organizations that objected to the deal.

The logging plan was consecrated in the name of fire prevention. The goal of the bill, Daschle said, "is to reduce the risk of forest fire by getting [logging] crews on the ground as quickly as possible to start thinning." It's long been the self-serving contention of the timber lobby that the only way to prevent forest fires is to log them first. The environmental movement has rightly countered that the real problem is a century of unbridled logging of old growth forests and fire suppression. In a single blow, the Sierra Club and Wilderness Society legitimized the timber industry's cockeyed claim.

Surprised that such a deed could originate in the office of Tom Daschle? Don't be. Despite what the League of Conservation Voters might allege, Tom Daschle's never been much of an environmentalist, especially in his home state. Indeed, the leader of the Democrats in the senate has always carried water for the big timber and mining companies that have done so much damage to landscape of South Dakota. Occasionally, he pipes up on high profile national issues, such as ANWR. But he rarely has his heart in it. Witness his woefully inept attempt to defeat the mad scheme to ship nuclear waste across the nation to Yucca Mountain.

The Sioux certainly have no love for Daschle. Daschle is a close friend and political ally of South Dakota governor William Janklow, known for his rabidly anti-Indian views. How anti-Indian is Janklow? In 1974 he told reporters: "The only way to deal with the Indian problem in America, is to put a gun to the AIM leaders' heads and pull the trigger." In 1983, Janklow sued writer Peter Matthiessen for $23 million in an attempt to stop publication of *In the Spirit of Crazy Horse*, Matthiessen's great book on the FBI's assault on the Pine Ridge reservation and the trial of Leonard Peltier. Janklow's suit was eventually thrown out of court.

Daschle also helped to organize the Open Hills Association, a group of ranchers, mining companies and timber groups that came together to oppose the return of the Black Hills to the Sioux. A recent Sioux newsletter described the Open Hills Association as espousing "overtly racist views."

In 1999, Daschle engineered the passage of the deceptively titled Wildlife Mitigation Act. The bill authorized the transfer of 90,000 acres of land along the Missouri River then controlled by the US Army Corps of Engineers to the state of South Dakota. The land is inside both the 1851 and 1868 Ft. Laramie Treaty boundaries and rightfully belongs to the Sioux tribe. A contingent of Sioux elders and members of the Lakota Student Alliance occupied LaFramboise Island, a sandbar in the Missouri River near the state capitol, for over a year as a protest against the transfer.

Daschle's also proven to be the kind of senator who is always willing to screw over the downtrodden to help a big time political contributor. An example. Around Christmastime of last year, Daschle quietly attached a rider to the Defense Appropriations Bill granting total legal immunity to the Toronto-based Barrick Gold Mining Company, which operates the Homestake Gold mine in the Black Hills. This mine, which was once owned by William

Randolph Hearst and has been in nearly continual operation since the Sioux were driven out of the mountains, has generated more than a billion dollars in revenue.

The Sioux haven't seen a dime. But they have seen the mine devour and despoil a huge chunk of their mountains. When the gold runs out, the Homestake mine will leave behind an environmental ruin of poisoned rivers, cyanide-laden leach ponds, toxic tailings piles and a hole in the earth a mile wide and 1,000 feet deep. Daschle's rider means that the US government assumes the costs of cleaning all this up, amounting to a $50 million bailout for a foreign corporation. "This re-affirms an unsurprising truth," says legal scholar Edward Lazarus. "This country deals far more generously with foreign corporations that buy our land than with the native peoples from whom we took it."

The latest Black Hills deal, it appears, was primarily geared to help Daschle's South Dakota colleague Tim Johnson, himself only slightly to the left of Attila the Hun when it comes to environmental issues, fend off a stiff Republican challenge for his senate seat from the green-bashing Rep. Jim Thune, who is currently the state's sole congressional representative. Of course, this scenario only works if green Democrats vote for Johnson in spite of his capitulations to the timber and mining industries.

It's an old story, one we've recounted time and again, that's taken an even darker, though entirely predictable, turn. The Black Hills are one of the most butchered national forests in the West. Less than five percent of the forest remains in an old-growth condition, the rest is fragmented by clearcuts and logging roads. Most of the remaining old-growth forest is located in the Norbeck Wildlife Preserve and the Beaver Park Roadless Area. In the 1990s, the Forest Service planned massive timber sales for both places.

The battle to save the Norbeck Wildlife Preserve goes back almost ten years, a back and forth war of appeals and lawsuits that culminated in 2001 with a landmark ruling by the Tenth Circuit Court of Appeals that the Norbeck timber sales were illegal. The environmentalists also won a court case stopping the Beaver Park sales.

In his defense of the deal, Daschle claims that it was reached through a consensus process of the "local stakeholders." This is untrue. In fact, two of the original plaintiffs in the lawsuits, Jeff

Kessler and Brian Brademeyer, objected to the proposed settlement. In recent testimony before congress, Mark Rey, the former timber lobbyist who now serves as assistant secretary of Agriculture in charge of the Forest Service, said plainly, "Our counsel have advised that there is no effective legal process to implement the modified agreement through the District Court, in the absence of the two non-settling plaintiffs." Rey advised that the only way to get the logging started was to steamroll the local enviros with a rider exempting the sales from judicial review. That's where Daschle, the Sierra Club and the Wilderness Society came in to save the day for big timber.

"We fought a decade to save those forests and finally won an appeals court victory," says Denise Boggs, director of the Utah Environmental Center. "Daschle and the big greens sold us out in ten minutes."

Some environmental big wigs have called Jeff Kessler, head of the Biodiversity Conservation Alliance, an obstructionist for not going along. He doesn't shy away from the charge. "You bet we're obstructionists," says Kessler. "We're obstructing the fruitless and environmentally damaging logging that won't significantly reduce risk to lives and property but that does mislead the public about fire safety, we're obstructing illegal activities by the Forest Service, we're obstructing stealth law-making that erodes our important environmental laws and the checks and balances designed by our founding fathers, and we're obstructing the loss of important old-growth forest and wildlife habitat."

But here's where the story takes off to another level. It's not just the Black Hills that have been put at risk. What's good for Daschle's backyard, the chainsaw delegation in Congress argues, must be good for the rest of the nation. Thus a little backroom deal in South Dakota can quickly metastasize into a cancer that ravages forests from Vermont to Alaska.

"After hearing all the hand-wringing from environmentalists downplaying the impact of appeals and litigation, it's nice to see that the highest-ranking Democrat in the nation agrees that these frivolous challenges have totally crippled forest managers," said Rep. Scott McInnis, Colorado Republican and chairman of the House resources subcommittee on forests and forest health. "It will be interesting indeed to find out if what's good for Mr. Daschle's goose is also good for the West's gander. We intend to find out."

And it's not just right-wingers like McInnis who are itching to use the Daschle rider as a template for a broader assault on the national forests and environmental laws. Senator Dianne Feinstein, a darling of the Sierra Club, announced last week that she intends to seek a similar exemption from environmental lawsuits for logging in California's national forests and may support an amendment that applies the provision to all national forests.

Daschle seems open to the idea. "I think the Black Hills could be a model for the rest of the country," Daschle told the *Rapid City Journal*.

This is an entirely predictable turn of events. But the Sierra Club remains blindly behind Daschle and refuses to denounce his bill as a mistake. "We appreciate the work of Senators Daschle and Johnson to bring all the parties to the table to hammer out a deal that would ensure the safety of South Dakotans and continued protections for America's National Forests," writes Sierra Club CEO Carl Pope in a defense of the deal. "This is how these matters should be addressed."

There's a lot of caviling with words here. Pope is getting expert at this kind of Clintonian parsing in his press releases. In the first place, the agreement wasn't supported by local environmentalists. In fact, the Sierra Club's own local representative, Brian Brademeyer, walked out of the talks once he saw where they were headed. He also quit his Sierra Club post. Pope's organization, it must be noted, is on record as opposing all commercial timber sales on federal lands, but that didn't prohibit him from signing off on logging in two of the most sacrosanct types of land in the national forest system: a roadless area and a wildlife preserve.

When Bush came into office, the mainstream enviros howled that he was putting timber industry flacks, such as Mark Rey, in charge of the national forests. A case of the fox guarding the henhouse, they charged. It's clear now that an equal threat comes from the leadership of the Democratic Party, in the form of Tom Daschle and Dianne Feinstein, and enviro bureaucrats who trade away forests, even in the sacred Black Hills, to keep them in power. There's a difference. No one can accuse Mark Rey of hypocrisy. He's never claimed to be a defender of nature.

That the Wilderness Society played a key role here is hardly shocking. After all, this was the group that was headed in the 1990s by a man who clearcut his own ranch in Montana and when he was exposed tried to blame the scandal on his wife. (See "Chainsaw Hypocrite" on page 52).

One of the principal deal cutters was Bart Koehler, now a flack for the Wilderness Society, whose main claim to fame rests on the fact that he was one of the founding members of Earth First! During Earth First! roadshows in the early 1980s, Koehler dressed up as a singing cowboy called Johnny Sagebrush. The act wasn't funny then; it's even less so now.

Koehler is only the latest of the founders of Earth First! to opt for a plush office and a plump salary. In 1989, Dave Foreman was arrested by the FBI on charges that he conspired to knock down powerlines in Arizona. He saved his hide by cutting a deal with prosecutors while his colleagues Mark Davis and Peg Millet were sentenced to six and three years in prison respectively. Then he renounced Earth First! and joined the Sierra Club board. Today he claims that Earth First! was really little more than a joke. Two other founders, Mike Roselle and Howie Wolke, both recently defended a deal that consigned thousands of acres in the Bitterroot Mountains of Montana to the chainsaw.

Edward Abbey must be grinding his teeth in his grave at how smoothly these green radicals have turned into political pimps for the Democratic Party, flashing their enviro credentials as they put their green stamp of approval on one clearcut after another. All in the name of pragmatism. Koehler and Foreman used to fume at the Wilderness Society and Sierra Club for just such sell-outs. To differentiate themselves they coined the phrase "No compromise in the Defense of Mother Earth" as a motto for Earth First! Nice slogan. Now it has come back to haunt their every step.

As aging green heroes, these former rads have coddled up to the very groups they used to revile as spineless sell-outs and have taken money from the same foundations they used to denounce as agents of big oil. It's all about getting big. And the budgets of the big environmental groups have bloomed since Bush got into the White House. The national Sierra Club now has more than 500 professional staffers. That's more than the timber industry and mining trade groups combined. Carl Pope, the Sierra Club's CEO, makes about $100,000 a year—or $96,000 more than the per capita income on the Sioux's Pine Ridge reservation, where 8 out of 10 adults are unemployed.

Yet, bigger isn't necessarily better. Go ask Enron and Worldcom.

Grassroots greens are getting angry as they've experienced the big groups undercut them time after time. "The actions of the Sierra Club and Wilderness Society in the Black Hills reinforces the accusations by the wise-use community that the environmental movement lacks integrity and accountability," says Denise Boggs of the Utah Environmental Center. "This is yet one more shameful example of the Sierra Club and Wilderness Society looking out for their political connections instead of for the land and wildlife that must actually live with the repercussions of their deal cutting."

In 1980, the Supreme Court ruled that the Sioux had been cheated out of the Black Hills. They awarded the tribe $106 million in compensation. The tribe told the court to keep its money. They wanted the land. Can you imagine the Sierra Club or the Wilderness Society doing the same?

The Black Hills have never seen such an act of betrayal since the Crow offered to scout against the Sioux for Custer. Return the sacred mountains of Crazy Horse now before Daschle and his cronies in Big Green can do even more damage.

Rapid City, 2002

Forty-One

Stolen Trust

Gale Norton, Native Americans and the Case of the Missing $10 Billion

Elouise Cobell comes right to the point. "Gale Norton should be thrown in jail." Cobell is a leader of the Blackfeet tribe, and lives along the Rocky Mountain Front in northwestern Montana. Norton, of course, is Secretary of the Interior and, as such, oversees the US government's relationship with Indian tribes.

Norton also controls the purse strings on federal trust funds holding more than $40 billion dollars owed to Indians across the nation. For her role in the mismanagement of the trust fund, Norton is facing a contempt of court citation from federal judge Royce Lamberth. If she gets slapped, she'll be in bi-partisan company. In 2000, Lamberth hit Bruce Babbitt and Treasury Secretary Robert Rubin with contempt citations for failing to halt the destruction of Indian trust account documents.

The case began in 1996 when Cobell, who has been called the Rosa Parks of Indian Country, filed a federal class action suit against the Interior Department, seeking both money that's been owed to Indian people and a radical change in how the trust fund is managed. Six years later, the case now stands as the largest class action suit in history, with more than 500,000 claimants. And, as it wound its way through the courts, it has tarnished two administrations and exposed the continuing war on Indian people by the federal government.

"We're not after money from the government," Cobell says. "The government has taken money that belongs to us."

Of course, stealing from Indians goes back to the origins of the republic. Mismanagement of Indian trust accounts was first noted by congress in 1823. But the Cobell suit is targeted at the notorious Dawes Act of 1887, which was an attempt to shatter Indian solidarity and culture by privatizing the reservations into 140 acre allotments put in the names of individual Indians. It was a set up, naturally. Indians were soon swindled out of more than two-thirds of their land, about 135,000 square miles in all. The remaining 57 million acres was put into a trust held by the Department of Interior. This too was a scam. With little or no input from the tribes, the land was leased out to white ranchers, oil companies, mining firms and timber companies. The land was stripped of its resources, often left in a ravaged condition.

The revenues from these leases (often sold at bargain-basement rates) goes into a trust fund administered by the Department of Interior. These days the fund receives about $500 million a year. Since 1887, more than $100 billion has gone into the accounts. Although the ranchers and oil companies have made a killing, little of that money has ever reached the tribes, where the per capita income hovers at less than $10,000 a year and unemployment rates hover near 70 percent. A new study shows that more than 90 percent of elderly Indians across the country are without access to long-term health care.

Lots of people have made money in futile and half-hearted attempts to straighten out the mess. In the early 1990s, Enron's favorite bookkeepers, Arthur Andersen was hired to make sense of the trust fund accounts. After two years, the accountants retreated in failure, but collected $20 million for their time.

"This scandal makes Enron look like a pimple," Cobell says. "It's worse than Enron, because it's the government that is lying, covering up and breaching its trust. They stole people's entire life savings. They robbed an entire race of people. If banks had ripped off white people, they'd be shut down in a New York second and everybody responsible would go to jail."

Before filing suit, Cobell tried to meet with Bruce Babbitt, then Clinton's Interior Secretary. Despite his high-minded rhetoric about environmental justice, Babbitt slammed the door in Cobell's face. She then sought out Janet Reno. Reno, too, brushed her aside. Cobell was disgusted at the hypocrisy and cowardice of the Clinton crowd. "They ought to have been ashamed," Cobell told one of Reno's deputies. "People are dying in all Indian communities. They don't have access to their own money."

In 1999, Lamberth ruled that the Interior Department had grossly mismanaged the accounts. "This case reveals a shocking pattern of deception," Lamberth wrote in his ruling. "I've never seen more egregious misconduct by the federal government." It was a huge victory for Cobell, who heard the news as she was driving across the wind-swept Blackfeet reservation. "I pulled over to the side of the road and I cried and cried," Cobell recalled.

But victory didn't prove that simple. Three years later, not a single Indian account has been straightened out and the government has done its best to defy the court and subvert its ruling. Incriminating emails were deleted. Subpoenaed documents were trashed, burned and shredded. The recalcitrance and malfeasance were so pervasive that Lamberth cited both Babbitt and Rubin with contempt of court.

Cobell thinks that the Clinton team was simply running out the clock, waiting to hand the mess off to the next administration. "It was crystal clear to me what the Clinton administration was up to," Cobell says. "Stalling, stalling and stalling."

When Norton took over, things got worse. Norton is a protege of James Watt, who once described Indian reservations as "the last bastions of socialism in the western world." Watt desperately wanted to revive the malicious spirit of the Dawes Act and sell off the rest of Indian country to the highest bidder. He was driven from office before he could realize this ambition, but Norton holds many of the same ideas and prejudices.

A few weeks after taking office, Norton told Judge Lamberth that she was intent on developing a plan that would restructure the Indian trust account system. In the year it took to develop, Norton and her team didn't consult once with the tribes. When the plan was unveiled nearly every tribe in the country denounced it.

Meanwhile, a string of special masters appointed to oversee the Interior Department's implementation of the rulings of the court have denounced Norton and her colleagues for tardiness, incompetence and "government malfeasance."

Norton claimed that the Department's new computer system would provide a quick fix to the problem. But last year a computer hacker successfully penetrated the site to demonstrate how easily the trust fund's records could be manipulated. Lamberth ordered the department to shut down all of its computer systems until the security problem could be fixed.

Norton's flacks used the ruling as a pretext to withhold dispatch of the year-end trust fund checks to 40,000 Indians. It was a move designed to punish the tribes and to try to undermine Cobell and her cohorts. Denied their money during Christmastime, several Indians called Cobell, blaming her for the bleak circumstances. "It was an act of retaliation," says Cobell. "They knew that Indians were starving, because they had no checks. Yet they did nothing."

Only a couple of members of congress were angered by these strong-arm tactics. "These people were subject to losing their car or their house," said Rep. Tom Udall, the Democrat from Colorado. "If this happened to security, all of Congress would be in an uproar."

But Lamberth was less tolerant. He has threatened to hold Norton and Bureau of Indian Affairs head Neal McCaleb in contempt. They could face jail and fines. Lamberth has already warned that the fines will be paid from their personal accounts and not government funds.

But Norton remains undeterred. In late July she engineered the forced resignation of Thomas Slonaker from his position as the special trustee for the Indian trust fund system. Slonaker, a Republican banking executive from Phoenix, had recently reported that the Interior Department had done little to make corrections to the trust account system. Slonaker had been called to testify before a senate hearing on the mismanagement of the trust fund and Norton instructed him not to submit his prepared testimony. When Slonaker refused, he was handed a letter of resignation by Steven Griles, Deputy Interior Secretary.

"It was like telling the emperor that she has no clothes," said Slonaker. "Sometimes, criticism is not welcome."

Cobell won't be so easy to get rid of. In the past, government officials have always counted on the poverty of Indian people as they trample over their rights with near impunity. But Cobell is a creative businesswoman and a master fundraiser. So far she has raised $9 million for the trust lawsuit from private sources and foundations, notably the Lannan Fund of New Mexico, which contributed $2 million to the cause.

She'll probably need every penny, because there's no indication that the Bush administration is backing down. "The government is going to fight this no matter what, even if it's morally, legally or ethically in the wrong," Cobell says. "That's a real country in itself." That's just the way things go in Indian country.

But Cobell also sees the litigation has having served to unite the tribes in a common front. "I actually see it as a miracle," Cobell says. "I've never seen tribes come together and work so hard."

Cut Bank, Montana, 2002

[Update September 2003: The Indian Trust case continues to rumble through the federal courts. Federal Judge Royce Lamberth, who is presiding over the bulk of the case, found Interior Secretary Gale Norton and her Deputy for Indian Affairs in contempt of court. He accused several government lawyers of unethical conduct in the case and called the Bush administration's proposed accounting schedule "a sham." The contempt finding against Norton and McCaleb was later overturned by the conservative DC Appeals Court, which ruled that they could not be held responsble for actions committed during the Clinton administration. The opinon was written by Judge Douglas Ginsburg, whose aspirations for a seat on the Supreme Court went up in smoke after reports of his indulgences with marijuana.]

Forty-Two

Totem Thieves

In 1899, railroad tycoon Edward Harriman put together an expedition of naturalists, scientists, painters and fellow robber barons to explore the coast of southeast Alaska. The shrewd Harriman, head of the Union Pacific, even rented the services of John Muir, the father of environmentalism and founder of the Sierra Club, thus striking a bond between corporate villains and mainstream greens that thrives to this day.

The object of the two-month foray, which was heralded as the largest survey of its time, was to size-up Alaska's riches (timber, gold, furs, oil) under the guise of scientific exploration. Karl Grove Albert, the famed geologist, picked at rocks. Bernard Fernow, the dean of the American forestry, cruised timber, calculating the number of board feet per acre. Edward Curtis lined up Haida and Tlingits for romantic mugshots and the painter Louis Agassiz Fuertes, taking Audubon's tradition to a new level of barbarity, shot thousands of animals in order to render them in his sketchbook.

Muir mused with the poet John Burroughs (pal of Walt Whitman) and imparted his transcendental thoughts about glaciers and grizzlies, while he dined with some of the high priests of Mammon—men he had previously excoriated as the defilers of the God's Temple.

Along the way, Harriman and his gang engaged in a good bit of plunder of native villages from Ketchikan to Wrangell. When they arrived at the Tlingit village of Gaash on Cape Fox, they encountered one of the most dazzling sites in North America: dozens of intricately-carved totem poles and the great grizzly bear house, exquisitely carved and painted.

The great Grizzly House of Gaash ranks as one of the most accomplished artworks produced in America during the 19th century, and rivals most 20th century art as well. It was certainly far beyond the talents of any of the artists mustered up by Harriman, although the paintings and (especially) the maps of Edward Dellenbach, who had also traveled down the Grand Canyon with

John Wesley Powell, are works of great beauty.

At the time Harriman arrived, most of the Tlingit villagers were away on a fishing expedition. Later the tycoon would claim that he thought the village was abandoned. This is almost certainly a lie. Harriman, known as the "Broker's Boy" by the trust-busters, is one of the most extravagant liars in American history and an apex capitalist, who not only created one of the great monopolies but also developed many of the tricks modern finance and accounting. Ken Lay is a piker next to the mighty Edward Harriman.

The totem poles at Gaash village were relatively new, many only a few years old. The lodges were tidy and clean. There were probably even elders still in the village. This was not Mesa Verde or Keet Seel, but a living community, whose history was carved on cedar: if anyone had taken the time to read it. The giant welcoming men, arms raised to the sky, the towering clan poles, where wolves chased frogs and ravens laughed at beavers and orca, and the austere grave poles that held the cremated remains of dead chiefs.

In any event, the team wasted little time documenting the site. Instead, Harriman ordered the totem poles cut down and removed the carved house posts and painted panels. The loot was packed up and shipped back to Seattle.

Harriman saw himself as a top tier philanthropist. He kept much of the plunder for his own enjoyment, of course, but donated a house post from Gaash to the Burke Museum of Anthropology at the University of Washington in Seattle.

The house post depicts a grizzly bear cradling a human figure in its mouth. This represents the story of Kaats, who married a grizzly. "Come here you bear, the highest bear of all bears," says the Tlingit story that goes with the posts.

The mate of this post went to the museum at the University of Michigan, but it was later acquired by the Burke Museum, where they were displayed together until last year when, after a 70-year long struggle, the Tlingit finally prevailed on the museum to return them.

Now the Burke is offering an exhibit on totem poles called Out of the Silence: the Enduring Power of Totem Poles. The exhibit includes numerous sculptures, panels and carvings, as well as a series of haunting photos by Adelaide de Meuil, who shot nearly 20,000 images of decaying totem pole sites in the 1960s. Naturally, this hardly makes up for the crime of housing stolen property for a century, but it's a compelling overview none-the-less that serves as an introduction to the powerful art of the Northwest tribes and tries to grapple with the unflattering, if not criminal, role played by collectors and anthropologists in robbing the tribes of their treasures.

Of course even at this late date, the Burke has not seen fit to return all of its ill-acquired pieces. They charge a hefty $9 to see the carvings. None of that money is going back to the tribes who produced the work. In fact, one of the masterpieces of the collection is a black 12-foot-long carved sea-lion that once perched on the ridgetop of a chief's lodge in the Tlingit village of Tongass, which gave its name to the magnificent rainforest of Southeast Alaska.

The sea-lion was stolen by a group of Seattle tycoons sent to southeast Alaska by the city's Chamber of Commerce with the express purpose of coming back with native art that could be displayed as "totems" for the Emerald City. Along with the sea-lion, the group sawed down Chief Kinninook's tall, elaborately-carved pole which told the story of the Chief-of-All-Women. It was one of the few Tlingit poles dedicated to a woman. Of course, it's not clear if the men from Seattle had any idea what the pole represented and it wouldn't have deterred them anyway. The pole was shipped back to Seattle, where it was erected as the "Seattle Totem Pole" in Pioneer Square. It stood there from 1900 to 1939, when it was burned down by an arsonist.

But the businessmen, who claimed the village of Tongass had been deserted when they raided it, had been seen by a Tlingit elder, who complained to federal officials. A grand jury was convened and indictments for theft were handed down against the thieves. Before the trial began, the businessmen invited the federal judge presiding over the case out for a night of carousing at an elite club in Seattle. The next morning the judge saw fit to dismiss all the charges. Ultimately, the Chamber of Commerce agreed to send the tribe $500 as recompense. But the money was mistakenly sent to the Tsimshian village at Metlakatla. The people of the Tongass never got a dime.

It could have been different. Instead of clinging on to these stolen fragments, the Burke Museum could have returned them to the tribes and hired tribal carvers to make replicas for the museum. This approach could have preserved the artworks and allowed the tribes to control their heritage, while giving work to a new generation of carvers.

Still the Burke's show at least provides hints at the remarkable range of the art form and the prowess of the artists: the carvings are powerful, haunting, funny, menacing and some as inscrutable as the strangest creations of Miró.

Human faces pop up in the carvings like gargoyles on cathedrals: on the tail of a beaver, in the blowhole of a humpback whale, on the wings of a raven and, more ominously, in the belly of a wolf, its tongue hanging out of a mouth studded with grinning teeth.

Some of the crests represent mythical figures from the time when the world was created. It's easy to imagine a Haida storyteller spinning tales to children in front of a beach fire, using a pole to bring the legends to life. There's Sisiutl, the double-headed sea dragon, who transforms himself into a speeding war-canoe; Fog Woman who brought the salmon to earth; Huxwhukw, the monster bird, with a long beak, sharp as a loggerhead shrike, which it uses to crack open the skulls of men and slurp out their brains; and mightiest of all the Thunderbird, which swoops down from the sky to snatch killer whales in its talons and carry them back to its mountain eyrie.

The poles and panels are almost always carved from a single western red cedar tree, an old-growth specimen with straight grain, few convolutions and knots and standing close to a river or cove so that the pole can be towed by canoe to the erection site. The art of tree selection is almost as demanding and nuanced as the carving itself. Imagine Michelangelo prowling the marble quarries of Carrera.

The felling of the tree is a complex undertaking. The Tlingit and Haida didn't have saws, never mind chainsaws. The technique for felling the large cedars, some 12 feet in diameter, was ingenious and certainly dangerous. First, the carver ringed the bark of the tree with an adze, then he would chisel out a hole in the trunk, place glowing hot rocks inside and wait for them to burn out the core of the tree so that it could be pulled down.

It's tough to build totem poles when all the old-growth cedar has been logged off by big timber companies operating on lands that once belonged to the tribes of the Northwest. That's the predicament facing today's carvers. Joe David is one of the Nuu-Chah-Nulth's greatest young carvers, a man of astounding ability. He lives near the village of Tofino, on heavily clearcut Vancouver Island. He says he finds it almost impossible to find trees tall enough for poles or thick enough for beamposts. Instead, he spends much of his time hiking the beaches looking for logs washed up by the tides. "We're down to sifting through loggers' litter now," he says.

Generally, the chief, like any picky patron, decides what goes on the pole. It is, after all, a symbol of his power, clan history, wealth and esteem. But he usually leaves it up to the artist to design the figures, which are first drawn on the pole with charcoal, then carved and painted, often in striking combinations of black, white and red.

The poles are raised to mark important events in the life of the village or the chief: to inaugurate a new house, hail a marriage, celebrate a birth, commemorate a death. Other poles had more down-to-earth purposes. One Tlingit pole shows an unflattering figure of a Russian, looking remarkably like a squat version of Drosselmeyer's nutcracker, who had seized chucks of tribal land without paying for it. It's a mockery pole and a wanted poster all in one. Another pole from a Nuu-Chah-Nulth village on Vancouver Island served as a kind of collection notice. This pole depicts Dzunuk'wa, the wild woman of the woods, a kind of tribal banshee, with outstretched arms, drowsy eyes, a howling mouth and pendulous breasts. The chief of the village placed this mocking monument in front of the lodge of his in-laws, who had failed to pay off their marriage debt.

The culture of the Northwest tribes revolved around the potlatch, the big party where debts and feuds were settled, alliances formed, marriages planned and history relived. Most of the totem poles were erected before or during potlatches. In 1884, the Canadian government, seeking to crush native customs and move the tribes off their lands, banned the potlatch. The exhibit deals cautiously with this attempted act of cultural genocide. It's unfortunate, because this more than any other factor brought to a close the great age of totem pole building.

The repression went far beyond that of course. The government and their Christian emissaries seized the tribes' ceremonial gear—dresses, masks, puppets, feast dishes and ladles—and carted them off to museums or hacked them apart in front of aghast tribal members. Children were abducted and sent off to government schools and fed Christian doctrine, a deft and proven way to kill off an oral culture.

It wasn't just the Canadian tribes who suffered. The Haida and Tlingit also saw their religious customs assaulted and their populations decimated by disease and forced eviction. A Forest Service survey of the Tongass region in 1900 tallied more than 800 totem poles. Thirty years later, fewer than 200 remained and most of those were "harvested" by the agency for museums in Washington, New York and Chicago.

The potlatches didn't die out completely. They went underground in remote coastal villages, mainly in lands of the Kwakiutl south of the Skeena River. But for the most part the pole raisings had to be abandoned, as they would be a dead giveaway to the persistence of the potlatch. It wasn't until 1951 that the bans were lifted and the old ways could be practiced openly again.

In the meantime, the Canadian government wasted no time in looting the remains of the cultures while they had a chance. In the early 1920s, government agents cut down hundreds of poles in Tsimshian villages and re-erected them miles away along the Canadian-Pacific Railway. The Jasper-to-Prince Rupert run offered a popular "Totem Pole Excursion."

Thus in one stroke the Canadian government moved to extinguish Tsimshian culture and give birth to ethno-tourism. Harriman would have been proud.

Seattle, 2002

PART VI

The Military Menace

Forty-Three

Doomsday At Deseret

On August 22, 1996 the US Army fired up the first furnaces on American soil designed to dispose of the world's deadliest gasses. The incinerator, located at the Deseret Chemical Depot fifty miles west of Salt Lake City, lies on the edge of the small Mormon ranch town of Tooele. Here, stored in rounded bunkers called "igloos," are 13,616 tons of chemical weapons, accounting for 44 percent of the nation's arsenal of mustard gas, Lewisite, the psychoactive agent BZ, GB (sarin) and VX nerve gasses.

These lethal materials are packed in 56,000 M55 rockets, more than one million artillery shells, thousands of mines, cluster bombs, spray tanks and ton-capacity containers. Some of the weapons date back to World War I, while others were upgraded to new levels of lethality during Reagan's arms buildup.

On August 25, 1996, less than 72 hours after it opened, the Tooele plant was forced to shut down after sarin gas leaked from filters above the furnace. Some days later the burners were again turned off when cracks in the concrete ceiling allowed a solution contaminated with nerve agents to leak into a utility room below.

In early September, an M-55 rocket loaded with explosives, propellant and sarin gas was being pushed through the furnace door by a robot when it jammed. Workers had to enter the chamber in rubber suits to dislodge the rocket with long spatula-type poles. All the while the furnace door was open, with the risk that the workers would be fried or exposed to the nerve agent.

These early "malfunctions" prompted the plant manager, Gary Millar, to urge the US Army and the plant's contractor EG&G Defense Materials, headquartered in Wellesley, Mass., to close the plant pending safety review and overhaul. Millar's urgings went unheeded and the nerve agents continued to leak out. On one occasion it took more than 24 hours to detect the source of the leaking sarin gas, which had again contaminated an area where unprotected personnel worked. Two of the workers who had been exposed to the leak, were later fired by EG&G.

By now Millar's efforts to get the plant closed down were having an effect on his own career. His employer, EG&G, told him to stay home for a few weeks, on the grounds that he was suffering from inordinate stress. Millar, who had put in twenty-two years with the defense contractor, says he was dismissed from the company because he insisted on "a level of safety and environmental performance required by state and federal laws and which any reasonably prudent person in my position would have insisted on."

"I started getting feedback that a number of the EG&G people saw me as a threat to their performance and choose to force me out rather than change to a higher level performance level and a safer culture," Millar says. "These managers spent as much time building and maintaining their turf boundaries as they did getting the job done."

In November, Millar sent a twelve-page letter to the chief executive officer of EG&G, Fred Barnes. He told Barnes that the plant was operating with hundreds of chronic technical deficiencies. He criticized Army managers and EG&G corporate officials who insisted on cutting corners and having "an attitude that didn't see safety as much as a risk."

"I can only conclude that current EG&G management actions are typical of the senior management at Three Mile Island before their nuclear incident or at NASA before the Challenger accident," Millar wrote. "I strongly believe that the [Tooele] operation poses a high risk potential to both employees and the public."

As Millar knew, there was scant point in turning to the US Army for muscle against EG&G's management. EG&G, amply stocked with former military officers, functioned merely as the Army's subsidiary. EG&G's Barnes brushed aside Millar's letter, saying that the manager had been relieved of his duties because of "a difference in philosophy at this particular site."

Millar finally began to send copies of his 10,000-word letter to the press and got some coverage on the AP wire. Public attention prompted the US Army to dispatch an investigative team to Tooele supposedly to examine Millar's charges and assess the safety of the plant. In blunter language: to organize a cover-up. On March 18 1997 the Army team released its report. Predictably the Army concluded that it could find no evidence that Millar had been fired because of his safety concerns. The plant was safe, the report said. It was Millar himself who was at fault for many of the problems that had occurred. With a nice line in bureaucratic throat-slitting, the Army report charged that "during his 15 months as general manager, Mr. Millar directed numerous documented and undocumented organizational restructurings and removed several key subordinate managers from their positions. These changes, overlaid on the complex operations of the plant as it progressed toward live-agent trial burn operations, created a turbulent, unfocused management environment." Echoing its assertions about Gulf War Syndrome, the Army also concluded that stress had indeed played a factor in Millar's supposed lapses.

The cover-up has gone well, but there's a problem: the plant continues to leak nerve gas. The Army's liaison manager at the plant, Tim Thomas, confirms that chemical alarms are going off at a rate of one to two times a week, and because of inadequate monitoring devices, the Army is unable to identify the precise chemical signaling the alarm.

For the US Army, EG&G and other defense contractors the stakes are extremely high. Scheduled for construction in the next five years are similar incinerators—each costing anywhere from $500 million to two billion—to be sited at Umatilla, Oregon (Raytheon has the contract); Anniston, Alabama (Westinghouse); Pine Bluff, Arkansas; Pueblo, Colorado; and the Blue Grass Army Depot in Kentucky. These plum contracts—totaling more than $10 billion—are only the beginning of the story. As a result of the Chemical Weapons Convention, the international market in chemical weapons disposal is hugely lucrative, with the total market estimated at nearly $75 billion. So it's scarcely surprising that Millar's letter got thrown in the trash.

The nerve agents stored at Tooele and the other sites are the most lethal in the world. VX, for example, has a toxicity ten thousand times that of its agro-industrial cognate, malathion. And, unlike sarin gas which dissipates quickly, VX is designed to persist in the environment at lethal levels for weeks. All the military nerve agents are closely associated with chemicals used in intensive agriculture and in fact were developed by Shell, Monsanto, FMC and DuPont under contract to the Army. A deadly dose of VX is about a

millionth the size of a grain of salt. Victims of VX and sarin poisoning die a wretched and painful death, typified by excessive saliva-
tion, uncontrollable tearing and urination, followed by seizures and
massive internal bleeding.

Even under the US Army's own conservative reckoning, a catastrophic incident at the Tooele plant involving VX would have a
"one percent kill radius of 60 miles," meaning that at 60 miles from
Tooele, one percent of the population would die. At 30 miles, 50 per
cent could be expected to die. At 15 miles, 75 per cent. As noted
above, the Salt Lake City metro area (population 750,000) is less
than 50 miles from Tooele.

Early in July, we were contacted by a member of the Army's
chemical weapons investigative team, the one that had deep-sixed
Millar. He told us that the conclusion of the Army's probe had been
"pre-ordained," and that it had been obvious from the start that
Millar was scheduled to be the scapegoat. The investigator said the
US Army team had been tightly controlled by Brigadier-General
Thomas Konitzer. Among other measures, Konitzer squashed an
assessment by our informant which had concluded that the Tooele
plant was "plagued by technical and organizational problems which,
under the current management regime, opened the potential for a
catastrophic incident."

But Konitzer was uninterested in anything but Millar's psycho-
logical mindset. "It's clear to me," our man concludes, "that the
Army is more concerned with controlling leaks to the media than in
securing the sound and safe operation of the plant. Was Gary Millar
under stress? Given what was going on out there, and the indifference of his superiors, he would've been insane not to be."

The Army investigator said that most of the flaws in the Tooele
plant were well known by the Army and EG&G since at least 1994,
when Steven Jones had pointed them out.

Jones was the environment and safety officer at the Tooele
plant until he was fired in 1994 for refusing to sign off on a document certifying that the incinerator was safe to operate. Jones pointed to a list of more than 3,000 safety violations at the facility, including some major design flaws. EG&G's president justified the dismissal of Jones on the grounds that the safety officer had approached
his work with "an overabundance of enthusiasm."

We reached Jones at his home in Provo, Utah. Ever since his dismissal in September 1994 he's been battling EG&G about his dismissal, and a possible settlement. And his criticisms of the plant of intensified. "All of the mishaps at the plant were predicted three years ago," Jones said. He told us unequivocally that if the plant is permitted to stay in operation without major changes there's going to "a catastrophe." Before taking the job at Tooele, Jones had served as an environmental and health officer for the Defense Department, overseeing what he called the military's "hot spots."

"Every day there are deficiencies being revealed," Jones says. "One of the biggest flaws is that the stack monitors don't work when they are exposed to heat, which means when the furnaces are burning. They have absolutely no idea what's coming out of the stack."

According to Jones, few of the employees have been trained to handle the extremely dangerous chemicals. A particular problem has developed with the operators of the forklifts used to move the M-55 rockets from their igloos (bunkers) to the furnace. Under the best of circumstances, the Army's own estimates suggests there's a one in 200 chance that a forklift is going to drop or puncture a rocket. Inside the rockets are volatile fuels, detonators, high explosives and enough nerve gas to kill 100,000 people. A forklift has already dropped a one-ton container of sarin gas, Jones reports.

Jones tells us the ventilator system at Tooele doesn't work, and that the overall approach to worker safety is abysmal. "The Army acts as if its immune from OSHA. They neither know nor care what's coming out of those stacks. They see their mission as merely to destroy the agent. If there are no dead bodies, they believe the mission is a success. But when the body count comes at Tooele or one of the other plants it's going to come quick and could be in the tens of thousands."

The description of the decommissioning process at the plant furnished to us by Jones is remarkable. A conveyer belt carries a rocket under a huge "laser-guided" slicer, which often fouls up, cutting the rocket in the wrong place, and dispenses the various sections of the rocket in the wrong furnace. Often, explosives end up in the furnace reserved for nerve agents and vice versa. Jones pointed out that at the Army's prototype incinerator operated by Raytheon at Johnston Atoll in the South Pacific, there have been numerous instances where the nerve agent kilns have been rocked and damaged by explosions. In its three years of operation, the Johnston Atoll incinerator has had 32 releases of nerve gas into the plant and the atmosphere.

"Never put anything negative about the plant in writing," Jones tells us he was told by his superiors. "This direction makes it impossible to do inspections because if you find deficiencies you can't write them up." Jones reckons that it would take EG&G at least three years to even get a grasp of the safety problems at the plant. But he's under no illusions that the company or the Army will come to their senses. In May, EG&G fired its environmental officer, Tina Campbell, after she complained about repeated violations. In late June, the plant experienced another large leak and remains temporarily shut down until the source can be located.

"The Army and the defense contractors are so heavily invested in this incineration technology that it looks like only a major disaster will derail them from building the other plants, which are exact clones of Tooele," Jones said. "But the risks climb for the Alabama and Pine Bluff plants where hundreds of thousands of people live near the site." Nearly fifty-percent of the people living near these two sites are black.

Inhabitants of Utah can scarcely take comfort from the reason plants like Tooele are located there. When the Atomic Energy Commission was justifying atmospheric testing of nuclear weapons at its Nevada site, the Commission agreed that it would only explode its bombs when the wind was coming out of the west, away from Las Vegas and Reno and towards the rural inhabitants of Utah, who were classified as "a low-use segment of the population". Eisenhower held a similar view of the expendability of Mormons, saying in 1956, the year the Dugway Proving Grounds conducted open air tests of sarin gas west of Tooele, that "We can afford to sacrifice a few thousand people out there in the interests of national security."

Afterword
Tooele: Triumph and Near-Disaster

Steven Jones, the former safety officer at the Army's chemical weapons incinerator in Tooele, Utah, won a tremendous victory on August 1, 1997 when federal labor Judge Ellin O'Shea ruled that Jones had been illegally removed from his job. In a fiercely worded 141-page finding, O'Shea ruled that Jones had been fired simply because he was trying to enforce environmental laws at the plant. She said testimony by officials from EG&G was "not credible or reliable" and that the reasons the company gave for dismissing Jones were "based on lie." O'Shea also singled out the Army for criticism, noting that the Tooele facility is "uniquely and solely controlled by and subject to [the] military."

The judge ordered EG&G to rehire Jones and pay him his full back salary since the date of his termination (roughly $250,000), and another $200,000 in economic and punitive damages. If EG&G decides not to reinstate Jones, the company must pay Jones another $500,000.

Jones said that he feels vindicated by the verdict and is ready to go back to work. The first thing he plans to do is to insist on an independent audit of the plant's operations. "They need some honesty and integrity out there," Jones said.

About the same time Judge O'Shea was putting the finishing touches on her decision in the Jones case, the Tooele plant experienced another brush with disaster. During the last week in May two delegations of congressional staffers and civic leaders from Oregon and Kentucky on a tour of the plant may have been exposed to sarin gas clinging to the casing of improperly stored MC-1 nerve gas bombs. The bombs were inspected by the group at close range. The group, which was unaware that the bombs had not been certified as decontaminated, wore no protective clothing.

Only a few hours after the group left Tooele, the Army tested the shell casings and discovered the presence of sarin gas. Instead of declaring "a chemical event," which would have triggered notification of federal and state environmental agencies and immediate medical attention for the tour group, the Army decided to cover up the mishap. The bomb parts were discreetly wrapped in plastic, stuffed into a metal container and moved to a storage area for "hot" materials.

The next day on anonymous caller tipped off the Utah Department of Environmental Quality about the events at Tooele.

DEQ officials called the Army, which confirmed the information but said the accident was inconsequential. According to an internal Army memo, "because of the recent interest, a decision was made to classify the agent detection within the bombs as a "chemical event." In other words, the Army admitted what had occurred only after it had been caught.

Still the Army took no action. Though half of the Oregon tour group remained in their hotel in Salt Lake City, the Army decided not to tell them about their possible exposure to the deadly gas. Two days later, the mayor of Hermiston, Oregon (the nearest community to the planned Umatilla chemical weapons incinerator, now under construction by the Army and Raytheon) got an anonymous call saying he had been exposed to nerve gas during the Tooele tour. The Army stayed quiet. Only on June 4, five days after the tour, did the Army contact members of the tour, inform them of the incident and assure them that they had never been at any risk. While members of the Oregon delegation were advised to have their blood checked for nerve agents, for some reason the people from Kentucky (site of the proposed Bluegrass incinerator near Richmond) were not told to seek any medical attention.

"The whole affair is abysmally stupid," says Oregon congressman Peter DeFazio. "If the safety of the group touring Tooele can't be assured, how can people trust the Army to protect their safety near these incinerators. This is a dubious technology that's extremely expensive and dangerous. A real mistake."

Tooele, Utah, 1997

Forty-Four

Chemical Weapons

As American As I.G. Farben

The US's lethal stockpile of nerve gas weapons is one of the darker chapters of the Cold War era. The story largely begins in Nazi Germany where, in 1936, I.G. Farben's chemical labs produced the first nerve agent, a toxic gas it marketed as Tabun. This was soon followed by Soman, Sarin and Zyklon-B. These nerve agents were thousands of times as lethal as the mustard gas and blistering agents deployed to such ghastly effect in World War I.

At the close of World War II, US intelligence agencies raided Farben's labs, seizing more than 1,000 tons of Tabun and Sarin gas, which it sent back to the US in large canisters labeled chlorine. Thither also intelligence agencies smuggled dozens of Nazi chemists. One of the more infamous was Walter Schreiber, a veteran of the grotesque aviation "medical" experiments at Dachau, where Nazi doctors—among other atrocities—injected insecticides into the blood and livers of concentration camp prisoners. Schreiber landed in Texas where he continued his chemical weapons research until he was exposed in 1952 by columnist Drew Pearson and fled to the friendlier terrain of Argentina.

In 1956, Rep. Gerald Ford pushed through a change in US policy giving the military "first strike" authority. But the big boom in US chemical weapons production occurred during the Kennedy administration, when annual spending on chemical weapons rose from $75 million to more than $330 million. The stockpiling of chemical weapons was overseen by Robert McNamara, who referred to the weapons as "a national asset." Under McNamara's direction, the US began deploying its chemical arsenal in Vietnam in 1964.

One of McNamara's assistants, Harold Brown (later Secretary of Defense, under Jimmy Carter), extolled the humanitarian virtues of chemical weapons: "Of particular interest is the possible use of nonlethal chemicals. That, of course, is an option which chemicals provide you that nuclear and high explosives do not. These weapons can incapacitate enemy forces with only a small percentage of fatalities."

During the Johnson administration, the Pentagon begged for the chance to use some of its arsenal against civil rights and anti-war protestors to demonstrate to the American people the "efficacy" of the chemicals. "By using gas in civil situations we accomplish two purposes: controlling crowds and also educating people on gas," said Major General J.B. Medaris. "Now everybody is being called savage if he just talks about it. But nerve gas is the only way I know of to sort out the guys in white hats from the ones in the black hats without killing any of them."

The US Army's chemical weapons program was a lucrative source of cash for dozens of universities, chemical and aerospace companies and academic researchers. Napalm was developed by Harvard scientist Dr. Louis Frisues, who also concocted a mad scheme to have bats drop tiny bombs on Japan during World War II. The Stanford Research Institute was given a $2 million federal grant to study the possibility of dispersing chemical agents from the exhaust of solid fuel rockets.

The research into biological weapons was just as bizarre. One of the biological agents developed for deployment in Southeast Asia was Rift Valley Fever, an extremely infectious virus to which Asians are particularly vulnerable. The LA-based Litton Industries, founded by Tex Thornton, a former spy for OSS, developed a delivery system for the virus. Litton's project was called "Supersonic delivery of dry biological agents." Meanwhile, the Air Force paid Goodyear more than $5 million to develop a packaging system for its virus, so the lethal germs could be safely transported around the globe.

Many of the research grants for biological and chemical weapons were funneled through the University of Oklahoma, disguised as funding for "ecological research in Alaska and Utah." These research projects were actually conducted at Ft. Greeley, Alaska and the Dugway Proving Grounds in Utah. Some of the funds went to study the feasibility of "seeding the winds with chemical and biological agents." But most of the research concentrated on the development of MEF, Mortality Enhancing Factors.

In 1984, Ronald Reagan complicated the current task of safely disposing of the weapons enormously by ordering over a half million M55 rockets retooled so that they contained high-yield explosives as well as VX gas. The Army now claims that many of these rockets are "unstable," are leaking nerve agent and may "self-detonate" if they are not destroyed by the year 2005.

                                                        Tooele, Utah, 1997

Forty-Five

Germ War

An American Chronology

As far as chemical and biological weapons are concerned," Madeleine Albright thundered, "Saddam Hussein is a repeat offender. He has used them against his neighbors and on his own people."

By Albright's criteria, Saddam has a way to go to catch up with the United States, which has deployed its CBW arsenal against the Philippines, Puerto Rico, Vietnam, China, North Korea, Laos, Cambodia, Cuba, Haitian boat people and Canada. Even more damning, the US Army, Navy and CIA CBW researchers have deliberately exposed hundreds of thousands of unwitting US citizens to an astonishing array of germ agents and toxic chemicals, killing dozens of people.

The US experimentation with bio-weapons goes back at least to 1900, when US Army doctors in the Philippines infected five prisoners with a variety of plague. At least four of the subjects died. In 1915, a doctor working with government grants allowed 12 prisoners in Mississippi to suffer untreated from pellagra, an incapacitating disease that attacks the central nervous system.

After World War I, the United States went on a chemical weapons binge, producing millions of barrels of mustard gas and Lewisite. Thousands of US troops were exposed to these chemical agents in order to "test the efficacy of gas masks and protective clothing." The Veterans Administration refused to honor disability claims from victims of these experiments. The Army also deployed mustard gas against anti-US protesters in Puerto Rico and the Philippines in the 1920s and 1930s.

In 1931, Dr. Cornelius Rhoads, then under contract with the Rockefeller Institute for Medical Investigations, initiated his horrific Puerto Rico Cancer Experiments. Rhoads infected dozens of unwitting subjects with cancer cells. At least thirteen of his victims died as a result. Rhoads, however, went on to head of the US Army Biological Weapons division and to serve on the Atomic Energy Commission, where he oversaw the gruesome radiation experiments on thousands of US citizens. In memos to the Department of Defense, Rhoads expressed his opinion that Puerto Rican dissidents could be "eradicated" with the judicious use of germ bombs.

In 1942, US Army and Navy doctors infected 400 prisoners in Chicago with malaria in experiments designed to get "a profile of the disease and develop a treatment for it." Most of the inmates were black, none where informed of the risks of the experiment. Nazi doctors on trial at Nuremberg cited the Chicago malaria experiments as part of their defense.

In 1947, the US Army put on its payroll Dr. Shiro Ishii, the head of the Imperial Army of Japan's bio-warfare unit. During World War II, Dr. Ishii had deployed a wide range of biological and chemical agents against Chinese and Allied troops. He also operated a large research center in Manchuria, where he conducted bio-weapons experiments on Chinese, Russian and American prisoners of war. Ishii infected prisoners with tetanus; gave them typhoid-laced tomatoes; developed plague-infected fleas; infected women with syphilis; performed dissections on live prisoners; and exploded germ bombs over dozens of men tied to stakes. In a deal hatched by Gen. Douglas MacArthur, Ishii turned over more than 10,000 pages of his "research findings" to the US Army, avoided prosecution for war crimes and was invited to lecture at Ft. Detrick, the US Army bio-weapons center in Frederick, Maryland.

In 1950 the US Navy sprayed large quantities of serratia marcescens, a bacteriological agent, over San Francisco, promoting an outbreak of pneumonia-like illnesses and causing the death of at least one man, Ed Nevins.

A year later, Chinese Premier Chou En-Lai charged that the US military and the CIA had used bio-agents against North Korea and China. Chou produced statements from 25 US prisoners of war backing his claims that the US had dropped anthrax-contaminated feathers, mosquitoes and fleas carrying Yellow Fever and propaganda leaflets spiked with cholera over Manchuria and North Korea. Secretary of State Dean Acheson dismissed Chou's accusations as being based on the "coerced confessions of brainwashed POWs."

Acheson blamed the outbreaks of disease in northern China and Korea on the "Communists' inability to care for the health of the people under their control." But in the fall of 1952 an International Commission looking into the matter produced a 700-page report supporting Chou's claims. The report noted that the insects found in the vicinity of the US "leaflet drops" were not native to the region. The Commission noted a "striking similarity" with the techniques perfected by Dr. Ishii during the Japanese occupation of Manchuria.

From 1950 through 1953, the US Army released chemical clouds over six US and Canadian cities. The tests were designed to test dispersal patterns of chemical weapons. Army records noted that the compounds used over Winnipeg, Canada, where there were numerous reports of respiratory illnesses, involved cadmium, a highly toxic chemical.

In 1951, the US Army secretly contaminated the Norfolk Naval Supply Center in Virginia with infectious bacteria. One type was chosen because blacks were believed to be more susceptible than whites. A similar experiment was undertaken later that year at Washington, DC's National Airport. The bacteria was later linked to food and blood poisoning and respiratory problems.

Savannah, Georgia and Avon Park, Florida were the targets of repeated Army bio-weapons experiments in 1956 and 1957. Army CBW researchers released millions of mosquitoes on the two towns in order to test the ability of insects to carry and deliver yellow fever and dengue fever. Hundreds of residents fell ill, suffering from fevers, respiratory distress, stillbirths, encephalitis and typhoid. Army researchers disguised themselves as public health workers in order photograph and test the victims. Several deaths were reported.

In 1965, the US Army and the Dow Chemical Company injected dioxin into 70 prisoners (most of them black) at the Holmesburg State Prison in Pennsylvania. The prisoners developed severe lesions which went untreated for seven months. A year later, the US Army set about the most ambitious chemical warfare operation in history.

From 1966 to 1972, the United States dumped more than 12 million gallons of Agent Orange (a dioxin-based herbicide) over about 4.5 million acres of South Vietnam, Laos and Cambodia. The government of Vietnam estimated the civilian casualties from Agent Orange at more than 500,000. The legacy continues with high levels of birth defects in areas that were saturated with the chemical. Tens of thousands of US soldiers were also the victims of Agent Orange.

In a still classified experiment, the US Army sprayed an unknown bacterial agent in the New York Subway system in 1966. It is not known if the test caused any illnesses.

A year later, the CIA placed a chemical substance in the drinking water supply of the Food and Drug Administration headquarters in Washington, DC. The test was designed to see if it was possible to poison drinking water with LSD or other incapacitating agents.

In 1969, Dr. D.M. McArtor, the deputy director for Research and Technology for the Department of Defense, asked Congress to appropriate $10 million for the development of a synthetic biological agent that would be resistant "to the immunological and therapeutic processes upon which we depend to maintain our relative freedom from infectious disease."

In 1971, the first documented cases of swine fever in the western hemisphere showed up in Cuba. A CIA agent admitted in 1977 that he had been instructed to deliver the virus to Cuban exiles in Panama, who carried the virus into Cuba in March of 1971. This astounding admission was met by a sepulchral silence by the US press.

In 1980, hundreds of Haitian men, who had been locked up in detention camps in Miami and Puerto Rico, developed gynecomasia after receiving "hormone" shots from US doctors. Gynecomasia is a condition causing males to develop full-sized female breasts.

In 1981, Fidel Castro blamed an outbreak of dengue fever in Cuba on the CIA. The fever killed 188 people, including 88 children. In 1988, a Cuban exile leader named Eduardo Arocena admitted "bringing some germs" into Cuba in 1980.

Four years later an epidemic of dengue fever struck Managua, Nicaragua. Nearly 50,000 people came down with the fever and dozens died. This was the first outbreak of the disease in Nicaragua. It occurred at the height of the CIA's war against the Sandinista government and followed a series of low-level "reconnaissance" flights over the capital city.

In 1996, the Cuban government again accused the US of engaging in "biological aggression." This time it involved an outbreak of thrips palmi, an insect that kills palm trees and other vege-tation first showed up in Cuba on December 12, 1996, following low-level flights over the island. The US has been unable to quash a United Nations investigation of the incident.

At the close of the Gulf War, the US Army exploded an Iraqi chemical weapons depot at Kamashiya. In 1996, the Department of Defense finally admitted that more than 20,000 US troops were exposed to VX and sarin nerve agents as a result of the US operation at Kamashiya. This may be one cause of Gulf War Syndrome, anoth-er factor is certainly the experimental vaccines given to more than 100,000 US troops. The doctors and the Pentagon knew the risks, the soldiers didn't.

Portland, 1997

Forty-Six

Glow Bugs

Hanford's Radioactive Ecology

In the spring of 1997, researchers conducting routine surveys of insect and plant life at the Hanford Nuclear Reservation, the vast Department of Energy site in eastern Washington which abuts the Columbia River, began to notice a strange and potentially horrifying phenomenon. More than a dozen new radioactive hot spots had sprouted up seemingly spontaneously across the 560-square mile site. Clearly, the radiation from the nation's chief nuclear complex was spreading, but how? The Hanford scientists pinned the blame for the contamination on "ecological transport." In other words, radioactive chemicals from supposedly contained areas had been transferred by bugs. The culprits include fruit flies, ants, worms, roaches and gnats.

In one instance, traces of strontium-90 were detected in a trailer used by Hanford workers as an office and a kitchen. According to an internal report obtained by *In These Times*, it was "determined that several items in the trailer were contaminated, including a cutting board, a countertop, a bench-seat, the floor, garbage cans and their contents, door handles and food wrappers." The review notes that the dumpsters near the trailer were emptied and transported not to a hazardous waste site, but in regular garbage trucks to the municipal landfill near Richland, Washington. The garbage trucks were later found to contain traces of radiation and were quarantined. The hot portions of the Richland landfill were cordoned off for weeks before the contaminated materials were excavated.

Although the Department of Energy claims there is no cause for alarm, there is evidence that Hanford workers who were not wearing protective gear were exposed to strontium-90. Several employees showed traces of radiation on their shoes and clothes. In at least one case, an ironworker at Hanford appears to have transferred the radiation to his home, where the carpet, floors, and laundry hamper tested positive for strontium-90 and other radioactive chemicals.

The presence of stronitum-90 has led investigators to conclude that the ultimate source of the radioactivity is a site known as B-Plant, a waste storage facility that is the only place at Hanford which stores strontium-90. The researchers believe that fruit flies, gnats, mice and other animals and insects have picked up traces of the deadly chemical and deposited it across the Hanford site and perhaps into the surrounding area.

The radiation is not just being spread by bugs and mice. A new study by the Government Accountability Project and scientist Norm Buske reveals that leaves from mulberry trees growing along the shores of the Columbia River are turning up disturbingly high levels of radioactive chemicals. Buske collected leaves growing from trees near a site known as N-Springs, where contaminated groundwater from Hanford seeps into the Columbia River. According to Buske's analysis, the mulberry leaves contained 32,000 picocuries per kilogram of strontium-90, more than 4,000 times the drinking water limit.

"Strontium-90, uranium and chromium are seeping into spawning grounds next to the old H-reactor," says Norm Buske, a physicist and oceanographer based in Spokane who heads Nuclear Free America. "The long-term health of the Columbia and Alaskan Pacific salmon fisheries is now threatened by the mix of radio-chemicals oozing from DOE's mismanaged Hanford wastes." This means that the radioactive legacy of the Cold War, once believed to be contained inside the confines of Hanford, is now moving inexorably off government land and into the communities, food and water supplies and ecosystems of the Pacific Northwest.

For nearly fifty years, Hanford manufactured uranium and plutonium to power the United States' nuclear arsenal, in a secretive operation with little regard for environmental safeguards. The activities at Hanford were not limited to bomb-making. They also included deliberate releases of radioactive iodine into the atmosphere to test fall-out patterns. Although the Department of Energy continues to deny any culpability, these releases are believed to be the cause of thousands of thyroid cancers in communities downwind from the weapons plant. With the collapse of the Cold War, the environmental ruins at Hanford were unveiled. It was called the most toxic site in North America, perhaps the world. So far Congress has spent more than $15 billion to deal with the contamination, with few results. The latest estimates suggests that the cleanup could take 50 years and cost more than $50 billion.

Through a quasi-privatization scheme launched in Clinton's first term, the day-to-day operations at Hanford are now run not by the Department of Energy but by the San Diego-based Fluor Daniel Corporation, an international construction conglomerate. As reported in earlier *In These Times* stories, Fluor used its political influence and massive campaign contributions to help win a record $5 billion contract to supervise the clean-up at Hanford. Fluor's existence has been a troubled one, marked by cost-overruns and a series of accidents, including an explosion last year which blew a hole in the Plutonium Processing Plant and released radioactive chemicals into the atmosphere.

Hanford watchers worry that Fluor is not up to the task of handling cleanup and that the new factor of radioactive bugs spreading the contamination only underscores the need for a radically different approach. "Fluor and DOE's approach to the Hanford site is really little more than multi-billion dollar spin-doctoring," said Tom Carpenter, director of the Government Accountability Project's Hanford program. "They had their chance to fix these problems, but failed."

Buske, and other Hanford activists, claim that the Department of Energy is incapable of handling the Hanford cleanup. "Their interest isn't cleanup, but keeping enough money pouring into Hanford to keep the bomb-building infrastructure in place," Buske says. "The only hope is to kill the nuclear weapons mission and turn over the site to an agency that is willing and capable of cleaning up the mess." One possible scenario brimming with irony is to hand Hanford over to the Department of the Interior, turning the irradiated wasteland into a national wildlife refuge.

Richland, 1997

Forty-Seven

Hot Property, Cold Cash

On May 14, 1997 at 10:47 p.m., a chemical tank exploded in a deserted factory at the Hanford Nuclear Reservation outside Richland, WA, the final resting place for more than two-thirds of the nation's high-level nuclear waste.

The explosion was extraordinarily powerful, blowing down steel doors and shattering windows throughout the building. The blast shredded the steel liner of a 1,500 gallon chemical drum laced with plutonium, sending the heavy metal lid hurtling through the ceiling, where it ruptured a water main and burst through the roof. Water poured into the room, streamed down four flights of stairs and flooded the nearby parking lot. A yellow-orange plume of toxic gases drifted over the Hanford site and nearby communities.

The explosion occurred less than 20 yards from a silo holding nearly 10 tons of plutonium, one of the largest caches of this deadly material in the world. If the blast had breached the plutonium silo, the destruction would have rivaled Chernobyl.

By all accounts, the scene in the wake of the explosion was chaotic. Plant managers were giving conflicting orders, emergency response codes were ignored, workers were ordered into contaminated areas without protective gear, other agencies were kept in the dark for hours and the public highway that runs near the site remained open to traffic.

At first, some suspected sabotage. The Department of Energy (DOE) has spent tens of millions of dollars to protect the plant from terrorist attacks. Black-suited guards with machine guns slung over their shoulders constantly patrol the site, which is ringed by electronic monitors, TV cameras and razorwire fences.

However, it soon became clear that the explosion was the result not of a bomb but of mismanagement by Hanford's lead contractor, Fluor Daniel, a wholly owned subsidiary of the Irvine, Calif.-based Fluor Corporation, a booming global construction company with annual revenues of more than $10 billion.

An internal DOE assessment of the near-disaster skewered

Fluor for numerous safety and reporting violations, noting that the chemical tank had not even been inspected for over six months despite signs that such an "autocatalytic explosion" was possible. Lloyd Pipe, a former acting manager of the plant, calls the DOE review "downright ugly." "We failed in some key areas of responsibility," he says. "Across the board, our actions in the wake of the explosion did not meet our expectations." Before the internal review was released to the public, Fluor's lawyers edited out key findings relating to possible violations of federal law, risks to human health and the extent of off-site contamination.

Gerald Pollet, director of the Hanford watchdog group Heart of America Northwest, sums up the incident more succinctly: "Fluor Daniel violated every rule in the book, put thousands of lives at risk and then, in the great Hanford tradition, tried to cover it all up and accuse the workers and nearby residents of mass hysteria."

For many long-time Hanford watchers, the explosion at the plutonium finishing plant wasn't a surprise. Environmentalists and seasoned DOE employees contend that Fluor snared the lucrative Hanford contract not because of its expertise in environmental cleanup, but due to the firm's inside connections to the Clinton administration and the six-figure contributions it made to the Democratic National Committee (DNC).

Hanford first burst into the national spotlight on August 9, 1945, when the Fat Boy bomb, armed with plutonium concocted at Hanford, incinerated Nagasaki, killing more than 39,000 people. Over the next 40 years, Hanford's atomic engineers churned out 54 tons of plutonium, 65 percent of America's nuclear arsenal. The engineers were proud of the bombs they had created, but much more cavalier about the toxic debris of the arms race. At Hanford, only the highest level nuclear waste—thick plutonium sludge—was tucked away into 177 underground tanks, each the size of Carnegie Hall. Nearly half of these tanks now are leaking plutonium in a steady drizzle toward the aquifer that lies beneath Hanford, while others are bubbling away in a dangerous and uncontrollable "self-boil." Most of the toxic waste—an estimated 400 billion gallons of contaminated liquid—was simply dumped, poured and sprayed right into the soil at Hanford, just meters from the Columbia River.

Fluor won the five-year, $5 billion contract to supervise the cleanup of Hanford in the summer of 1996, after a string of disastrous accidents cost Westinghouse, Hanford's previous contractor, its contract. The government awarded Fluor the contract over the objections of several senior DOE officials who felt that the company was not experienced enough for such a complex and dangerous operation. "Fluor is basically a big construction company with a get-in and get-out quick mentality," says a longtime DOE staffer. "But Hanford is something else entirely. This is a 100-year cleanup where the slightest mistake could spell disaster and put a million lives at risk."

Fluor's recent experience with the DOE was another cause for concern. In 1993, the company was awarded a contract to manage the Fernald nuclear site outside Cincinnati. Fluor agreed to clean up the toxic residue at this former uranium processing plant, which houses more than 20 million pounds of radioactive materials, for $2.2 billion. But in Fluor's four years at Fernald, the company has been accused of massive overbilling, shoddy work performance and false record keeping. Fluor was also cited by the DOE for more than 1,000 serious safety violations, ranging from lax rules to exposure to radiation.

The allegations against Fluor surfaced in a remarkable series of stories by investigative reporter Mike Gallagher in the *Cincinnati Enquirer* beginning in February 1996. Gallagher's exposes prompted a DOE investigation, an audit by the General Accounting Office and congressional hearings. Fluor's Fernald operation has been hit with a record $34 million in fines for worker injuries, poor job performance and bad bookkeeping. Most disturbingly, Fluor has been cited for violating guidelines on nuclear criticality, the potentially explosive buildup of radiation that occurs when tanks of radioactive waste are stored too close to each other.

DOE officials knew Fluor's record at Fernald when they awarded it the contract to oversee operations at Hanford. How, then, did a company with Fluor's reputation for shoddy and reckless work end up with such a lucrative and dangerous deal to oversee the cleanup of what the DOE itself calls "the single largest environmental and health risk in the nation?"

The answer is political connections. At the onset of the Clinton era, Fluor recognized the potential for huge deals involving the cleanup of hazardous waste sites on federal properties. For help, the company turned to Peter S. Knight, a key Washington, D.C., fixer with close ties to Al Gore. For 13 years, Knight served as chief of staff for Gore during his tenure in the House and Senate. Knight ran Gore's failed 1988 presidential campaign and headed his 1992 vice-presidential run.

After the election, Knight was named to Clinton's transition team where he oversaw appointments of subcabinet positions at the Environmental Protection Agency and the Interior and Energy departments, including the choice of Thomas Grumbly as assistant secretary of energy. It was Grumbly who awarded the Hanford contract to Fluor, gave the company money to design part of the controversial Yucca Mountain nuclear waste storage plant and resisted demands that the company's troubled Fernald contract be canceled.

Knight left the transition team in January 1993 to join the powerful Washington law firm of Wunder, Diefenderfer, Cannon and Thelen. Knight was startlingly upfront about using his ties to Gore and other high-ranking Clinton officials as a way to recruit clients. In a solicitation letter to one client, Knight boasted he was "very familiar with DOE and close to Secretary Hazel O'Leary's new team." Knight soon became one of the outfit's top lobbyists, racking up an impressive roster of high-profile clients including Disney, Lockheed-Martin and Molten Metal Technologies. In his first year, Knight registered more than a million dollars in billings. His standard fee was between $10,000 and $25,000 a month.

By the end of 1994, Knight and his clients were poised to make a killing off his pal Gore's Reinventing Government Initiative, which proposed to "streamline" government programs and hand over some functions to the private sector. The scheme to privatize many of the DOE's most sensitive operations was particularly lucrative. The DOE offered more than 200 different projects, where private firms would be handsomely paid to run government operations like the cleanup at Hanford. For corporations such as Fluor and Lockheed, this was a no-lose situation: fat government contracts and minimal oversight. "These contracts are one of the great scandals of the Clinton era," says Pollet of Heart of America Northwest. "There's no financial risk no matter how badly you botch the job."

The $5 billion Hanford "integrated management" contract was

the biggest prize of all. Thirteen big firms put in bids for the Hanford project, led by defense giant Raytheon. Knight pleaded Fluor's case. It was a hard sell, given the company's track record at Fernald. But as a final inducement, Fluor sent a check to the DNC for $100,000 on May 3, 1996. (Fluor gave the Democrats a total of $203,000 during the 1995-96 election cycle.) A few weeks later, Grumbly awarded Fluor the contract. "Everyone thought Raytheon had the deal sewed up," says Todd Martin from the Hanford Environmental Action League. "Raytheon certainly did. They'd already opened an office near Hanford. When DOE gave the contract to Fluor, it came as a total shock."

Fluor assumed control of operations at Hanford on October 1, 1996. The company was supposed to have developed an integrated work safety plan prior to that date. After requesting several extensions, Fluor finally produced in January 1997 what one DOE staffer described as a "mishmash of confusing and conflicting guidelines." It wasn't until the following September, nearly a year after being awarded the contract, that Fluor finally produced an acceptable safety plan. But over that year, the company's safety record was riddled with accidents, including explosions, electrical fires, injuries and chemical spills.

"They haven't met with the community, haven't consulted with public interest groups and don't listen to their workers," says Tom Carpenter, a lawyer with the Government Accountability Project in Seattle. "Many of Fluor's managers are former military men who remain mired in a Cold War mentality. They're addicted to secrecy and dismiss safety questions as a secondary concern. This is a nonunion company that isn't used to listening to its workers and isn't comfortable with even the slightest criticism. When workers speak up, they're simply fired."

Carpenter has represented numerous Hanford workers who have risked their careers to expose dangerous operations at the site. This summer, Carpenter filed a whistleblower complaint with the Department of Labor on behalf of seven pipefitters who were fired by Fluor after they objected to the use of faulty valves on a pipe used to carry high-level nuclear waste from one storage tank to another.

How much will it cost to mop up the mess at Hanford? The Department of Energy says $40 billion over the next 30 years. But other economists estimate that the figure may soar to as high as $300 billion in an operation that could drag out over the next 75 to 100 years. Over the past decade, more than $10 billion has been spent at Hanford with almost nothing to show for it. Fluor is already more than $100 million over budget, and the DOE, in an internal review in November, rated the company's performance in key areas as "marginal" (the equivalent of a D). Fluor even submitted bills to the DOE for two lobbyists it hired to weaken Washington state's hazardous waste laws.

Despite this sordid record, the DOE has no plans to terminate the contract. In fact, Fluor seems poised to cash in on performance bonds that could net the company a $54 million bonus for its first year at Hanford and, according to sources inside the DOE, the company may be in line to get a five-year extension of the contract, worth another $5 to $7 billion.

Meanwhile, in September 1997, congressional investigators subpoenaed 64 boxes of records from the DOE and Fluor regarding the Hanford contract. Knight and Grumbly have been forced to undergo grueling depositions. They both deny any wrongdoing. The Republicans in Congress have used the scandal as a way to bludgeon Gore.

There's a joke going around Hanford these days. What has Fluor done in a year that Westinghouse couldn't do in 10? Make Westinghouse look good. To those who live downwind from Hanford, the punch line carries a morbid edge. "I'm afraid to go out there now," says Carpenter. "Fluor's management of the place is simply incompetent. At Hanford, the slightest screw-up can have the deadliest consequences."

Seattle, 1998

Forty-Eight

Depleted Uranium

Cancer as Weapon

[This story was written during the NATO bombing campaign against Yugoslavia. Since then depleted uranium weapons have been used in the US wars against Afghanistan in 2001 and Iraq in 2003. DU is most commonly used in armor plating for tanks and personel carriers and as casing for rockets and bombs. In the most recent war on Iraq, environmental scientists with Britain's Royal Society estimate that more than 3,000 tons of DU weapons were used by US and British forces. The Royal Society called for removal of the radioactive debris to protect the health of Iraqi citizens and occupation forces. The Pentagon rebuffed the request, maintaining that the DU posed no health risks.]

At the close of the Gulf War in 1991, Saddam Hussein was denounced as a ferocious villain for ordering his retreating troops to destroy Kuwaiti oil fields, clotting the air with poisonous clouds of black smoke and saturating the ground with swamps of crude. It was justly called an environmental war crime.

But months of bombing of Iraq by US and British planes and cruise missiles has left behind an even more deadly and insidious legacy: tons of shell casings, bullets and bomb fragments laced with depleted uranium. In all, the US hit Iraqi targets with more than 970 radioactive bombs and missiles.

More than 10 years later, the health consequences from this radioactive bombing campaign are beginning to come into focus. And they are dire, indeed. Iraqi physicians call it "the white death"—leukemia. Since 1990, the incident rate of leukemia in Iraq has grown by more than 600 percent. The situation is compounded by Iraq's forced isolations and the sadistic sanctions regime, recently described by UN secretary general Kofi Annan as "a humanitarian crisis," that makes detection and treatment of the cancers all the more difficult.

"We have proof of traces of DU in samples taken for analysis and that is really bad for those who assert that cancer cases have grown for other reasons," says Dr. Umid Mubarak, Iraq's health minister.

Mubarak contends that the US's fear of facing the health and environmental consequences of its DU bombing campaign is partly behind its failure to follow through on its commitments under a deal allowing Iraq to sell some of its vast oil reserves in return for food and medical supplies.

"The desert dust carries death," said Dr. Jawad Al-Ali, an oncologist and member England's Royal Society of Physicians. "Our studies indicate that more than forty percent of the population around Basra will get cancer. We are living through another Hiroshima."

Most of the leukemia and cancer victims aren't soldiers. They are civilians. And many of them are children. The US-dominated Iraqi Sanctions Committee in New York has denied Iraq's repeated requests for cancer treatment equipment and drugs, even painkillers such as morphine. As a result, the overflowing hospitals in towns such as Basra are left to treat the cancer-stricken with aspirin.

This is part of a larger horror inflicted on Iraq that sees as many as 180 children dying every day, according to mortality figures compiled by UNICEF, from a catalogue of diseases from the 19th century: cholera, dysentery, tuberculosis, e. coli, mumps, measles, influenza.

Iraqis and Kuwaitis aren't the only ones showing signs of uranium contamination and sickness. Gulf War veterans, plagued by a variety of illnesses, have been found to have traces of uranium in their blood, feces, urine and semen.

Depleted uranium is a rather benign sounding name for uranium-238, the trace elements left behind when the fissionable material is extracted from uranium-235 for use in nuclear reactors and weapons. For decades, this waste was a radioactive nuisance, piling up at plutonium processing plants across the country. By the late 1980s there was nearly a billion tons of the material.

Then weapons designers at the Pentagon came up with a use for the tailings: they could be molded into bullets and bombs. The material was free and there was plenty at hand. Also, uranium is a heavy metal, denser than lead. This makes it perfect for use in armor-penetrating weapons, designed to destroy tanks, armored-personnel carriers and bunkers.

When the tank-busting bombs explode, the depleted uranium oxidizes into microscopic fragments that float through the air like carcinogenic dust, carried on the desert winds for decades. The lethal dust is inhaled, sticks to the fibers of the lungs, and eventually begins to wreck havoc on the body: inducing tumors, hemorrhages, ravaged immune systems, leukemias.

In 1943, the doomsday men associated with the Manhattan Project speculated that uranium and other radioactive materials could be spread across wide swaths of land to contain opposing armies. General Leslie Grove, head of the project, asserted that uranium weapons could be expected to cause "permanent lung damage." In the late 1950s, Al Gore's father, the senator from Tennessee, proposed dousing the demilitarized zone in Korea with uranium as a cheap failsafe against an attack from the North Koreans.

After the Gulf War, Pentagon war planners were so delighted with the performance of their radioactive weapons that they ordered a new arsenal and under Bill Clinton's orders fired them at Serb positions in Bosnia, Kosovo and Serbia. More than a 100 of the DU bombs have been used in the Balkans over the last six years.

Already medical teams in the region have detected cancer clusters near the bomb sites. The leukemia rate in Sarajevo, pummeled by American bombs in 1996, has tripled in the last five years. But it's not just the Serbs who are ill and dying. NATO and UN peace-keepers in the region are also coming down with cancer. As of January 23, 1999, eight Italian soldiers who served in the region have died of leukemia.

The Pentagon has shuffled through a variety of rationales and excuses. First, the Defense Department shrugged off concerns about depleted uranium as wild conspiracy theories by peace activists, environmentalists and Iraqi propagandists. When the US's NATO allies demanded that the US disclose the chemical and metallic properties of its munitions, the Pentagon refused. It has also refused to order testing of US soldiers stationed in the Gulf and the Balkans.

If the US has been keeping silent, the Brits haven't been. A 1991 study by the UK Atomic Energy Authority predicted that if less than 10 percent of the particles released by depleted uranium weapons used in Iraq and Kuwait were inhaled it could result in as many as "300,000 probable deaths."

The British estimate assumed that the only radioactive ingredient in the bombs dropped on Iraq was depleted uranium. It wasn't. A new study of the materials inside these weapons describes them as a "nuclear cocktail," containing a mix of radioactive elements, including plutonium and the highly radioactive isotope uranium-236. These elements are 100,000 times more dangerous than depleted uranium.

Typically, the Pentagon has tried to dump the blame on the Department of Energy's sloppy handling of its weapons production plants. This is how Pentagon spokesman Craig Quigley described the situation in chop-logic worthy of the pen of Joseph Heller: "The source of the contamination as best we can understand it now was the plants themselves that produced the depleted uranium during the 20 some year time frame when the DU was produced."

Indeed, the problems at DOE nuclear sites and the contamination of its workers and contractors have been well-known since the 1980s. A 1991 Energy Department memo reports: "during the process of making fuel for nuclear reactors and elements for nuclear weapons, the Paducah gaseous diffusion plant... created depleted uranium potentially containing neptunium and plutonium."

But such excuses in the absence of any action to address the situation are growing very thin indeed. Doug Rokke, the health physicist for the US Army who oversaw the partial clean up of depleted uranium bomb fragments in Kuwait, is now sick. His body registers 5,000 times the level of radiation considered "safe." He knows where to place the blame. "There can be no reasonable doubt about this," Rokke recently told British journalist John Pilger. "As a result of heavy metal and radiological poison of DU, people in southern Iraq are experiencing respiratory problems, kidney problems, cancers. Members of my own team have died or are dying from cancer."

Depleted uranium has a half-life of more than 4 billion years, approximately the age of the Earth. Thousand of acres of land in the Balkans, Kuwait and southern Iraq have been contaminated forever. If George Bush Sr., Dick Cheney, Colin Powell and Bill Clinton are still casting about for a legacy, there's grim one that will stay around for an eternity.

Portland, 1999

Forty-Nine

Amchitka

30 Years After

Amchitka Island sits at the midway point on the great arc of Alaska's Aleutian Islands, less than 900 miles across the Bering Sea from the coast of Russia. Amchitka, a spongy landscape of maritime tundra, is one of the most southerly of the Aleutians. The island's relatively temperate climate has made it one of the Arctic's most valuable bird sanctuaries, a critical staging ground for more than 100 migratory species, as well as home to walruses, sea otters and sea lions. Off the coast of Amchitka is a thriving fishery of salmon, pollock, haddock and halibut.

All of these values were recognized early on. In 1913, Amchitka was designated as a national wildlife refuge by President William Howard Taft. But these ecological wonders were swept aside in the early '60s when the Pentagon and the Atomic Energy Commission (AEC) went on the lookout for a new place to blow up H-bombs. Thirty years ago, Amchitka was the site of three large underground nuclear tests, including the most powerful nuclear explosion ever detonated by the United States.

The aftershocks of those blasts are still being felt. Despite claims by the AEC and the Pentagon that the test sites would safely contain the radiation released by the blasts for thousands of years, independent research by Greenpeace and newly released documents from the Department of Energy show that the Amchitka tests began to leak almost immediately. Highly radioactive elements and gasses, such as tritium, americium-142, plutonium and cobalt-60, poured out of the collapsed test shafts, leached into the ground water and worked their way into ponds, creeks and the Bering Sea. At the same time, thousands of Amchitka laborers and Aleuts living on nearby islands were put in harm's way. Dozens have died of radiation-linked cancers. The response of the federal government to these disturbing

findings has been almost as troublesome as the circumstances surrounding the tests themselves: a consistent pattern of indifference,
denial and cover-up continues even today.

There were several factors behind the selection of Amchitka as
a test site. One most certainly was the proximity to the Soviet
Union. These explosions were meant to send a message. Indeed, the
tests were designed to calibrate the performance of the Spartan anti-
ballistic missile, built to take out the Soviet nuclear arsenal.
Publicly, however, the rationale offered by the Atomic Energy
Commission and the Defense Department was simply that
Amchitka was a remote, and therefore safe, testing ground. "The site
was selected—and I underscore the point—because of the virtually
zero likelihood of any damage," claimed James Schlesinger, then
chairman of the AEC.

What Schlesinger and his cohorts overlooked was the remarkable culture of the Aleuts. Amchitka may have been remote from
the continental United States, but for nearly 10,000 years it had
been the home of the Aleuts, who left Amchitka in the 1880s after
Russian fur traders had wiped out the sea otter population. However,
the Aleuts continued to inhabit nearby islands and relied on the
waters near Amchitka for subsistence. Indeed, anthropologists
believe the islands around Amchitka may be the oldest continuous-
ly inhabited area in North America. The Aleuts raised forceful
objections to the tests, pointing to the risk of radiation leaks, earthquakes and tsunamis that might overwhelm their coastal villages.
These concerns were never addressed by the federal government. In
fact, the Aleuts were never consulted about the possible dangers at
all.

In 1965, the Long Shot test exploded an 80 kiloton bomb. The
$10 million test, the first one supervised by the Pentagon and not
the AEC, was really a trial run for bigger things to come. But small
as it was, there were immediate problems. Despite claims by the
Pentagon that the test site would not leak, radioactive tritium and
krypton-85 began to seep into freshwater lakes almost instantly. But
the evidence of radioactivity, collected by Department of Defense
scientists only three months after the test, was kept secret for five
years. The bomb site continues to spill toxins into the environment.
In 1993, EPA researchers detected high levels of tritium in ground

water samples taken near the test site.

The contamination from Long Shot didn't deter the Pentagon bomb-testers. In 1969, the AEC drilled a hole 4,000 feet deep into the rock of Amchitka and set off the Milrow nuclear test. The one megaton blast was 10 times as powerful as Long Shot. The AEC called it a "calibration test" designed to see if Amchitka could withstand a much larger test. The evidence should have convinced them of their dangerous folly. The blast triggered a string of small earthquakes and several massive landslides; knocked water from ponds, rivers and lakes more than 50 feet into the air; and, according to government accounts, "turned the surrounding sea to froth."

A year later, the AEC and the Pentagon announced their plans for the Cannikin nuclear test. At five megatons, Cannikin was to be the biggest underground nuclear explosion ever conducted by the United States. The blast would be 385 times as powerful as the bomb dropped on Hiroshima. Cannikin became a rallying point for native groups, anti-war and anti-nuke activists and the nascent environmental movement. Indeed, it was opposition to Cannikin by Canadian and American greens, who tried to disrupt the test by taking boats near the island, that sparked the birth of Greenpeace.

A lawsuit was filed in federal court, charging that the test violated the Limited Test Ban Treaty and the newly enacted National Environmental Policy Act. In a 4 to 3 decision, the Supreme Court refused to halt the test. What the Court didn't know, however, was that six federal agencies, including the departments of State and Interior and the fledgling EPA, had lodged serious objections to the Cannikin test, ranging from environmental and health concerns to legal and diplomatic problems. Nixon issued an executive order to keep the comments from being released. These documents, known as the Cannikin Papers, came to symbolize the continuing pattern of secrecy and cover-up that typified the nation's nuclear testing program. Even so, five hours after the ruling was handed down on November 1, 1971, the AEC and the Pentagon pulled the switch, detonating the Cannikin bomb.

In an effort to calm growing public opposition, AEC chief Schlesinger dismissed environmental protesters and the Aleuts as doomsayers, taking his family with him to watch the test. "It's fun for the kids and my wife is delighted to get away from the house for awhile," he quipped.

With the Schlesingers looking on, the Cannikin bomb, a 300-foot-long device implanted in a mile deep hole under Cannikin lake, exploded with the force of an earthquake registering 7.0 on the Richter Scale. The shock of the blast scooped a mile wide and 60-foot-deep subsidence crater in the ground over the test site and triggered massive rockfalls.

The immediate ecological damage from the blast was staggering. Nearly 1,000 sea otters, a species once hunted to near extinction, were killed—their skulls crushed by the shockwaves of the explosion. Other marine mammals died when their eyes were blown out of their sockets or when their lungs ruptured. Thousands of birds also perished, their spines snapped and their legs pushed through their bodies. (Neither the Pentagon nor the Fish and Wildlife Service has ever studied the long-term ecological consequences of the Amchitka explosions.) Most worrisome was that a large volume of water from White Alice Creek vanished after the blast. The disappearance of the creek was more than a sign of Cannikin's horrific power. It was also an indication that the project had gone terribly wrong; the blast ruptured the crust of the earth, sucking the creek into a brand new aquifer, a radioactive one.

In the months following the explosion, blood and urine samples were taken from Aleuts living in the village of Adak on a nearby island. The samples were shown to have abnormally high levels of tritium and cesium-137, both known carcinogens. Despite these alarming findings, the feds never went back to Adak to conduct follow-up medical studies. The Aleuts, who continue their seafaring lifestyle, are particularly vulnerable to radiation-contaminated fish and marine mammals, and radiation that might spread through the Bering Sea, plants and iceflows.

But the Aleuts weren't the only ones exposed to Cannikin's radioactive wrath. More than 1,500 workers who helped build the test sites, operate the bomb tests and clean up afterward were also put at risk. The AEC never conducted medical studies on any of these laborers. When the Alaska District Council of Laborers of the AFL-CIO, began looking into the matter in the early '90s, the Department of Energy claimed that none of the workers had been exposed to radiation. They later were forced to admit that exposure records and dosimeter badges had been lost.

In June 1996, two Greenpeace researchers, Pam Miller and Norm Buske, returned to Amchitka. Buske, a physicist, collected water and plant samples from various sites on the island. Despite claims by the DOE that the radiation would be contained for hundreds of years, the samples taken by Buske revealed the presence of plutonium and americium-241 in freshwater plants at the edge of the Bering Sea. In other words, Cannikin continues to leak. Both of these radioactive elements are extremely toxic and have half-lives of hundreds of years.

In part because of the report issued by Miller and Buske, a new sense of urgency was lent to the claims of laborers who said they had become sick after working at the Amchitka nuclear site. In 1998, the union commissioned a study by Rosalie Bertell, a former consultant to the Nuclear Regulatory Commission (which replaced the AEC). Bertell found that hundreds of Amchitka workers were exposed to ionizing radiation at five times the level then recognized as hazardous. However, the research is complicated by the fact that many of the records from the Amchitka blast remain classified and others were simply tossed away. "The loss of worker exposure records, or the failure to keep such records, was inexcusable," Bertell says.

One of the driving forces behind the effort to seek justice for the Amchitka workers and the Aleuts is Beverley Aleck. Her husband Nick helped drill the mile-deep pit for the Cannikin test. Four years later, he died of myelogenous leukemia, a type of cancer associated with radiation exposure. Aleck, an Aleut, has waged a multi-year battle with the DOE to open the records and to begin a health monitoring program for the Amchitka workers. In April of this year, the Clinton administration finally agreed to begin the first health survey of the Amchitka workers. The study was supposed to begin this summer, but it is languishing without funding.

Will the victims of the Amchitka blasts ever get justice? Don't count on it. For starters, the Aleuts and Amchitka workers are specifically excluded by the Radiation Exposure Compensation Act from receiving medical assistance, death benefits or financial compensation. There is a move to amend this loophole in the law, but even that doesn't mean the workers and Aleuts would be treated fairly. The DOE has tried repeatedly to stiff arm other cases by either dismissing the link between radiation exposure and cancer or, when that fails, invoking a "sovereignty" doctrine, which claims the agency is immune from civil lawsuits.

Dr. Paul Seligman, deputy assistant secretary of the DOE's Office of Health Studies, writes it off as the price of the Cold War. "These were hazardous operations," Seligman says. "The hazards were well understood, but the priorities at the time were weapons production and the defense of the nation."

At a time when the mainstream press and Republican politicians are howling over lax security at nuclear weapons sites and Chinese espionage, a more dangerous betrayal of trust is the withholding of test data from the American public. China may use the Los Alamos secrets to upgrade its tiny nuclear arsenal, but the Amchitka explosions already have imperiled a thriving marine ecosystem and caused dozens of lethal cancers in Americans.

The continuing cover-up and manipulation of information by the DOE not only denies justice to the victims of Amchitka, but indicates that those living near other DOE cites may be at great risk. "DOE management of the U.S. nuclear weapons complex is of the old school in which bad news is hidden," says Pam Miller, now executive director of Alaska Community Action on Toxics. "This conflicts with sound risk management and makes the entire system inherently risky. The overwhelming threat is of an unanticipated catastrophe."

Juneau, 2000

Fifty

One of Our H-Bombs Is Missing

T hings go missing. A few weeks ago an electric power company in New Hampshire admitted that they'd lost track of four highly radioactive cooling rods from its nuclear power plant. It's to be expected. Even at the Pentagon. Though we rarely hear about it. In October 2001, the Inspector General for the Pentagon reported that the military's accountants had misplaced a destroyer, several tanks and armored personal carriers, hundreds of machine guns and rounds of ammo, grenade launchers and some surface-to-air missiles. In all, nearly $8 billion worth of weapons were AWOL.

Those anomalies are bad enough. But what's truly chilling is the fact that the Pentagon has lost track of the mother of all weapons, a hydrogen bomb. The thermonuclear weapon, designed to be capable of incinerating Moscow, has been sitting somewhere off the coast of Savannah, Georgia for the last 40 years, steadily becoming more and more dangerous. The Air Force has gone to greater lengths to conceal the mishap than to locate the bomb and secure it.

On the night of February 5, 1958, a B-47 Stratojet bomber carrying a hydrogen bomb on a night training flight off the Georgia coast collided with an F-86 Saberjet fighter at 36,000 feet. The collision destroyed the fighter and severely damaged a wing of the bomber, leaving one of its engines partially dislodged. The bomber's pilot, Major Howard Richardson, was instructed to jettison the H-bomb before attempting a landing. Richardson dropped the bomb into the shallow waters of Warsaw Sound, near the mouth of the Savannah River, a few miles from the city of Tybee Island, where the pilot believed the bomb would be swiftly recovered.

The Pentagon recorded the incident in a top secret memo to the chairman of the Atomic Energy Commission. The memo has been partially declassified. "A B-47 aircraft with a [word redacted] nuclear weapon aboard was damaged in a collision with an F-86 aircraft near Sylvania, Georgia, on February 5, 1958. The B-47 aircraft attempted three times unsuccessfully to land with the weapon. The weapon was then jettisoned visually over water off the mouth of the Savannah River. No detonation was observed."

Soon search and rescue teams were sent to the site. The sound was mysteriously cordoned off by Air Force troops. For six weeks, the Air Force looked for the bomb without success. Underwater divers scoured the depths, troops tromped through nearby salt marshes, and a blimp hovered over the area attempting to spot a hole or crater in the beach or swamp. Then just a month later, the search of Warsaw Sound was abruptly halted when the Air Force reassigned its forces to deal with another self-inflicted crisis of the Cold War. In Florence, South Carolina, another H-bomb had been accidentally dropped by a B-47E. The bomb's high explosive material exploded on impact, sending radioactive debris across the landscape. The explosion caused extensive property damage and several injuries on the ground.

The search teams never returned to Tybee Island and the affair of the missing H-bomb was discreetly covered up. The end of the search was noted in a partially declassified memo from the Pentagon to the AEC, in which the Air Force politely requests a new H-bomb to replace the one it lost. "The search for this weapon was discontinued on 4-16-58 and the weapon is considered irretrievably lost. It is requested that one [phrase redacted] Weapon be made available for release to the DOD as a replacement."

There was a big problem, of course, and the Pentagon knew it. Over the last 55 years, the United States has lost eleven nuclear weapons. In the first three months of 1958, the Air Force had four major accidents involving H-bombs. The Tybee Island bomb remained a threat, as the Atomic Energy Commission acknowledged in a June 10, 1958 classified memo to Congress: "There exists the possibility of accidental discovery of the unrecovered weapon through dredging or construction in the probable impact area...the Department of Defense has been requested to monitor all dredging and construction activities."

But the wizards of Armageddon saw it less as a security, safety or ecological problem, than a potential public relations disaster that could turn an already justifiably paranoid population against their ambitious nuclear project. The Pentagon and the AEC tried to squelch media interest in the issue by a doling out a morsel of candor and a lot of misdirection. In a joint statement to the press, the DOD and the AEC admitted that radioactive material could be "scattered" by the detonation of the high explosives in the H-bombs. But the letter downplayed possibility of that ever happening: "the likelihood that a particular accident would involve a nuclear weapon is extremely limited." In fact, that scenario had already taken place and would again.

That's where the matter stood for more than 42 years until a deep sea salvage company, run by former Air Force personnel and a CIA agent, disclosed the existence of the bomb and offered to locate it for a million dollars. The disclosure this spring, along with recently declassified documents, prompted fear and outrage among coastal residents and calls for a congressional investigation into the incident itself and why the Pentagon stopped looking for the bomb.

"We're horrified because some of that information has been covered-up for years," says Rep. Jack Kingston, a Georgia Republican. The cover up continues. The Air Force, however, has told local residents and the congressional delegation that there was nothing to worry about. "We've looked into this particular issue from all angles and we're very comfortable," says Major Gen. Franklin J. "Judd" Blaisdell. Blaisdell is Director of Nuclear and Counterproliferation and Deputy Chief of Staff for Air and Space Operations at Air Force headquarters, Washington, D.C. "Our biggest concern is that of localized heavy metal contamination," says Blaisdell.

The Air Force has even suggested that the bomb itself was not armed with a plutonium trigger. But this contention is disputed by a number of factors. Howard Dixon, a former Air Force sergeant who specialized in loading nuclear weapons onto planes, said that in his 31 years of experience he never once remembered a bomb being put on a plane that wasn't fully armed.

Moreover, newly declassified 1966 congressional testimony by the then-assistant secretary of Defense W.J. Howard describes the Tybee Island bomb as a "complete weapon, a bomb with a nuclear capsule." Howard said that the Tybee Island bomb was one of two weapons lost up to that time that contained a plutonium trigger.

Recently declassified documents show that the jettisoned bomb was an "Mk-15, Mod O" hydrogen bomb, weighing four tons and packing more than 100 times the explosive punch of the one that incinerated Hiroshima. This was the first thermonuclear weapon deployed by the US Air Force and featured the relatively primitive Teller-Ulam design. The only failsafe for this weapon was the physical separation of the plutonium capsule (or pit) from the weapon.

In addition to the primary nuclear capsule, the bomb also harbored a secondary nuclear explosive, or sparkplug, designed to make it go thermo. This a hollow plug about an inch in diameter made of either plutonium or highly enriched uranium (the Pentagon has never said which) that is filled with fusion fuel, most likely lithium-6 deuteride. Lithium is highly reactive in water. The plutonium in the bomb was manufactured at the Hanford Nuclear Site and would be the oldest in the US. That's bad, not good, news. Plutonium gets more dangerous as it ages. In addition, the bomb would contain other radioactive materials, such as uranium and beryllium.

The bomb is also charged with 400 pounds of TNT, designed to cause the plutonium trigger to implode and thus starting the nuclear explosion. As the years go by, those high explosives are becoming ever more flaky, brittle and sensitive. The bomb is most likely now buried in 5 to 15 feet of sand and is most likely slowly leaking radioactivity into the rich crabbing grounds of the Sound.

If the Pentagon can't find the Tybee Island bomb, others might. That's the conclusion of Bert Soleau, a former CIA officer who now works with ASSURE, the salvage company. Soleau, a chemical engineer, says that it wouldn't be hard for terrorists to locate the weapon and recover the lithium, beryllium and enriched uranium—the essential building blocks of nuclear weapons.

The Russians must be watching these events unfold with grim amusement. After all, the US has repeatedly scolded Russia for losing track of its nuclear materials, contributing to the loose nukes scenario that is now being used to partially justify junking the Anti-Ballistic Missile Treaty and embarking on the new $60 billion Star Wars scheme.

What to do? Coastal residents want the weapon located and removed. "Plutonium is a nightmare and their own people know it," says Pam O'Brien, an anti-nuke organizer from Douglassville,

Georgia. "It can get in everything—your eyes, your bones, your gonads. You never get over it. They need to get that thing out of there."

The situation reminds many nuke watchers of the Palomares incident. On January 16, a B-52G bomber, carrying four hydrogen bombs, crashed while attempting to refuel in mid-air above the Spanish coast. Three of the H-bombs landed near the coastal farming village of Palomares. One of the bombs lodged itself in a dry creek bed and was recovered, battered but relatively intact. But the TNT in two of the bombs exploded, gouging 10-foot deep holes in the ground and showering uranium and plutonium over a vast area. Over the next three months, more than 1,400 tons of radioactive soil and vegetation was scooped up, placed in barrels and, ironically, shipped back to the Savannah River site, where it remains. The tomato fields near the craters were burned and buried. There's no question that due to wind and other factors much of the contaminated soil dispersed across the region. "The total extent of the spread will never be known," concluded a report by the Defense Nuclear Agency.

The clean up was a joint operation between US Air Force personnel and members of the Spanish civil guard. The US workers encased themselves in what passed for protective clothing. Army scientists monitored them for radiation exposure. Similar precautions weren't taken for the Spanish workers. "The Air Force was unprepared to provide adequate detection and monitoring for personnel when an aircraft accident occurred involving plutonium weapons in a remote area of a foreign country," the Air Force commander in charge of the clean up later testified.

The fourth bomb hit in the Atlantic Ocean 8 miles offshore and was missing for several months. It was eventually located in 2,850 of water by an Alvin mini-submarine, where it rests to this day.

Two years later, on January 21, 1968, a similar accident occurred when a B-52G caught fire in flight above Greenland and crashed in ice-covered North Star Bay near the Thule Air Base. The impact detonated the explosives in all four of the plane's H-bombs, which scattered uranium, tritium and plutonium over a 2,000 foot radius. The intense fire melted a hole the ice, which then refroze, encapsulating much of the debris in ice, including the thermonuclear assembly from one of the bombs. The recovery operation, conducted in near total darkness at temperatures that plunged to minus 70 degree Fahrenheit, was known as Project Crested Ice. But it was known by the work crews as Dr. Freezelove.

More than 10,000 tons of snow and ice were cut away, put into barrels and transported to Savannah River and Oak Ridge for disposal. Other radioactive debris was simply left on site, to melt into the bay after the spring thaws.

More than 3,000 workers helped in the Thule recovery effort, many of them were Danish soldiers. As at Palomares, most of the American workers were offered some protective gear, but not the Danes, who did much of the most dangerous work, including filling the barrels with the debris, often by hand. The decontamination procedures were primitive to say the least. An Air Force report noted that they were cleansed "by simply brushing the snow from garments and vehicles."

Even though more than 38 Navy ships were called to assist in the recovery operation and it was an open secret that the bombs had been lost, the Pentagon continued to lie about the situation. In one contentious exchange with the press corps, a Pentagon spokesman uttered this classic bit of military doublespeak, "I don't know of any missing bomb, but we have not positively identified what I think you are looking for."

When Danish workers at Thule began to get sick from a slate of illnesses, ranging from rare cancers to blood disorders, the Pentagon refused to help. Even after a 1987 epidemiological study by a Danish medical institute showed that Thule workers were 50 percent more likely to develop cancers than other members of the Danish military, the Pentagon still refused to cooperate. Later that year, two hundred of the Danish workers filed suit against the US under the Foreign Military Claims Act. Ultimately, the suit was dismissed. But the discovery process revealed thousands of pages of secret documents about the incident, including the fact that US Air Force workers at the site, like the Danes, have not been subject to long-term health monitoring. Even so, the Pentagon continues to keep most of the material on the Thule incident secret, including any information on the extent of the radioactive (and other toxic) contamination at the site.

These recovery efforts don't inspire much confidence. But the Tybee Island bomb presents an even touchier situation. The presence of the unstable lithuim deuteride and the deteriorating high explosives make retrieval of the bomb a very dangerous proposition—so dangerous, in fact, that even some environmentalists and anti-nuke activists argue that it might present less of a risk to leave the bomb where it is. In short, there aren't any easy answers. A problem that is exacerbated by the Pentagon's failure to conduct a comprehensive analysis of the situation and reluctance to fully disclose what it does know.

"I believe the plutonium capsule is in the bomb, but that a nuclear detonation is improbable because the neutron generators used back then were polonium-beryllium, which has a very short half-life," says Don Moniak, a nuclear weapons expert with the Blue Ridge Environmental Defense League in Aiken, South Carolina. "Without neutrons, weapons grade plutonium won't blow. However, there could be a fission or criticality event if the plutonium was somehow put in an incorrect configuration. There could be a major inferno if the high explosives went off and the lithium deuteride reacted as expected. Or there could just be an explosion that scattered uranium and plutonium all over hell."

Savannah, GA, 2001

Fifty-One

Battlefield Alaska

Star Wars Comes to the Arctic

The Kodiak Launch Complex was marketed to Alaskans as one of the nation's first commercial space ports. Many promises were made to lure public support: high-paying, year-round jobs; better roads; a fancy cultural center; new schools with real astronauts helping out in the classrooms; peace and prosperity.

The whole multibillion-dollar project, located on Narrow Cape, a remote tip of Kodiak Island 250 miles west of Anchorage, was supposed to be run by a state-chartered outfit called the Alaska Aerospace Development Corporation. In 1996, the state and the feds turned over 3,500 acres of public land for the project, which would house two launching pads, a space vehicle assembly plant, a radar station, a command center and other support facilities. Its backers claimed that a new age of commercial space traffic was dawning, and that Kodiak Island was one of the world's best locations for "launching telecommunications, remote sensing, and space science payloads" into orbit.

Local skeptics weren't thrilled at the prospect of their wilderness redoubt being transformed into an Alaskan Cape Canaveral. After all, Kodiak was already one of Alaska's most popular tourist destinations, with tens of thousands of people coming to fish for salmon and halibut, hike the wilderness, photograph the great grizzlies and view one of the few thriving populations of gray whales in the Pacific—people who might think twice about visiting with missiles screaming overhead. Others worried their villages might be vulnerable to misfires and toxic fallout. Some wondered how Kodiak, one of the most remote islands in North America, could possibly be the epicenter of a profitable commercial enterprise. There were suspicions that something a bit more nefarious might be in the offing.

These concerns were briskly swept aside by state and federal officials. A brief environmental analysis was slapped together, with much of the data concealed from public scrutiny, and construction began in 1998. Not long thereafter, the Alaska Aerospace Development Corporation announced it was having financial problems, and the federal government came to its rescue with a timely handout and the promise of sustained appropriations. But there was a catch: instead of sending into orbit commercial satellites and the cremated remains of rich Trekkies, the Kodiak site was going to work very closely with the Air Force and its legion of defense contractors.

There's some compelling evidence that this was the plan all along, starting with the man tapped to head the Alaska Aerospace Development Corporation: Pat Ladner, a former Air Force lieutenant colonel who served in the '80s as the program manager for a secretive project called the Single Stage Rocket Technology Program (SSTR). This program was a component of the initial burst of funding for Reagan's version of Star Wars. But by the early '90s, with public and congressional support lagging, the Pentagon made a decision to "privatize" much of the development and testing for many of its Star Wars projects. Ladner retired from the Air Force in 1993 and joined the Alaska Aerospace Development Corporation. The facilities at Kodiak were designed by the Defense Advanced Research Project Agency, the same shadowy wing of the Pentagon that had supervised the SSTR program on Ladner's watch.

So the launching pads at Narrow Cape turned out to be just another off-shoot of the National Missile Defense program. On November 5, 1998, the Kodiak site fired off its first rocket, an experimental Air Force missile that is part of the Pentagon's "atmospheric interceptor technology program." The rocket arced across the sky for more than 1,000 miles before slamming into the Pacific somewhere off the southern Oregon coast. A second rocket was launched from Kodiak on September 15, 1999.

Since those initial launches, a steady stream of Star Wars experiments have been ongoing at Kodiak, projects steered there by the guiding hand of Sen. Ted Stevens, the ranking member of the Appropriations Committee. Stevens is a master at manipulating the flow of federal dollars back to military projects in Alaska, often as last-minute amendments to Defense Supplemental Appropriations bills, where they receive little public scrutiny. This is how Star Wars has continued almost uninterrupted since its inception in 1983. The next round of tests at Kodiak will involve a much more potent and unnerving rocket, a Polaris missile packed with a payload of simulated nuclear warheads. In August 2001, a Polaris was fired from Kodiak and streaked 4,300 miles to Kwajalein Atoll in the Marshall Islands of the South Pacific, where interceptor missiles tried (and failed) to shoot it down. Over the next five years, Kodiak is slated to launch more than 20 Polaris rockets. (The other Polaris launching site is on the Hawaiian island of Kauai.)

Even though the test rockets only pack simulated nukes, they are still dangerous. The missiles' three-stage booster engines carry highly toxic materials, including magnesium, hydrazine and radioactive thorium. The boosters fall to the ocean and are not recovered. The exhaust trail itself leaves behind a poisonous plume of smoke. "Each rocket first stage releases a minimum of 8,000 pounds of aluminum oxide at lift-off," warns Brad Stevens (no relation to the senator), a biologist with the National Marine Fisheries Service in Kodiak. "Much of this will wind up in local streams that drain into Twin Lakes and the Fossil Beach tidepools and kelp beds, which provide nutrients and shelter for juvenile marine species. Documented fish kills in waterways around Cape Kennedy attest to the fact that rocket emissions can destroy aquatic life." (Also under the flight path of the missiles are rocky beaches on small islands that serve as haul-outs for Stellar sea lions, an endangered species.)

One of the launch trajectories will send missiles over the fishing villages of Akhiok and Old Harbor and across one of the world's most pristine salmon spawning grounds. The Pentagon has told the people living there not to worry: they will clear the waters of boats before each launch and build two hardened bunkers in each town. The bunkers serve as stark reminders that the townspeople not only are potential victims of an accident, but a target of Russian and Chinese defense systems designed to counter Star Wars.

Alaskans are old hands at this by now. Indeed, there's a grim irony in the fact that Alaska, the most frigid of states, has been one of the most ravaged battlegrounds of the Cold War. Over the past 55 years, Alaska has witnessed: early warning radar erected onto the fragile tundra in the early '50s; the intentional irradiation of more than 100 unwitting Alaskan native peoples in 1955 to test the acclimation of humans to sub-zero temperatures; Project Chariot, a mad scheme to excavate a naval harbor at Cape Thompson by exploding five nuclear bombs at the mouth of a coastal creek (the bombs were never detonated, but the site was left a toxic and radioactive mess); and the Cannikin nuclear test in 1971, one of the largest ever, which permanently contaminated Amchitka Island and continues to ooze radioactive debris into the Bering Sea. Kodiak alone already suffers from 17 toxic dumps left by previous Pentagon operations on the island. Even the push to transform the Arctic National Wildlife Refuge into a forest of oil derricks has lately been justified on the grounds of national security.

So it shouldn't come as much of a surprise that Alaska seems poised to bear the brunt of Bush's new Star Wars plan. The Kodiak site is just one of more than a dozen enclaves of assorted anti-missile paraphernalia that will be scattered across the state, from the Aleutians to the Arctic plains. In addition to Kodiak, Congress approved the construction of a $500 million radar dome on remote Shemya Island in the Aleutians. Shemya, the site of an old CIA listening post, is more than 1,500 miles from the nearest active military base. A top Pentagon official told *The Washington Post* that it posed difficult construction problems, and that when completed the site would be "very, very vulnerable" to attack.

Ted Stevens also has pushed to make Fort Greely Military Reserve, an Army outpost on the Tanana River about 90 miles southeast of Fairbanks, a base for the 100 interceptor missiles once the Stars Wars scheme becomes operational. Constructed in 1945, Fort Greely already has a dark history as a kind of outdoor laboratory for some of the Army's most malign experiments. In 1953, the Army authorized the use of Fort Greely and the adjacent Gerstle River Proving Ground to test chemical and biological weapons. Of course, these operations were kept secret from the surrounding population of homesteaders, miners, trappers and the Goodpastor tribe of Athabaskan Indians.

In the early '60s one of the biological weapons tests went terribly wrong, and 21 people were infected with tularemia, an often fatal disease characterized by raging fevers. After the Army stopped testing chemical and biological weapons at the site, it did a cursory cleanup and buried most of the contaminated canisters and shell-casings in shallow pits next to the river and several lakes and ponds, where the lethal detritus continues to seep out.

In 1962, the Army built a small nuclear reactor at Fort Greely, which it claimed was needed as a power station. This claim proved to be an elaborate cover. The reactor did generate some electricity, but it also produced weapons-grade plutonium. The background of this project is revealed in a startling report released by physicist Norm Buske and Pam Miller, director of Alaska Community Action on Toxics. Among their findings: the Army dumped nuclear waste into Jarvis Creek for 10 years; disposed of liquid radioactive waste into groundwater that was used as a drinking source by the village of Clearwater; and used radioactive steam from the reactor to heat the military base. "Army leaders were more committed to producing special nuclear materials for battlefield nuclear weapons than they were to assuring the safety of the operation," Buske and Miller concluded.

Fort Greely was slated for decommissioning as part of the military's base-closure program. A convincing theory holds that Stevens and the Pentagon want to transform this Arctic outpost into the deployment site for 100 interceptor missiles as a convenient way to disguise the extent of the contamination and to evade accountability for what went on up there through the '60s.

What's more, the Fort Greely site is a major sticking point with the Russians and Chinese. Under the Anti-Ballistic Missile Treaty, each nation is permitted only one site for missile defense. Currently, the US site is in Grand Forks, North Dakota. Plans to begin pouring concrete for the new site at Fort Greely clearly violate the accord. Stevens, Alaska's senior senator, dismissed concern that these early Star Wars projects might breach the treaty, saying, "Construction of the Shemya radar in and of itself is not a violation of the ABM treaty until it is integrated into a defense system."

Why Alaska? It's not that all Alaskans welcome the Pentagon. In fact, an organized campaign defeated Edward Teller's nightmarish Project Chariot scenario. And in 1983, Alaskans approved the nuclear freeze initiative by an overwhelming vote. But in a state this large and sparsely populated it's relatively easy for big money to overwhelm citizen opposition, especially when those billions are backed by the lobbying might of the military, the nuclear labs and their contractors.

At present estimates, the Star Wars program will unleash a $60 billion spending spree. In Republican Sens. Frank Murkowski and Stevens, Alaska sports two pitiless hoarders of Pentagon pork. Even Alaska's Clintonesque governor, Democrat Tony Knowles, has gotten into the act, investing a chunk of state money with lobbyists to help steer as much of the Star Wars business to Alaska as possible.

It will surprise no one who is familiar with the symbiotic relationship between Stevens and the arms makers that the treasurer of his Northern Lights Leadership PAC, Richard Ladd, is also president of Robinson International, a top DC lobby shop that specializes in representing defense contractors. In the past two election cycles, the Northern Lights PAC has raked in more than $300,000, largely from corporate executives, many with ties to defense firms. The PAC recycled all that money back into Republican campaigns. In return, the defense companies, led by Boeing and Lockheed-Martin, have been very generous to Stevens. From 1995 to 1999, the senator received $255,650 in PAC contributions from missile defense-related firms, second only to Virginia's John Warner, who, as head of the Senate Armed Services Committee, pulled in $330,000.

Earlier this year, in an interview with the *Alaska Journal of Commerce*, Stevens boasted about how he almost single-handedly had steered hundreds of millions of dollars in defense contracts to Alaska, even under President Clinton. He predicted that much more federal loot was ready to flow north in the Bush regime. The money comes in, but it doesn't stay long. Most of it ends up in corporate coffers in Alabama, California and Washington State. Even Ladner, the head of the Alaska Aerospace Development Corporation, recently admitted that the year-round jobs at the Kodiak launch site would probably only amount to a few security and maintenance positions. It's the old Cold War routine repeated once again: the money goes south, but the risk and the waste stays up in Alaska.

Kodiak, 2001

Fifty-Two

When We Bombed the World

The Cold War (as we once knew it) may be over but its legacy remains quite hot—hot and deadly. A new report estimates that fallout from open-air nuclear testing has killed more than 15,000 Americans and caused at least 80,000 cancers. Ominously, the report concludes that nuclear testing has exposed to radiation nearly everyone who has resided in the United States since 1952.

The new report, conducted by the National Cancer Institute and Centers for Disease Control, is remarkable for several reasons, not least because it represents the first time the US government has released an assessment of the spread and consequences to human health of radioactive fallout from global nuclear testing. It's also the first time that the government has owned up to the fact that a substantial number of cancer deaths nationwide have been caused by nuclear testing. Previously, the government had only admitted adverse health consequences to "downwinders," residents in states adjacent to the Nevada test site.

The report was commissioned by Congress in 1998 following public uproar over a 1997 study by the National Cancer Institute that investigated the fallout of only one radionuclide, iodine-131, and its link to thyroid cancers. That study looked mainly at the so-called "milk pathway" to exposure. Iodine-131 was dropped as fallout across dairy country, where it was consumed by cows and goats. The iodine then showed up in a concentrated form in cow and, particularly, goat milk.

This examination of global fallout is much broader, tracking, among other things, exposure to cesium-137. In addition to charting fallout from the Nevada Test Site, the National Cancer Institute study also looked at fallout from US tests in the Marshall Islands and Johnston Atoll, British explosions at the Christmas Islands and Soviet testing at Semipalatinsk and Novaya Zemlya.

The irradiation of the global environment has been a uniquely cooperative endeavor, with all of the world's nuclear superpowers contributing to the toll. The US has carried out 1,030 nuclear weapons tests (the last on 23 September 1993); the former Soviet Union: 715 tests; France: 210 tests. Britain 45 tests; China: 47 tests.

The body count from fallout is insidious, largely hidden in the slow but relentless accumulation of cancers, such as thyroid (2,500 deaths), leukemia (550 deaths), radiogenic cancers from external exposure (11,000 deaths) and radiogenic cancers from internal doses of carbon-14, tritium and cesium-137 (3,000 deaths).

"This report and other official data show that hot spots occurred thousands of miles away from the test sites," said Dr. Arjun Makhijani, president of the Institute for Energy and Environmental Research. "Hot spots due to testing in Nevada occurred as far away as New York and Maine. Hot spots from US Pacific area testing and also Soviet testing were scattered across the United States from California, Oregon, Washington, and in the West to New Hampshire, Vermont and North Carolina in the East."

Even so the conclusions are far from comprehensive. The CDC/NCI study only included tests conducted from 1951 through 1962. That means that it excluded Chinese tests, most French atmospheric testing in the Pacific, pre-1951 testing in the Marshall Islands and by the Soviet Union, the 1945 New Mexico tests. the Hiroshima and Nagasaki bombings and ventings from underground tests by the US and the Soviet Union.

In addition, the NCI/CDC did not include calculations for Alaska and Hawaii, which certainly experienced heavy fallout from the Novaya Zemlya and Marshall Islands tests respectively.

And this only tells a small part of the story. The fallout statistics don't account for the deaths and illnesses of other civilians, including uranium miners, nuclear plant workers and people who live near places such as Hanford and Rocky Flats.

The National Cancer Institute/Centers for Disease Control study has been gathering dust for at least six months, as the Bush administration and congress tussled over how to control the import of its grim conclusions. Even in the 1950s, the Pentagon and the old Atomic Energy Commission knew that radioactive fallout from explosions at the Nevada Test Site was spreading across the country and into Canada and Mexico. Yet, they largely chose to conceal this information from the public. Although, the United States has been grievously tardy in owning up to inflicting this horror on its own people, it is ahead of the other nuclear testing nations, which have remained morbidly quiet on the subject.

The tally of the innocent dead and dying from 50 years of nuclear testing doesn't seem to have given the nuclear hawks in the Pentagon the slightest pause. Indeed the Bush administration's new Nuclear Posture Review calls for the development and testing of a new generation of nuclear weapons, the so-called bunker-busters. The plan would not only abridge the test ban treaty, but it would put another generation at risk.

"Today's nuclear arsenal continues to reflect its Cold War origin, characterized by moderate delivery accuracy, limited earth penetrator capability, high yield warheads, silo and sea based ballistic missiles with multiple independent reentry vehicles, and limited retargeting capability," write the authors of the review that the Pentagon submitted to Congress in January.

"New capabilities must be developed to defeat emerging threats such as hard and deeply buried targets...to find and attack mobile and relocatable targets, to defeat chemical or biological agents, and to improve accuracy and limit collateral damage," they argue.

"While the United States is making every effort to maintain the stockpile without additional nuclear testing, this may not be possible for the indefinite future," warned Defense Department strategists. "Increasingly, objective judgments about capability in a non-testing environment will become far more difficult."

Before Bush signs off on a new round of nuclear weapons testing, he should closely scrutinize the fallout maps that accompany the NCI/CDC study. They are eerily similar to the famous electoral map of the 2002 election. In other words, the cancers have fallen most heavily on the American heartland that, along with the Supreme Court, handed Bush the White House.

Of course, it would be too much to expect that the next time Bush barks about Saddam Hussein killing his own people he would reference our own government's frightful history of atomic victims.

Portland, 2002

Fifty-Three

Fallon's Fallen

Is the US Navy Killing Children in Nevada?

In June of 2002, Adam Jernee died from acute lymphocytic leukemia, a remorselessly fast-moving cancer of the blood. He was eight-years old and had fought the cancer for more than two years of his short life.

Adam and his father lived in Fallon, Nevada. This small ranching town of 8,000 people in the Carson Desert 50 miles east of Reno may have the highest per capita rate of childhood leukemia in the nation. The children of Fallon are more than 100 times more likely to be stricken with leukemia then children elsewhere in country.

Last week, another Fallon child was diagnosed with leukemia. That makes 17 kids from Fallon who have been contracted leukemia since 1997. Adam is the second child to have died within the past year. In September, Stephanie Sands succumbed to the cancer after battling it for two years. She was 21.

Cancer isn't the only problem. Kids and adults in Fallon and surrounding Churchill County are coming down with a myriad of other rare diseases, such as Myelodysplastic Syndrome and aplastic anemia. These diseases also relentlessly attack the bone marrow.

The kinds of cancers and other illnesses that have cropped up in the Fallon area are almost certainly caused by some kind of exposure to toxic chemicals. The source of that poison almost certainly sits a few miles outside the town of Fallon—somewhere on the 240,000-acre Fallon Naval Air Station, one of the Navy's largest bombing ranges, and home of the Top Gun fighter pilot training school.

But good luck getting the Navy to take responsibility or even look very hard to find out what the problem might be. Years have passed and the Navy has done next to nothing, except deny culpability and try bully anyone who demands answers from naval brass. Apparently the Navy doesn't even care if the cancers are killing children of its own officers. The Navy has known about high levels of cancer among the children of Fallon workers and Navy officers since at least 1991; yet, the Pentagon has done little except try to conceal information on levels of pollution at the base and stiff-arm investigators.

"Our frustration level is very high," says Brenda Gross, whose six-year old son has been sick with leukemia for two years. "This should have been found and stopped a long time ago. But you can't get anything out of the Navy."

Local residents think they know the answer: jet fuel spills and fuel dumping by Navy aircraft. JP-8 jet fuel, a combination of kerosene and benzene, is a known carcinogen and has been linked to leukemia and other bone marrow diseases.

The Navy has summarily ruled out jet fuel as a cause of the Fallon cancers, but records from the state of Nevada show that the Fallon air base has at least 26 toxic waste sites, 16 of them contaminated by jet fuel. Most of the Fallon area is playa, a dry lakebed over shallow groundwater. According to the Geological Survey, several distinct plumes of jet fuel have entered the water table beneath the air base.

Nearby residents charge that Navy fighter pilots routinely dump excess fuel into the desert prior to landing at Fallon. The Navy says this is a rare occurrence, with emergency fuel dumps happening about three times a year. However, Navy records show that in a single instance a few years ago more than 800 gallons was dumped into the Carson playa.

In 2000 alone, according to the Navy's own statistics, Fallon-based fighters and bombers consumed 34 million gallons of jet fuel, much of it is pumped in on a jet fuel pipeline, which runs from Sparks, Nevada to Fallon. Locals and environmentalists say that the pipeline regularly leaks the poisonous gas into the desert.

Publicly, the Navy contends that the pipeline spills are minor and inconsequential, averaging less than 45 gallons a year. But two whistleblowers at the air base told Navy investigators that more than 30,000 gallons of fuel had leaked from the pipeline and from a truck in 1988 and 1989 alone. Initially, the Navy dismissed the allegations, but later admitted that there had in fact been two major spills.

While Navy officials claim that the jet fuel is not the cause of the Fallon cancers, they admit that there's been no independent monitoring of jet fuel inventories at the base, even though federal officials demanded an oversight system in 1989.

There have been persistent rumors that Navy contractors have been dumping fuel at the base in order to increase fuel purchases. Because of the lack of oversight, the Navy has almost no idea how much fuel it has on the base or where it goes. In 1990, the base commander, Cpt. Rex Rackowitz, admitted that he couldn't account for the whereabouts of more than 350,000 gallons of fuel.

Another source of jet fuel contamination of Fallon area water is the three old underground storage tanks. A report filed with Congress two years ago revealed that underground saltwater has seriously corroded the 45-year old tanks (each with a capacity of more than a half million gallons) and noted that the tanks lack any kind of overfill and leak protection.

"I lean toward the base as the cause," says John Posey, a former aircraft mechanic at Fallon, whose daughter was diagnosed with leukemia in 1990. "Jet fuel dumping, radar and electronic emissions, jet fuel spills. All that is dangerous stuff."

Despite the rising cancer rate and the deaths, the people of Fallon have gotten few answers from state and federal government. The parents of sick kids feel they are being stonewalled. "I think there's a potential cover up here," said Richard Jernee, Adam's father. "I don't have faith in any of these people. How many kids have to die before we get to the truth?"

The jet fuel spills may well be one source of the cancers. But another study suggests that there may be a more ominous explanation. A 1994 survey of groundwater in the Fallon area by the US Geological Survey showed that 31 of 73 drinking water wells showed high concentrations of radioactive minerals. It was only revealed to the public in 2002 by a former USGS staffer who thought it might have a bearing on the Fallon illnesses.

The radiation may in part come from depleted uranium expended by bombs and missiles at the Fallon bombing ranges. Navy statistics show that more than 7 million pounds of ordinance is dropped on the Fallon bombing ranges, including the notoriously cratered B-20 site, every year.

Now the Navy wants to move some of its Vieques bombing training missions to Fallon. It recently renewed its 20-year lease on the B-20 bombing range and acquired another 50,000 acres of BLM lands for target practice. "The Cold War is over," says Kalynda Tilges of the Reno-based Citizen Alert. "The Navy is ignoring the consequences of its pollution, and the nation continues to throw money into a big, black hole."

Fallon isn't the only airbase with a leukemia cluster. Seven children have recently been diagnosed with childhood leukemia in Sierra Vista, Arizona, adjacent to the Davis-Monthan Air Force Base.

"When are these people going to do something real?" says Floyd Sands, whose daughter Stephanie died of leukemia last year. I haven't seen them do anything real so far."

So much for Bush's bluster about Iraq being an international demon-state for poisoning its own people.

Fallon, 2002

PART VII

Excursions

Fifty-Four

Disquiet on the Western Front

The Paranoid War on the West
(with James Ridgeway)

Here in the high desert of Nevada's basin and range landscape, down roads with names like the Alien Extra-Terrestrial Highway that run off into the sky, and where the wrangler and the miner still call the shots, there's full-scale insurrection afoot.

You can drive through country for hundreds of miles and never see another car. Then, suddenly, you come across a man sitting by the side of the road staring off into the distance of a bombing test range, watching for the latest version of the Stealth fighter or maybe a UFO. This is Edward Abbey country, home to loners and drifters, people on the lam, desert anarchists.

Sitting in the corner of a Tonopah coffee shop, called the Station House, next door to the incessant cacophony of the casino, where the old ladies play the slot machines and the men gather in the ambient smoke around the roulette wheels, sits Wayne Hage, a top icon of the Wise Use Movement. Hage stands for Western tradition and its fight against the evil doers in Washington.

Here at the Station House, Hage sits, day after day, drinking bottomless cups of bitter cowboy coffee and looking out the window at the tottering remnants of mining derricks strewn across the town. Trucks thunder past, and in the sky, the odd Japanese tourist teeters precariously with his camera from a hot air balloon that carries him past the wonders of the old mining world, being celebrated at the annual Jim Baker Days, a three-day drunkfest in honor of the miner who, the story goes, discovered Tonopah's silver load when his mule kicked at him and dislodged some rocks that glistened in the sun.

It is Wayne Hage you go see if you really want to know what's going on in the Wise Use Movement's battle against environmentalists and the federal government. Hage was reluctant to meet us this blistering day in early June. He said he'd been hammered by the press too often, especially by the environmental press with an ax to grind against the Wise Use Movement.

The Wise Use movement claims to consist of more than a thousand local organizations across the country, representing nearly three million people—people who fear the infringement of their property rights, mostly by what they see as oppressive federal government regulations. Many of these groups are simply out after money: they want the government to pay them considerable sums in exchange for changing traditional uses of their property that have run afoul of federal laws or even in exchange for cutbacks in the commercial use of public lands.

Other Wise Use groups have congealed as a political force to demand unrestricted access to federal land, whether it be to log, run cattle, or for less than environmentally friendly recreational pursuits, such as off-road motorcycling and snowmobiling. Corporate America has also invested heavily in certain factions of the Wise Use movement, using them as a grass-roots stalking horse in their efforts to preserve the archaic laws and regulations that allow them heavily subsidized entry to the wealth of the public domain. Now with the active help of a conservative Republican congress and a weak executive branch, the big transnationals are intensifying their efforts to exploit the land, notably through the revival of gold mining and extensive oil and gas drilling.

The federal lands are now at the center of a growing political struggle over the concept of property rights. Making up one-third of the nation, the public domain is managed by the federal government and encompasses what remains of the nation's valuable minerals, old-growth forests, native grasslands, and the extremely valuable oil and gas reserves on the outer continental shelf.

Although appearing a lush green on the road map, much of this territory has been grotesquely transformed by big companies into a kind of industrial wasteland, consisting of millions of acres of atomic and other bombing ranges, ammo dumps, military and energy facilities, strip mines, clearcuts, dammed, dredged and scoured rivers, and leaching mounds of cyanide. Still, though victim to a century of abuse and neglect, the public lands also hold the last remnants of wild America, its salmon and trout, elk, grizzlies, owls, and wolves, its forests, deserts and mountains—the American wilderness.

The Wise Use Movement has crafted a profile of its enemy. The way people like Wayne Hage see it, they are engaged in an aggressive chess game with elite legions of the environmental movement, who are covertly carrying out a sinister master plan, a vast socialist experiment to depopulate the rural West. As evidence, they point to the Wildlands Project and to quotes from environmentalists calling for a 50 percent reduction in North America's population by the year 2100. The Wise Use movement often suggest that the real goal of the environmental movement is to clear real Westerners off the land, so that the West can be returned into an "eco-theme park" for the pleasure of vacationing suburbanites.

In order to advance their socialist agenda, the Wise Users argue, environmentalists have infiltrated the federal government. Under Bill Clinton, the thinking goes, environmentalists have embedded key leaders in powerful positions inside the EPA, Interior and Agriculture Departments, and then, acting through their positions on government regulatory bodies, the environmentalists have set out to first reduce and then eliminate all grazing and logging on federal lands and sharply curtail mining by driving up the cost of doing business.

Furthermore, Hage argues, through the Endangered Species Act, environmentalists are turning fights over such seemingly innocent figures as the coho salmon, spotted owl, and gray wolf into national symbols of a broad land use planning instrument. Chief among Wise Use enemies is Clinton's Interior Secretary Bruce Babbitt, who has initiated the National Biological Survey, known in the ominous parlance of the Wise Use movement as the NBS. "The NBS is fascist, man, it's socialist," said Chuck Cushman, head of the American Land Rights Association, based in Battle Ground, Washington. "These guys map your property with infrared satellite photos, looking for plants, you know, then they can actually come on your property without your permission. If they find one of those plants, you know you're screwed worse than if they found dope."

But, of course, in the minds of people like Wayne Hage, the real menace lies not with the environmentalists, but with the political and financial powers that prop them up. It is the big Eastern foundations who now provide the principle financing of the major environmental organizations that are pulling the strings. And who is hiding behind the foundations? The Rockefellers, the Pews, the Mellons and other titanic American families made rich through the Standard Oil Trust and its like. Through their securities portfolios, naturally, these foundations are interlocked with the multinational corporations that run the world, and who eye the public lands as a source of cheap wealth when times get hard. And thus it is, according to Hage, that the small rancher in the Nevada high desert is to be driven off the land by Forest Service and the BLM rangers who are nothing more or less than agents of the Rockefellers.

"It's not some deep dark conspiracy," says Wayne Hage. "The information is out there for anyone to see. Most people don't pay attention to economics. And when they do, they say, 'My god, it's one of those conspiracy theories.' No it isn't. It's just the record. So you have the environmental movement as a stalking-horse used to carry out the transfer of private rights of individuals over to the hands of government and the multinational corporations, which serve the function of the old nobility under the monarchists. And look at who owns these damn gold mines out here...foreign consortiums."

Hage is the Nevada rancher whose cattle were impounded and sold by Forest Service agents in 1991 after he blatantly overgrazed his allotment on the Toiyabe National Forest. Hage promptly closed down his cattle operation and filed a $24 million suit against the Forest Service in federal claims court alleging that "taking" of his grazing rights. Hage was later arrested after he logged juniper trees along a creek without a permit.

Hage is the author of *Storm over Rangelands*, which presents his historical overview of the western United States. Today, Hage and his book have become part of a carefully crafted legend that occupies center stage in the Wise Use and the property rights movements.

According to Hage's interpretation of western history the public lands were always a means to be sold off, and even though they never were, the actual ownership at the end of the 20th century has become a melange of various tangled interests, both public and private—the so-called split estate. In fact, Hage argues, there's no such thing as public lands. Of course, that didn't stop the government from expropriating them, nationalizing the lands over and over again.

As an example of this kind of thought lurking in the shadows of American history, Hage points to Carl Schurz, Interior Secretary under President Rutherford B. Hayes. Hage writes in *Storm over Rangelands*, "Schurz's efforts to prevent the establishment of private property rights on the public lands may have sprung from his socialist background. Schurz was a controversial German immigrant who had fought along with Karl Marx in the Revolution of 1848, came to America, was elected senator from Missouri, and supported the radical Republicans' reconstruction plans."

So, says Hage, with the nation deeply in debt after the Civil War, the European banking houses, led by the Rothschilds, conspired with the federal government to use the western lands as collateral against repayment of war debt. The government reneged on the Spanish land grants and sent out the cavalry to kill off the Indians, who had real and justifiable land claims, to clear off any obstacles to this loan repayment scheme. Then European financial interests joined forces with the big Eastern families to build the railways, control the new towns and farms and, through the American Cattle Trust, turn the livestock business into a huge monopoly.

It was, after all, that great hero of environmentalism, Clarence King, the explorer of the Sierra Nevadas, the father of the Smithsonian Institution and Geological Survey, the very father of federal science, who secretly sent his geology students from Ivy League universities to rustle cattle for his own profit on the western plains during summer vacation, abetting his huge cattle operation.

As time went on, according to Hage's interpretation of history, western lands were set aside through the conservation movement, starting with Yellowstone National Park, then Yosemite. These shrines to conservation were in fact part of a vast project of "nationalization," the equivalent, Hage says scornfully, of "crown lands" in England.

Hage also cites how the Taylor Grazing Act, which organized and regulated public domain grazing during the 1930s, "created the collateral base for funding of Roosevelt's New Deal." According to Hage similar expansions of federal authority over western lands coincided with the Vietnam War (Wilderness Act) and Clinton's health care plan (Babbitt's range reform initiative and the National Biological Survey).

Hage is one of the leaders of a group called Stewards of the Range, headquartered in Boise, Idaho, and run by Hage's attorney Mark Pollot, a former assistant Interior Secretary under James Watt during the early Reagan years. During his tenure at the Interior Department, Pollot authored Executive Order #12630, which required the government to attest that all federal agencies compensated lands-owners if their regulations or actions infringed on property rights. Today, Pollot's group, Stewards of the Range, has become the legal battering ram in the ranchers' running resistance against federal authority, backing, for example, Cliff Gardner's willful trespassing of his cattle in the Ruby Mountains on the Humboldt National Forest.

A thousand miles away in the posh Seattle suburb of Bellevue, Washington, are the offices of the group that published Hage's screed: the Center for the Defense of Free Enterprise. This group is run by Ron Arnold, who along with his business partner, Alan Gottlieb, serve as field marshals and media packagers for the property rights movement.

Arnold was a former draftsman for Boeing, a public relations man for different companies, a writer and film-maker, while Gottlieb makes his money (lots of it, too) from direct mail operations for Republican candidates, and most significantly, for gun groups, including the Second Amendment Foundation and the Citizens Committee for the Right to Bear Arms. Gottlieb also publishes a magazine called, *Women and Guns*.

The Wise Use movement is a significant political grouping. "There are 1200 to 1500 groups we can identify," says Arnold. "Few of these groups ever got any real money from big corporations. Neither are they especially aligned with small business. In fact, probably a third of our members are housewives." Altogether Arnold and Gottlieb estimate there are as many as three million people on their mailing list.

Much of the Wise Use movement has a strong, though peculiar, libertarian bent. "There is a strain that runs through it that is upset with government interfering in their lives," says Gottlieb. "Not just libertarian or conservative, but an awful lot of people who are to the left of center and they are very upset with the government telling them what to do."

"It's a diverse collection," says Arnold. "I'm pro-abortion and Alan is not. I'm for legalization of marijuana. We never got into immigration. We did try to see if there is a bridge between the Wise Use groups and the gun movement, but no. Wise Use people pretty much support gun rights. But it doesn't work the other way around. Gun rights people don't do much for the property rights movement. And that's the part that really pisses me off."

Even though the Wise Use movement may attract people from diverse political and ideological heritages, it was also lustily embraced by Newt Gingrich's anti-government revolution. The Wise Use movement nestles comfortably among the organizations and tendencies on the rightwing of the Republican party now in ascendancy on Capitol Hill and in many statehouses.

It is a world that Ron Arnold knows very well. During the early 1980s, Arnold was brought in by Paul Weyrich of the Free Congress Foundation to write a glowing authorized biography of James Watt, then viewed by the media and most of America as a kind of neo-fascist, born-again lunatic from Wyoming.

Watt, of course, was the messiah of the Sagebrush Rebellion, the precursor of the Wise Use movement, which helped put Ronald Reagan in the White House. Once installed, Reagan began talking about privatization and Watt soon had people thinking he would sell off the public lands to the highest bidder.

But, according to Arnold, shortly after Watt took over at Interior, he told the more radical factions of the Sagebrush rebels, people like Wayne Hage, to knock it off. "Privatization was scrapped," Arnold recalls, "because Watt and the others discovered you can't sell off what you don't own. If you try to auction off pieces of 'public' property, you can't do it because the ownership is split. There are so many stratifications you could never figure out who really owned what. So notions of ownership looked more and more like a commons than a capital asset."

Among many in the Wise Use movement, however, there is a deeper feeling of betrayal associated with Watt's tenure, a belief that Watt came to be entranced by the corridors of power, that he was seduced by the sense of control he had over the public lands. As an example of this, people like Hage point to the "good neighbor policy," developed by Watt, which allowed the governors of the western states to work with Watt's office in developing policy for federal lands.

Until the Oklahoma City bombing in April of 1995, Wise Use was building a great deal of political momentum. Now it is backpedaling furiously to get away from both the militia and county supremacy movements, which threaten to drag them onto the dangerous edges of the anarchist right.

Political investigators, such as Chip Berlet, Dan Junas, Tarso Ramos, and David Helvarg, have attempted to link elements of the Wise Use movement to both the racist Posse Comitatus and the militias. Ramos and Helvarg point to the role some of the Wise Use leaders have played in the National Federal Lands Conference, headquartered in Bountiful, Utah. Ron Arnold, for example, once served on the board of advisors of the conference, and Wayne Hage was its former president. The conference is the leading force behind the county supremacy movement in the West.

More to the point, the conference enthusiastically endorsed the creation of the militias in its October 1994 newsletter, urging interested individuals to get in touch with, among others, the Militia of Montana. The article argues that militias are needed to defend states from an overbearing federal government poised to enforce "seizure orders which can be enacted with the stroke of a bureaucratic pen," plunging the nation into "an absolute dictatorial, martial law mode of repression."

Arnold bristles at questions about the conference, saying he cut all association with it years ago. With this one article, however, investigators, journalists, and opponents of the Wise Use movement have been able to paint them as little more than a group of pistol-packing wackos, aligned with the most paranoid and dangerous elements of the far right.

The county movement, as it's called, is centered on some 70 western counties that are surrounded by the public domain and are defiantly declaring their independence from it. No better example of this insurgency can be found than in Wallowa County in eastern Oregon. Bounded on one side by Hells Canyon, the deepest gorge in

North America, and on the other by the serrated, snow-capped peaks of the Wallowa Mountains, Wallowa is one of the most remote and isolated counties in Oregon, 50 miles of hard driving from the nearest highway.

Thirty years ago, ranching, logging, and mining formed the economic backbone of Wallowa. Over the past 10 years, however, Wallowa County has been undergoing a dramatic structural transformation. First, the small sawmills closed, victims of their own rapacious appetite for old-growth Ponderosa pine, which had been nearly eliminated from the county's mountains by the late 1980s. Then, in the early 1990s, the corporate mills, owned by transnational timber giant Boise-Cascade moved out. While they blamed the closures on environmental regulations and lawsuits, the prime factor was a desire to find more efficient locations for their new high tech mills.

Meanwhile, there are only 46 ranchers left in a county the size of Delaware. And according to one economic study, total farm income in the county represented only 8 percent of total employment in 1992. Of this, ranching represented less than 2 percent. More people work in the county's art galleries. Today, the biggest single employer in Wallowa County (and most of the rural West, for that matter) is the federal government—in this case the Forest Service.

Wallowa County's demographics are also changing. Young people are fleeing the county for better paying jobs in Lewiston, Boise or Portland. This is a phenomenon at work across the entire region. Indeed, the contemporary West is a much more urban landscape than the east. More than 80 percent of Westerners live in cities.

As the children of ranchers, loggers and sawmill operators flee into the cities, new kinds of urban refugees are moving into the county. And these new immigrants are bringing with them many of the trappings of their cosmopolitan lifestyles. In the past year alone, the small town of Joseph, named after the great Nez Perce chief who was born near here, has seen the opening of two herb farms, an organic farmers' market, an artists' cooperative, a designer coffee shop and a microbrew pub.

In short, Joseph has become something of a yuppie vacation retreat, a wannabe Jackson, Wyoming. And the locals don't like it one bit. They fear rising property tax rates, pressures from their mortgage holders, displacement from traditional lifestyles. All they see are urbanites throwing cash around while they lose their jobs in the timber and ranching industries.

For the ranchers of Wallowa County no better symbol of these changing conditions can be found than Andy Kerr's move to Wallowa County. Kerr, executive director of the Oregon Natural Resources Council, is the state's most prominent environmentalist. He and his wife Nancy relocated from Portland to Joseph in the spring of 1994. Soon afterwards, someone threw a rock at Kerr's window and began harassing a woman who was house-sitting while he was away from home. In the fall of 1994, Kerr and fellow enviro Ric Bailey were hung in effigy at a big property rights rally in Joseph.

Recently the town's lone Chevron dealer told Kerr to get lost when he stopped in for gas. He announced he wasn't going to sell gas to a guy who put people out of work. Kerr noted that he'd been selling him gas for six months. "Well, not any more," the dealer snarled.

The way the town elders see it, it's the federal government that's to blame. In 1994, county residents voted to adopt an ordinance aimed at kicking the federal government off lands they insist belong to the state of Oregon, and in so doing, turned Wallowa County into a firebase Charlie of the West's war against the federales.

Arleigh Isley, a local administrative law judge and one of the county fathers, declares: "I have found nothing in the Constitution that provides for the federal government to own large tracts of land, nor have I found any amendment to the Constitution that could allow it to do that. As a consequence I have to conclude they are doing it without proper authority." Isley adds that part of the law that set aside the public domain lands was "written in after Congress adjourned. They knew it was illegal!"

So far, Wallowa County has not taken any steps to enforce its ordinance. County commissioner Ben Bosworth, widely regarded as the lone moderate on the commission, explains why: "The day after the election we could've had 200 people with guns on the courthouse lawn, saying let's kick the bastards off. But the sheriff here is too much of a lapdog. So far we've just used the ordinance as a negotiating tool."

Deal Potter, a former Vietnam chopper pilot who ran unsuccessfully for county commissioner, is another keen adherent of county rule. In fact, Potter drafted the Wallowa County ordinance, and organized the rally at which bags of straw with Bailey's and Kerr's names written on them were hung from a mock gallows. The "War on the West" signs posted in windows and on telephone poles throughout the county were made by Potter, as were the "Bag Bailey's, Babbitt and Kerr" stickers that adorn the rear bumpers of nearly every two-ton Chevy truck in town. He thinks that the Endangered Species Act is more than just an environmental measure. "It's become a tool to change the political system," says Potter. "To expand the authority of the federal government into completely new areas. It's a tool for social engineering."

When asked if he didn't feel some sympathy with commercial salmon fishermen, put out of business by declining runs of chinook and coho, Potter said, simply and without a trace of irony: "No, that's just the price of doing business."

Potter also describes recent sightings of "black helicopters" in Wallowa County. "I got calls from lots of worried folks about six weeks ago, complaining about black helicopters hovering over their property," Potter says. "They knew my background as a pilot. So I looked at them, and they were DEA-type choppers. I think they were on loan to Babbitt's Biological Survey, out there doing GIS mapping."

"A lot of people in the East view the West as simply their playground," says Jim Walker, another unsuccessful candidate for Wallowa County commissioner. Walker, a Mormon with biceps the size of sledgehammers, operates a small ranch at the foot of the Wallowa Mountains, where he also runs a mail order backpacking supply company. "They want a government-provided playground," Walker says. "And it is not supposed to be that way. Every state is supposed to enter the union on an equal footing, which means that the state is to own and control the disposition of all the lands within its borders—just like out East. The only property the feds are supposed to own here is the post office."

Isley, Potter and Walker are up-front county power advocates. They represent a growing and increasingly confrontational faction of the Wise Use/property rights movement. It is a situation that makes some of the old-time Wise Use leaders squirm.

Ron Arnold, for example, is trying his best to distance the mainstream property rights movement from the out-of-favor militia and county supremacy movements. "I deplore them," Arnold says. "I think the notion of taking up arms to defend what we're trying to defend is wrongheaded. It's stupid. I tell them: Look, if you take up arms against the United States government that's called insurrection. And you'd better be prepared to deal with the consequences, which will be quite severe."

Today, Arnold seems not to have any use for the county movement or its constitutionalist adherents. "I don't know where people like Dick Carver are coming from, Arnold says, referring to the Nye County, Nevada county commissioner who forced a confrontation with the federal government over the control of the public domain and has become a hero of the county rights crowd, speaking at rallies across the West, including the Jubilee, a convention of neo-Nazi and racist groups in California.

"Carver obviously hasn't read very many legal documents from the time of the revolution, if he thinks the government has no authority to own those lands," Arnold says. "Constitutionalists? I call them tub-thumpers. There are no lawyers associated with the Wise Use movement who do anything but shake their heads at these guys.

"It has nothing to do with what I envision as part of the Wise Use movement," Arnold says of the county supremacy advocates. "If these people fall under that umbrella in your opinion, you make up the theory, because it's not mine. Any time somebody asks me what the Constitution says, I tell them the Supreme Court will tell you, go ask them."

All this from Arnold, who only last fall made an incendiary speech at the Wallowa rally, organized by Dale Potter, where Kerr and Bailey were hung in effigy.

"I got a bunch of people together who said, we'll just hang Bailey and Kerr in effigy here, and so we just hung 'em up in Joseph," says Potter with a snicker. "Well, I found out that all you gotta do is take a bag of straw, put some old clothes on it, and put a name on it and, shit, you've got everybody in the United States wanting to talk to you."

Kerr chuckles at this and retorts: "Potter made the local paper and lost his election, but thanks to him, Bailey and I received sympathetic coverage in *Newsweek* and on CNN."

The attorney generals of Nevada, Oregon, Montana and New Mexico, four states where the county movement is most strident, have cited a wealth of case law that establishes federal precedent in contests with state and local governments over public lands.

"The county power guys are making it up," says Kerr on the constitutional basis of these claims. "It's a theory they have to believe. I don't see anybody suing on it. They say they are proceeding carefully. No, they are not. They are faking it."

Up until the mid-90s, the property rights movement had been a major public relations success, only now challenged because it is suddenly saddled with the unwelcome baggage of the militia. But even when taken apart from the ideological fringes, the property rights movement isn't all that it appears to be. Until the last few years, the federal managers of the public lands under the control of the BLM and the Forest Service have, if anything, maintained a beneficent relationship to the logging, mining and ranching interests they were meant to regulate and superintend.

The federal agencies have bent over backwards to mind their interests, fixing fences, digging wells, constructing water holes, and building other "improvements" on the public range for the ranchers who lease it at a fraction of what they would pay for commercially equivalent rangeland. Ranchers who possess public lands allotments are allowed to take those subsidized contracts and, using them as collateral, borrow from financial institutions, notably the federal farm and land banks, whose operations are insured by the federal taxpayer.

Not only did public lands ranchers not pay market costs, the ranchers on BLM lands are still allowed to sublease the public range out at a much higher price, thereby taking for themselves the profit from this publicly-owned land. On top of that, 25 percent of the gross receipts from all commercial use on the public lands is returned to the counties—hundreds of millions a year.

The political power of the Western rancher is grossly disproportionate. In a time of blind budget cutting, their water and grazing subsidies remain sacrosanct. Moreover, in 1993 when Jim Baca, the reform-minded BLM chief of the early Clinton years, tried to make some modest changes in federal grazing policy, the ranchers rose up and engineered his ouster. Baca was replaced by Mike Dombeck, a man with a much friendlier attitude toward the ranching industry. In fact, Dombeck authored an internal memo suggesting that 100 million acres of BLM lands could either be returned to the states or sold off outright.

As for the so-called constitutional underpinnings of the property rights and county supremacy movements, one need only consider that most of the federal land west of the 100th meridian is arid desert—worthless without water. Yet the water rights that give the land economic value, whether for grazing farming, mining, or urban development, are controlled not by the federal government, but by the states.

Wayne Hage, for example, complains about the vast federal monolith that is destroying his ranch in order for the environmentalists and their hidden Eastern money manipulators to get at his clear mountain water and sell it to greedy developers in Los Angeles. In fact, Hage, according to friend and colleague Ron Arnold, is trying to sell his own water to Las Vegas, the fastest growing city in the West.

In the most profound sense, the entire rhetorical construct of the property rights movement in the West is make-believe. It is a PR gambit, designed to transform the real anger and anxiety over the changing economic conditions of the West into a forceful political movement that can be dominated, manipulated and, finally, no doubt, abandoned by the Republican rightwing, whose ties have always been with corporations and not people. "The untold story here is that the Wise Use Movement is really a front for rightwing politicians and multinational corporations," says Jim Nelson, the supervisor of the Toiyabe National Forest, who cracked down on Hage and other renegade ranchers.

Admittedly, Wayne Hage, Jim Walker and Cliff Gardner are not making millions on their federal range allotments. However, behind the ranchers in the Wise Use movement lurk gold conglomerates, oil and gas companies, and developers poised to makes tens of billions from the deregulation of public lands—entities with much less sympathetic public profiles than the Western rancher.

That the ranchers have aligned themselves in a political movement with these transnational corporate forces, which, in the long run, also threaten their interests, shows the real and resounding success of Ron Arnold, who has expertly used the rancher to put a more pleasing, almost mythological, face on the property rights movement.

That is not to say that these ranchers haven't made an awful mess of the public range. As Edward Abbey wrote: "The rancher (with a few honorable exceptions) is a man who strings barbed wire all over the range; drills wells and bulldozes stock ponds; drives off elk and antelope and bighorn sheep; poisons coyotes and prairie dogs; shoots eagles, bears, and cougars on sight; supplants the native grasses with tumbleweed, snakeweed, poverty weed, cowshit, anthills, mud, dust, and flies. And then leans back and grins at the TV cameras and talks about how he loves the American West."

A New West is coming. And in it the rancher appears to be a doomed species. The recent spasm of resistance now occurring may turn out to be little more than a kind of ghost-dancing, a violent nostalgia for a time long since past. The question is: into whose hands will the New West fall? The owners of the resurgent gold mines and the timber conglomerates or the transplanted urbanites escaping metropolitan blight-the new Western pioneers?

Wells, Nevada, 1995

Fifty-Five

High and Dry in the Mojave

Let this be a lesson to you all: don't try to con teenagers when it comes to spring break. It can be done, of course, but the consequences are bound to be unspeakably harsh.

This winter when we were all sitting around the table in our house in Oregon City, facing the prospect of six more months of gloom and rain, the four of us decided that an escape to someplace sunny, dry and hot in April might recharge us, making it possible to trundle on through the sunless Oregon spring.

For years, I've wanted to spend some time in the Mojave desert. I've driven across its basins and mountains many times, but always on the way to or from someplace else. There was a spot on the map that had long intrigued me: Twentynine Palms, California, a small desert town at the northern entrance to Joshua Tree National Park. I suggested this as a potential destination. Apparently, when I said Twentynine Palms, our kids, aged 19 and 17, heard Palm Springs, that sprawling cancer of a city 50 miles to the south. They were enthused for once and, ridiculously, I did nothing to discourage their fantasy.

Dumb move on my part.

We flew from Portland to Sacramento to Ontario, California. I detest airplanes and this was the first time I'd flown since 9-11. The rest of the family, frequent fliers all, had already become inured to the groping searches, the demands to remove shoes (which in our son Nat's case could, depending on the shoes, be a noxious event in itself), the ceaseless checking for photo ID, the seizure of knitting (though not crochet) needles and nail clippers. As it turned out, self-consciously liberal Portland conducted the most intrusive searches of the three cities, with the lines slushing forward at the pace of the Wisconsin Glaciation.

Having arrived bleary-eyed at PDX three hours early, I had a chance to watch dozens of searches and try to make sense out of who was being singled out and why. By and large the pat-downs at the gate seemed to be dictated by a simple quota system—ten to twelve individuals per flight, roughly twice as many men as women. (Nat and I were searched four times in four flights. Our daughter Zen once. Kimberly not at all.)

A demographic note. In Portland, nearly all of the people charged with doing the searches were black; most of us being searched were white. It was a fetching irony, and a situation that might do more than anything else to instill popular resentment toward the relentless incursions of the Surveillance State. There's nothing like a good frisking to convince even the most stalwart Republican that perhaps Ashcroft has gotten a little carried away.

I'd say one out of four passengers who'd been selected for inspection huffed, pouted and acted indignant, many of them snapping at the searchers with boisterous declarations of their patriotism. And, for the most part, the searchers kept their cool, trying to keep the searchees calm enough so that they wouldn't be booted from the airport as, to give an old phrase new meaning, "flight risks." Many of them snickered, shook their heads and imparted knowing winks to their colleagues. One could easily imagine situations where blacks who objected to similar searches by cops on the shoulder of, say, the New Jersey Turnpike ended up being hauled off to jail or to the morgue.

Ontario was a different story. The searches here were more cursory. Instead, this rather puny airport had opted for a robust show of military force, with more than a dozen (all white, as far as I could tell) national guard troops prowling the corridors in full combat gear, including M-16s, giving young women the once over. It had the creepy atmosphere of the airport in Buenos Aires during the height of the Dirty War.

From Brand Hell to the Devil's Garden

We headed east on Highway 10 out of Ontario. This must be one of the blandest roads in America: a smog-drenched corridor of car lots, cloned subdivisions, billboards promoting phone sex and Indian casinos—the latter day rubble of the California dream.

The monotony is broken only by the brooding hulk of the San Bernardino Mountains and by Cabazon, home of the giant truckstop dinosaurs featured in PeeWee's Big Adventure and the Desert Hills

Premier Outlet Mall.

If you thought we'd drive right past Cabazon, you don't know our daughter, who as a taskmaster would shame even merciless old Ward Bond from Wagon Train, the sixties TV western sponsored by the Borax Company, the mining conglomerate that has done more than just about anyone to ravage the outback of the Mojave.

This may be the world's hautiest outlet fashion mall. It's an orgy of brand retailing wrapped in a kind of faux-Venetian architecture. The stores hawk discards from an array of designers, from Donna Karan and Gucci to Barney's of New York and Versace. In the Giorgio Armani Exchange a near brawl broke out among about 20 Japanese teens, each fighting for possession of as many of the impossibly tight tops as they could grab. Still, most people seemed mainly interested in toting around a bag with some elite store's name and brand on it. Others, quite sensibly, headed straight for the Godiva Chocolatier.

The whole scene is so overwhelming that it's possible to imagine that even Naomi Klein—the Boadacea of the battle against Brand Culture—might feel faint at the prospect an afternoon trolling the aisles. I finally took refuge in the Bose speaker store, found a CD by The Kinks and cranked up You Really Got Me loud enough to awaken the San Andreas Fault.

About 20 miles outside of Cabazon we came to the junction of I-10 and Highway 62. In the notch between these roads, there's a patch of Sonoran desert known as the Devil's Garden. By most accounts, it was once to the world of American cacti what the Hoh Valley is to temperate rainforests: the most exuberant expression of the biome on the continent.

In 1906, George Wharton James, in his book *Wonders of the Colorado Desert*, described the strange cactus jungle this way: "When we find ourselves on the mesa, we begin to understand why this is called by the prospectors 'the devil's garden.' It is simply a vast, native, forcing ground for thousand varieties of cactus. They thrive here as if specially guarded…I know of no place where so many are to be found as in this small area near the Morongo Pass."

Twenty-five years later it would all be gone, plundered by Los Angeles real estate developers—the great barrel cacti and ocotillo uprooted for replanting in the obligatory cactus gardens that adorned nearly every house in southern California.

The passing of seventy years has done little to restore the damage. There should be a sign somewhere commemorating this spot as one of the great battlefields in the history of environmentalism, the Antietam of the desert preservation movement.

The cause of the desert was taken up by one of the great unsung heroes of the environmental movement, Minerva Hamilton Hoyt. Hoyt wasn't a female John Muir. She wasn't a mountaineer or a desert rat. She was an LA socialite.

Hoyt proved to be tenacious, visionary and connected. She soon got FDR's ear, and more importantly, face time with his Interior Secretary, the original Harold Ickes. Ickes pere was a titan of his time, nothing like his son, Harold Jr., the weasely hatchet man of the Clinton White House. Ickes took Hoyt's maps and within three months had withdrawn from private looting more than a million acres of land from Morongo Pass east to the Colorado River, then still a river in flow as well as name.

Over the years, the mining firms and ranchers and Pentagon whittled away at the monument, seizing anything of commercial or strategic value. In 1993, when Clinton and Dianne Feinstein pushed through the California Desert Protection Bill, creating Joshua Tree and Mojave national parks, it turned out to be a far cry from the original vision hatched by Hoyt and Ickes. The deal was another Clintonesque win-win gesture, designed to grab headlines but save precious little.

Highway 62 is a 175-mile-long arc of road cutting through the heart of the Joshua tree country from Palm Springs to the Colorado River town of Earp, at the foot of the Whipple Mountains. The road climbs up out of the carbon monoxide-glutted haze of the Coachella Valley past the shadow of Mt. San Gorgonio onto what the locals call the Hi Desert and we know as the southwestern tip of the Mojave. We moved quickly past the towns of Morongo Valley, Yucca Valley and Joshua Tree, increasingly inhabited by the service workers for Palm Springs, who have been priced out of the absurdly inflated land values in Coachella Valley.

The original Highway 62, now buried under asphalt and the ubiquitous DelTaco drive-thrus, was known during the prohibition era as the Bootlegger's Highway. At night, giant Joshua trees (including the largest known tree in existence) were soaked with kerosene and lit on fire, like giant tiki torches, to mark the perilous path to John Shull's place near Indian Cove canyon. Shull was the clubfooted genius of Mojave moonshine, whose potent concoctions found their way to the speakeasies and casting rooms of LA.

It was after nine when we finally pulled in at the Inn at 29 Palms, a small resort, perched on the edge of a fan palm oasis, consisting of about a dozen nicely kept adobes built in the 1920s. There were immediate remonstrations from the backseat. Apparently, this wasn't exactly (or even remotely) the kind of spring break getaway our kids had in mind. Their worst fears were confirmed by the hotel: no phone, out of cell range, no video games, no nearby shopping district and a television the size of a cantaloupe.

Revenge would be swift and unsparing and it would come in the form of…Palm Springs.

Windmills and Liberace's Bathroom

Kimberly and I awoke early to golden sunshine, the insistent call of a Scott's oriole and unremitting demands for reparation.

"Yes?" I say.

"Time to go."

I was being double-teamed now. Even Nat, once a reliable hiking companion, had defected.

"Go? Go where?"

"Palm Springs."

"Good lord. Why?"

"There's nothing happening here."

"Precisely."

"There's nothing to do."

"Take a hike. Read Twain. Bask in the sun."

"You won't let us. Skin cancer, remember?"

Checkmated again. Palm Springs it was.

Of course, this elegant bit of sophistry didn't stop Zen from trying to attain in a matter of five days the same bronze tones Georgia O'Keefe acquired after a period of 60 years of sustained exposure to desert sun. She got the requisite tan, a kind of living proof for her running mates back in soggy Eugene that she had made a desert pilgrimage, and, after day three, a nasty case of sun poisoning, which, naturally, didn't deter her in the least from two more days of noon-to-dusk broiling.

Palm Springs has been a spring break haven ever since Troy Donahue stripped his shirt off and presided over a poolside rave-up in Palm Springs Weekend. But I blame our kids' obsession with the place all on Carson Daley and those MTV spring break hot tub shows. And why not.

From the west, the entrance to Palm Springs is heralded by a sprawling windfarm, operated by the Wintec Corporation. Simply put: it's a blight masquerading as an example of enlightened environmentalism. More than 4,000 wind mills clot the San Gorgonio Mountain pass, blotting the scenery for miles, and shredding untold thousands of migrating birds. Perhaps only the pesticide-sated waters of the Salton Sea, forty miles to the south, present a more lethal hazard to our avian cousins in this region.

Some of the windmills are 150-feet tall, armed with blades half the length of a football field. When fully-deployed, the three twirling arms of the windmills look like nothing so much as Mercedes-Benz hood ornaments. It's certainly appropriate. By some accounts, the Coachella Valley boasts more Benzes per capita than any other conclave of fat cats in North America.

First Palm Springs, then the Nevada Test Site. The radioactive wastes of the NTS are slated to become the next big windfarm. In a deal hatched between the DOE and Siemens Energy, and brokered by Nevada Senator Harry Reid, the blast site windfarm will consist of the 325 turbines whizzing out 260 megawatts of electricity.

There we have it. Windmills are a greenwashed form of political pork, big capital-intensive projects that spurt lots of money into the accounts of energy conglomerates (even nuclear firms), and keep people wired into the current utility system. Under green energy marketing, the energy brokers and utilities can even con consumers into paying more for each kilowatt of wind power, a feel-good green premium.

You can drive down the fog-curtained Oregon coast and find more solar panels than you'll ever see here in the valley of perpetual sun, a place that could easily disconnect entirely from the power grid.

But it's all about growth. Even the windmill power plant is getting into the real estate development business. Here's how Wintec describes their new Green Mall project: "Most of the property has never been developed. A small portion of the property is improved with large utility grade wind turbine generators which have already become a large tourist attraction. The property is visited by several thousand tourists per week. All can safely share the property, each complimenting the other. The property is well situated in the emerging commercial/industrial sector of the City of Palm Springs and enjoys a tremendous competitive advantage for commercial mall development."

Shopping malls on previously undeveloped desert...that's the kind of environmentalism that would have made Sonny Bono gleam with pride.

Of course, in a perverse way the contamination of what the landscape ecologists call the "viewshed" of the Coachella Valley may be all for the good, the dispensation of a kind of historical and ecological justice on the perpetrators of so much destruction and misery (not mention horrid cinema). After all, Palm Springs was always the favored desert colony of Hollywood's most noxious right-wingers and their allies in the world of big business: Bob Hope, Bing Crosby, Walter Annenberg, Frank Sinatra, Sonny Bono. Some of these early pioneers still survive deep into their dotage, who seems to exist on some far-out kind of life-support system reminiscent of the devices in Frederic Pohl's Gateway series of SF novels. Call it the mummification effect, where the process of decay unfolds so slowly it's ever so difficult to detect the living from the dead.

Palm Springs (and its associated enclaves, Cathedral City, Desert Springs, Palm Desert and Rancho Mirage) is like a Chinese box of private enclosures, restaurants, bars, resorts, condos, spas, plastic surgeons, sex clubs. But at the heart of it all is, of course, the golf course.

Palm Springs is the Luxor of the hacking classes. There are more than 100 courses in and around the city, all of them prodigious consumers of water, piped in from the poor Colorado River or sucked out of the Palm Springs aquifer. Back in 1987 (the most recent full-blown study I could come across), Palm Springs' links soaked up a more than 130,000,000 gallons of water on an average summer day. It's certainly much more than that now, with a new 18-hole course being bulldozed into the desert nearly every year.

In the arid West, turf watering accounts for up to 60 percent of urban water use. To keep its course a shimmering, almost surreal green, the Palm Springs Country Club extracts 430 million gallons of water from the aquifer every year—that's five times the average for golf courses nationwide—and enough water to meet the daily needs of 11,000 people (and untold humpback chubs, the great, now vanishing fish of the Colorado).

Tiger Woods has a lot of explaining to do. After Woods does his penance for being a frontman for sweatshops, he needs to account for his shameless promotion of Palm Springs as a golfing Mecca for millionaires. Woods used to mouth pieties about bringing public golf courses back to urban neighborhoods and chafe about country clubs that catered only to whites. Now he pimps for one of the most exclusive—and exclusively white—enclaves in America, hawking courses that are built and maintained on the backs of Mexican immigrant labor. These workers are paid so stingily that they could toil for a month and not afford the green fees for a single round at many of the elite clubs.

Rarely have so many billions been mustered to so little purpose. There are few public spaces in Palm Springs, and its outliers, that aren't solely geared toward channeling you into retail outlets or overpriced restaurants. We tried to eat on the cheap. But it was impossible to get away with a lunch for less than $50. Those producers at CBS should forget about using remote places like the Marquesas Islands as a setting for Survivor and instead hand the contestants $100 and see if they could survive in Palm Springs for two weeks—they'd make the cannibals of the Donner Party look like a bunch of vegans.

The art museum is decidedly third-rate and the city's buildings fall victim to the same kind of civic-ordered mundaneness that destroyed Santa Fe and dozens of other towns across the New West. To find interesting architecture here you've got to venture up into the side canyons and foothills of Mount San Jacinto, and peer with binoculars into gated communities looking for the odd house designed by a Neutra, Venturi or Schindler, though in the case of Neutra this is becoming an uncertain proposition. Around the time we were visiting Palm Springs, Neutra's famous Maslon House, built there in 1963, was being sold to a Mr Richard Rotenburg, who promptly tore it down. The former owner could have attached a preservation easement to the deed, but that might have lowered the value of the lot.

There are better ways to quench the voyeuristic impulse. Go to the bookstore and pick up two indispensable guides to the sleazier side of the valley, Jack Titus's *Palm Springs Close Up* and Ray Mungo's *Palm Springs Babylon*, which provide vivid accounts of the political, financial and sexual escapades of the city.

Palm Springs is where Nixon came to lick his wounds after resigning the presidency, Mamie Eisenhower to get tanked and Betty Ford to dry out. It's also where JFK had his fateful assignation with Marilyn Monroe on March 25, 1962, at Bing Crosby's estate.

It wasn't supposed to come down that way. Frank Sinatra, who had shuttled dozens of starlets to the Kennedy brothers, had been expecting JFK to make his house a presidential getaway. Indeed, Sinatra had sunk a lot of cash into a new security system and a helicopter pad just for Kennedy's benefit. Then pious Bobby intervened, citing Sinatra's fruitful relationship with Sam Giancana, among other mobsters. Sinatra fumed and shifted his loyalties to the Republicans. In 1969, he hosted Spiro Agnew, who, upon arriving in town, announced to the press corps: "It's nice to be in Palm Beach."

One redeeming virtue of old Palm Springs is that it served as a relatively safe harbor for many Hollywood gays, from Rock Hudson to Liberace, who partied at places like the Desert Palm Inn and the New Lost World Resort (formerly Desi Arnez and Lucille Ball's compound), which has become one of the most opulent gay and lesbian getaways on the planet. (Of course, the city was also a refuge of last resort for wealthy butchers, such as the family of the Shah of Iran. But out here that just comes with the territory.)

If gays were tolerated, the same can't be said for other oppressed classes, such as Jews and blacks. Until the early Fifties, Jews were permitted to stay in only one hotel in town and that one discreetly identified them with a "J" beside their names in the desk ledger. Blacks were simply not welcome at all, except as golf caddies, as Jack Benny discovered when he tried to book a room for his partner Rochester.

But the great Palms Springs dream is distilled to its essence in this passage from Mungo describing The Cloisters, Liberace's house:

"The house is across the street from a Catholic church, Our Lady of Solitude, where sandwiches are passed out daily to the homeless who loiter in the vicinity. Inside, Liberace's toilet is a throne, with arm-rests and a high back done up in red velvet. The shower curtain features replicas of Michelangelo's David, while the wallpaper is decorated with Greek couples fucking in every imaginable position. There is a Gloria Vanderbilt suite, a Rudolph Valentino room (Liberace's middle name was Valentino, and the Great Lover was an early Palm Springs celebrity who made several pictures here in the twenties), a room wallpapered in tiger skin, a Marie Antoinette suite, a bath with mirrored walls and ceiling and a pool-sized Jacuzzi, and a collection of strange bric-a-brac and junk no thrift could unload, including plastic birthday cakes and a life-sized stuffed male doll with erect penis. Into this world he introduced his young escorts, took his pills and kept his cranky mother."

Yes, those were the halcyon days; it's all been downhill since.

The Oasis of Mara

Our little hotel sits beneath the Queen and Pinto mountain ranges on the northern edge of Joshua Tree National Park at the Oasis of Mara. This fan palm oasis used to be known as Indian Gardens, after the beanfields laboriously tended by the Serrano Indians. Mara is the name the Serrano gave to the place, meaning "place of small springs and tall grasses."

The Serranos were part of the "toloache" cult, whose rituals were brought to life by psychedelic trips induced through the smoking of that noted member of the datura family, jimson weed. The hallucinations were induced primarily for religious rites, but they also had more pragmatic applications, such as to assure luck in gambling.

By most accounts, the Serrano tribe proved to be masters of a complex desert agriculture, cultivating beans, melons, gourds and Devil's claw, a plant domesticated for use in weaving the tribe's extraordinarily beautiful baskets. They also gathered the fruit of the fan palm and the sugar-sweet seedpods of the honey mesquite.

The Serrano, and their neighbors the Cahuilla and Fernandeno tribes, were pacifists and not uncommonly led by a woman chief.

This rooted and nonconfrontational mode of existence suited life in the desert, but became problematic when the more aggressive Chemeheuvi band of Paiutes showed up at the Oasis in 1867, having been driven westward from their homelands along the Colorado by Mormons and miners.

Life for these tribes under the Spanish occupation was miserable, but it got even worse when California became a state, especially after the gold rush. In 1851, California's second governor, John McDougal, laid out the state's genocidal gameplan: "a war of extermination will continue to be waged between the races until the Indian race becomes extinct." They were duly denied citizenship rights, voting rights and the right to testify in court.

California was admitted to the union as a free state. But this bit of enlightened thinking didn't apply to Indians, who were routinely rounded up by ranchers, railroad companies and mining firms and made to work as slaves. This appalling situation was made official state policy with the passage of the Indenturement Act of 1850. Often slaughter accompanied enslavement. Indian parents were killed and the children kidnapped and sent off to work as slaves until the age of 30. The practice wasn't outlawed until 1867, four years after the emancipation proclamation.

By 1902, the wars, disease, murders and kidnappings had taken their toll on the both Serrano and Chemeheuvi tribes. In that year's census, only 37 Indians remained at the Mara Oasis. Today there's little evidence of the Indians at all, except for a small cemetery of unmarked graves just west of the oasis.

From the Mind of Edgar Allen Poe

The Mojave isn't easy to get a handle on. In general, it's a high elevation landscape, relatively cool and wet, as far as deserts go—and surprisingly barren. The Sonoran desert, by contrast, is lower, searingly hot, parched and astonishingly diverse. On the other hand, the Mojave boasts the hottest spot in North America, the most sunken (Death Valley), and the driest (Baghdad, California).

The signature plant of the Mojave is the Joshua Tree, which an early desert ecologist described as springing full-grown from the mind of Edgar Allen Poe. Joshua Trees are monicots, grotesquely oversized lilies, with contorted limbs and trunks armored with spikes, which are used skillfully by the loggerhead shrike to impale its prey. They reminded me of the gruesome gibbets haunting the backgrounds of so many of Pieter Breugel's paintings. Indeed, there is something deathlike about the Joshua Tree. Rot is its signature feature, from the inside and out. Most mature Joshua Trees are hollow, the pithy core having flaked away.

These vegetable beasts (explorer John Fremont called them the most repulsive member of the plant kingdom) grow at an excruciatingly slow rate, something on the order of 1.5-2 centimeters per year. Even so, there are some gargantuan specimens in the park. One multi-headed titan in the Covington Flats is 40 feet tall and 14 feet in circumference, making it something on the order of 800-years old, about the age of the ancient Douglas firs of the Oregon cascades.

Joshua Tree National Park contains a confluence of deserts, the meeting ground of the Mojave and the Sonoran, which in California, for obscure politico-etymological reasons, is referred to as the Coloradan.

Like most of the western parks, Joshua Tree was pretty well picked over by the mining companies before (and even after) it was set aside as a national monument and later a park. The fabled prospectors (and Joshua Tree had many) upon whom so much of the myth of western libertarianism has been constructed were in reality little more than hard rock sharecroppers for the big mining companies in San Francisco, New York and London. The most productive mine in Joshua Tree yielded little more than $2.5 million in ore, mainly gold. Certainly not worth all the bother and bloodshed.

On Tuesday morning, I went for a walk up Ryan Mountain, a relatively modest ascent of about 2,000 feet. Modest unless you are a flatlander, who spends 80 percent of his waking hours in front of a Macintosh at 200 feet above sea level. I huffed and puffed my way, being passed by a cadre of extreme runners who sprinted to the summit and back down before I had even made it half way. Trip on a cholla, I muttered, as they rumbled by.

They call it Ryan Mountain, after Jep and Tom Ryan, owners of the Lost Horse mine, who lived near its base in a house built by a nefarious character named Sam Temple. By most accounts, Temple was a sadist and unrepentant Indian killer, who served as the model for the murderer in Helen Hunt Jackson's novel *Ramona*. I don't know what the Serranos called this humpbacked peak. But it must have been a primo place to imbibe jimson weed.

The view from the top was worth the pain of the climb. Dust devils sprouted and zigzagged across the yucca plain below, which stretched for miles to the lavender-colored Little San Bernardino Mountains. The horizon was smudged by a dingy haze, bubbling up like steam from a witch's cauldron, which signaled the presence of Palm Springs. I watched a ferruginous hawk lost in a lazy spiral beneath me, far too high to be searching for prey, apparently just joyriding on a thermal.

Lacking a stash of jimson weed or any other kind of hooch, I found a flat slab of rock, toasted by the sun, and fell asleep. But a few minutes later I was jolted awaked by a growl from the sky. A few hundred feet above me, six Apache attack helicopters cut northward across the turquoise sky. They were no doubt headed for the Marine Air Combat Training Center, a 596,000 acre bombing range located a few miles north of Twentynine Palms.

The Mojave is military land. During World War II, the Pentagon seized more than five million acres of the desert for military training grounds and bombing practice. The man in charge of running the show in the early days was none other than Gen. George S. Patton.

I can't escape the sense that this place is haunted: so many thousands of practice invasions, carpet bombings, decimations of virtual armies and cities. This is where they practiced the bombings of Libya, Iraq, Serbia, Afghanistan and, now, Iraq once again.

And there have been many real deaths up there, too. Beyond the coyotes, antelope, lizards and desert tortoises wiped out by explosions or pulverized by roving columns of tanks, many young American soldiers have been lost. In training exercises during World War II, more than 1,100 men perished in the Mojave. Most died of dehydration. The brutal Patton limited the soldiers to one canteen of water per day as they were sent on forced marches across the sun-scorched terrain, apparently thinking it would toughen them up for the North African campaign. "If you can work successfully here, in this country," Patton ranted to his troops, "it will be no difficulty at all to kill the assorted sons of bitches you meet in any other country."

The man was sadistic and stupid. He graduated near the bottom of his class at West Point and it's easy to see why. He apparently had no understanding of how intense heat and low humidity dry up the human body, conditions that would put even the best-conditioned athlete at risk of heat stroke. It's a wonder more didn't die.

But Patton remains an icon. Down the road at Chiriaco Summit, there is a museum honoring the general. It's all hagiography and it must disgust many of the men who served under him. Most Americans know that Patton slapped two shell-shocked soldiers who'd sought refuge in an Army hospital bed during the Allies' invasion of Sicily in August 1943. In the most famous incident, a sobbing Private Paul Bennett told Patton that his nerves had been "shot by the shelling." Patton responded with a slap across the face and his infamous rebuke, "Your nerves, hell. You are just a goddamned coward, you yellow son-of-a-bitch. Shut up that Goddamned crying… You're going back to the front lines and you may get shot and killed, but you're going to fight. If you don't, I'll stand you up against a wall and have a firing squad kill you on purpose. In fact, I ought to shoot you myself, you Goddamned whimpering coward."

This quote is taken from the official report on the incident filed by Lt. Col. Perrin H. Long, head of the unit's Medical Corps. Long's report, which had been suppressed by Patton's friend Gen. Omar Bradley, eventually reached Eisenhower, who was outraged enough to sideline Patton from his command for a few months.

The Patton cult persists in spite of this, a fact attested to by the thousands who pour into the Chiriaco Summit museum. Many even say the poor soldiers deserved the rough treatment. But one suspects that attitudes toward Patton would be different if it was more widely known that following a similar merciless logic the general had sent those 1,100 young men to their deaths in the desert—sacrificing them to the unforgiving Mojave sun and his own stupidity.

Disney Does Joshua Tree

I left Ryan Mountain and headed for Hidden Valley, a bewildering maze of rock south of the town of Joshua Tree. As I pulled into of the parking lot at the trailhead, I was accosted by a pair of coyotes standing in the middle of the road. They weren't the hipster creatures portrayed in the poetry of Gary Snyder. These coyotes seemed straight out of a Dickens street gang. They had the scruffy look of expert pick-pockets and petty thieves.

I shouted at them that I wasn't about to hand over my lunch and they should be ashamed of themselves for resorting to such undignified panhandling. They grunted and shuffled off, looking for a more sympathetic mark.

The place was a jumble of granite walls, strangely eroded slabs and domes of quartz monzonite, beaten soft by desert winds and almost fleshlike in color, glowing in the early evening sun with the hue of Bardot's skin in that unforgettable opening shot of Contempt.

The narrow side canyons here created a moister microclimate that allowed for desert grasses to flourish. But its remoteness, sheltered conditions and forage also attracted the attention of a band of cattle rustlers known as the McHaney Gang. By all accounts, they ran a complex operation, involving rebranding, bribery, and a thriving interstate trade in both horses and cattle.

None of this did the idiosyncratic ecology of the valley much good. By the time the Park Service got its hands on the property the grasses were pretty much gone and, from photos taken in the 30s, so was nearly every other form of vegetation. Things have started to come back to life. I didn't see many grasses, but the valley floor was crowded with yuccas, prickly pear, cholla, Joshua Trees, the strange two-headed nolina plant and, sunning herself on a boulder, a chuckawalla, the giant iguana-like lizard whose saggy skin looks three sizes too large for its body.

In a guide to the Hidden Valley nature trail, the Park Service pats itself on the back for having evicted the cows. But other parasites have taken their place, none so ubiquitous or annoying as the legions of rock climbers, in their insect-like gear, clinging from pastel-colored ropes to the sheer granite faces of the valley.

A couple of miles east of Hidden Valley is a small rockshelter with a panel of petroglyphs featuring fish and turtles on it. The Park

Service calls them the Movie Petroglyphs. In October of 1961 some morons at the Disney Studios thought it would be good to feature the petroglyphs, originally pecked into the rock by Serranos and Paiutes, in a film called Chico: the Misunderstood Coyote. But the director didn't think the images looked quite Indian enough, so he instructed the art department to paint over the glyphs and carve a batch of new figures. The Disneyfied images have all the verisimilitude of a Donald Duck cartoon. Even worse, the Park historian told me that the Park Service (50 years after the passage of the Antiquities Act, which made looting of Indian artifacts a felony) gave Disney the okay to paint over the rock art as long as they used "removable paint."

The originals weren't good enough. They stood in the way of something considered more cinematic and profitable. Now they are no more. Forget the tired theories of Frederick Jackson Turner: that's the real metaphor for the history of the West in a nutshell.

Willie Boy Was Here

The Yucca Valley is the scene of one of the Old West's last great myths, the story of Willie Boy, a young Paiute-Chemeheuvi Indian accused of two brutal killings. The white version of the story goes something like this. In 1909, a drunken Willie Boy got into a fight with a Paiute chief named Indian Mike in the town of Banning, slaying the older man with a six-shooter. Willie Boy kidnapped the chief's daughter Isoleta, fled on foot east up to the Yucca Valley into the Hi Desert, dragging the poor girl with him as a hostage. When the young woman began to slow him down, Willie Boy raped her repeatedly and then shot her in the back.

Eventually, so the story goes, he made his way to the Oasis of Mara outside Twentynine Palms, where only a few Indians remained, tending their beanfields near the giant fan palms. Willie Boy raided their huts for food and weapons and headed for the Pinto mountains. He was finally cornered in a small canyon and, in a final blaze of glory, gunned it out with the sheriff's men. He wounded a couple of men, but finally turned the gun on himself.

Willie Boy's exploits became a huge national story, because what passed for the White House press corps happened to be in

Riverside, California at the time, covering William Howard Taft's cross-country rail trip promoting his latest piece of tariff legislation. Bored to tears by Taft's bloated stump speeches the reporters seized on Willie Boy's story, hyping it as the ruthless murder of an Indian chief and the kidnapping and slaying of an Indian princess. It dominated the national papers for weeks.

In 1969, the great Abraham Polonsky, the director of Body and Soul and Force of Evil, whose career was wrecked by the blacklist, returned from his enforced exile to shoot a fairly good film about the grim story, called Tell Them Willie Boy Was Here, with Robert Redford and Robert Blake (now facing trial for the murder of his wife) once again playing the role of a misunderstood killer. In Polonsky's version we are given a kind of reversal of the Kasper Hauser/Wild Child story that François Truffaut (and later—to better effect—the German director Werner Herzog) was exploring at about the same time in his film L'enfant Sauvage.

In the Polonsky film, Willie Boy is an Americanized Paiute Indian who, upon being accused of committing a horrendous crime (the killing of the chief) based on little more than racial stereotyping, reverts into a kind of Hollywoodized version of Indian "savagery," leaving behind a trail of blood worthy of a Jacobean revenge play.

Neither of these recitations share much relation to what really happened back in 1909, according to the local Paiutes who knew the story from the inside. The Hunt for Willie Boy: Indian-Hating and Popular Culture, by James A. Sandos and Larry E. Burgess, a brilliant new work of ethnohistory, sets the record straight. Sandos and Burgess use Indian recollections of the event and historical records to recreate what really happened. It seems that Willie Boy and the girl were engaged, a relationship that was not viewed warmly by her father the chief, who came after the young Indian one day with a gun. In a struggle, the gun went off and the chief died. There's also no evidence that Willie Boy was a drunk. He and Isoleta fled together, hounded by one of the largest posses ever mounted. Sandos and Burgess believe that far from being raped and murdered by Willie Boy, the young woman was actually shot by one of the posse's leaders.

Not far from where Willie Boy met his end nearly a century ago is a new Indian gaming casino, throbbing with neon, that seemed to be doing a brisk business taking money from military types and ranchers. Perhaps after all these years the Paiutes have exacted a certain kind of revenge after all.

Blame It on Reyner Banham

The Inn at 29 Palms is one of those wind-blown and sun-hammered places that could have appeared as the setting in a desert noir by Horace McCoy or Jim Thompson. Life at the inn centers on the pool and the adjacent restaurant, where the cooks conjure up the best food in the Valley, if not the entire Mojave.

That the word is out about the quality of the Inn's food is attested to by the steady flow of local customers, a kind of daily parade of Hi Desert society: real estate agents, retirees from the Bay Area, gay couples, artists, cops and Marine Corps officers. The secret is the fresh vegetables, grown on the grounds, in a lovingly tended garden.

I spent a few hours by the pool flipping through Reyner Banham's book *Scenes from American Deserta*. Banham was a prickly English architectural critic who settled in southern California in the 1960s and wrote a book that I greatly admire, *Los Angeles: The Four Ecologies*. Growing up in Indianapolis, I'd inherited the Midwesterner's reflexive hatred of LA, as a smog-clotted, car-obsessed, Sodom of narcissists, mountain-rapers and apocalyptics.

True enough, of course. But LA can also be great fun. And Banham's book, like Robert Venturi's on Las Vegas, provided an intellectual rationale for joining the party—and a key to understanding why going to LA, contrary to all my Hoosier conditioning, was worth the hassle of clogged freeways and damaged lungs.

As much as I liked Banham's book on LA, I came to despise his take on the California deserts—not so much for Banham's aesthetic, which in a way isn't so different than Edward Abbey's reveries about his boyhood haunts in Appalachia, as for what the forces he found beautiful and bounding with creative energy have done to the land and its human and ecological communities. In a sense, Banham practices a kind of hit-and-run aesthetic, rarely sticking around long enough to appreciate the consequences of the constructions he adored.

Banham had a taste for unplanned, accidental landscapes, studded with gadgets and gizmos in various states of use and disrepair, utility, fancy and ruin. That's pretty much what this part of the desert was, an architectural free-for-all, a scattering of human structures with no real aspiration to be architecture. Naturally, that's an empowering state of play for a critic, who sets himself up as an interpreter of chaos.

Banham is right about an important point: the deserts of California are not natural landscapes. Almost every square inch has been rearranged in some degree by human use or abuse, intentional and accidental. The myth of ecological purity is one that environmentalists pursue at their own peril. Indeed, such thinking led groups like the Sierra Club to support Senator Dianne Feinstein's Mojave National Park legislation and promote it as kind of unblemished wilderness, when in fact it contains gold mines, cows, off-road vehicles and nearly every other contemporary curse of desert ecosystems.

But it's one thing to recognize the imprint of humans, from the sophisticated desert agriculture of the Serrano to the riverside nuclear waste dumps of US Ecology, and quite another to fetishize it, as Banham so often does. He exudes about the nearby Salton Sea, for example, which is a man-made disaster, a kind of ecological root-canal gone horribly awry. Today, this water-wasteland, which Sonny Bono tried to hawk into a desert Riviera, is a kind of toxic sludge pit, where the water sucked out of the Colorado River and irrigated through the fields of the Imperial Valley, returns to die, loaded with pesticides and the other chemical detritus from industrial agriculture.

Yes, as Banham notes, it's possible to see a certain kind of strange beauty in the contraptions surrounding a gold mine, set starkly against a purple sky and blood red cliffs, and but you must also recognize that you're staring a grave dug in the earth a thousand feet deep and a mile wide and know that hundreds of miles of streams, so precious in this arid land, have been fouled with cyanide. This is the context that undermines Banham's aesthetic.

Banham once said that the thing he'd miss most about rural California is the air-shows. He liked Watsonville's fly-in the best, which didn't have any stars or celebrities or commercialized gimmicks. It succeeded as a kind of planned anarchy, a spectacle governed by no one. That's not the kind of air show that goes on out here in the Mojave every day. Surely even Banham would have cringed at the black billion dollar monsters that prowl these skies.

Gram Parsons BBQ

On our final morning in the Mojave, I walked a mile or so up to the Park headquarters, rather indelicately entrenched in what was once the southern tip of the Mara Oasis, looking for information about the demise of one of rock'n'roll's legendary bad boys, Gram Parsons. As I was talking to the park historian, the sky darkened, the wind whipped up, thunderclaps rattled the windows and, finally, the rains came down to wild cheers inside the ranger station. The rangers took turns prancing around outside in the downpour. "It's been a year since we've seen rain like this," one of them shouted.

Even an Oregonian like me, who had come to the desert to trade our 8 months of rain for a week of steady sun, could appreciate that this storm was a beautiful thing, indeed. The desert pulsed to life almost immediately at the first hint of the rain squalls. Even the small, reddish barrel cactuses seemed to perk up. And the smell of the Mojave after a drenching rain is an unforgettable pleasure, a scent flush with the pungent odor of creosote bush, mesquite and sand verbena.

As the skies lightened up, the ranger pulled out a topo map and pointed to the spot I wanted to visit: Cap Rock.

I'm of mixed views on Gram Parsons, the former member of the Byrds, founder of the Flying Burrito Brothers and originator of California country-rock. I like much of his music. He had a sweet, doom-ridden voice and he wrote some great songs, the beautiful Hickory Wind, for example. He re-introduced the steel guitar to rock, and gave new life to old tunes by the Louvin Brothers and Hank Williams. On the other hand, he was a trust-fund rocker with a sprawling sense of entitlement who deliberately shattered his considerable talent and spawned a genre of seventies soft rock that haunts the FM airwaves to this day, from the humorless perfection of the Eagles to the formulaic crap of Pure Prairie League and Poco.

Parsons was born in Waycross, Georgia. His mother, Avis

Snively, came from money. The Snivelys owned one of the largest orange groves in Florida and the Snively property in Winter Haven was turned into the Cypress Gardens theme park, a big pre-Disney attraction. His father, "Coon Dog" Connor, was also wealthy, coming from a family of retailers in Tennessee. These were rich but not happy people. By all accounts, both were drunks and battled depression. In 1958, Coon Dog blew his brains out with a .38 revolver. It was the first in a string of tragedies.

Soon thereafter, Gram's mother married a fortune hunter named Bob Parsons and drank herself to death a few years later. The death was attributed to alcohol poisoning. Parsons, who had adopted Gram and his sister Little Avis, moved them to Florida and married the family babysitter a few months later. Gram always suspected that Bob Parsons had a hand in his mother's death.

The Snively money bought Gram a draft deferment and sent him to Harvard, where he discovered hard drugs, developed a deeper sense of his own alienation, avoided any alliance with fellow southerner Al Gore and perfected his brand of post-rockabilly southern rock.

By 1969, Parsons was in LA, challenging Roger McGuinn for leadership of the Byrds. They collaborated on one masterpiece of country rock, Sweetheart of the Rodeo, before Parsons split with fellow Byrd Chris Hillman to form the Flying Burrito Brothers.

While in Southern California, Parsons became good friends with Rolling Stone's guitarist Keith Richards. Evidently, Parson's turned the Stones on to country music (for better or worse) and he and Richards would often escape up to the Mojave to listen to Chet Atkins records, sample a vast menu of drugs and scan the desert skies for UFOs.

Before going on tour in the summer of 1973, Parsons and a few friends went up to the small town of Joshua Tree, where they stayed in the Joshua Tree Motel, a nice but modest establishment on Highway 62. Parsons (who, for the curious, stayed in room number 8, which contains a plaque commemorating the event) went on a three-day binge of Jack Daniels, morphine and heroin. On the night of September 19, he overdosed, choked on his own vomit and died. His body was ultimately taken to LAX, where it was scheduled to be flown to New Orleans for burial.

Like most junkies, Parsons tended to brood on his own death. And he repeatedly told his friend and road manager Phil Kaufman that when he died he didn't want to be buried in the ground: "You can take me out to the desert in Joshua Tree and burn me. I want to go out in a cloud of smoke." What follows is a screwball escapade that could have made a great Preston Sturges film.

Kaufman, one of the more outlandish characters in the LA rock scene, took it upon himself to fulfill Parsons's final wish. He borrowed an old hearse, dummied up some paper work and went to LAX, where he conned the people working for Continental Airlines' mortuary services into turning over Parsons's coffin. Kaufman and his pal Michael Martin were so drunk at the time that they ran the hearse into a wall as they left the airport.

On the drive to Joshua Tree, Kaufman and Martin stopped at a gas station to buy more beer and a couple of gallons of high test gasoline. "I didn't want him to ping," Kaufman later wrote in his madcap autobiography *Road Warrior*.

The two ended up at Cap Rock, a bizarrely eroded dome of granite near Ryan Mountain. Kaufman says they stopped there because he was too drunk to drive any further. They unloaded the coffin and hauled it to a small alcove at the base of the rock monolith. Then Kaufman noticed headlights approaching and told Martin that it must be the cops. They quickly poured the gasoline over Parsons's corpse, lit it on fire, then sped away, across open desert.

They didn't drive very far before Kaufman passed out. When they awoke the next morning they found themselves stuck in the sand. They had to hike to a gas station and get a tow truck to pull them out. Their adventures weren't over. Just outside LA, the hearse got into a multi-car pile up. When a California Highway Patrol officer ordered Kaufman and Martin out of the hearse, empty beer bottles fell to the pavement, and the officer put them in handcuffs. As the cop interviewed the other drivers, Martin slipped out of his cuffs, started the hearse and the two escaped.

At first the cops tried to blame the corpse theft and pyre on a satanic cult. But a few weeks later Kaufman turned himself in. He and Martin were fined $1,000. To raise the money, Kaufman threw a party. He called it the Koffin Kaper Koncert.

The spot where Kaufman ignited Parsons's coffin has become an informal memorial. There's a large stone at the spot with the words Safe at Home (title of a Parsons's song) painted on it in red letters. People leave things at the site: syringes, plastic flowers, CDs, St. Christopher medallions. Others have scrawled scraps of Parsons' lyrics on the face of Cap Rock itself.

I wanted to get a photo of the Gram Parsons BBQ pit from a small shelf on the rock above. There was only one way up. It involved a scramble over a scree pile, then a bit of free-climbing up a fissure in the granite. As I neared the ledge, I stuck my hand in a slot in the rock. Then I heard a kind of hollow buzzing, steady and insistent. I froze. I'd heard that sound before, though not quite so distinctly.

I looked down and saw about six inches from my hand a neatly coiled, blonde rattlesnake with the telltale slashes beside each eye, its erect tail chattering away like a drum groove laid down by Elvin Jones.

This was not your ordinary rattlesnake. No. This was Crotalus Scututalus. The Mojave rattler, a snake with a reputation for a foul temper and a deadly bite. Indeed, the herpetologists describe the Mojave's venom, rather cagily under the circumstances, as "unique." Uniquely poisonous. The Mojave's venom contains a strange brew of more than 100 distinct neurotoxins, a concoction so complex even the mad scientists at Monsanto can't duplicate it.

This all makes ecological sense. The Mojave is a harsh environment. The opportunities to nab a meal of delicious Kangaroo rat don't present themselves that often. The venom (an offensive, not a defensive weapon) increases the likelihood of a strike resulting in a kill.

Time slowed down. And I began to calculate the odds, like some backcountry bookie. A phrase flickered across my mind: you're more likely to be struck dead by lightning than to be bitten by a rattlesnake. It was strangely comforting. But only for a moment. Surely, those odds were calculated for the population of the country at large. Most people never see a rattlesnake. What were the odds of someone in my circumstance? Eyeball to eyeball with C. Scututalus, with me the intruder in his small patch of dust?

Those are precisely the kind of percentages they don't give you, probably with good reason. It turns out the snake/lightning analogy is false, a bit of well-intentioned pro-rattler propaganda designed to keep the roughnecks from slaughtering any more snakes than they already do.

In fact, rattlesnakes inflict more than 8,000 bites on humans in the US every year. That's a respectable number by any standard. The snake scientists say that 75 to 80 percent of rattler bites are considered "illegitimate"—an odd bureaucratic descriptor for a boneheaded move on the part of a human. Illegitimate touching of a pit viper.

One of the park rangers had told me that the last person to die of a snakebite in Joshua Tree was an English teacher who had led a field trip to the park with his students. Someone discovered a Mojave rattler lounging under a picnic table at the Jumbo Rocks campground. The teacher decided to use the snake as a prop (was he a fan of Harry Crews' strange novel, A Feast of Snakes?), picked it up by the tail, began to discourse on the pacifist nature of the snake, when the rattler, quite properly, bit him in the stomach.

Of course, I too was a damn English major. And I had just made an illegitimate, boneheaded move. Used to scrambling over boulders and rockpiles in the rattler-free Oregon Cascades, where at worst you're likely to be scolded by a pika, I hadn't bothered to look where I was sticking my hand. It was all up to Mister Scututalus, now.

But the little Mojave didn't strike. He no doubt figured it wasn't worth wasting his precious payload of venom on this bonehead, who could just as easily kill himself by slipping off the slick granite and smashing his skull on the makeshift cenotaph for a long-forgotten rocker. And for that I'm grateful.

We left Cap Rock and drove off into the desert evening, chasing those distant storms, behind a van bizarrely adorned with two whitewater kayaks (a true Banham moment), my foot tapping the floorboard to the beat of that most urbane of all bluesmen, Memphis Slim:

> You may own half a city,
> Even diamonds and pearls.
> You may own an airplane, baby,
> And fly all over this world.
> But I don't care how great you are,
> Don't care what you are worth—

'Cause when it all ends up
You got to go back to Mother Earth.
Yeah, Mother Earth is waitin',
And that's a debt you got to pay.

Right you are, Slim. But not today.

Twentynine Palms, 2002

Fifty-Six

Something About Butte

Butte isn't a mining town. It's a mined town.

The core of the city is hollow, tunneled out. Beneath the shattered surface of the Hill, there are more than 10,000 miles of underground passages and thousands of shafts, glory holes descending deep feet into the bedrock. Every now and then, holes will open in the crust of the earth, swallowing sidewalks, garages and dogs.

Houses, black as ravens, are sunk into mine waste heaps and slag piles, the exhumed geological guts of the billion dollar hill, once coveted and swiped by America's dark lord, John D. Rockefeller, during the end game in the War of the Copper Kings. People still live in the hovels.

Gallows frames prick up through the town like quills on a porcupine. Once, these steel derricks cranked the miners down into the depths in hoist cages, now they resemble the frightful gibbets that haunt the backgrounds of Bruegel's paintings from the years of the Black Death. Indeed, many that went down never came up. The tunnels of Butte are also a catacomb, holding the bones of more than 2,500 miners.

In the 1880s, Butte was the biggest and wildest town between Denver and San Francisco. It boasted 75,000 people and the most opulent opera house west of Manhattan. There were whorehouses and banks, theaters and bars, French restaurants and the Columbia Gardens, one of the world's fanciest amusement parks.

It's the place where Cary Nation's sobriety campaign came to a crushing end, when the madame of Butte's leading brothel pummeled the puritanical crusader to the floor of the bar, as hundreds cheered, beer steins raised high.

The mine barons didn't live in Butte, where the day mansions were stained black by the smoke of the smelters, but up in Helena, which harbored more millionaires per capita than any other city in the nation.

Those days are gone.

Today, Montana has a crop of millionaires, but they've made

their money in Hollywood, Atlanta, or New York City and now hide out, like the James Gang, in large compound-like ranches, sprawling over mountains and trout streams. Otherwise, Montana's economy is on the rocks, beleaguered by chronic high unemployment and wages as depressed as you'd find in rural Mississippi.

And Butte leads the way. Fewer than 30,000 people live here now and the number erodes every year. There's only intermittent mining being done now and few miners remain, except some old-timers, many of whom wear oxygen masks along with their cowboy hats.

Butte has gone from being the richest hill on earth to the world's most expensive reclamation project and the nation's biggest Superfund site. The only good paying jobs in town these days go to the supervisors of those charged with cleaning up the mess and to the medical technicians who routinely test the blood of Butte's children for arsenic and lead.

The Superfund designation doesn't end in Butte. It follows the entire 130-mile-long course of Silver Bow Creek to Milltown Dam at the confluence with the Clark Fork River outside Missoula. Silver Bow Creek: that's what the Butte Chamber of Commerce handouts call it. But that's not how it's known to the locals. They call it Shit Creek, for its sulphurous stench and sluggish orangish-brown water. For decades, this stream served as little more than an industrial colon for the fetid effluent of Butte's mines. It is a dead river and a deadly one, too.

The Milltown Dam holds back six million cubic tons of toxic sludge: cadmium, arsenic, copper, lead, manganese, zinc. It continues to pile up year after year. No one knows what to do with it, though some have suggested trucking it to ARCO's headquarters in downtown Los Angeles.

On the east side, the town of Butte comes to an abrupt end. The Berkeley Pit yawns across nearly a square mile of terrain. The gaping pit is filling inexorably with waters so acidic that they can't sustain life of any kind.

Over it all presides the Madonna of Rockies, a 100-foot tall statute perched on the Continental Divide that glows at night like a slab of radium. Her arms are outstretched in piteous benediction of the hellish wasteland below. The locals call her Our Lady of the

Tailings. She was erected in 1985 by a group of miners in hopes that the boom time would return.

It hasn't.

Not to fear. The town fathers have a plan to recharge Butte's flatlined fortunes. They want to turn Butte into a tourist haven, a kind of toxic wonderland. After all, they figure, people can't help looking at traffic crack-ups, the bloodier the better. Why wouldn't they throng to the nation's most poisoned city?

Perhaps they could call it Poisonville National Park. Poisonville. That's the name Dashiell Hammett, America's hard-boiled Dante, gave to Butte in *Red Harvest*, his strange nocturnal novel of corruption and corporate filth. "The city wasn't pretty," writes Hammett on the opening page of *Red Harvest*. "Most of its builders had gone in for gaudiness. Maybe they had been successful at first. Since then the smelters whose brick stacks struck up tall against a gloomy mountain to the south had yellow-smudge everything into uniform dinginess. The result was an ugly city of forty thousand people, set in an ugly notch between two ugly mountains that had been all dirtied up by mining. Spread over this was grimy sky that looked as if it had come out of the smelters' stacks."

That was written in 1929. The skies are clearer now that the smelters are shut down. But the town looks much the same. Only there's less of it.

There's a precedent, of sorts, and it's close at hand. Down the road 23 miles to the west is the town of Anaconda, once the biggest and foulest smelter complex in the world. The ore from the Anaconda mines was taken by the Company's railroad to Anaconda where it was chunked into the giant blast furnaces and melted down to commercial copper. The waste rock was piled in mammoth dumps. The smelters belched out their lethal smoke 24 hours a day, seven days a week, for decades. The smelter fallout turned the daytime sky dark and coated the land with poison in a radius of fifty miles or more.

Now, all that's left is a single dark smelter stack 534-feet tall and the sinister heaps of poison rubble, Montana's version of the tower of Isengard in Tolkien's *Lord of the Rings*. Today the stack and the hill it sits on are within a state park. But the ground is so polluted the public isn't permitted entry. It's a roadside photo-op, like the cooling towers of Three Mile Island.

But the big draw in Anaconda these days is the world class $8 million golf course, designed for ARCO by Jack Nicklaus and built on toxic mine wastes. The sand traps are black ash, culled from the burnt slag swept out of the smelters' ovens. It gives a whole new meaning to sand hazard.

"Odd as it sounds, those dumps are historic resources," says Mark Reavis, a Montana architect who is pushing the scheme to make Butte a national park. "The preservation community here is worried we're going to lose, bury and cover-up all signs of mining. Butte should be a monument to a societal decision: the quest for minerals. I'm trying to preserve. They're trying to clean up."

This mad scheme appeals to Bush's haughty Interior Secretary Gale Norton, for whom slag heaps seem to exude an almost aphrodisiacal allure. The Bushites are desperate to jettison the troublesome notion of corporate liability for Superfund cleanups entirely. If they can do it in Butte under the banner of historic preservation so much the better.

* * *

On this fall day, fierce winds blow down off the spine of the Rockies, whipping the tailings into metallic dust devils that swirl down the streets, blowing by the great, decaying mansions of the mine bosses, the banks and the bordello museum, the courthouse and zinc bars, coating cars and people in a powder the texture of crushed bone.

My friend Larry Tuttle and I walk into a bar to get out of the toxic wind. Tuttle runs a green group called Center for Environmental Equity. It's a small outfit, but they carry a big stick and they like to whack big companies. Indeed, Tuttle may be the mining industry's biggest pain in the ass. He's seen it all, from the poison ruins of Summitville to the huge gash in the Little Rockies made by the Zortmann-Landusky mine. But even Tuttle seems awed by the Butte's 150 years of self-abuse. And he's been here before.

"You can't believe it until you see it," he says. "Then when you do, you feel as if you can't trust your eyes. It's the smell that makes it real."

On the wall of the bar is a ratty poster from last August promoting Evel Week, a festival celebrating the exploits of Butte's most famous native son, the daredevil Evel Knievel. I'm sorry I missed it. Our waitress tells us that Joan Jett and the Blackhawks kicked ass on the final night, "as fireworks lit up the sky like bombs over Baghdad." Jett's brand of leather-metal seems perfectly geared to the sensibilities of Butte. This isn't a town for rodeos, but machines. Heavy ones.

"Evel cares about this place," the waitress tells us. "That's a lot more than you can say about the bosses at ARCO or those people at EPA. They don't give a damn."

It strikes me that Evel Knievel is the perfect hero for the post-industrial West. His body is as broken as his hometown. Knievel's doomed aspiration led to him attempt to jump his jet-cycle across the maw of the Snake River Canyon. It was the perverse denoue-ment of a bizarre career. Each Knievel event was an audacious flirta-tion with suicide, each one grander than the one before it. Meaning the odds of death were greater. In Knievel's world, the motorcycle jump replaced the public hanging as a spectacle.

We drain our beers and head west down Park Street, past the shuttered storefronts and EPA projects to decontaminate the front lawns of row after row of houses, many of them empty. The road takes us to Montana Tech, once the great mining school of this com-pany town. The school gets a cut from the proceeds of almost every mining and logging operation in the state of Montana, a financial incentive to keep churning out students to work as unquestioning zombies for the very industries that are laying waste to the state.

Our destination wasn't the college, but the sedulously adver-tised World Mining Museum located on a backlot of the campus. The museum turned out to be little more than an enclosure of min-ing detritus—a gallows frame, hoist cage, rail cars, sheave wheels, dick shovels—with a few utterly unapologetic interpretive displays.

At the entrance to the Montana Tech campus is a bronze stat-ue of Marcus Daly, the financial trickster who transformed Butte from a roughneck mining camp into the biggest boom town in the Rockies during the late 1800s. The bronze is by America's most gift-ed sculptor, Augustus Saint-Gaudens. You get the idea Daly would-n't have had it any other way. He saw himself as the Cosimo de Medici of Butte and Saint-Gaudens as his Cellini. Saint-Gaudens, it seems, had other ideas. His Daly is hardly a triumphal figure. The statue, erected two years after the robber baron's death, depict a porcine and blustery man. It reminds me of Melville's Confidence Man, a smirking demon cackling up at the Madonna of the Rockies.

Butte got its start in 1864 when gold was discovered along Silver Bow Creek. But Butte wasn't destined to be a gold rush town. The real money was in a cheaper mineral that ranked second only to iron as the most important metal of the industrial revolution: copper. And, in 1876, Daly laid his hands on one of the purest veins of copper in the world, the Alice claim on Butte's hill. "The world doesn't know it yet," the squat Irishman boasted. "But I have its richest mine."

Daly headed back to San Francisco where he rustled up an impressive retinue of California gold rush millionaires as financial backers for his scheme to develop the Butte copper mines, including George Hearst, Lloyd Tevis and James Haggin. Haggin was dark-skinned and reportedly of Turkish descent. When Daly's arch-rival, William Clark, publicly smeared Haggin as "a nigger," it launched a decade-long feud that became the first shot in the famous War of the Copper Kings.

Of course, time and circumstances heal all wounds among industrial magnates and eventually Daly and Clark patched things up in the name politics and profit. Clark went on to become a US senator from Montana, where he shepherded the interests of the mining conglomerates and became a favorite target of ridicule for Mark Twain. "He is said to have bought legislatures and judges as other men buy food and raiment," Twain wrote of Clark. "By his example he has so excused and so sweetened corruption that in Montana it no longer has an offensive smell. His history is known to everybody; he is as rotten a human being as can be found anywhere under the flag; he is a shame to the American nation, and no one has helped to send him to the Senate who did not know that his proper place was the penitentiary, with a ball and chain on his legs. To my mind he is the most disgusting creature that the republic has produced since Tweed's time."

Daly's company took its name from one of the nearby mines, which supposedly derived from Horace Greeley's ridiculously optimistic assessment in the early days of the Civil War that Gen.

McClellan's troops would encircle and squeeze the life out of Robert E. Lee's forces "like a giant Anaconda." It may not have been an apt description of McClellan's rather timid performance, but it did come to serve as the perfect totem for the nature of Daly's company.

Daly bought up or squeezed out nearly every other claim in town. Eventually, Anaconda's mines would yield up 20 billion tons of copper, fully a third of all the copper used by the US from the 1870s through the 1950s. Before the final frenzy, Anaconda's mines would generate more than $20 billion worth of copper.

Daly pumped the profits back into his operations. He built the town of Anaconda to smelter the Butte ore and it became an industrial complex to rival the steel mills of Gary. It wasn't just mineral claims Anaconda acquired. It owned more than a million acres of timber land, hundreds of sawmills, railroads, banks, and the rights to most of the water in western Montana. During its heyday, Anaconda would employ two-thirds of the workers in the entire state. And, naturally, it owned politicians, judges and every newspaper in Montana except one, the *Great Falls Tribune*.

By the 1890s, Anaconda was a true behemoth, a regional monopoly that few dared to tangle with. Its soaring profits soon captured the attention of the big daddy of trusts, Standard Oil, which made haste to acquire Anaconda in 1899. The people of Butte were warned that the travesties of Daly's reign would seem benign compared to what awaited them under the iron fist of Henry Rogers and Standard Oil. In a prophetic speech on the steps of the Butte courthouse, Augustus Heinz, the last independent operator in town, told 10,000 angry mine workers: "These people are my enemies: fierce, bitter, implacable. But they are your enemies, too. If they crush me today, they will crush you tomorrow. They will cut your wages and raise the tariff in the company store on every bite you eat and every rag you wear. They will force you to live in Standard Oil houses while you live, and they will bury you in Standard Oil coffins when you die."

Heinz was in the midst of a fraught battle with Anaconda over ownership a particularly rich vein of copper that zigzagged through the Hill in a maze-like pattern. Anaconda took Heinz to court to seek sole possession of the vein. When the Company's handpicked judge refused to resolve the dispute in favor of the Company,

Anaconda shut down its operations, threw 6,500 miners out on the streets, and held the town hostage until got its way. Heinz was defeated and Anaconda seized complete control of Butte. Then it turned its sights on destroying the only force that stood in its way: Butte's labor unions.

The extractive industries of the West—the logging camps and mines—were as brutal on workers as they were on the land. In Butte alone, more than 2,500 miners lost their lives in the tunnels and glory holes. Perhaps, 250,000 were injured, many seriously. Others got sick from foul water and cancerous air. A health survey of 1,000 miners in 1914 found that at least 400 of them suffered from chronic respiratory diseases. The maimed and ill were forced to work until they dropped, then they were discarded like human mine tailings.

Thus it's not surprising that Butte, the nation's biggest mining colony with some of the most wretched working conditions imaginable, became one of the birthing places of the American labor movement. In 1878, Marcus Daly tried to cut wages at his mines from a miserly $3.50 a day to $3. More than 400 miners walked off their jobs and paraded through town behind a brass band in protest. Then they formed the first union in town, the Butte Workingmen's Union. Daly got the point.

Soon there was only one mine that operated as a non-union shop, the Bluebird Claim. On June 13, 1887, union members marched to the mine and took the Bluebird miners to the Orphean Hall to induct them into the union. They told the befuddled mine boss they were there to: "gently intimate to the men that the shutting down of the mine would be in accordance with the eternal fitness of things."

A few years later, Butte's workers played the key role in forming the Western Mining Union. The Butte Miner's Union became Local Number One. By 1900, more than 18,000 laborers in Butte belonged to various trade unions: waitresses and bartenders, typesetters and sawmill workers, blacksmiths and brewers, teamsters and theatrical employees, hackmen and newsboys.

By and large, Daly got along with the workers and their unions. He'd worked as a laborer in the gold and silver mines in California and, to some degree, sympathized with the plight of the miners. He was also practical. Daly wanted to increase productivity as fast as possible and would do almost anything to avert a strike or a slowdown.

This state of affairs changed immediately after Standard Oil absorbed Anaconda. Standard Oil had no tolerance for labor unions and set out to destroy the miners' unions of Butte. They hired Pinkerton agents to infiltrate the unions, finger the lead organizers, and sabotage the unions from the inside. The Pinkerton men developed a blacklist of union leaders that Anaconda used to summarily fire 500 workers, saying they were Socialists. Workers were required to sign the equivalent of loyalty oaths, identifying their political and union affiliations. Workers deemed radicals and agitators weren't called to work.

In the meantime, although the price of copper had soared from 8 cents a pound in 1878 to 20 cents a pound in 1914, Anaconda's wage-scale had remained the same: a flat $3.50 a day. This prompted a strike and violent counter-attack in 1914 that culminated in the dynamiting of the Miner's Union Hall. A few weeks later, Anaconda refused to recognize the legitimacy of the Western Federation of Miners.

But the union organizers kept at it, largely in the person of the IWW's Frank Little, a mesmerizing speaker who was running the IWW's Free-Speech campaign in Butte—the model for the Free Speech Movement in Berkeley. He spoke out against the wretched working conditions that lead to the Granite Mountain catastrophe, where 168 miners died agonizing deaths in the Speculator Mine. He also urged miners to reject the draft and refuse the call to fight in World War I, a message that appealed strongly to the Irish, Germans and Serbs who made up the bulk of Butte's mine workers.

But the Company had had enough. In the early morning hours on August 1, 1917, Little was rousted from his bed in a boarding house by Anaconda goons. They tied him to a rope behind their truck and dragged him down the main road in Butte. Then they lynched him from a railroad trestle. More than 7,000 people came to his memorial service.

But the Company had won the day. The state of Montana bowed to their murderous masters at Anaconda HQ and officially banned the IWW and then enacted the Sedition Act that outlawed "disloyal, profane and scurrilous" writings and speeches of any kind—made by working people naturally.

Future labor uprisings would be crushed for Anaconda with the help of the National Guard and the US Army. From 1917 through 1921, Butte was on occupied town. The US Army captain sent to police Butte was none other than Omar Bradley, later a five-star general and commander of US Forces in Europe during World War II, who arrived in Butte with the Army's Company F in January of 1918. During his time in Butte, Bradley's troops crushed two strikes, occupied two union halls, and arrested more than 100 striking workers, charging them with sedition—Posse Comitatus Act be damned.

"When my men are ordered to do a thing, I believe they will do it," Bradley said after the raids. "We got orders to quell a riot and had no alternative but to quell it. I am glad nobody got seriously hurt, but I would rather have seen a lot of people hurt than to feel that my boys had let me down."

Thus Anaconda now gave orders to the US Army operating on domestic soil. Sixty years later, the Company, now a global giant, would call on Henry Kissinger and the CIA to protect its interests in Chile, where the government of Salvador Allende had nationalized Anaconda's copper mines. Allende fell and Pinochet's dictatorship, loyal to big copper, took its place, installing a 25-year long reign of terror. This time around thousands of people got maimed, tortured and killed.

* * *

To get the best view the Berkeley Pit, you must enter a tunnel that could double as a runway for one of Evel Knievel's mad jumps. You emerge into a void: before you is a hole in the earth a mile and a half wide and more than 2,000 feet deep. The flesh-toned terraced slopes look like a ziggurat in the making. It is the Mammoth Cave of quarries.

A man next to us is leading a tour. He tells a group of retirees that as big as it is the Berkeley Pit isn't the largest open pit mine on earth. That honor belongs to the Kennecott mine south of Salt Lake City.

"Yes," Tuttle interjects. "But the Kennecott mine wasn't allowed to fill with water. Not yet, anyway."

The Berkeley Pit is filled with 44 billion gallons of acidic water and it's growing every day. From the viewing platform, it looks like

Montana's evil version of Crater Lake.

By 1955, Butte had become the most relentlessly mined patch of land on the planet. But the richest veins of copper were beginning to run out. Anaconda, driven by the remorseless logic of efficiency, made a crucial decision to switch from mining the underground tunnels to excavating a giant open pit. It was a move that slashed jobs and trashed an already mangled landscape.

There was a minor obstacle. Half of Uptown Butte stood on the site Anaconda wanted to dig up. These blocks included old mansions, the Columbia Gardens amusement park, the opera house where Twain spoke and Caruso sang, and the Irish community of Dublin Gulch, where miners once pelted J.P. Morgan himself with rotten tomatoes. It was yet another of Anaconda's hostage-taking schemes: allow us to gobble up your town or we'll shut down and move our operations to Arizona or Chile. The town fathers relented, of course, as they had always done. So did labor, even though it meant fewer jobs and lower pay.

So a new age was inaugurated in Butte: the era of open pit mining and chemical processing. New technologies and bigger machines allowed Anaconda to simply gnaw up the bedrock, pulverize it and strip out the metals in a chemical wash, leaving behind toxic waste heaps taller than any hill in Indiana. This noxious method would soon spread across the West. As so often before, Butte served as a working laboratory for some of the mining industry's worst ideas.

How long does it take to excavate a hole this big? About 20 years of 24 hour a day blasting. By the 1970s, the giant pit was pretty much played out. The price of copper had plunged. Recently enacted environmental laws began to nag at the company. Anaconda tried one last blackmail scheme in 1974, saying that to continue operations it would have to consume the rest of downtown Butte. The town's politicians got behind Anaconda's scheme to blow up the old core of the city, in a kind of civic suicide pact. But wiser heads urged caution and Anaconda lost interest. They shut down operations at the pit later that year.

In 1977, Anaconda sold off its operation to ARCO. The deal must surely go down as one of the most lame-brained acquisitions in American history. ARCO claimed that it felt too tied down to oil and gas operations and wanted to diversify into minerals. That might sound compelling in a prospectus, but investors must have shook their heads at the decision to acquire an ailing mine that hadn't turned a profit in years. Perhaps they were looking for tax write offs.

What they got was something quite different. In 1982, Butte was declared the nation's biggest Superfund site and ARCO was named the responsible party, culpable for financing the clean-up of Anaconda's toxic playpen. Of course, the mess could never be cleaned up, but the bill for what locals call the "suck, muck and truck" operation could tally in the hundreds of millions of dollars.

Then ARCO committed one of the great environmental crimes of our time. The company turned off the pumps that kept the tunnels of Butte from flooding with water. The internal plumbing of Butte had been permanently wrecked by the thousands of miles of underground tunnels that had pierced through the water table. When the pumps were shut off, the water poured through the tunnels, leaching a periodic chart of poisons out of the earth, and found their way into the Berkeley Pit. The waters flow there at the rate of more than five million gallons a day. Every day. Forever.

The waters of the Berkley Pit permit no life to exist within them. It is a lake of sulfuric acid, powerful enough to dissolve metal. The cobalt-colored waters lure migratory birds in from the flyway to and from Canada. It's a lethal pitstop, since only a sip of these metallic waters is enough to kill. Over the years, thousands of geese, ducks and swans have perished here. In 1996 there was a mass poisoning when nearly 400 snow geese died in the pit's foul waters. Autopsies showed that the birds burned to death from the inside out—for the snow geese one taste of that water was like downing a pint of Drano.

In fifteen years or so, the poisonous waters of the pit will have risen to a level that will permit it to spill into the local aquifer, wiping out springs, wells and creeks. ARCO has belatedly begun construction of a pumping station near the pit at Horseshoe Bend, but there's no guarantee that it will work. Or that if it works, it will work in time to save the aquifer.

Meanwhile, ARCO continues to play political games with the clean up. The governor of Montana is Judy Martz, a slaphappy Republican who used to run the Butte garbage company. ARCO has financed her political career, but not without the stench of scandal. In 1999, when Martz was lieutenant governor, she and her husband bought 80 acres of land from ARCO along Silver Bow Creek. They paid only $300 an acre for the property, less than half the going rate for similar parcels in Butte. Martz chose not to publicly disclose the transaction, even though at the time the state was involved in litigation against ARCO over the cleanup of the very same Silver Bow Creek.

Martz is a kook, but she's ARCO's kind of nutcase. In her campaign for governor Martz proudly vowed to be "a lapdog of industry." And she's tried to keep her word, going so far as to call the wildfires that scorched the West in 2002 "acts of environmental terrorism." Where is Mark Twain when you really need him?

* * *

Yes, history does continue to repeat itself in Butte. But not for much longer. The town has nearly reached its geographical limit.

In 1984, soon after ARCO pulled the plug on operations at the Berkeley Pit, financier Dennis Washington opened a new deep pit mine a few hundred yards away. He paid ARCO $18 million for the land. Then he engineered tax breaks from the nearly bankrupt city and the state, won waivers of environmental liability, got subsidized power and other inducements. And in a final blow to Butte's historical identity, Washington's East Continental Pit mine operated as a non-union shop. The mighty Gibraltar of Labor had finally been mined to dust.

Naturally, Washington made a killing. Perhaps as much as a billion dollars on that $18 million investment. Then in 2000 his mine too suspended operations. Of course, there's no requirement to restore the land. So now an extra 2.5 million gallons of acidic water streams into the toxic pit. It's the oldest story in the West: privatize the profits, socialize the costs, the risks and the fallout.

Perhaps the idea of a park here isn't such a bad idea after all. But it should be a national battleground, like the bloody fields of Antietam or Little Big Horn—hallowed ground where both labor and the environment were laid low.

The headstone on the grave of the Wobblies' great martyr Frank Little reads: "Slain by capitalist interests." It's a fitting epitaph for Butte as well.

Butte, 2002

Index

Jeffrey St. Clair edits, with Alexander Cockburn, the investigative newsletter and website CounterPunch.org, which has been callled "the best political newsletter in America." He is a contributing editor of *In These Times* and writes the weekly Nature and Politics column for the *Anderson Valley Advertiser*. His reporting has appeared in *The Washington Post, San Francisco Examiner, The Nation, The Progressive, New Left Review* and many other publications. His books include *Whiteout: The CIA, Drugs and the Press, Al Gore: A User's Manual, Five Days That Shook the World: The WTO, Seattle and Beyond, The Politics of Anti-Semitism* (all with Cockburn), and *A Guide to Environmental Bad Guys* with James Ridgeway. A native of Indiana, he now lives in Oregon with his wife Kimberly, daughter Zen and son Nat.